Justice Brennan

JUSTICE BRENNAN

The Great Conciliator

Hunter R. Clark

A Birch Lane Press Book
Published by Carol Publishing Group

To Hillel Black,
for helping me find my voice as a writer,
and for giving renewed voice to the vision
of an America that lives up to her ideals.

Copyright © 1995 by Hunter R. Clark

A Birch Lane Press Book
Published by Carol Publishing Group
Birch Lane Press is a registered trademark of Carol Communications, Inc.
Editorial Offices: 600 Madison Avenue, New York, N.Y. 10022
Sales and Distribution Offices: 120 Enterprise Avenue,
Secaucus, N.J. 07094
In Canada: Canadian Manda Group, One Atlantic Avenue, Suite 105,
Toronto, Ontario M6K 3E7
Queries regarding rights and permissions should be addressed to
Carol Publishing Group, 600 Madison Avenue, New York, N.Y. 10022

Carol Publishing Group books are available at special discounts for
bulk purchases, sales promotion, fund-raising, or educational
purposes. Special editions can be created to specifications. For
details, contact: Special Sales Department, Carol Publishing Group,
120 Enterprise Avenue, Secaucus, N.J. 07094

Book design by Ardashes Hamparian

Manufactured in the United States of America
10 9 8 7 6 5 4 3 2 1

Library of Congress Cataloging-in-Publication Data
Clark, Hunter R.
Justice Brennan : the great conciliator / by Hunter R. Clark.
p.   cm.
"A Birch Lane Press book."
ISBN 1-55972-261-4 (cloth)
1. Brennan, William R.   2. Judges—United States—Biography.
3. United States.   Supreme Court—Biography.   I. Title.
KF8745.B68C55   1994
347.73′2634—dc20
[B]
[347.3073534]
[B]   94-16681
CIP

Contents

Preface vii

Acknowledgments xi

1   The Perfect Match of Mind and Heart   3

2   "Everything I Am"   12

3   Harvard Law School   21

4   Counselor and Soldier   26

5   A Major Scandal   34

6   Reforming the Courts   43

7   The Hinge of Fate   51

8   The Shamrock and the Robe   58

9   Ike's Second-Biggest Mistake   71

10   Life in Georgetown   85

11   Justice Brennan Versus Senator McCarthy   104

12   "An Incredibly Buoyant Person"   113

13   Faubus, Little Rock, and Justice Brennan   129

14   Outwitting the Conservatives   151

15   Empowering the Suburbs: One Person, One Vote   164

16   Obscenity   182

17   *New York Times v. Sullivan*   207

18   The Conservative Backlash   233

19   Fighting a Rear-Guard Action   252

20   Brennan's Legacy   275

Appendix   287

Notes   291

Index   331

Preface

WHEN I MET JUSTICE BRENNAN IN 1970, I was fifteen years old, attending Capitol Page School in the Library of Congress, and working as a page in the U.S. Supreme Court. I was entirely too young at the time to appreciate the nature and scope of his contributions as a justice or to gauge in any way his historical significance. As an African American whose parents were contemporaries of Thurgood Marshall, I had grown up in a home in which Marshall was revered as a role model. My father was thrilled that I had been hired at the Court and by the prospect that my proximity to Marshall would inspire me to become the great civil rights lawyer he dreamed I would one day be.

But though I had heard of Thurgood Marshall's legendary achievements in the struggle for racial equality, I was a child of the 1960s, and Marshall's commitment to "working within the system" was entirely too mundane for me. I and my contemporaries were "Black and Proud"! We wanted freedom *now*! Little did I know or comprehend that Marshall, an icon to my parents but an Uncle Tom to me, was really one of the most courageous, visionary, and iconoclastic leaders in our nation's history.

At the time, Justice William O. Douglas was more my style. I followed him around as much as he would let me, always hung around his chambers asking for things to do, read all his latest books (which seemed to come out one right after the other), and worshiped the ground he walked on. He was someone I could relate to, even if he was seventy-two. He talked my modern language. African Americans were "Black"—not "Negro" or "colored," Uncle Tom terms to any self-respecting young militant. He saw the youth movement as a rejuvenation, as a renaissance of the revolutionary ideas advanced by Thomas Jefferson and James Madison. He was critical of the Establishment and called for an end to the Vietnam War, for which I would soon be of draft age and eligible.

I never gave any thought to Justice Brennan. Frankly, I had never heard of him. But I could sense that he was somehow special from the first time I met him. I remember he walked into the chief justice's outer office for the justices' weekly conference alongside Justice Marshall. Marshall was an enormous, blustering man who dwarfed him. Brennan was giggling like a schoolboy at something Marshall had muttered out of the side of his mouth. He even put his hand to his lips to keep from bursting into laughter.

When I opened the door for the two men to enter the conference room, Brennan stopped, welcomed me to the Court, and locked my adolescent hand in his longshoreman's handshake, which I thought would crush my knuckles. He put his other hand on my right elbow and drew me close to his face, smiling broadly and catching his breath from laughing so hard at whatever Thurgood Marshall had just said.

In an instant he was gone. I stood there grinning soph-omorically. That smile stayed on my face all day. I don't know why. About a quarter-century later, when I started writing this book, I learned that he had the same effect on most people.

When I wrote to retired Justice Brennan in 1992 to ask for his assistance with this biography, he wrote back saying that he already had a biographer, Steve Wermeil, who used to cover the Court for the *Wall Street Journal*. He said, therefore, that his direct involve-ment with me would be inappropriate. Characteristically, he added that he and his wife, Mary, were proud of me for all my success since high school.

I plunged ahead anyway. And although he never assisted my efforts directly, he facilitated my research by making available to me the information contained in his "vertical file" in the Supreme Court library—a compilation of all his speeches and articles—together with all the interviews he had sat for over the years and virtually every published article about him. It was with these files that I began my research.

Later I requested access to his case files in the Library of Congress, which he had donated in seven installments between 1967 and 1990. These files occupy some 346.8 linear feet of shelf space and consist of roughly 305,000 items that span the length of his service on the Court—early drafts of opinions, memorandums from law clerks or among the justices, correspondence, and so on.

Access to these documents is restricted to those having the written permission of Justice Brennan himself, and the justice was kind enough to grant his permission for me to review all but one of the files I asked for.

Research of these Library of Congress files was invaluable in tracing the evolution of Brennan's thinking and the forces and ideas that influenced his jurisprudence. They are in some instances like a clearly marked road map through his mind.

I found nothing in the files that was of a sensational nature or that might be considered an embarrassment to the other justices or to the Court as an institution. Liberals and conservatives disagree. Sometimes liberals and conservatives disagree even amongst themselves. That is to be expected. There is nothing controversial about the existence of disagreement, passionate or strongly worded.

Yet when Thurgood Marshall's Library of Congress files were made available to the public shortly after his death in 1993, their release touched off a firestorm of controversy. The fact is that the U.S. Supreme Court is, with the possible exception of the U.S. intelligence agencies, the most secretive area of the government, and that secrecy is guarded jealously.

In fact, according to Justice Sandra Day O'Connor, she and other justices have, in the wake of the controversy surrounding the release of the Marshall papers, "stripped" their files of provocative material. If this is indeed so, then Justice Brennan's decision to accord me access to his case files may have bestowed upon me a privilege which in hindsight will become especially significant, precious, and rare. He may have provided me with the kind of candid insights into the mind and passions of a modern Supreme Court justice that will not be available again to the American public for a very long time.

Justice Brennan did not, however, go so far as to allow me access to his "histories"—detailed journals written by his law clerks that chronicle each of his thirty-four terms on the Court. He offered no explanation for denying my request to see these materials, and at the time we corresponded concerning them, he was undecided as to their ultimate disposition. Perhaps his attitude toward the histories remains essentially the same as it was when he was questioned about them by Nat Hentoff for a profile that ran in the March 12, 1990, edition of *New Yorker* magazine.

He told Hentoff, "It's a very troublesome question for me as to what the hell to do with them [the histories]. I have a very clear memory of how angry Hugo Black and Bill Douglas were when Alpheus Mason used Chief Justice Harlan Fiske Stone's private notes in a biography about him. They were memoranda of cases, histories of cases—the voting, the reactions of the members of the Court, and so forth. Black and Douglas were furious. They insisted that Stone's histories were one-sided and didn't tell the whole story. They said it was all a goddam lie. That's why Hugo Black insisted he was going to burn every damn paper of his. He said, 'I'm not going to have any colleague of mine in a position where he can say I've lied about what happened.' His instructions weren't carried out completely, but some of his papers were destroyed. What concerned Hugo Black bothers me, too."

Consequently, it may be a long time before the contents of Brennan's histories are revealed, if they are ever made available.

To complete the story of William Brennan's life and career, I relied upon interviews with former law clerks and those who worked for him or with him and others who, for whatever reason, knew him well or came within his sphere. Many of these sources wish to remain anonymous, and I fully intend to respect their wishes. Where possible, however, I have cited whatever information I have relied upon to support my perspectives and conclusions.

This biography is intended to make the general public aware of this wonderful man's contributions to American democracy and to popularize his views in the hope that his dreams for all of us may someday come to pass.

Acknowledgments

THERE ARE CERTAIN PEOPLE without whose help this book could not have been written. Unfortunately, many of them wish to remain confidential sources, and so I cannot express my gratitude publicly. But those whose assistance can be revealed I would indeed like to thank.

- Esme Bahn, of Howard University's Moorland-Spingarn Research Center, for nurturing this project with valuable research assistance when it was in its embryonic stages.
- The U.S. Supreme Court library staff for graciously facilitating my use of the Court's files relating to Justice Brennan.
- The staff of the Library of Congress manuscript division for their assistance with Justice Brennan's case files.
- The Drake University Law School Library staff for making no single piece of information beyond more than a few hours' reach.
- The Office of the Curator of the U.S. Supreme Court for helping me compile photographs from the Collection of the Supreme Court of the United States, each one of which encapsulates a story worth more than a thousand words.
- Nicholas T. Christakos, former president of the Harvard Club of Washington, D.C.
- Professor Catherine B. Shannon, former president of the Charitable Irish Society, for her insights into the history and culture of the American Irish.
- Hillel Black, my editor, for the reasons stated in the Dedication of this book, and everyone else at Carol Publishing who worked on this project.
- Edward A. Novak III, my literary agent.
- Justice Brennan's sons, William Joseph Brennan III and Hugh Leonard Brennan, for guiding me through the twists and turns of their family's history.

• And above all, Justice Brennan, for granting me the access to sources and information that I would not otherwise have gained without his consent. I pray my efforts have advanced the traits and ideals embodied in this great American, whom I love so deeply and admire beyond measure.

Justice Brennan

CHAPTER 1

The Perfect Match
of Mind and Heart

[A]n examination of [Justice] Brennan's opinions, and his influence upon the opinions of his colleagues, suggests that there is no individual in this country, on or off the Court, who has had a more profound and sustained impact upon public policy in the United States for the past 27 years.

—*National Review* (May 18, 1984)

JUSTICE THURGOOD MARSHALL was watching television on July 26, 1990, when he learned that President George Bush had named David Hackett Souter to replace Marshall's close friend and liberal ally William Brennan on the U.S. Supreme Court. Irate at the prospect of the obscure New Hampshire judge's ascending to the seat occupied by a man who Marshall declared "cannot be replaced," he flew into a rage. He made an angry phone call to ABC News and hastily arranged a press conference. Later that evening in his home he derided Souter on ABC's *Primetime Live*, telling his interviewer Sam Donaldson, "When his name came down, I listened to television, and the first thing I called my wife and asked, 'Have I ever heard of this man?' She said, 'No, I haven't either.' So I promptly called Brennan. And his wife answered the phone, and...she said, 'He's never heard of him either.'" Marshall went on to ridicule the president who had made the appointment, saying angrily, "It's said that if you can't say something good about a dead person, don't say it. Well, I consider him dead."[1]

It was an inauspicious Washington beginning for Souter, a gaunt, frail-looking New Englander with a perpetual five o'clock shadow, cast as he was in the unenviable role of heir to the Brennan legacy. He admitted that by the time he arrived for his first day at the Court, his self-esteem had sunk about as low as a man's can go. It seemed incongruous, therefore, to find him seated comfortably next to Brennan on the dais at a Harvard Club of Washington, D.C., reception in Brennan's honor, held in the grand ballroom of the National Press Club on the evening of September 30, 1992. The two chatted amiably, exchanged warm glances, and on occasion clasped hands firmly. From among all his distinguished acquaintances and fellow Harvard alumni on and off the Court, the liberal stalwart Brennan had chosen Souter, the New Hampshire conservative, to serve as his toastmaster for the evening.

Souter related in his tribute the story of their first meeting at the Court, where the custom is for the junior justice to move into the chambers of his predecessor. He went to pay a call on Brennan to make the appropriate arrangements. "I had come to the Court, of course, in succession to the seat that he had held for nearly 34 years," he explained.[2] "I did not know how he would feel about that. And I certainly did not know how he would feel about the fact that I was not what might be called a Brennan liberal. I did not know what kind of reception I would get from him.

"I found out when I called on him the first time in his chambers. He saw me, the door was open, he saw me standing in the outer reception room and he came forward to greet me. I got ready for a handshake and what I got instead was a bear hug. Justice Brennan just threw his arms around me and he hugged me and he hugged me and he went on hugging me for a very, very long time.

"Quite simply," he went on, tears welling in his eyes, "Justice Brennan is a man who loves. And I rest my case that the Brennan mind, which held a share of the judicial power of the United States, has met its match in the Brennan heart through which that other power passes and indeed has its origin. And in their perfect match, I think, lies the secret of the greatness of our friend."[3]

He spoke of Brennan's contributions as a justice, reciting by rote the holdings of his major decisions. "One can agree with the Brennan opinions and one may disagree with them," he said.[4] "But their collective influence is an enormously powerful defining force in the contemporary life of this republic. And their author will live in them as what I will call our great contemporary for as long as those opinions exert their power and for as long as we and our successors register the force that they exert.

"The fact is that the sight and sound and thought of our contemporary world is in a great measure the reflection of Justice Brennan's constitutional perceptions. And I may add to that that his influence will affect the fortunes of whatever agenda the Court or country may set in the years ahead. And just as Justice Brennan's influence will endure, he is bound to remain as much our contemporary in the world ahead of us as he is our contemporary this evening."[5]

Souter ranked Brennan among Harvard's most fabled alumni, a group that includes Oliver Wendell Holmes, Louis Brandeis, and Felix Frankfurter, all of whom sat on the Supreme Court. He told the audience, "You have chosen to honor a graduate of the law school not only among the most eminent of our age but the most eminent of any age that the college and the law school have known or will know." As he spoke, caterers passed glasses of champagne all around.

Earlier in the evening, Harvard Club president Nicholas T. Christakos read statements submitted by Harvard University officials for the occasion. University President Neil L. Rudenstine praised Brennan as "one of Harvard Law School's most revered and courageous alumni."[6] His message read, "Justice Brennan, you have spoken up for the voiceless, given strength to the powerless and wisdom to us all. You have brought both reason and passion to bear on the major issues of our time, and you have read our Constitution as the living document it surely was meant to be."

Rudenstine concluded, "If there was a Supreme Court of today's Harvard alumni, we could do no better than to have you as our chief justice. We salute you, and we thank you."[7]

Law School dean Robert C. Clark drew a smattering of hisses for a faxed statement that, though laudatory, was more subdued. "We are enormously proud of the Justice and grateful for his continued devotion and assistance to the school," Clark wrote.[8]

"His appearances at the school have special meaning for students who are always struck by the warmth and modesty of one who has left such an important mark on the law."[9]

More recent Harvard Law School graduates appointed to the Court, such as Justices Antonin Scalia and Souter, have not shared Brennan's liberal views. Most often, they have positioned themselves at the opposite end of the political spectrum.

Souter raised his glass. The audience, peppered with dignitaries and high government officials, rose to its feet. "I pray you," he began, "whether you are liberal or conservative, whether you are old or young, drink with me now to our great contemporary Justice Brennan!"[10] From the crowd came shouts of "Hear, hear!"

Those who are intimately familiar with the modern history of the Court and its internal workings know that William Joseph Brennan Jr. was the seminal justice of the twentieth century. His greatness lay not only in his writings, voluminous and visionary though they are, but also in his force of personality. He was the consummate coalition builder on the Court during its liberal heyday in the 1960s and on into its conservative retrenchment of the 1970s and 1980s. When necessary, he was an indefatigable infighter behind closed doors, possessed of an uncanny gift for forging consensus among his Brethren of differing, if not warring, views.

He was overshadowed in the media throughout his long and illustrious tenure by the likes of Earl Warren, Hugo Black, William O. Douglas, and Thurgood Marshall. But the conservative *National Review* was correct in 1984 when it offered a begrudging accolade to him as a formidable philosophical adversary:

"Today, after more than a quarter-century of service on the High Court—a tenure exceeded by only a handful of Justices—William Brennan remains a figure largely overlooked by the public. Yet an examination of Brennan's opinions, and his influence upon the opinions of his colleagues, suggests that there is no individual in this country, on or off the Court, who has had a more profound and sustained impact upon public policy in the United States for the past 27 years."[11]

Calling him "a study in ironies," the article went on, "A Catholic, he has played an instrumental role in the unfettered availability of abortion across the country and has found tuition tax credits and legislative chaplains unconstitutional; appointed to the Court by a Republican because of his ostensibly conservative views and because of his experience as a state court judge, it is he who mandated the reapportionment of every state legislative system in the country and who has made a substantial contribution to the shift of power from the states to the federal courts; the son of hard-working Irish immigrant parents, he nevertheless has made significant strides in elevating the welfare state to constitutional status."[12]

His goal was always double-edged: attract moderate justices to the liberal fold and move the Court's conservative members more to the center by having them write their opinions more narrowly. Usually, he tried to accomplish his objectives by writing his Brethren personal letters setting forth his thoughts about cases under review rather than through face-to-face confrontations or formal legal memorandums. Frequently he would rely on his law clerks to mingle and share his thoughts with the other justices' clerks. His hope was that they, in turn, would influence the justices for whom they worked.

Often, however, he engaged in direct, personal diplomacy to great effect. Thurgood Marshall once said of the man his grandson William was named after, "There's nobody here that can persuade the way Brennan can persuade. Brennan will sit down with you and talk to you and show you where you're wrong. Well, there's nobody with that power on the Court today."[13]

In his speech to the Harvard Club, Souter quoted from an open letter to Brennan from a former law clerk, describing the justice's technique: his use of irresistible personal charm to gain sway. "'You were talking to someone in the hallway or stairs, a guard, a gardener, a janitor. You pick up your previous conversation with him and remember it as if he were your closest friend. You talk about him and never about yourself. You use his name in every sentence or you call him pal. You grasp onto his arm while talking and never let go as long as the conversation lasts. We used to call it taking the pulse.'"[14]

Turning to Brennan, Souter remarked, "I would bet that each of your law clerks at some point dreamt up some inane topic to discuss with you just to feel the assurance of your grip."[15]

He completed his recitation, "'As you part, you reiterate how delighted you are to have seen him. And he believes he has made your day just by talking to you. He feels that way not because you put on a good act but because it is true.'"[16] Souter added his own emphatic conclusion, "And it *is* true."[17]

With thirty-six years of service, longtime supply manager Henry Johnson was one of the few people who worked at the Court longer than Brennan. He remembered the justice from his early days at the Court. "Justice Brennan was very friendly," Johnson recalled in a 1990 interview.[18] "He would see you in the hall and remember you as a person. He knew you by name. It was like he'd been knowing you for a long time."[19]

Alan C. Kohn can attest to that. Later the founding partner of a St. Louis, Missouri, law firm, Kohn served as a law clerk to Justice Charles E. Whittaker from April 1957 to September 1958, shortly after Brennan joined the Court. He remembered happening onto the justices' elevator one day and coming face-to-face with Brennan. "Imagine my shock and surprise when, before I could say anything, he said to me, 'Hi, Alan. How are you? How do you like working for Justice Whittaker?'

"To have him remember me at all," Kohn recalled, "much less my first name and for whom I was working, was overwhelming. He had an incredibly outgoing and friendly personality which went hand in hand with his consummate political skill. It is easy to understand how he became a great influence on the Court with such a personality to go along with his strong intellectual capacity. And, certainly, it made a lasting impression on me and taught me the lesson that humility and warmth, together with strong, mutual reciprocal relationships, are important ingredients in achieving some happiness and success in life."[20]

Justice John Paul Stevens came under Brennan's spell shortly after he joined the Court in 1975. In a conversation with Brennan soon after his appointment, Stevens mentioned in passing that he had received an invitation to the prestigious Gridiron Club's annual awards dinner but lamented having left his tuxedo home in Illinois.

Brennan sized him up quickly. Noting that they were of equal stature, he offered to lend Stevens his tuxedo for the affair. Stevens accepted and thus was properly attired for his social debut in the nation's capital.[21] Perhaps it should come as no surprise that although Stevens was considered a moderate when President Gerald R. Ford appointed him, he has since moved to the center and is even regarded as disappointingly liberal in some conservative circles.

Souter, too, has come under Brennan's influence. A conservative by reputation, he moved to the center during the Court's 1991–92 term.²² His conservative supporters were especially disappointed by his refusal in *Planned Parenthood v. Casey*²³ to vote to overturn *Roe v. Wade*,²⁴ which in 1973 had established a constitutional right to abortion.

Planned Parenthood involved a Pennsylvania statute that required, among other things, a twenty-four-hour waiting period for abortions, which the Court upheld; parental consent for minors, which was also upheld; and notification of husbands, which the justices struck down. Overall, the Court's lengthy, fractured ruling revised *Roe* significantly. Nonetheless, Souter joined with Justices Sandra Day O'Connor and Anthony Kennedy to form a centrist plurality that reaffirmed *Roe*'s essential holding: A woman has a constitutional right to choose to have an abortion.

One reason cited for upholding *Roe* was the need for the Court to maintain its credibility by adhering to legal precedent—*stare decisis*—rather than shifting wildly each time presidents and the justices they appoint or public opinion changes. On this point, Souter was most eloquent. Reading from the bench the portion of the plurality opinion which he had written, he declared, "Where, in the performance of its judicial duties, the Court decides a case in such a way as to resolve the sort of intensely divisive controversy reflected in *Roe* and those rare, comparable cases, its decision has a dimension that the resolution of the normal case does not carry. It is the dimension present whenever the Court's interpretation of the Constitution calls the contending sides of a national controversy to end their national division by accepting a common mandate rooted in the Constitution."²⁵

He went on, "The Court is not asked to do this very often, having thus addressed the Nation only twice in our lifetime, in the decisions of *Brown* [*v. Board of Education*] and *Roe*. But when the Court does act in this way, its decision requires an equally rare precedential force to counter the inevitable efforts to overturn it and to thwart its implementation. Some of these efforts may be mere unprincipled emotional reactions; others may proceed from principles worthy of profound respect. But whatever the premises of opposition may be, only the most convincing justification under accepted standards of precedent could suffice to demonstrate that a later decision overruling the first was anything but a surrender to political pressure, and an unjustified repudiation of the principle on which the Court staked its authority in the first instance."[26]

He concluded, "So to overrule under fire in the absence of the most compelling reason to reexamine a watershed decision would subvert the Court's legitimacy beyond any serious question."[27]

To underscore their solidarity, the *Casey* trio presented their plurality opinion as the first jointly written Supreme Court decision since the Court's 1958 ruling in *Cooper v. Aaron*,[28] the Little Rock, Arkansas school desegregation case. In *Cooper*, all nine justices were listed as coauthors of an expansive ruling that reaffirmed their undivided commitment to school desegregation and their 1954 ruling in *Brown*.

To those who study the Court, the significance of the ruling in *Casey* transcended even the complex, politically and socially pervasive question of abortion with which the decision ostensibly dealt, for *Casey* did much more than merely reaffirm *Roe*. As author David J. Garrow has observed, "*Casey* also signaled the unexpected failure of the right-wing judicial counterrevolution that the Reagan and Bush administrations had hoped to bring about by naming staunch conservatives to the Federal bench."[29]

Evidently David Souter, as Brennan's heir, aspires to a wisdom that he associates more with Brennan's emphasis on reasonableness and consensus than with ideological extremism of any stripe.

Despite his success and the admiration that Brennan commands among his friends, colleagues, and others familiar with his work, he has always been a humble, self-deprecating man. After being named to the Supreme Court, he likened himself to "the mule that was entered in the Kentucky Derby. I don't expect to distinguish myself," he demurred, "but I do expect to benefit from the association with so many who collectively and individually do so much."[30]

As he was honored by the Harvard Club, he demonstrated the same modesty and reserve. A bespectacled, diminutive Irishman with twinkling eyes and animated gestures, nicknamed "Yoda" by a former law clerk[31] after the sage alien in the "Star Wars" films, he moved unsteadily to the rostrum. At the age of eighty-six, he evidenced the ravages of radiation therapy for throat cancer and the strokes that had impaired his short-term memory. He stood silently until the thunderous applause subsided, then delighted the elite Harvard faithful with a self-deprecating yarn about his first day as a trial lawyer, defending an indigent accused of car theft and armed robbery. His voice grew stronger and his brogue more pronounced the longer he spoke, though he lost his train of thought every two or three sentences, turning each time for prompting from his wife.

"I asked the witness, a retired policeman, whether he was familiar with the defendant's reputation for veracity. He looked confused, then responded, 'Yes, he is a very good driver.'

"I thanked him for that observation, then asked him again whether he was familiar with the defendant's reputation for veracity. Again he answered that the defendant was a very good driver.

"When I asked him a third time, he looked like he was about to get up out of the chair and come after me. He was a big Irish guy. So I turned to the judge and asked him to direct the witness to answer my question.

"The judge looked perturbed. He leaned over and said to the witness, 'Officer so-and-so, Mr. Brennan wants to know the defendant's reputation for telling the truth. But because Mr. Brennan went to *Harvard*, he has to use a word like "veracity" instead of just asking you a simple question.'"[32]

He concluded his remarks quietly, "These wonderful things you have said about me here this evening—I am not all of that."[33]

He departed the dais unsteadily, supported by a cane on one side and his wife on the other. He was handed his coat and prepared to leave while the crowd offered a thunderous ovation. Harvard Club President Christakos moved to the lectern and asked those in attendance to delay their departure so that their applause, while the justice was leaving, would "follow him down the hall and ring in his ears all night." Those who admire him hope it did, just as his words and deeds will ring in America's collective mind and heart forever.

CHAPTER 2

"Everything I Am"

Everything I am I am because of my father.
—William J. Brennan Jr.

THEY CAME IN THREE WAVES, starting at about the time of the American Revolution. First to arrive were the so-called "Scotch-Irish" who emigrated from Ulster, now Northern Ireland. Protestant and Anglicized, they assimilated rapidly into the interior of their new, melting-pot nation. They were renowned for their pioneer spirit.

The second wave came after 1830, Irish Catholics who, because of their religion, were the first conspicuously different ethnic group. They were commonly thought of as "famine immigrants," but other factors combined with crop failure to inspire their exodus, including British military domination, political and religious persecution, and overpopulation. Lacking frontier skills, they settled in the great cities, like Boston, New York, and Philadelphia, where they segregated into urban ghettos, working as laborers and domestics, hauling cement, laying trolley-car tracks, and digging ditches.

Unlike their Scotch-Irish predecessors, they remained identifiable as a group. Differentiated from the mainstream by their religion, they developed their own subsociety, social, cultural, and political. They resented Anglo-Americans, "Yankees," whom they likened to the British oppressors back home. The antipathy was mutual: Anglophiles vilified them with stereotypes—they were "dumb," "incapable of being educated," "drunken," "brutish," "culturally inferior," and "religiously misled"—and with racial slurs—they were "micks," "paddys," and "shanty Irish." Want ads and job postings commonly advised that "Irish need not apply."

The third wave consisted of Irish Catholics who came to the United States in a steady but dwindling stream from about the time of the Civil War to the turn of the century. By the time the stream finally slowed to a trickle, it had culminated in a migration of epic proportions.

"No other country has lost so high a proportion of its population to emigration," historian Marjorie R. Fallows has written of Ireland, "for today, many times more Irish live outside their homeland than in it and there is scarcely an Irish family that does not have part of its lineage in America."[1] The heritage the Irish Catholics who came to the United States during the nineteenth century shared was "an outlook on life formed by centuries of defeat, subjugation and alien occupation of their native country and a Catholic religion darkened by the same past."[2]

William Joseph Brennan Sr. came in the third wave. At the age of twenty, he arrived in Trenton, New Jersey, from his native County Roscommon in 1893 and worked as a laborer.[3] He moved to Newark three years later in search of a better job, and it was there that he met his wife, Agnes McDermott, also a County Roscommon native.

"My dad was born and brought up in Frenchpark and my mother was born and brought up in Castlerea," Bill Jr. told Sean O Murchu in an interview for *Irish America* in 1990.[4] "Now, Castlerea and Frenchpark are really only about 10 miles, if that much, apart, but they never met until they came to the States.

"My mother came to the States to live with an aunt, a Mrs. Butler, who had a boarding house in Newark," he went on.[5] "My father came from Trenton. He had been working on building the canal at Trenton, didn't like it very much, and had a chance to get a job in Newark shoveling coal at Ballantine's brewery. He needed a place to live and somebody, I don't know who, told him about a Roscommon lady who had a boarding house. So he went down, applied and was accepted. My mother was about 17 or 18 at the time. That's how she met him."[6]

His parents, he said, "saw a chance for a better life in America.

That's what I think. I don't know all the details because neither
mother nor father talked about it that much."[7]

What other transplanted Roscommoners of the era remembered
was a place where there was little for a man like Bill Sr., a strapping
six-footer, brawny, muscular, and adventurous, to do. Located
northwest of Ireland's center, landlocked County Roscommon was
far removed from the mystery and challenge of the sea. The
landscape was dotted with hardscrabble family farms, and sheep
grazed the rolling fields. Fresh, clearwater lakes yielded abundant
fish, and iron ore and coal were mined in the hills. But aside from
the raw beauty of the land, the place held little appeal. Although
Bill Sr.'s village of Frenchpark, in western Roscommon, was only
some seven to ten miles northeast of Castlerea, Agnes's home,
neither Bill Sr. nor Agnes were surprised that they had never met.
"That's Roscommon for you," Bill Sr. exclaimed over dinner when
they met. "Nothing ever happens there!"[8]

Agnes agreed. "There's simply nothing to do in Roscommon,"
she said.[9]

Their host, Mr. Butler, proclaimed the world to be small place,
offering, "Well, now, this is Newark, New Jersey, for you!" The
romance was born. They married later that year, 1903.[10]

According to Fallows, "Politics was a career open to the self-
made man as were few others, and along with the priesthood and
union leadership it became one of the most heavily traveled roads to
success for the Irish."[11]

So it was with Brennan Sr. He rose through the ranks of the
trade-union movement and later gained elective office, becoming
Newark's public safety director, the city's most powerful public
official.

"Actually what happened was that when he started shoveling
coal at Ballantine's, he thought the conditions were bad for ordinary
workers," Bill Jr. told O Murchu.[12] "He started organizing within
Ballantine's and then spread around to the other breweries around
the city. Remember, there were no trade laws to help you in those
days. You just had to fight your way through. He did it so well that
he moved up within the organized labor hierarchy around Newark.
At the same time he was going up locally, he was also going up
internationally in the International Brotherhood of Firemen and
Oilers."[13]

Bill Jr. was born on April 25, 1906, the second of eight children. According to one account, his twenty-four-year-old mother went into labor on the night of April 24th, which sent his father dashing into the street calling for a doctor in his thick Irish brogue.[14] A Dr. Haggarty from New Brunswick, New Jersey, in town for a wedding, was passing by in a horse-drawn carriage at just that moment and responded to the emergency. He delivered the future Supreme Court justice in the early hours of the following morning.[15]

Two years later, Brennan's thirty-six-year-old father became business manager of the union local and, in 1909, was elected president of the Essex County Trades and Labor Council, the umbrella group for all county trade unions.[16] It was from that office that the elder Brennan launched his political career, his ambition fired by a bitter and incendiary trolley drivers' strike that lasted, off and on, for three years.

The strike began in 1913. Brennan Sr. started agitating for better wages for Newark's trolley-car drivers, going from union hall to union hall advocating "unity and unionism," often with Agnes and young Bill Jr. at his side.[17] A statewide strike ensued, but ultimately the drivers were defeated.

As Bill Jr. related to O Murchu, "[T]he transit company was headed by Thomas McCarter. The McCarters were the powerful family in Newark and in the state generally. One brother, Easel McCarter, was head of the largest bank in the state, the Fidelity Union Trust Company; Robert N. McCarter was the attorney general in the state and the senior partner in the leading law firm in the state. They really ran the state. They had a grip on the local police department in Newark, and the strike was defeated because the police were on the side of the McCarters."[18]

A defining moment in Bill Jr.'s young life occurred in 1916 when, at the age of ten, he saw his father brought into the house by union men after he had been bloodied and beaten by police during a labor protest.[19] In fact, Bill Jr. told O Murchu that the anti-union police violence and the jailings and beatings of union leaders to break the strike "led to a movement, in which my father was very active, to change the form of government in Newark."[20]

Up to that time, Newark had a mayor-alderman form of government under which power was concentrated in the hands of a single chief executive. Bill Jr. went on, "And before it was changed—in an effort to prevent the change—my father was appointed a police commissioner by the mayor."[21] In fact, Newark's Republican mayor Thomas L. Raymond was so anxious to slow or derail the reform movement that he made the appointment despite staunch Democrat Bill Sr.'s assurance that he had voted against him in the last election[22] and intended to remain loyal to the Democratic Party.[23]

It came as no surprise when the Republican attempt to placate the elder Brennan did not work. Bill Jr. said that after his father's appointment, "he promptly showed where he stood in the labor disputes and then that led to one fight after another. And, by God, they changed it. They changed the form of government from what was a mayor-alderman form to a mayor-councilman form, with commissions, and labor got representation. But that wasn't enough for them. They swept away the whole government—councilman, mayor, alderman and all that business—and substituted it with a city commission of five, and each commissioner was assigned departments."[24]

He continued, "The Department of Public Safety [in Newark] was in charge of the police, firemen and licensing—the most powerful in the whole city. Well, they had a city election to elect the commissioners and the first five were the elected commissioners. There were 80 candidates and my father finished third and was assigned the Department of Public Safety. The term was for four years. He was third in 1917, he was second in 1921; and he was first in 1925 and 1929. And, by all odds, the most powerful public figure in the city in those days."[25]

By the time his father was first elected in 1917, eleven-year-old Bill Jr. was already contributing to the family by working "every kind of job in the world."[26] His father's new position paid better than shoveling coal in the brewery. In fact, his $5,000-a-year salary was good money in those days. "But," Bill Jr. was quick to point out, "there were eight of us."[27]

Besides, the elder Brennan was determined to see his children take full advantage of the opportunities America offered, so he instilled in them an uncompromising work ethic. "Oh, yes," Bill Jr. explained, "with my dad, you had to be doing something all the time, working at something, preferably at something you liked."[28]

Fortunately, young Bill liked doing all sorts of things. By that time, the family lived in a spacious three-story house at 119 Munn in Vailsburg, an ethnic neighborhood that was predominantly Irish and German.

"Across the street from us," he recalled, "was a dairy farm and my brother Charlie, at five in the morning, would milk the cows, and by the time they had cooled it and bottled the milk, I would walk across the street and deliver it all the way up to the school, which was two miles away, and then in the afternoon I would deliver papers.

"Oh, sure, and not only that, but in the transit system, which was a trolley-car system, the fare was five cents and in rush hour there would be a mob running for a trolley car downtown. The transit company dreamed up the bright idea of having high-school kids carry a change purse and go up and down the trolley aisles with change so there would be no delay in getting on. That paid $5 a week."[29]

His father also imbued him with pride in his Irish heritage. "My father kept me, all of us, well aware not of not only the Friendly Sons but the Ancient Order of Hibernians," he recalled.[30] "He used to subscribe to the *Irish World* and some others. And St. Patrick's Day was a big holiday for us.

"Back when I was growing up," he continued, "there were any number of Irish associations, and Irish affairs that my mother and dad used to go to all the time."[31] He recalled that his parents had a player piano and that his mother's favorite "was John McCormack, the great singer, and there wasn't anything of his that was recorded that we did not have the day it came out."[32]

The couple managed one return to the Old Sod, the Emerald Isle, visiting relatives and friends in 1928.[33] "That happened to be my first year in Harvard Law School," Bill Jr. recalled. "You got your grades sometime in the summer and I remember how impossible it was to get telephone service in those days. My father sent telegrams saying, 'Did you get your grades, did you get your grades?'"[34] One thing Bill Jr. always said about his dad was "He was going to make a lawyer of me, by golly."[35] Asked years later whether his father would have been surprised by his appointment to the Supreme Court, he replied, "No, he would have expected it."[36]

Perhaps it was his experience as an Irish Catholic that made the senior Brennan empathetic to the plight of other minorities. This empathy, too, he imparted to his son. When William Ashby, the Newark Urban League's first director, complained early in Brennan's tenure of bias against African Americans in police hiring, the new public-safety director put more African Americans on the force.[37]

His mother, Agnes, for her part, was content to remain in the background while her domineering husband's political fortunes and influence rose. "I wish I could do justice to her," he said. "Mother was just absolutely extraordinary really, she was a sweet, caring woman, fending off my dad when he got upset with something we were doing. She would protect us."[38]

She outlived her husband by some thirty-five years, for which Bill Jr. was grateful as it allowed her to witness and share in the fruits of her sacrifice. "Thank God she survived until my appointment here [to the U.S. Supreme Court]," he told O Murchu. "I was here for about ten years before she died."[39]

As a labor leader, Bill Sr. had built his reputation through his outspoken commitment to the interests of working people. As a politician, he made his name by cleaning up the city government. One of his first moves as director of public safety was to order a crackdown on those who violated the liquor law. Under what became known as "Brennan's law," taverns were ordered closed promptly at 1:00 A.M. in accordance with what was in fact an existing ordinance that saloonkeepers and landlords had for years routinely bribed police not to enforce.[40]

In 1923, he "notified all fourteen of the captains in the police department that the city must be rid soon of vices, particularly gambling, or they would be suspended and placed of [sic] trial for dereliction of duty."[41] He also made clear that police brutality and forced "confessions" would not be tolerated. "The use of unnecessary force in making arrests, and violence in any form towards the citizens, has been done away with," he boasted during his 1925 reelection campaign.[42] "Nightsticks should last a long time. The police have been made the servants of the people and not their masters."[43]

He even went so far as to defy the policemen's union. In 1921, he rejected a pension plan proposal that he regarded as overgenerous.[44] The conservative *Newark Daily News*, which had opposed his election, lauded his efforts. "Originally elected as a labor man,

Brennan has shown honest independence for the city's interests and unusual courage in public service," the newspaper opined.[45] "He is inexperienced, but strong in honesty and grit."[46] *The Newark Evening News* offered similar praise for his stubborn defiance of vested interests, declaring, "Brennan doesn't give a tinker's damn what people think, when he thinks he is right."[47]

Every man has a public life, a private life, and a secret life, however, and by at least one account the elder Brennan's private behavior did not always match his public persona, especially not as he got older. He "flatly refused to condemn gambling."[48] Moreover, he "paid mere lip service to the idea of enforcing Prohibition."[49] "He hated drunkenness, but was not opposed to a sociable cocktail if it was handled with adult aplomb."[50]

In addition, he indulged in the petty perquisites of high office: a city-owned cabin by the reservoir and a car paid for by the government.[51] He may have had some role in a hit-and-run fatality involving the car for which he managed to escape both liability and responsibility. Evidently Brennan Sr. was driving or riding in the vehicle that struck and killed Oscar Santholm in Kearny, New Jersey, on the night of March 2, 1918.[52] Santholm's widow subsequently brought suit against Brennan and the automobile manufacturer for $50,000.[53]

The trial judge declared a "nonsuit" in regard to Brennan, finding that he was "merely a guest" in the vehicle.[54] The driving instructor who was present and the manufacturer, Whiting Motor Car Company, were held jointly liable for $8,000 in damages.

But whatever might have been William Brennan Sr.'s ambitions, responsibilities, or foibles, he was devoted to his family, and his son Bill Jr. loved him. "Even though there were eight of us and he was on call 24 hours a day, he never neglected us," he said.[55] In 1986, he told an interviewer, "Everything I am I am because of my father."[56]

Yet he was, in fact, more of a momma's boy growing up in Newark. He walked hand in hand with her to Mass on Sunday.[57] And he sided with her in family arguments when she stood up to his father.[58]

Nevertheless, he complied with his father's demand for academic excellence. "I wasn't a hellraiser as a child, that's something my father would never tolerate," he told an interviewer in 1989.[59] "He was quite a disciplinarian, and his one absolute determination was that each of us would get everything in the way of education."[60] He went on, "I had four sisters and three brothers and it was a strict Catholic household, the old kind that is. We all went to parochial schools and if there weren't any, we went to public schools."[61]

Bill Jr. "got A's, but had to work for them."[62] His teachers described him as a "perfect young man, thoughtful and polite, never a cutup."[63] A high school classmate said, "Bill took home so many academic prizes from school, none were left for the rest of us."[64]

His father decided early on that his eldest son would be a lawyer, not a politician following in his footsteps. "Lad," his father once told him, "you argue well around the house and I've no doubt you'll make a fine lawyer. But as for politics, I think you'd be happier out than in."[65]

Bill Jr. explained, "Well, in his position, my dad had a number of very close friends who were lawyers and he was so taken with this whole bunch of Irish lawyers. They were the leaders of the bar and they were close friends of my father's, and my dad encouraged me to do it and got them to encourage me."[66]

They did, and Bill Jr. was persuaded. By the time he was graduated from Newark's public Barringer High School, his sights were set firmly on practicing law. In the fall of 1924, he left home to attend the University of Pennsylvania's undergraduate Wharton School of Finance and Commerce. In 1928, he was graduated with honors and a degree in economics. In the fall of that year, he entered Harvard Law School.

CHAPTER 3

Harvard Law School

Most of us learned very little about how to be a lawyer and practice law....Bill Brennan, however, did get some taste of the real world and a chance to deal with people's problems first hand.

—Frederick W. Hall, a friend, Harvard
Law School classmate, and New Jersey
state supreme court justice

BILL BRENNAN DISTINGUISHED HIMSELF at Wharton the way he did in all his endeavors for the rest of his life, by combining a prodigious capacity for hard work and self-discipline with an unswerving commitment to a long-range goal. Wharton proved to be a sensible choice. A lawyer who might one day be in practice for himself needed to develop a good business sense. He placed his academic emphasis on finance and business-related subjects.

In his extracurricular pursuits, he exploited his penchant for detail, his commitment to exhaustive preparation, and his affinity for the supporting, rather than the leading, role. As secretary for his fraternity, he kept minutes of meetings, recorded membership and attendance, and organized activities and events. As student manager of Penn's football team, he was in charge of uniforms, equipment, towels, and the water bucket. His social life, meanwhile, was focused on a woman named Marjorie Leonard.

He met Marjorie at a tea at the Washington Hotel in Newark during his sophomore year of high school.[1] He found her "fascinating and bright," he told his friends, and he was undaunted by the fact

21

that she had come escorted by someone else.[2] Her father had been Hugh Leonard, the New York Athletic Club's wrestling coach, killed when he was struck by lightning when she was only five.[3] She was orphaned six years later when her mother died, and she was raised and educated by her two older sisters who were school-teachers in the tiny Genessee River town of Belfast in southwestern New York.[4] She was living in East Orange, New Jersey, at the time she met Bill Jr., and they began courting.[5] They married on May 5, 1928, in Baltimore, Maryland, a month before his college graduation.

She was twenty at the time; he was twenty-one. It was a marriage that would produce three children—William Joseph III, Hugh Leonard, and Nancy—and last some fifty-four years, until her death in 1982.

Four months after their wedding, Bill Jr. was on his way to Harvard Law School in Cambridge, Massachusetts. His father had made him a Harvard man. Columbia University Law School in New York City was the "school of choice" in those days.[6] Columbia's former dean Harlan Fiske Stone, who later became chief justice of the United·States, had recruited an impressive, research-oriented faculty.[7] This being the case, it would have been natural for a student with Bill Jr.'s fine record to aim high for Columbia. But in the twilight of the roaring twenties, Manhattan's social temptations made Bill Sr. uneasy about sending his son to law school there.[8] So he sent him to Harvard in stodgy Cambridge instead.[9]

Not that Harvard was by any means second-rate. The case method developed there by Dean C. C. Langdell and others during the nineteenth century was the paradigm for how law should be taught. The case method based legal research on the study of actual cases rather than textbooks. In addition, the faculty boasted legendary professors like Roscoe Pound; Austin Wakeman Scott and Samuel Williston, whose names were synonymous with trusts and contracts law, respectively; and Felix Frankfurter, to name but a few. Harvard could also point to an impressive array of alumni who had served on the U.S. Supreme Court, including two giants, Oliver Wendell Holmes and Louis D. Brandeis. No, the problem for Bill Brennan was not Harvard's stature; his problem was money or, rather, lack of it, which was why he went to Cambridge alone.

When they married, Marjorie vowed to become "the same kind

of shy but loyal Irish wife Agnes [his mother] had always been."[10] Now that promise was put to the test. His father had seven other children to support on his government salary. Some of them would soon be college age. There was no way Bill Sr. could shoulder the entire financial load of Bill Jr.'s tuition. Bill Jr. turned to Marjorie and asked her to pay for his law-school education. Dutifully and enthusiastically she complied. When he left for Cambridge, she stayed behind to work as a secretary and proofreader for a local newspaper in New Jersey.[11]

Bill Brennan liked Harvard Law School. He thrived on the fast-paced, intellectual challenge of it and the voluminous workload. But he struggled at first to find his niche. Harvard was geared more toward theory than practice; its faculty and curriculum emphasized the law's theoretical underpinnings and abstract, philosophical concepts. By contrast, young Bill was sensible, mundane, and practical. He picked a goal and went after it. It might take patience and a great deal of work. He understood that whatever he wanted he could get with time, patience, and work. He was, in short, result-oriented, more concerned with the outcome than with the method needed to achieve his goal.

In this sense, Harvard played to his weaknesses. He could do the work despite its theoretical or philosophical nature. But it was still not the kind of work on which he could bring to bear such strengths as his forceful and appealing personality and powers of persuasion. He was personable, warm, pragmatic, a good problem solver—and he had a good bit of the blarney in him to boot. Harvard did not grade on those qualities. Hence Bill failed, initially, to make much of an impression. Years later when he achieved renown, classmates recalled him vaguely as a "workaholic" and "prodigious note taker."[12]

He failed to win a position on the *Harvard Law Review*, a top honor achieved by only the most outstanding students. But although he was not the brightest star in Harvard's constellation, his grades were good enough to earn him the opportunity to work for the Harvard Legal Aid Society located downstairs in the *Law Review*'s plain white, frame building on Massachusetts Avenue. This work brought out the best in him.

The Harvard Legal Aid Society gave students the chance to handle actual cases and practice in court representing indigent clients in divorce, bankruptcy, landlord–tenant, and other civil matters. In short, it was *real* lawyering on behalf of *real* people. Harvard's emphasis on theory over practice was evidenced by the fact that no academic credit was given for the clinical work done at the Society, no matter how skillful or successful.

Hence, for those who participated it was a labor of love on behalf of the poor. And yet it was worthwhile by any measure for the invaluable experience it provided, especially to those like Bill Brennan who aspired more to being practitioners than academicians or scholars. For Brennan it was a chance to cultivate his "intangible assets," such as client counseling, negotiating, and crafting litiga-tion strategy.

According to Frederick W. Hall, a classmate and friend who later served on the New Jersey state supreme court, Harvard law students of the era "learned very little about how to be a lawyer and practice law. Through the Ames [Moot Court] competition we did acquire some experience in brief writing and appellate argument so that when we graduated we perhaps could argue an appeal but could not safely advise a client or try a case in the lowest tribunal. Bill Brennan, however, did get some taste of the real world and a chance to deal with people's problems first hand through his membership in the Legal Aid Society—at that time gained purely on the basis of grades."[13] Unfortunately, no sooner had he found his niche than his financial needs were complicated by the illness and death of his father during his second year of law school.

Bill Sr. was only fifty-seven years old in 1930, but his health was poor and he had aged beyond his years. His red hair had turned pure white, his kidneys troubled him, and, irritable from not feeling well, he had a temper and a short fuse. A petty turf battle over taxicab licenses early in the year almost brought him to blows with the city's licensing commissioner. According to one account, "Brennan ripped off his glasses and lunged at the younger man with fists clenched."[14] Meanwhile his decision to prohibit employees under his control from working second jobs earned him the sobriquet "Simon Legree"[15] after the heartless slave master in Harriet Beecher Stowe's *Uncle Tom's Cabin.*

His doctor prescribed rest. But when he finally managed to get away in mid-May he contracted pneumonia during a weekend trip to the Pequannock watershed[16] in western New Jersey. Two weeks later he died. His wife, Agnes, and mother, Bridgett, were at his bedside when he passed away, along with two of the eight children—Kathleen, at twenty-five the eldest, and Charles, twenty-one, then enrolled at Penn.[17] Bill Jr. stayed in Cambridge throughout his father's sudden illness to study for his second-year final exams.[18]

"He had a remarkable reputation," Bill Jr. said of his father years later.[19] His dad was indeed loved, and when he died, Newark grieved. One headline declared, "Whole City Mourns at Brennan Funeral."[20] He lay in state and was then taken to his final rest in a funeral procession that was a mile long.[21] In addition to his mother, wife, Kathleen, Bill Jr., and Charles, he was survived by the five other children: Betty, seventeen; Margaret, fourteen; Helen, twelve; Tom; and Frank, the youngest at ten.

An honest politician, Bill Sr. had supported his large family on nothing but his salary, spending up to every penny of it, with little to leave behind when he died.[22] With the United States in the midst of the Great Depression, prospects looked bleak indeed for the Brennan family, especially for Bill Jr., who, even with Marjorie's support, had no way to pay for his final year of law school. The alumni foundation at Harvard refused, however, to permit the loss of a promising student.[23] Bill Jr. was granted a scholarship to complete his studies based on scholastic achievement and need. For spending money, he waited tables at a fraternity house and also did other odd jobs.[24]

The year after his father's death, he was graduated "high in his law class."[25] Next, he set about the business of making a career for himself and helping to care for the large family his father had bequeathed him.

CHAPTER 4

Counselor and Soldier

To ignore the conditions of the many underpaid people in the
United States is as foolish as it would be to ignore public health,
crime and the need for education.

—Robert Wood Johnson,
chairman of the board,
Johnson & Johnson Company

B Y THE TIME BILL BRENNAN was graduated from Harvard Law
School in 1931, there was little of the open discrimination
against the Irish that had been common in his father's day. None of
the elite corporate law firms, all bastions of WASP power, would be
so crass as to declare outright, "Irish Need Not Apply." Yet being
both Irish and Catholic were strikes against him as he sought his
first job. In those days no top-flight Wall Street firm hired
Catholics.

He considered hanging out his shingle as a sole practitioner or
founding a partnership with Donald Kipp, a friend since the first
year of law school. But he worried about being able to attract
enough paying clients to make a living. "What if one day no one
walks in the door?" he used to ponder aloud to Kipp.[1] After all,
times were hard. It was the Great Depression, and most people
needed food, not lawyers.

Corporations, however, needed lawyers all the time, Depression
or no, and what the large corporate law firms paid was irresistible,
When he heard there might be a permanent position available with

Pitney, Hardin & Skinner, the top big firm in his hometown of Newark, he pursued it.

Pitney, Hardin had never hired a Catholic on a permanent basis, although Brennan had clerked there the summer following his second year of law school.[2] Founded around the turn of the century by John Oliver Halstead Pitney, whose older brother Mahlon Pitney served on the U.S. Supreme Court from 1912 to 1922, the firm was quintessentially blue-blood. Its tradition was, in fact, to hire only Princeton men, though its partners' law degrees varied because Princeton had no law school.[3] The firm's corporate clientele included the Duke Power Company, New Jersey Bell, Howard State Bank, and United New Jersey Railroad.[4] Its specialty was strike breaking.[5]

Shelton Pitney, the managing partner of Pitney, Hardin, decided to break with tradition. Justice Mahlon Pitney had little involvement with the firm his younger brother John Oliver had founded.[6] But the justice's son Shelton took over as managing partner after his uncle's death in 1928.[7] His father, who had died in 1924, had been a conservative justice. He had voted to strike down state minimum-wage and maximum-hour laws.[8] He had also written the majority opinion upholding the conviction of accused child slayer Leo Frank,[9] who had obviously been railroaded and was later lynched by an anti-Semitic mob in Georgia.

At the same time, however, Justice Pitney was "sensitive to the vagaries of the industrial workplace,"[10] and, oddly, "his most enduring contribution to the development of American constitutional law was his support for state workmen's compensation statutes."[11] According to liberal Justice Louis D. Brandeis, "But for Pitney we would have had no workmen's compensation laws."[12]

Evidently Shelton Pitney inherited a streak of his father's anomalous liberalism. He decided that the firm had to change to keep pace with the times. He made young Bill the firm's first Catholic hire and assigned him to what was then an arcane but promising aspect of the firm's practice, labor law. Thus Bill Jr. found himself cast in a role that placed him squarely at odds with his own legacy, for Pitney, Hardin represented management, not labor. In fact, one of his father's best friends referred to the firm derisively as "Pluck'em, Hook'um and Skin'um."[13] Bill "Unity and Unionism" Sr. must have turned over in his grave.

There were two ways to succeed in big law firm practice. One was to be a "rain maker"; the other was to be a "ditch digger." Rain makers made profits for the firm by using their social connections to bring in high-paying clients. Ditch diggers, by contrast, justified their salaries through invaluable long hours of grunt labor. If the former was the high road and the latter the low, then Bill Brennan started down the low road at Pitney, Hardin. What he lacked in family wealth and business connections he compensated for with hard work. It was typical for him to arrive at the office at 8:00 A.M. and stay until 2:00 A.M. the next day.[14]

At the same time, he managed to study for and gain admission to the bar. Under New Jersey's bar rules in the 1930s, would-be lawyers were required to serve a yearlong "clerkship," in effect an apprenticeship, with someone already admitted to practice before taking the attorney's examination.[15] Candidates who were successful on that exam had to pass a second test three years later in order to qualify as a counselor-at-law.[16] Brennan passed the attorney's exam in 1932 and was admitted to practice as a full counselor in 1935.[17]

Meanwhile, Shelton Pitney marveled at his young associate's inexhaustible energy. He took him under his wing, adopting him "as his personal associate for complicated tax and labor work."[18] Brennan "rose rapidly, gaining considerable experience in corporate law and management–labor problems"[19] that were on the cutting edge of the New Deal. In 1935, Congress passed the Wagner Act, which set up the National Labor Relations Board and established the rights of unions to organize and bargain collectively. According to friend and classmate Frederick Hall, Brennan "proved particularly adept at dealing with people at point-blank range in [labor] negotiations."[20]

His talent and commitment paid off. His "keen analytical mind, awesome discipline, and prodigious capacity for sustained work were winning him a fine reputation in the legal profession."[21] In 1937, Pitney, Hardin made him a partner.[22] Six years out of law school, he was thirty-one years old.

"All appeared serene."[23] In addition to his career success, "there were then two healthy children in Brennan's household,"[24] William III and Hugh Leonard, five and two years old, respectively, and in around 1938 the family moved to a comfortable house at 2 Brookwood Road in South Orange, New Jersey.[25]

The young lawyer was forced, however, to limit his life to the practice of law. Bill Brennan led a sedentary existence. Whereas his father had loved to fish and drive cars, Bill Jr. had no hobbies and did not particularly enjoy movies or the theater.

Only rarely did he get home from the office in time to have dinner with Marjorie and the boys. When he did, the boys were put to bed afterward and he and Marjorie sat up reading. He enjoyed biographies and Irish poetry—*Plutarch's Lives* and the works of W. B. Yeats were among his favorites—which he might peruse while smoking a pipe from the extensive collection his father had left him. Marjorie, for her part, liked detective novels. Summer vacations, when he was able to take time away from work, were typically spent on the beach in a rented cottage on Cape Cod.

World War II changed everything, shattering his comfortable if banal calm and buffeting the Brennan clan with grief and worry. Charlie, his beloved brother with whom he had milked cows and delivered milk in the early morning hours of his childhood years, was killed during the American army's invasion of the Philippines at Leyte Gulf in October 1944.[26] Another brother, Frank, was shot down over Germany that same year but managed to parachute back to earth and survive the remainder of the war in a German POW camp.

Bill Jr. entered the army himself in July 1942.[27] He was thirty-six. He recalled, "I was asked to come into the service and head up the labor end of the Ordnance Department, which had the task of procuring munitions from all over the country."[28] The man who "asked" him to enlist was Robert Wood Johnson, whose father had invented adhesive tape and founded the multi-million-dollar Johnson & Johnson company in 1896.[29] As chairman of the company's board of directors, Robert Wood Johnson had been one of Brennan's clients at Pitney, Hardin.[30]

A man of vision and compassion, Johnson had worked closely with Brennan to fashion an innovative package of workers' benefits for his employees as the 1930s drew to a close.[31] "To ignore the conditions of the many underpaid people in the United States is as foolish as it would be to ignore public health, crime and the need for education," he once declared in a speech at Catholic University in Washington, D.C.[32] A zealous patriot, Johnson enlisted after the attack on Pearl Harbor, was commissioned a colonel, and in May

1942 was assigned to the army's Ordnance Division in Washington.

According to Johnson, at that time the army's entire ordnance operation was conducted by six officers, including himself, and six stenographers, from "a room that measured about twenty by twenty with loops of telephone and light wires dangling in spiral festoons from the ceiling."[33] He said, "We undertook to spend some $36 billion for army ordnance. We placed orders wherever there was most likelihood of immediate and substantial deliveries and we sought justification in the old army motto: 'You never get court-martialed for ordering too much.'"[34]

When he decided he needed a good lawyer, he thought of Bill Brennan, the man he had turned to for help in reshaping his company's labor relations. He approached his superior, Major General Levin Campbell, about bringing Brennan on board.[35] Campbell acceded to Johnson's request, called Brennan, who was vacationing on Cape Cod, and asked him to enlist.[36] "I hadn't thought particularly about going into the army," he said later, "but the first thing I knew, I was in uniform."[37]

Commissioned a major, he joined Johnson's operation in Washington, where "his knowledge and experience in labor law proved of great help."[38] Within a year, he was promoted to lieutenant colonel and put in charge of the labor resources section of the Office of the Chief of Ordnance.[39] Meanwhile, Johnson transferred out of Washington to New York in January 1943, leaving Brennan to work more closely with Undersecretary of War Robert P. Patterson, who was in charge of army procurement.[40]

The two had much in common and worked well together. Brennan was the son of Irish immigrants; Patterson's paternal grandfather, a Protestant minister, had emigrated from County Sligo,[41] a northwestern province contiguous to County Roscommon. Both were graduates of Harvard Law School. Both had been in corporate law practice, Patterson with a big Wall Street firm.[42] Patterson was older and had served with distinction in World War I, during which he was awarded the Purple Heart and the Distinguished Service Cross for valor.[43]

Patterson "adopted Brennan as his primary aide-de-camp."[44] Together with Lieutenant General Bill Knudson, peacetime president of General Motors, they "feverishly tackled the problems of the warplane industry."[45] They organized a rally to promote patriotism and the war-weapons industry that was attended by tens of thousands of people at the Los Angeles Coliseum in late 1943.[46] They also traveled the West Coast delivering speeches, promoting better conditions for factory workers, and introducing innovations like staggered shifts to avoid traffic snarls.[47]

By 1943, Brennan was chief of the army Ordnance Department's Civilian Personnel Division.[48] It was in that role that he made some of his most controversial decisions of the war. The biggest issue he faced concerned the discharge or furlough of servicemen in Europe after the war against Hitler was over.

He was confronted with requests from major industries and their allies in Congress that frontline soldiers who were skilled workers in certain occupations be discharged or furloughed ahead of others. For example, the transport of war supplies and materiel from the East to West coast for shipment to the Pacific theater was logjammed. The railroad companies blamed the army, complaining that many of their best-skilled workers were stuck in Europe when they should have been back home assisting in the delivery of supplies for the continuing war against Japan.

Brennan insisted, however, on equal treatment for all servicemen. Despite strong political pressure, he refused to allow discharges or furloughs based on occupational preferences. He feared that favoritism, or the appearance of favoritism, would undermine morale.

In 1945, the U.S. Senate established what became known as the Mead Committee, a special panel to investigate the national defense program, chaired by Senator James Mead of New York. The committee held hearings in Washington shortly after V-E Day, on July 18, 23–24, 27, and 31, and on August 16, 18, and 21–24. Among other things, the committee took up the question of Brennan's refusal to grant furloughs and discharges based on occupational preferences. Brennan, who was by that time chief of the army Service Forces labor branch, was called to testify and to defend his steadfast position.

At one point, he was questioned pointedly by Chairman Mead about his refusal to permit the 719th transportation battalion to be released from duty in June 1945, immediately after European hostilities ended. Located in Italy, the 719th was composed primarily of railroad men whose mission was to handle the European railroads during the war. Mead demanded of Colonel Brennan, "Why has this not been done?"[49]

Brennan replied, "In response to the general discharge program, the point system was developed, as you know, after consultation with the GIs themselves regarding what factors should be taken into account in making discharges, and it is the GIs who said that they wanted four factors which the discharge program uses—length of service, of service overseas, of combat experience, and number of children. They had an opportunity to vote on the occupational qualification as a factor, and they turned it down overwhelmingly."[50]

Mead pressed on. "We have no objection to the arrangements with the GIs," he insisted. "We think that is very laudable on the part of the Army and that it is good coordination, but if you had a crisis in the country that would interfere with the Japanese war effort, it occurs to us that the furloughing temporarily of experienced men...would not in any way interfere with any arrangements."[51]

Brennan held his ground. "Let me say, Senator, we had furlough programs prior to the end of the European war. You may recall we had them in ammunition plants, rubber plants, and cotton duck [small sails] plants. And the GIs who were still fighting in fox holes in Europe made a very real issue of the fact that some of their buddies, no better qualified than they, were permitted the soft spots in industrial employment while they had to continue fighting in Europe."[52]

He continued, "The point I am trying to make is that the guys who still have the war to fight in the Pacific are the fellows to whom it is not fair and who will first resent any deviations from the point system of discharge, because to the extent you make an exception for a single soldier there is somebody eligible for discharge whose discharge is delayed or perhaps doesn't come about for a long time."[53] He insisted, "We cannot explain to the soldier why this kind of problem can't be solved with civilian labor."[54]

Brennan had made his point. He was not long for the military anyway, though he did not know it at the time. Asked years later about his army experience, he replied, "Sure I regret not having seen more of the front lines. I expected to when I was ordered to Manila in 1945 before we dropped the bomb. General Styer was there setting up what was called AFWESPAC—Army Forces, Western Pacific—the outfit that was going to invade Japan. I was ready to head up personnel in the Philippines, but the *Enola Gay* stopped that."[55] The *Enola Gay* was the name of the B-29 bomber that dropped the atomic bomb on Hiroshima. In September 1945, he separated from the army at the rank of full colonel, having been awarded the Legion of Merit for his contributions to the military's procurement programs.[56]

CHAPTER 5

A Major Scandal

[I]t seems to me that men in high places should be like Caesar's wife, beyond suspicion.

—John Slezak, chief of the
Chicago Ordnance District

BILL BRENNAN'S AWESOME SELF-DISCIPLINE and the fervor with which he attacked the challenges he confronted as an army procurement officer belied his peaceful spirit, his gentle soul. By the time the war finally ended, he was more than ready to go home. As a decorated veteran with friends in high places like Robert Patterson, whom President Harry S. Truman elevated to secretary of war in September 1945, he might well have enjoyed a successful Pentagon career on either the civilian or service side of the military. But he never even considered it. Instead he concluded justifiably that he had done his duty, having served his country in the way that made the most of what a man like him had to contribute.

In business suit and tie, his wife, Marjorie, at his side, he boarded a train headed north for New Jersey in September 1945 wondering as he pulled out of Union Station whether he would ever again return to Washington. The train was full of servicemen still in uniform, returning to their wives and families. Most were younger than Bill, closer in age to his brothers Frank and Charlie.

As the whistling locomotive whisked him through what was no longer just the American capital but now the capital of the free world, past the Negro tenements jumbled alongside the railroad tracks in the segregated city, he bade a forlorn farewell to the Capitol dome glistening in the distance in the afternoon sunlight. He took the white linen handkerchief from the breast pocket of his coat and wiped the lenses of his wire-rimmed glasses, which had misted. He bit his lip and said a silent prayer for his dead brother to hear. Marjorie squeezed his bicep. His mind was a camera whirring with images of Charlie.

Ironically the aftermath of the war that had demanded so much and cost the Brennan family so dearly was about to open opportunities for the thirty-nine-year-old ex-colonel that were beyond any he could have planned. The conquest of Germany and Japan had united the nation, including management and labor, which set aside their differences with the overriding goal of maximizing output for the war effort. Now peacetime unleashed all the festering hostilities and grievances. No sooner had the country extricated itself from the military conflict abroad than it found itself embroiled in labor upheaval at home. When Bill Brennan returned to private practice with his old firm, the nation was rife with slowdowns, work stoppages, and strikes over such issues as higher wages, improved working conditions, and better workers' benefits—all of which had been postponed because of the war.

As a labor-law specialist, he had talents that were in great demand. His law firm realized his potential for bringing in business and advertised his presence by making him a name partner in what now became Pitney, Hardin, Ward, and Brennan. "He practiced law, including labor law, with competence and courtesy."[1] Meanwhile, he "resumed the comparatively even tenor of private life."[2]

His share of the partnership earnings was roughly $50,000 annually, comfortable for the times by any measure.[3] He worked long hours, as always, but occasionally found time for golf, which Marjorie also enjoyed. Then two events occurred that altered the course of his life.

The first took place on December 7, 1945, four years to the day the Japanese bombed Pearl Harbor, when John Ralph Hardin, the firm's principal business-getter, died suddenly at his desk.[4] The second followed about a month later when Shelton Pitney, the firm's managing partner, who had originally hired Brennan and been his mentor, died unexpectedly of a heart attack.[5] Home just five months from the war, Brennan found the firm that now bore his name suddenly shaken by the loss of its two most prominent and renowned members, upon whose contacts much of the firm's business depended.

With so much at stake personally and professionally, he tried to move in and fill the void created by Hardin's and Pitney's untimely deaths. The result, unenviable despite its material rewards, was that he became both ditch digger and rain maker.

At first, he wore both hats with aplomb. According to Tom Dunn, future mayor of Elizabeth, New Jersey, who at the time was a union leader at Western Electric, which Brennan represented, Brennan's polished demeanor and elegantly understated conservative apparel made him an impressive opponent during a labor dispute that began in late 1945 and carried over into the spring of 1946. Dunn recalled that Brennan "looked like one of the blue bloods from Essex County," that he had the "look of a guy who was really on his way up the ladder."[6]

Yet he was gracious and humane, a gentleman, and fair. Dunn recalled that shortly before the start of a hearing in their litigation, Brennan approached him unexpectedly and said, "I just want you to know I've asked the judge to postpone our case. I just found out your father has [recently] passed away. We'll have the hearing another day."[7]

Another opponent, Morton Stavis, future founder of the Center for Constitutional Rights, remembered how Brennan assisted him generously so that the issues raised in a couple of cases they worked on could be presented clearly for the court.[8] He recalled, "He was a vigorous, overwhelmingly able, and above all gracious opponent. I was inexperienced in litigation at the time and was guilty of a number of procedural oversights. Not only did he not take advantage of them but he went out of his way to help me correct the record so that the cases would be tried fairly on the merits. Result: he won one case, I won the other."[9]

On April 1, 1946, Brennan enhanced his reputation and name recognition tremendously with a speech to the Essex County, New Jersey, Bar Association in which he made an impassioned plea for organized labor to reform itself. His remarks were reprinted a month later on the front page of the May 9 edition of *The New Jersey Law Journal*, the state's weekly legal newspaper, of which he was an editor, under the title "Formulae for the Settlement of Labor Disputes."

Claiming to speak neither "for management generally, nor for any managements particularly," he declared, "I do *not* believe that all strikes are bad. I think that an industrial democracy inevitably must have some of them when collective bargaining doesn't resolve differences. Strikes, with the exception, perhaps, of stoppages in industries of vital public importance, such as utilities, are not too great a penalty for industrial freedom." He warned, "The alternative [to strikes] is solution of disputes by government fiat and that is a dead end road destructive of the interests of management and worker alike."

He went on to call for "remedial legislation" that would recognize organized labor's "present day great strength and power." He observed, "Unions now have 14 million members, as compared to 4 millions in 1935. Their membership totals almost 50% of the industrial work force in industries where unions are active. And 10 and 1/4 millions of these members are under closed or union shop or union maintenance agreements."

At the same time, however, he criticized labor's "tendency toward abuses" of its power, which, he said, "cry out for some measures of control." Alluding to the American public's "irritation with the recent strike epidemic," he called upon labor unions to be grateful for their recent progress. He explained, "In the circumstances of labor shortage prevalent throughout the war, the balance of bargaining lay with them and most unions did not hesitate to press their advantage to the full. Maintenance of membership, that potent weapon for increasing and holding membership, was the most important, but great gains in vacation benefits, paid holidays, sick leave and other valuable and very desirable improvements in working conditions were achieved without any real struggle."

Urging the unions to exercise self-restraint, he admonished them, "Free enterprise succeeds only when each group furthering its common aims practices a high degree of self-government, self-discipline and self-reliance and accepts its responsibilities not wrongly to invade or trample upon the rights of other groups," including management.

He concluded with a call to outlaw as unfair labor practices the "coercion and intimidation of individuals to become and remain union members," as well as racial discrimination in union representation or membership, which was common.

Successful within his law firm, well respected within his profession, young and vigorous, Bill Brennan was prospering. His future indeed looked bright, despite the demands of his high-profile rain making. But before he could move forward and reap the benefits of his prodigious labors, he would have to retrace and defend his recent past. In the summer of 1946, he was called back to Washington to testify again before the Mead Committee. This time, he would have to defend himself against charges of corruption relating to a wartime procurement scandal that had become popularly known as the "Garsson war profits case."[10]

The scandal broke when the Mead Committee learned that some $48,000 had been paid by a government weapons contractor, the Chicago-based Garsson combine, to a nonexistent lumber concern whose agent happened to be Congressman Andrew May of Kentucky, chairman of the House Military Affairs Committee.[11] In other words, May had been bribed to steer arms contracts to Garsson during the war.

Further investigation revealed that the Garsson brothers' Batavia Metal Products Company had been awarded the contract to produce crucial 8-inch artillery shells, despite the brothers' shadowy backgrounds.[12] Henry Garsson had been fired as an Internal Revenue Service agent following bribery charges.[13] Murray Garsson, for his part, was known for associating with such notorious gangsters as Dutch Schultz and Owney Madden.[14] In what it charged was a major scandal, the Washington Post alleged that army procurement officers had been unduly influenced by May's "pressure tactics" in both the awarding of contracts and the handling of matters related to the Garssons.[15]

Robert Patterson was mentioned in the Post by name. Brennan was implicated by virtue of his efforts to get the manpower ceiling for Batavia raised late in the war when most workers were away in the armed forces and labor was at a premium. Increased manpower in the Garsson plants created the potential for the award of more government contracts. It also increased the opportunity for "pirating," shifting workers from one weapons project to another without permission, or away from arms production to the profitable manufacture of scarce consumer goods.

According to the *Post*, "His [May's] interference, it is plain, was considered an adequate excuse for according special favors to Garsson companies in connection with war contracts. The Army-Navy E Award of Merit was bestowed on one of them over the protest of Army Ordnance officers, at the instigation of the then Undersecretary, now Secretary of War Patterson."[16]

The *Post* concluded, "In our opinion, the motives behind this facile yielding to Congressman May's appeals should be thoroughly probed. And whatever Mr. May may have done, he should not be regarded as an isolated target for attack behind which others open to criticism can seek shelter. For if Mr. May had been dealing with Government officials impervious to the voice of influence he certainly could have done very little for his contractor friends."[17]

The dispute regarding the manpower ceiling began in February 1945 when Henry Garsson was advised by the Chicago-area office of the War Manpower Commission that Batavia could have no more than 789 employees.[18] Garsson immediately called Patterson directly to insist that he needed the ceiling raised by at least 75 to fully man the plant, cover absenteeism, and avoid a 25 percent reduction in production of 8-inch shells.[19] Brennan traveled to the Chicago plant in the spring of 1945 on Patterson's orders. Those orders came in response to repeated complaints from General Dwight D. Eisenhower about inadequate supplies of artillery ammunition following the Normandy invasion.[20]

On February 28, 1945, Patterson had sent a memorandum to Brennan explaining, "The 8-inch shell program, as you know, is of the most critical importance. It seems silly to me for the War Manpower Commission to split hairs in a case of this kind, where a plant is devoted wholly to urgent war programs and where the production output is excellent."[21] During his Mead Committee testimony, Brennan was asked by one senator, "You interpreted that memorandum to be instructions to you to get the manpower ceiling raised, if you could, Colonel Brennan?"[22]

Brennan replied, "I did, sir."[23]

Under tough questioning it became clear that whatever actions Brennan had taken on Batavia's behalf were at the behest of higher-ranking officers, such as Patterson, and against his own better judgment. Patterson, for his part, seemed to have been operating with an attitude of "Damn the torpedoes, full speed ahead!" insofar as optimizing the plant's artillery shell production. There was no evidence of corruption on either man's part.

As the citation accompanying the Distinguished Service Medal awarded to Patterson in September 1945 read, "Owing largely to his dominating integrity there had hardly been even a suggestion of malfeasance" during his tenure as head of military procurement.[24] It was, truly, an extraordinary commendation. During World War II, Patterson's department executed contracts worth over $100 billion, the "largest amount of business ever done by any single organization in the history of the world."[25]

The committee members were moved by the testimony of former Colonel John Slezak, who had been chief of the Chicago ordnance district and whose assistance Brennan had enlisted in his effort to raise Batavia's manpower ceiling. Slezak told the senators, "[I]t seems to me that men in high public places should be like Caesar's wife, beyond suspicion, and when you are frequently being called, directly or indirectly, from someone who is chairman of the Military Affairs Committee, it makes it tough on you. You can't help but feel you are being duressed into something that you don't want to be duressed into."[26]

He concluded, "It is my personal opinion that it is not good public policy."[27]

But Brennan had more, much more, to rely on in his own defense than Slezak's testimony. Members of the panel were astounded when he introduced into the record transcripts of his telephone conversations, which he had recorded, that were related directly to the Batavia affair. One was of a conversation with Slezak, dated March 5, 1945. In it, Brennan complained about the pressure coming from higher up the chain of command.

He told Slezak, "You know that man Garsson. He made me so angry sometimes. You see, he called over your head; he called over our head; he called over [General] Hardy's head and he got Patterson all exercised and got us in the position we are now in of having an order that we must accomplish that [manpower] ceiling of a thousand, and we are supposed to accomplish it by this week."[28]

Slezak responded, "You see, when we were there [at the Batavia plant], the Undersecretary [Patterson] promised Garsson any ceiling, almost—you remember, you were there."[29]

Brennan replied, "I know; I was there."[30]

After reading from the transcript, one senator asked Brennan, "That is pretty strong language, isn't it, Colonel?"[31]

He replied, "Very strong language, very strong language. I had a very tough job to do. And if I overstated it, it is in the way of trying to sell Colonel Slezak on doing a job that neither of us wanted to do."[32]

By the time Brennan was excused as a witness, Chairman Mead, speaking on behalf of the committee, was prepared to offer both thanks and praise for a job well done. Addressing his remarks to both Brennan and Slezak, he stated, "The afternoon session has brought forcibly to my mind the evil effects of meddling in the proper routine of Army procedure. I can see why you men were suffering from a mental hazard as a result of unnecessary interference with the work that was being done properly and at the proper level."[33]

He went on, "I can see where a few men, eager for favors they were not entitled to, as is evidenced in the case of the men who were operating these plants, can disrupt, at times even demoralize the activities and the proper functioning of agencies and regional systems all over the country."[34]

He added, "The higher and more powerful the meddler may happen to be, the more widespread is the chaos and the confusion."[35]

In closing, he remarked, "I think you are to be commended for standing up under the pressure and serving as well as you did under those circumstances."[36] He went on, "I am very glad that you men came here and spoke so frankly and forthrightly to us this afternoon."[37]

Earlier, however, Mead and others on the panel had expressed some dismay at the idea of Brennan's tapes. "I would like to have you tell us," Mead demanded, "how long this practice has been in operation in the War Department, this practice of recording telephone calls."[38]

Brennan responded matter-of-factly, "I can only speak from my personal experience, Senator. I know that when I arrived in the War Department in July of 1942 there was made available to me a recording device. I used it I think for a short time."[39]

He explained, "I had a button on the telephone for that purpose, or it depended upon the make of the mechanism. Some of them had little levers on the machine that were set up alongside of the phone. I know that every phone available to me was wired for some such machine to be used."[40]

"You wouldn't call it wire tapping, would you?" another senator asked angrily.[41]

Brennan replied, "It was just recording a telephone conversation. It served many useful purposes."[42]

He went on, "Depending on how busy we were—and some of us were very busy indeed in those days—it was helpful to have a record of a telephone conversation as a memorandum to remind you of things to be done or otherwise."[43]

When news of Brennan's wiretapping was reported by the *Washington Post*, Speaker of the House Sam Rayburn joined House Republican leader Joe Martin in condemning it as "a mean practice."[44] But whatever any lawmaker's opinion, one thing was clear: William Brennan knew how to cover his ass. With his latest Washington travail behind him, he self-confidently boarded a train back home to New Jersey.

CHAPTER 6

Reforming the Courts

The spirit if not the letter of justice requires a prompt hearing and settlement of suits; otherwise an injustice is perpetuated and aggravated.

—William J. Brennan Jr.

DESPITE HIS RELATIVE YOUTH, his drive, and his vigor, Bill Brennan would eventually begin to crack under the weight, volume, and pressure of the work and high profile he had assumed. No wonder. Not least among the challenges that he undertook in late 1946 was to help spearhead the drive to rewrite New Jersey's antiquated constitution in order to reform the state's judicial system.

By 1946, New Jersey's court system, established under an article of the state constitution that was more than a century old, was decrepit and had all but ground to a halt. The system of seventeen autonomous courts lacked cohesive structure and had no set of comprehensive administrative rules. The jurisdictions of the various courts overlapped and were duplicative. Furthermore, judges were unaccountable. As Brennan later wrote, it was a system "free of any sort of control from within or without, the judges concerned with their own court only and brooking no interference from judges of other courts, or indeed even from members of their own court."[1]

As a result, the administration of justice was painfully slow. Delays of eight to ten years in bringing cases to trial were not unknown.[2] Moreover, cases that could have been settled instead proceeded to trial because there was no effective pretrial settlement procedure. The situation was exacerbated by New Jersey's population explosion following World War II, and the suits resulting from the increased number of cars on the streets and highways.

Worst of all, however, was the lack of pretrial discovery that would require the disclosure of pertinent evidence and other information to the opposing side. As Brennan put it, "[N]either side of a lawsuit ever knew until the actual day of trial what the other side would spring in the way of witnesses or facts. The technique was to play the cards close to the vest and hope by surprise or maneuver at the trial to confound one's adversary or, more important, to confuse the jury sufficiently to carry the day whether or not right and justice lay on the side of one's client."[3]

He concluded, "It was and is great sport, but hardly defensible as a system for determining causes according to truth and right."[4]

The court-reform movement in the United States was begun by Harvard Law School dean Roscoe Pound in 1906 with a speech in St. Paul, Minnesota, entitled "The Causes of Popular Dissatisfaction with the Administration of Justice."[5] Among those sparked to action by Pound's call for reform was Arthur T. Vanderbilt, "one of that small band of valiant crusaders who carried the torch the length and breadth of the nation."[6]

Vanderbilt was born in Newark in 1888, the son of a wealthy railroad executive.[7] He received his law degree from Columbia University in 1913,[8] founded his own firm across the street from Pitney, Hardin,[9] and established himself among the foremost members of the legal profession. He was especially renowned for his involvement in the representation of Norman Thomas, leader of the Socialist Party. In a controversial and celebrated case, Thomas brought suit against Jersey City mayor Frank Hague after Hague barred him from speaking publicly. Vanderbilt, a leading liberal Republican, was named chief spokesperson for the American Bar Association (ABA) when that organization intervened in the suit on Thomas's behalf in 1938.[10] The case eventually went to the U.S. Supreme Court, which ruled unconstitutional the city ordnance upon which Hague had based his actions.[11]

In 1930, Vanderbilt had been named chairman of the Judicial Council of New Jersey, a post he held for a decade.[12] In 1941, he was made a member of the New Jersey State Constitutional Convention, where he trumpeted his call for the reform of New Jersey's anachronistic judiciary.[13] He succeeded in recruiting the help of a young attorney at his firm, a Harvard Law graduate by the name of Nathan L. Jacobs, who was a classmate and friend of Bill Brennan's.

As Brennan later recalled, "He [Jacobs] enlisted me in that cause [court reform] in 1946 when he and I joined seven other lawyers to form the editorial board of the *New Jersey Law Journal*. The *Journal* played a significant part in helping organize support for constitutional reform."[14] In a series of lengthy *Journal* editorials, Brennan pleaded the reformers' case, attacking what he called the "century old horse and buggy court structure that is ours."[15]

When a constitutional convention was called in June 1947 to revise the state's 103-year-old charter, Brennan served as the *Journal's* spokesperson before the committee that dealt with the judicial article.[16] After the convention, he "threw himself into the successful fight for the adoption of the recommended new document which provided a court system since generally recognized as a model to the nation."[17] He also "labored long and effectively with Jacobs and others preparing the rules of court promulgated by the new Supreme Court under the broad rule-making power bestowed by the new charter."[18]

The new judicial article, which took effect on September 15, 1948, consisted of only "six short sections and twenty-seven pithy paragraphs."[19] Yet it embodied a revolutionary model for the effective administration of justice. Brennan summarized it by explaining, "New Jersey borrowed from industry and commerce one of America's great contributions, namely, the principles of business management which have done so much to advance this nation to the place of the world's greatest productive economy."[20]

Vanderbilt had attributed the legal profession's reluctance to embrace modern business management principles to a mistaken way of looking at the proper role of judges. He once said, "I suspect that the real reason for the lack of concern with the administration of the courts is attributable primarily to the fact that the time-honored concept that a judge must be completely free and independent in his judicial determination has resulted in the invalid assumption that each judge must also be completely independent in matters of administration as well."[21]

He went on, "The deep-seated abhorrence of change on the part of the members of the legal profession has helped perpetuate this misunderstanding of the proper place of administration in a court system notwithstanding the tremendous advances made in closely related fields of governmental operation as well as in business management and the obvious inability of the courts with their horse-and-buggy ways to keep pace with the times."[22]

By virtue of his undergraduate training at Wharton, which emphasized managerial competence, Brennan was uniquely qualified to contribute mightily to the reform movement. Yet when all was said and done he gave the ultimate credit for the movement's success to Vanderbilt. "Arthur T. Vanderbilt labored for twenty-five years in New Jersey for adoption of a judicial structure embodying these attributes," Brennan wrote in 1957.[23]

"The great contribution of Arthur T. Vanderbilt," he continued, "is that he provided the positive proof that the cause of justice need not suffer from delays, technicalities or the evils of maneuver and surprise. No longer is business-like administration of the courts rare and suspect."[24]

So great, in fact, was his admiration for Vanderbilt that he compared him with Sir Thomas More, author of *Utopia* and Lord Chancellor of England during the reign of Henry VIII. He once wrote, "Several centuries ago another great judge was famed for his ability to bring order and efficiency to the courts. He was Sir Thomas More. When he took office the docket was crowded with cases, some of them twenty years old. He, too, knew how true it was that the spirit if not the letter of justice requires a prompt hearing and settlement of suits; otherwise an injustice is perpetuated and aggravated. So great was his skill in devising processes to bring cases to the point of prompt hearing that the day arrived when not a matter or man was left to be heard. A jingle commemorates his achievement:

> "When More some time Chancellor had been
> "No more suits did remain.
> "The like will never more be seen
> "Till More be there again."[25]

Of Vanderbilt's achievements, he declared, "The inevitable march of all jurisdictions toward improved administration proceeds daily at an accelerated pace. Arthur T. Vanderbilt's conspicuous service in bringing this to pass has earned him an indelible place not only in our profession but in the heart of every grateful citizen conscious that 'Justice, sirs, is the chiefest interest of man on earth.' "[26]

Under the new system that Vanderbilt and his young Turks like Brennan and Jacobs put in place, five features stood out. First, New Jersey adapted the Federal Rules of Civil and Criminal Procedure to its courts. According to Brennan, "The Federal Rules represented the most comprehensive, the most flexible, the most modern existing set of rules to accomplish the objective of ruling the disposition of particular cases according to their merits and to prevent their disposition for mere procedural reasons. Those rules represented years and years of work of outstanding experts and reflected the thoughtful criticisms of thousands of individual lawyers throughout the country. They were ours for the asking and it was natural that we should have taken advantage of our opportunity."[27]

Second, an Office of the Administrative Director of the Courts was established. The administrative director's primary responsibility, Brennan explained, was "to gather and interpret statistics concerning the stuff of court business, which, of course, is litigation. How many cases are there—where are they pending—how long have they been pending—is the number of new cases on the up or down grade—the necessity for such information is apparent."[28] The administrative director was also charged with "important housekeeping tasks, budget responsibilities, and the duty continuously to study operations and develop procedures the better and more efficiently to process court business."[29]

Third, each judge was required to file a weekly report with the administrative director. Among other things, the reports were to include information on the names and types of cases handled each day, the number of hours the judge spent on the bench, and the amount of time devoted to each matter. "I suppose one of the complaints most often heard from litigants and the public before the new system became effective," Brennan wrote, "was that too often the judge was not found on the bench during working hours. The public was not always satisfied with the answer that he was working in chambers. Though the suspicion was not justified, people felt uneasy about the conduct of public business in chambers."[30]

Fourth, pretrial discovery and pretrial conference procedures were made mandatory; the kinds of surprise and maneuvering that Brennan deplored were eliminated. He wrote, "I am so fully convinced that these tools accomplish better justice, not only in bringing about settlements and avoiding time-wasting trials, but of far more importance, in assuring that right and justice shall have the most favorable opportunity of prevailing in cases that are tried, that I have almost a closed mind to any argument opposing the mandatory requirement."[31]

Fifth and last, the chief justice of the Supreme Court was given "assignment" power, meaning the authority to send judges out of their regular counties to sit elsewhere when needed because of increased court workload or other necessity. The chief justice was also empowered to appoint from among trial level judges a chief judge, or assignment judge, for each county, whose duty, as Brennan explained it, was "to be in his county administratively the vice president or branch manager of the system. In addition to his regular judicial duties, the Assignment Judge keeps close tab on the dockets in all the courts, assigns cases to other judges from the master list prepared at his direction, and has general administrative authority within the county."[32]

Eight years after the system was implemented, Brennan was able to point to an impressive record of improved judicial administration, especially with regard to speedier trials. He regarded settling or trying cases swiftly as crucial to achieving just results and at one point called court congestion and delay "the most serious problem in the administration of justice."[33] He once said, "Justice delayed is essentially bad justice. Witnesses die, memories fail and the right may not prevail when it takes years for a case to reach a decision."[34]

He wrote, "In September 1948, when we started, trial lists were two or more years in arrears, and some cases were pending up to eight years. Within three years, by 1951, all arrears were cleared up, and current cases were being tried, if not previously settled, at least within nine months and more often within six months after complaint was filed."[35]

He was also pleased with the tremendous reduction in the number of cases that actually went to trial. He observed, "[N]ow only a little more than one out of every four or five cases ever gets to trial. The best we did in the old days was to settle half the cases; the other half were tried."[36]

He attributed the reduced number of trials to the mandatory pretrial discovery and pretrial conference procedures, explaining, "Each side knows the strengths and weaknesses of his own and his adversary's cases, and, given that knowledge, settlement results almost as a matter of course when both sides see that it is to the best interest of each to settle."[37]

In 1948, liberal Republican Governor Alfred E. Driscoll, whose administration was marked by government reform and civil rights and other social advances, appointed Vanderbilt chief justice of the New Jersey state supreme court, making him head of the state's revamped judiciary. A short time later, Driscoll offered Jacobs a superior court, or trial-level, judgeship, as part of his policy of "farming out promising young lawyers to judgeships in the lower courts for seasoning."[38] Driscoll's idea was that in this way, "when vacancies in the higher courts occurred they could be filled with experienced men who were still vigorous."[39]

According to Brennan, Jacobs "accepted appointment to the bench in 1948 from conviction that one who fought to create the new system should help make it work."[40] He added, "He influenced me to follow his example."[41]

Others did. John J. Francis, Alfred C. Clapp, G. Dixon Speakman, and Joseph Harrison, all of whom worked with Jacobs and Brennan on the *Journal's* editorial board, accepted judicial appointments, taking their places in the new system they had helped create.[42] At first, however, Brennan was reluctant to leave private practice.

Money was his primary concern. Judges certainly earned a great deal less than name partners in corporate law firms like Brennan's. Besides, trial judges were at the very bottom of the pay and prestige ladder. As a trial judge, his annual income would drop from between $50,000 and $60,000 to roughly $20,000.[43]

He had responsibilities. It was 1948. He was forty-two. He had his mother to support, along with several sisters who lived at home.[44] He had his own wife, Marjorie, and the boys, now fifteen and twelve, to think of. In just three years, William III would be ready for college. Hugh would soon follow. A judgeship simply did not seem feasible. He told himself that his concern should be with making more, not less, money.

Vanderbilt wanted him on board, however, and courted him indirectly through his friends like Donald Kipp, who worked in Brennan's firm. Vanderbilt reportedly told Kipp that Brennan would move quickly up the ranks from the trial to the appellate level and that, in the words of Vanderbilt, who was then some sixty years old, "If I last, he will be on the [state] supreme court."[45]

In January 1949, Brennan relented. He accepted Governor Driscoll's offer of a judgeship.[46] Thus, like his father before him, his first appointment in civilian government came from a Republican official. Yet Driscoll's reaching out to him came as no real surprise to those who knew Brennan, for, as Frederick Hall later wrote, "While he had many friends in high places, he was never active in politics and his was a nonpolitical appointment."[47]

What did come as a surprise, according to Hall, was Brennan's acceptance of Driscoll's offer. "In view of his prominence and assured success at the bar," Hall wrote, "it was surprising to outsiders when he turned to a judicial career in 1949 by accepting appointment to the superior court, the tribunal of general jurisdic-tion."[48] In Hall's view, "They did not realize the depth of his conviction and dedication to the cause of justice under law for all and his determination to assist in making the year-old New Jersey system work."

That was probably true. But what outsiders, acquaintances, and even some close friends also did not know was the extent to which the demands of his firm were taking their toll on him. As Bernard M. Shanley, a lifelong friend of Brennan's who later became President Eisenhower's appointment secretary, explained, "His law practice was so heavy that it became a depressive thing, and that influenced his decision to accept a judgeship."[49] In fact, the strain on his health and spirit had grown so great that some friends and family members feared he was on the verge of a nervous breakdown.

In any event, he was saved. And when he donned the robe of a New Jersey superior court judge in January 1949, the hinge of fate, to borrow a phrase from Winston Churchill, swung William Brennan's way.

CHAPTER 7

The Hinge of Fate

The overwhelming number of final and vital decisions upon which depend life, liberty, and property...are decisions of the state courts.

—William J. Brennan Jr.

BEING A TRIAL JUDGE was no less demanding than being a name partner in his law firm. Indeed, Judge Brennan worked almost as many hours as had counselor-at-law Brennan in private practice. But those hours were more regular, and they were spent in the library, in his chambers, or at home with his family. Freed from the hustle of rain making, he was his own boss, free to think, decide, and write as he saw fit.

Moreover, he was temperamentally suited to the judicial role. No fit could have been more perfect. He brought to the bench the keen instincts of a masterful trial lawyer. He could sense when people were lying and he knew when they were telling the truth, and the ascertainment of truth appealed to him innately much more than advocacy. As a lawyer, he was sworn to represent his clients zealously, and although his practice may have been courteous, the bottom line was always to win; truth and right were often secondary. He had grown tired of the advocate's role. He had been literally sick of it.

By contrast, his years as a New Jersey state judge were to be among the happiest of his life. Somehow, he managed to make ends meet financially. At the same time, he was liberated both personally and intellectually by a job that emphasized his strong suits, which were his intuitive gifts, and writing and research. As a result, he blossomed. In fact, "[h]is rise in the judiciary was just as meteoric as had been his climb up the legal ladder as an associate at Pitney, Hardin & Ward."[1]

Nevertheless, it was not until years later, after he had served on the U.S. Supreme Court for almost two decades, that he was really able to see, in hindsight, his job as a state judge in the proper perspective, to appreciate fully the importance, the significance of the state judge's role. In a tribute to Nathan Jacobs in the *Rutgers Law Review* in 1974, he wrote, "The spotlight is often focused upon the decisions of the United States Supreme Court. Too often, I think, that focus tends to divert attention from the vital role of the state courts in the administration of justice."[2]

He explained, "Actually the composite work of the courts of the 50 states has greater significance in measuring how well America attains the ideal of equal justice under law for all. It is important to stress that the Supreme Court of the United States has power to review only those decisions of state courts that rest on federal law. I suppose the state courts of all levels must annually hand down literally millions of decisions that do not rest on federal law, yet determine vital issues of life, liberty, and property of countless human beings of the nation."[3]

He emphasized, "The overwhelming number of vital decisions upon which depend life, liberty, and property thus are decisions of the state courts."[4]

As a trial judge, Brennan sat primarily in Hudson County, where Jersey City was a veritable snake pit of corruption under the entrenched political machine of perennial mayor Frank Hague. He took on the Hague machine in an important voter-fraud case, *Casey v. MacPhail*.[5] In *Casey*, he ruled that a candidate for the office of commissioner of Jersey City had a right to inspect voter-registration rolls to make sure that "only those who legitimately have a right to vote in the municipal election shall in fact vote at that election."[6] He also managed through his tireless labors to clear the court's docket of backlogged cases.

Arthur Vanderbilt was impressed with his efforts and named him assignment judge for the county.[7] Then in September 1950, barely a year and a half after his initial appointment to the bench, Vanderbilt elevated him to the appellate division of the superior courts, which had jurisdiction over all appeals from the trial courts and was only a step below the supreme court, the state's highest tribunal.

Brennan's duties as an appeals judge were different from those at the trial-court level. As one commentator has written, "While one is not generally faced with the need for instantaneous decision," such as snap judgments on motions or objections as at the trial level, "the responsibility imposed is ordinarily greater and much more far reaching. Although the primary task is to decide the present case, the precedential effect of a decision is a matter of concern. Opinions should be clear, sound expositions of why the case is decided the way it is—not just homilies, philosophical essays or mere conclusory recitals. All this requires the highest degree of legal scholarship, common sense and farsightedness."[8] Brennan proved himself "amply possessed of these talents."[9]

At first, he proceeded slowly, conservatively. The judicial liberalism that would later manifest itself was for the most part latent at this point in his career. He was a stern taskmaster, a stickler, holding judges and defendants alike to the strict letter and detail of the law.

In *Palestroni v. Jacobs*,[10] for example, jurors deliberating a contract dispute asked the trial judge for a dictionary in order to define the word *wainscot*, which had been used in a contract specification. Brennan ruled that the dictionary amounted to "extraneous evidence" and that the definition it provided might have contradicted the judge's instructions to the jurors at the end of the trial.

Declaring that the judge erred in providing the dictionary without first informing the defendant's counsel, he ordered a new trial. He explained, citing a precedent, "The stringency of the rule is not mere formalism; the rule is 'imperatively required to secure verdicts based on proofs taken openly at the trial, free from all danger of extraneous influences.'"[11]

In another case, *Ex Parte Graham*,[12] he upheld the conviction of a man found guilty of incest. The defendant contended that because he had not been present when the verdict was delivered, his "substantial constitutional rights" had been violated.[13] Brennan disagreed. He conceded that "when testimony is presented or the jury is instructed, the accused has the right to be present because he is entitled under the Constitution to confront the witnesses against him and make his defense upon the merits with the assistance of counsel."[14] Nevertheless, he went on, "such reasons for his presence do not obtain after the jury has concluded its deliberations and those constitutional provisions cannot be construed as requiring his presence when the verdict is reported."[15]

In two other cases, he construed the constitutional rights of individual citizens narrowly. In *Cortese v. Cortese*,[16] he held that a mother in a paternity suit could not refuse a blood test for herself or her child based on a right of privacy. He wrote, "The citizen holds his citizenship subject to the duty to furnish to the courts, from time to time and within reasonable limits, such assistance as the courts may demand of him in their effort to ascertain truth in controversies before them."[17]

And in *In re Pillo*,[18] he held that the privilege against self-incrimination contained in the Fifth Amendment to the U.S. Constitution did not apply to the states. He conceded, "We should interpret the privilege [against self-incrimination] liberally in light of its wholesome service to the cause of personal freedom."[19] But, he concluded, quoting from an earlier case, "to interpret and apply the privilege without regard to the public interest and without striving to accommodate that interest...would be unrealistic and doctrinaire."[20]

After just two years in the appellate division, Governor Driscoll appointed Brennan to the six-member state supreme court, along with Jacobs, his Harvard classmate who had sparked his initial interest in judicial administration. Brennan recalled, "He [Jacobs] and I took our seats on the supreme court on the same day, March 13, 1952. He was sworn first, and was therefore my senior. We sat in the end seats on the bench and were at times referred to—not always to flatter us—as the 'Harvard ends.'"[21]

Brennan was "classed as one of the 'liberal' members of the court,"[22] probably because of his demonstrated commitment to judicial reform.

That same year, he moved his family some forty miles south to the town of Rumson, in Monmouth County, where he purchased a refurbished, converted carriage house on Conover Lane that was to be home for the next four years. He managed to maintain a comfortable lifestyle on his modest annual salary of $24,000.[23] He arranged for there to be more quiet evenings at home with Marjorie, spent reading and smoking, or chatting quietly while sipping a drink. Marjorie, for her part, involved herself in a range of community activities during the day, from the Rumson community appeal board to the county public-health nursing organization.[24] She also took up needlepoint.[25]

The New Jersey supreme court functioned much like the Supreme Court of the United States. The court had a "selective jurisdiction," meaning the justices heard only those cases that they decided were of particular importance or interest.[26] In terms of the process by which cases were decided, they studied briefs submitted by opposing counsel in advance of oral arguments, drafted their own opinions, and met in conference following the oral arguments in an effort to reach consensus.[27] The six judges met in Trenton, the capital, on Monday and Thursday of each week that court was in session. Brennan spent the rest of his time in Red Bank, about an hour south of Newark, where his chambers were located.

It was during his tenure on the New Jersey state supreme court that he began to express the liberal views with which he would forever be identified, especially his expansive views on free speech and the rights of criminal defendants. Writing for the majority of the court in 1953, for example, he overturned the denial of a permit to a prospective burlesque theater operator in Newark.

His opinion in the case, *Adams Theatre Co. v. Keenan*,[28] interpreted the First Amendment somewhat restrictively. Again relying on precedent, he declared, "There are 'narrowly limited classes of speech' which are not given the protection of the First Amendment."[29] He went on, "[O]ne such exception is speech which is outrightly lewd and indecent."[30]

Nevertheless, he ruled that the license denial was an unacceptable form of censorship and prior restraint. He cited the 1952 edition of *Webster's New International Dictionary* for the proposition that "burlesque" as a form of theater need not necessarily be lewd or indecent.[31] Therefore, he concluded, Newark officials lacked sufficient grounds for concluding that the theater owner would necessarily offer performances that were beyond the scope of the First Amendment's protection.

Citing an earlier decision, he concluded that the censorship power "is so abhorrent to our traditions that a purpose to grant it should not be easily inferred."[32]

During the same 1952–53 term, he broke ranks sharply with Vanderbilt over the scope of a criminal defendant's right to pretrial discovery. Writing for the court in *State v. Tune*,[33] Vanderbilt held that the defendant, convicted of murder, had no right to inspect the confession he had given to police. Claiming not to have remembered the confession's contents, the defendant had argued that access to the document was crucial to his counsel's preparation for trial.

Brennan dissented. He wrote, "It shocks my sense of justice that in these circumstances counsel for an accused facing a possible death sentence should be denied inspection of his confession which, were this a civil case, could not be denied."[34] He concluded bitterly, "To shackle counsel so that they cannot effectively seek out the truth and afford the accused the representation which is not his privilege but his absolute right seriously imperils our bedrock presumption of innocence."[35]

By 1955, he was ready to reconsider his earlier, limited view of the privilege against self-incrimination as expressed in his opinion in *In re Pillo*. Writing for the majority in *State v. Fary*,[36] he took a dim view of a witness's refusal to testify before a grand jury. But he wrote eloquently of the overall importance of the privilege against self-incrimination in the context of a democratic society. He stated, "The privilege of a witness against being compelled to incriminate himself, of ancient origin, is precious to free men as a restraint against high-handed and arrogant inquisitorial practices."[37]

He added, "It has survived centuries of hot controversy periodically rekindled when there is popular impatience that its protection sometimes allows the guilty to escape. It has endured as a wise and necessary protection of the individual against arbitrary power; the price of occasional failures of justice under its protection is paid in the larger interest of the general personal security."[38]

The defense of the Fifth Amendment privilege against self-incrimination was a theme Brennan would return to repeatedly in the coming years against the backdrop of intrusive congressional investigations into suspected communist influences in and out of American government, and the various smear campaigns against progressive thinkers and nonconformists. In fact, the restoration

and revitalization of the full gamut of rights and privileges guaranteed under the U.S. Bill of Rights but eroded during the communist
purges of the 1940s and 1950s would be his next great personal
crusade.

He would undertake his new mission with the same fire and
tirelessness that he had brought to his earlier efforts to force the
reform of organized labor and the New Jersey judiciary, respectively.
Ultimately, he would succeed, as he always had. He would make
formidable adversaries in the process, but the means by which he
would arrive at his ends would distinguish him for his unique
understanding and use of power.

CHAPTER 8

The Shamrock and the Robe

The thing that sort of disgusts me—and I mean disgusts—there are so many Irish who would rather not claim it [being Irish]. I resent it, I just think it's so sad.

—William J. Brennan Jr.

S T. PATRICK, IRELAND'S PATRON SAINT, was born in western Britain during the fifth century A.D. His father was a church deacon and minor government official. At the age of sixteen, Patrick was kidnapped by Irish raiders who held him in slavery for six years. During that time, he had a spiritual awakening and found the Lord. Eventually he managed to flee his captors and find passage back to Britain. But according to his *Confessio*, or spiritual autobiography, he had a vision that he should return to Ireland. That he did, embarking on his "laborious episcopate" to evangelize the heathen.

Risking martyrdom, he roved beyond the known reaches of the Christian world, baptizing and converting, using an indigenous three-leafed plant, the shamrock, to explain the mystery of the Holy Trinity—three Persons in one God: Father, Son, and Holy Ghost. He railed against injustice and denounced British chieftains for their ill treatment of Irish prisoners of war. According to legend, he performed at least one miracle, driving all the snakes out of Ireland

58

and into the sea. He was a man, it has been said, whose "moral and spiritual greatness shines through every stumbling sentence of his 'rustic' Latin."[1] By the time his mission was over, he had established Christianity in Ireland. A millennium and a half after his death, it thrives there today.

To William Brennan, ethnic pride was a virtue. "The thing that sort of disgusts me," he told an interviewer in 1990, "and I mean disgusts—there are so many Irish who would rather not claim it [being Irish]. I resent it, I just think it's so sad."[2] In 1954, after two years as an associate justice of the New Jersey state supreme court, he was proud to be one of the most prominent members of the nation's Irish Catholic community.

Therefore he was honored to accept an invitation from the Charitable Irish Society of Boston to deliver the keynote address and to respond to the traditional toast "To the Day We Celebrate!" at the organization's 159th annual St. Patrick's Day dinner.

He was all the more gratified at the prospect of sharing the platform with such notables as United Nations ambassador Henry Cabot Lodge, and high Massachusetts government officials, including Republican Senator Leverett Saltonstall; Republican Governor Christian A. Herter, who would respond to the toast "To the Commonwealth of Massachusetts!"; and Democratic Mayor of Boston John B. Hynes for the response to the toast "To the City of Boston!"

Vice President Richard M. Nixon had declined the Society's invitation to attend. Lodge was there in his place to respond to the toast "To the United States of America." Nixon's future rival for the presidency, Democratic Senator John F. Kennedy, also sent his regrets, having previously agreed to address the Friendly Sons of St. Patrick in New York City on the same night.

On St. Patrick's Day, the whole world claims Irish lineage. March 17, 1954, was no exception, especially not in Boston, the most Irish city in the United States. Under the auspices of the all-male Charitable Irish Society, locally prominent Irish-American men joined their male counterparts of every ilk and political stripe—about a thousand distinguished guests in all—in the grand ballroom of the posh Sheraton Copley Hotel downtown for a fine meal, a full roast beef dinner for $7.50 a plate. As a six-piece band engaged by the Society for $103.50 played Irish music, they paid homage to Irish heritage and to surging Irish-American political power.

Each guest wore a green carnation in his tuxedo lapel. And, as was the custom, each table was decorated with potted shamrocks shipped in for the occasion from the Old Sod itself, a tradition begun in the previous century by the wife of John Boyle O'Reilly, the storied poet, editor, and adventurer.

At the head table, Brennan was joined by, among others, the Right Rev. Joseph M. Fitzgibbons of the Archdioceses of Boston; the Honorable Joseph J. Shields, consul general for Ireland; Daniel A. Binchey, senior professor of the Institute of Advanced Studies, Dublin, Ireland; Captain Joseph A. Callaghan, representing Admiral Momson of the U.S. navy; Paul Tierney, president of the Eire Society of Boston; Andrew J. Keith, president, Scots Charitable Society; Ronald A. Forth, president, British Charitable Society; Dr. John F. Conlin of the Massachusetts Medical Society; Boyle; Herter; Saltonstall; and Lodge.

Founded in Boston on St. Patrick's Day in 1737 by two dozen or so "Gentlemen, Merchants, and Others of the Irish Nation," the Society was the oldest Irish organization in the United States. According to past president Henry Lee, the purposes for which the Society was founded were "alleviating suffering and of cultivating a spirit of fellowship among all of Irish birth and descent."

Over the centuries the Society boasted a broad-based membership of Protestants as well as Catholics, Irish as well as Anglophile and other philanthropists. The organization had contributed to such causes as Irish famine relief and immigrant settlement, and a host of local charities. Following a tradition that began in 1795, its St. Patrick's Day dinner served, in Lee's words, as "a forum for eminent figures, both American and Irish."

Patriotism was a consistent theme of those dinners. As Lee put it, "whatever their political views and whatever their personal struggles, members have affirmed the Society's pledge to the Eagle of America."

Over the course of the previous century, Boston's proud Old Guard, the WASP elite, had watched their influence dwindle. The rising tide of immigration caused by British repression and famine back home had swelled the voter rolls with the masses of Irish stevedores and bottle washers, cooks, domestic servants, ditch diggers, and bootleggers. By exercising their right to vote, the Irish gained political power.

"They did not have the education to go into business at any high level, and they did not have the capital to become farmers," one historian has written.[3] "They were left only with menial, low-paying jobs that were not going to lead to any degree of affluence in industry, commerce, or agriculture. The only legitimate route open to them was politics."[4]

Political office produced patronage, which, in turn, provided access to better-paying jobs with government benefits. The Irish swelled the state and municipal workforces as they had the voter rolls, occupying positions once denied them by discrimination. Police forces, fire departments, teachers' unions, and municipal bureaucracies became their domains.

Irreversibly, the Brahmin Boston of the Adamses, Quincys, and Lodges, of the descendants of Oliver Wendell Holmes, Ralph Waldo Emerson, and Louisa May Alcott, became the stronghold of the Irish political bosses, men like Boston's perennial mayor James Michael Curley, Michael Doherty, Patrick Maguire, Michael Cun-niff, and Thomas Gargan.

Six years later, the nation would elect a grandson of former Boston Mayor John F. "Honey Fitz" Fitzgerald as its first Irish Catholic president. John Fitzgerald Kennedy would narrowly defeat Nixon and his running mate, Lodge, who personified the Brahmin legacy. As he took his place beside him on the dais, Brennan understood the significance of Lodge's being there to cultivate as best he could the Irish Catholic constituency. Lodge's self-professed goal was to "liberalize" the Republican Party by broadening its base to include the Irish working class.[5] Within two years, Brennan himself would be elevated to the U.S. Supreme Court in part because of President Eisenhower's desire to attract Irish Catholic voters.

But his thoughts that day were not so much of his own future prospects as they were, more fittingly, of his heritage, his past, and the future of his country, America, and the broader Irish-American community within it. His views, his feelings, were forged and tempered by the centuries-old Irish struggle for dignity.

At the age of forty-eight, he had developed an acute sensitivity to the plight of working people, the downtrodden, and those whose political views were held in disfavor or contempt. As journalist Nina Totenberg has written, "He grew to maturity at a time when there was incredible poverty and repression, a time when children worked as laborers twelve and fourteen hours a day, a time when attempts at unionizing workers were put down with ruthless force, and [he] witnessed some of those struggles firsthand."[6]

Brennan once told an interviewer, "What got me interested in people's rights and liberties was the kind of neighborhood I was brought up in. I saw all kinds of suffering—people had to struggle. I saw the suffering of my mother, even though we were never without. We always had something to eat, we always had something to wear. But others in the neighborhood had a harder time."[7]

The 1950s were particularly virulent; the nation's peacetime affluence was beguiling. The GIs who had returned home from World War II were lavished with unprecedented benefits, including employment preferences and low-cost government loans to buy their first homes or complete their higher educations. Housing boomed, and modern suburbs spread out from the cities. Financial security spawned a baby-boom generation that recollects white picket fences, mothers who did not have to work, and streamlined, chrome-appointed automobiles with powerful V-8 engines. The New York Yankees were on top. God, it seemed, was an American.

But beyond the expansive confines of the burgeoning white middle class, injustice was rampant. As Yale law professor Owen Fiss, who clerked for Justice Brennan during the Supreme Court's 1965–66 term, has written, "In the 1950's, America was not a pretty sight. Jim Crow reigned supreme. African Americans were systematically disenfranchised and excluded from juries. State-fostered religious practices, like school prayers, were pervasive. Legislatures were grossly gerrymandered and malapportioned.... The heavy hand of the law threatened those who publicly provided information and advice concerning contraceptives, thereby imperiling the most intimate of human relationships. The states virtually had a free hand in the administration of justice. Trials often proceeded without counsel or jury. Convictions were allowed to stand even though they turned on illegally seized evidence or on statements extracted from the accused under coercive circumstances. There were no rules limiting the imposition of the death penalty. These practices victimized the poor and disadvantaged, as did the welfare system, which was administered in an arbitrary and oppressive manner. The capacity of the poor to participate in civic activities was also limited by the imposition of poll taxes, court filing fees, and the like."[8]

In addition, the nation was in the grip of an anticommunist frenzy, a "Red Scare" attributable in large part to the military challenge posed by the Soviet Union and the fear that communists had somehow infiltrated the U.S. government. Beginning in the late 1940s and continuing on throughout the decade of the 1950s, communists, alleged communists, and their suspected sympathizers were, as University of Texas law professor Michael E. Tigar has written, "remorselessly driven from the trade union movement, the civil service, the professions, the sciences and every influential area of American life. Their rights to hold jobs, to engage in professions, or to hold positions of trust in the trade unions were systematically abridged and denied."[9]

The U.S. Congress was swept up in the anticommunist frenzy and passed any number of laws of questionable legality, aimed broadside at the political left. The Internal Security Act of 1950 required communist groups to register with the government and to divulge their leadership, membership, and funding sources. Under the statute, popularly known as the McCarran Act, members of suspect organizations could be denied jobs in the defense industry as well as passports for foreign travel.

The Communist Control Act of 1954 provided for criminal prosecutions or deportations of suspected radicals, established loyalty-security programs, and loyalty-oath requirements. The law even went so far as to "officially" designate certain organizations as subversive.

Meanwhile, many who were subpoenaed to appear before the House Un-American Activities Committee invoked the Fifth Amendment privilege against self-incrimination when questioned as to their beliefs and associations. But invoking the privilege proved stigmatizing, tantamount to an admission of some sort of guilt.

The Supreme Court was part of the problem, not part of the solution. In *American Communications Association v. Douds* (1950),[10] the justices upheld the constitutionality of denying communists the right to hold office in labor unions covered by the collective bargaining provisions of the Taft-Hartley Act. Not since the turn of the century had the labor movement as a whole, its left-wing members under suspicion, suddenly found itself under attack and so divided.

The Court also gave the government broad power to arrest and prosecute suspected communists under the Smith Act, which made it a crime to advocate the overthrow of the U.S. government by force or violence. In *Dennis v. United States* (1951),[11] the Court upheld the Smith Act's constitutionality under the First Amendment, and leading members of the American Communist party went to jail—not for what they had actually done, but for the mere espousal of their beliefs.

The impact of all this was to chill not just communists or suspected communists in the government or labor movement but virtually any liberal, social activist, or progressive thinker who dared not risk being pinned with the communist label. The resulting repression of free speech had the intended result of severely constricting public debate on progressive ideas and principles.

"After all," according to Tigar, "one purpose of the purge was to tame and to capture the scientific and intellectual community. When the nonconformists had been driven from its ranks, the remainder could be welcomed into the 'think tanks,' 'research projects,' 'centers,' 'institutes,' and other ghettos erected by the military, the intelligence agencies and corporate America."[12]

The man who had come to personify the purge was himself an Irish Catholic, Republican Senator Joseph R. McCarthy of Wisconsin. Using hearings before the Senate internal security subcommittee as his forum for rooting out so-called communists across a broad spectrum of government, academia, the arts, and sciences, he grabbed headlines with his grandstanding style and outrageous accusations. The allegations, innuendoes, smears, and outright lies—and the period itself, known as the McCarthy era—will forever be associated with his name.

As an American patriot, William Brennan went to Boston that St. Patrick's Day to take a stand against McCarthyism, for he saw great, counterproductive danger in it. "Few then had the bravery to remind McCarthy and the public that the Bill of Rights still had living validity," one commentator has recalled.[13] But Brennan "refused to be silent when he felt the great charter of freedom was under attack."[14]

As a leader of the Irish-American community, he went to make his feelings known on the broader subject of anticommunism, which had stirred considerable debate and division among Irish Catholics. As historian William V. Shannon wrote in his now-classic *The American Irish*, "McCarthyism was a major crisis in the coming of age of the Irish Catholic community in the United States. It derived strength from the worst, the weakest, and the most outdated parts of the Irish experience in this country. But it also tested the best in that experience."[15]

A Gallup poll taken in January 1954 at the height of his power indicated that McCarthy was regarded favorably among American Catholics (58 percent) more than among Protestants (49 percent) or Jews (15 percent).[16] McCarthy's "closest political allies were Protestant Republican senators from the Middle West and Far West— William Jenner of Indiana, Karl Mundt of South Dakota, and Herman Welker of Idaho—and the Republican Party in these areas provided him with his political base."[17] Nevertheless, according to Shannon, "The discrepancy among religious groups would probably have been wider if the poll had asked the question only of Irish Catholics, instead of all Catholics."[18]

He explained, "Many Irish Catholics who fell for McCarthy's appeal had at the bottom of their minds a conviction they would not articulate in intellectual terms, but which they deeply felt. This was the belief that very few Americans outside the Catholic faith have any real religion or understand what it means to take religion seriously.

"Only the Catholics, so this feeling goes, believe that God is literally present in their churches; only Catholics make a great point of going to church every Sunday in foul weather or fair, in summer vacations or in winter snow. Since one sees everyone but fellow Catholics as in various stages of backsliding toward agnosticism and atheism, it naturally follows that if religious freedom is to be kept alive in this country it is up to the Catholics."[19]

He concluded, "It follows, furthermore, that only Catholics can fully grasp the sinister nature of communism, an avowedly anti-religious movement."[20]

The religious persecution experienced by Irish Catholics in

America only hardened these sentiments. As Catherine B. Shannon (no relation), president of the Irish Charitable Society from 1990 to 1991 and the first woman to serve in that role, has written, "The staunch Catholicism of the 19th and early 20th century immigrants, originating in communal pride...was reinforced by the pervasive anti-Catholicism of the dominant Anglo-Saxon Protestant establish-ment and culture. Irish-American Catholic solidarity, if not ex-clusiveness, was a natural corollary of nativist prejudice and the violence often visited upon Catholic churches, convents and Irish neighborhoods by mobs during the Know-Nothing era in New York, Boston, Philadelphia, and Lowell [Massachusetts]."[21]

She went on, "The Catholic clergy and the close-knit Catholic parishes provided spiritual sustenance as well as an effective, if informal, social welfare network that enabled the immigrants and their children to survive the early decades of social isolation, exhausting manual labor, poverty and generally poor living conditions."[22]

In William Shannon's view, "The cultural isolation and the residual resentment against past discrimination convinced many Irish that they had a special mission to save America for religion in the struggle against communism. They felt that only they knew what the struggle was all about and that the liberals and the atheists and the Jews and the half-agnostic Protestants did not know."[23]

By the mid-1950s, however, a "historic dichotomy between Irish Americans' conservative religious values and their more liberal political and social values"[24] was manifest. Obviously, the Irish-American community was split along class lines. In fact, there had been so much assimilation into the mainstream culture that some Irish-American intellectuals questioned whether an "Irish Ameri-can ethnic sense" would survive for longer than a few more decades.[25]

By the early 1960s, William Shannon was ready to write: "Undoubtedly the tensions and conflicts of middle-class life made some Irish peculiarly responsive to the appeals of McCarthy, but the Irish have been advancing socially and economically in the open competition of American life for many decades before McCarthy appeared in 1950 and have continued in the years afterward. Their 'touchiness,' their resentment at social snubs, their desire to assert their American patriotism, and their desire to 'make good' socially were much more intense thirty or forty years earlier."[26]

He went on, "By 1950, many of these status concerns had faded out, and most Irish were mellowed by the feeling that they had comfortably arrived. Moreover, McCarthy did not have his strong-est support in the Irish community among the more successful and those actively rising on the social scale. The blatancy and crudeness of his appeal were vaguely disturbing and offensive to these wall-to-wall [carpeting], two-cars-in-the-garage Irish. Like suburban voters of other nationality backgrounds, these Irish more typically pre-ferred the blandness of Dwight Eisenhower or, later, the well-mannered, Ivy League liberalism of John Kennedy."[27]

He explained, "McCarthy was strongest in the poorer, old-line Irish neighborhoods in South Boston, Brooklyn, and Chicago where working-class and lower-middle-class families still lived. These were the people who had been left behind in the scramble; they did not suffer status anxieties due to social and occupational mobility for the simple reason that they were not mobile. They had not advanced beyond where they were a generation or two generations earlier. Their suspicions, prejudices, and resentments were of a simpler, more old-fashioned, more primitive kind."[28]

According to the March 18, 1954, edition of *The Boston Daily Globe*, Lodge in his remarks "said the cause of human dignity and freedom is bound to prevail [over communism] because it is based on the will of God."

The Globe went on to report, "He [Lodge] said recent actions by the United States indicated this country has seized the initiative from Soviet Russia in the Cold War," in part because "President Eisenhower's proposal for sharing the atom stockpile for peace won the United States new friends in the United Nations."

When William Brennan of suburban South Orange, New Jersey, the risen and well-to-do son of a coal-shoveling union organizer, spoke, he tried to bridge the gap between the Irish-American classes.

The ostensible theme of Brennan's speech was the religious nature of this nation and its people. "Yes," he told his audience, "this America, like the Irish since St. Patrick planted the seed of Christianity in Ireland in the year 432, is and always has been theistic."[29] But tucked into his address along with references to "the constitutional guarantees of religious liberty" were allusions to "the guarantees of other human liberties to be found in the Constitution."[30]

Proclaiming that the "Irish love of individual liberty has naturally flowered in this America where the promise of that liberty has been realized as nowhere else on earth," he warned of the dangers of communism.[31] "Organized atheistic society," he declared, "is making a determined drive for supremacy by conquest, as well as by infiltration. We are at a crucial hour, and Americans of all faiths have a common stake in the outcome and are commendably on the alert."[32]

At the same time, however, he cautioned against the loss of freedom and civility: "Americans of all races and creeds have closed ranks against the godless foe. Whatever of treasure, of time, of effort required to defeat him, we will provide, and gladly. But we cannot and must not doubt our strength to conserve, without sacrifice of any, all of the guarantees of justice and fair play and simple human dignity which have made our land what it is."[33]

Without mentioning him by name, he asserted that by under-mining American democratic traditions and ideals, McCarthy was, in effect, giving aid and comfort to the enemy. And, his flat brogue rising, blood pounding behind his eyes, he issued a stern warning to the Soviets: "The enemy deludes himself if he thinks he detects in some practices of the contemporary scene reminiscent of the Salem witch hunts, any signs that our courage has failed us and that fear has palsied our hard-won concept of justice and fair play. These are but passing aberrations even now undergoing systematic deflation."[34]

He concluded to thunderous applause, "America, the leader and hope of free men everywhere, has supreme confidence in the irresistible strength of our free society to meet and vanquish today's imperialism, so utterly devoid of hope and offering man only the promise of a degrading slavery."[35]

Early in his speech, Brennan had regaled the assembly with a history lesson, recounting Irish attempts to overthrow British rule in the late eighteenth century. In 1791, an alliance of Irish Protes-tants and Catholics, the Society of United Irishmen, was founded for the purpose of instigating a rebellion. Their leader, a young

Protestant lawyer named Wolfe Tone, had enlisted the support of France, and a French fleet was on its way to Ireland. But a traitor to the Irish cause, Thomas Reynolds, managed to infiltrate the Society's small leadership circle. Reynolds informed the British military commander, Lord Cornwallis, of the Society's plans, and the leaders of the revolt were arrested and hanged, their weapons seized, before the French fleet landed.

Afterward, according to Brennan, the British army "loosed upon the Irish people a terror with few parallels, so ruthless that even the enemy military commander lost control of his troops and in his words protested to London, 'Every crime, every cruelty that could be committed by Cossacks and Calmuchs has been committed here. The way in which the troops have been employed would ruin the best in Europe.'"[36] Brennan finished, "So what Benedict Arnold and Lord Cornwallis could not do in America, Thomas Reynolds and Lord Cornwallis accomplished in Ireland."[37]

His storied reference to an infamous traitor to freedom's cause was to prove apocryphal, for somewhere in the audience that night was Brennan's own Thomas Reynolds. As he might have suspected based on his knowledge of history, he was himself at that moment the object of betrayal. No sooner had he finished speaking than the gist of his outspoken attack was communicated to Senator Joseph McCarthy and his allies in Washington.

Yet for all their force, fervor, and fury, the words of one still relatively unknown New Jersey state supreme court justice had less to do with McCarthy's ultimate undoing than McCarthy himself. In December 1954, he was formally censured by the Senate for his tactics and misconduct.

Two months later, in a February 23, 1955, address to New Jersey's Monmouth County Rotary Club, Brennan reiterated his earlier St. Patrick's Day themes and welcomed McCarthy's apparent demise.[38] He upheld the Fifth Amendment's privilege against self-incrimination and defended its use by those called to testify before congressional investigating committees.

"Frankness with ourselves," he declared, "must compel the acknowledgment that our resentment toward those who invoked its protection led us into a toleration of some of the very abuses which brought the privilege into being so many centuries ago. The abuses took on modern dress, it is true—not the rack and the screw, but the distorted version of the happenings at secret hearings released to the press, the shouted epithet at the hapless and helpless witness.

"And woe betide him who cried protest at this perversion of the legislative inquiry. He was thrust in the mold of a sympathizer with and protector of those who plead the fifth amendment. Intentionally conceived or merely misguided, the result has been to engender hate and fear by one citizen of another, to have us distrust ourselves and our institutions, to have us become 'a nation afraid.'"[39] He cautioned, "That path brings us perilously close to destroying liberty in liberty's name."[40]

With regard to the Senate's censure of McCarthy, who, at the time of Brennan's speech, was "investigating" suspected communists at nearby Fort Monmouth, he stated, "[T]here are hopeful signs in recent events that we have set things aright and have become ashamed of our toleration of the barbarism which marked the procedures at some of those hearings. It is indeed reason for pure joy and relief that at long last our collective conscience has sickened of the excesses and is demanding the adoption of permanent and lasting reforms to curb investigatory abuses."[41]

In two short years, the men would meet face-to-face for the only time. McCarthy would be a ruthless inquisitor, Brennan this time the hapless witness. The occasion would be Brennan's confirmation hearings. Joe McCarthy would be all that stood between William Brennan and a seat on the U.S. Supreme Court.

CHAPTER 9

Ike's Second-Biggest Mistake

I made two mistakes as President and they are both sitting on the Supreme Court.

—President Dwight D. Eisenhower, referring to Earl Warren and William J. Brennan Jr.

THE LATE YALE LAW PROFESSOR Fred Rodell observed, "Prediction in print is a preoccupation of the foolhardy."[1] This is especially true with regard to prognostications about how people will vote once they are appointed to the U.S. Supreme Court. Associate Justice Sherman "Shay" Minton, who served from 1949 to 1956, was certainly no exception.

Appointed to the high bench by President Harry Truman in 1949, Minton had up to that time been regarded as a liberal. In fact, during his years in the U.S. Senate from 1935 to 1941, where he met and befriended then–Missouri Senator Truman, Minton, a Democrat from Indiana, was one of the most enthusiastic supporters of Franklin Roosevelt's New Deal, including FDR's plan to "pack" the Supreme Court in order to liberalize it. Roosevelt rewarded his fealty by naming him to the U.S. Court of Appeals for the Seventh Circuit after Minton lost his Senate reelection bid in 1940.[2]

By 1956, however, Justice Minton was considered a conservative. He had embraced the philosophy of "judicial restraint," believing that judges "should allow the executive and legislative branches the greatest freedom to create policy and programs with the minimum of interference from the judiciary."[3]

In addition, he was enthusiastic about the era's anticommunist zeal. He wrote the majority opinion in *Adler v. Board of Education*[4] in 1952, upholding a New York state law that barred "subversives" from teaching public school. That same year, he voted with the majority in *Carlson v. Landon*,[5] allowing the attorney general to seize and hold without bail any alien communist considered to be a threat to the national security.

Minton was generally nondescript. He caused a stir in August 1956, however, when, returning from a European vacation, he told reporters bluntly that he hoped Democrat Adlai Stevenson would wrest the presidency from Dwight D. Eisenhower in November.[6] His feelings, he explained, were based on his belief that Ike was "terribly handicapped physically" by the severe heart attack the president had suffered in September 1955.[7]

Ironically, it was Minton's health that failed. On Friday, September 7, 1956, he announced his retirement from the Court, citing a circulatory problem in his legs, pernicious anemia.[8] The disease, he told journalists, was "like diabetes—you can do something about it but you can't cure it."[9] Then sixty-five, he had walked with difficulty for some time and had been using a cane for the past year.[10]

The *New York Times* noted in passing the culmination of his "quiet career," commenting dryly, "It is likely that the publicity attendant upon his retirement from the court is the first that many of his younger countrymen will have heard of him."[11] Eisenhower, for his part, graciously offered "appreciation" for Minton's service on both the high court and the court of appeals.[12]

His departure provided the president with the opportunity to name his third Supreme Court nominee, Earl Warren and John M. Harlan having been the first and second, respectively. According to Eisenhower's attorney general Herbert Brownell, Ike took "an unusual personal interest in judicial appointments."[13] Brownell recalled, "Unlike some of his successors in office, he did not rely on the White House staff to screen potential nominees and to interview them about their judicial philosophy and legal views. Instead, the attorney general was the president's chief adviser on these matters."[14]

Eisenhower had four basic criteria that he used to select nominees for the federal bench, up to and including associate justices of the Supreme Court. They were youth, relatively speaking; and favorable recommendations from the American Bar Association (ABA) Committee on Judicial Appointments; from the candidate's local bar; and from the FBI, based on a character background check.[15]

Eisenhower regarded the chief justice's role as somewhat different from that of the associate justices. For example, the chief justice, as head of the judicial branch, would need to involve himself fully in matters of judicial organization and administration.[16] Ike therefore felt that in selecting a chief justice, "previous experience in public affairs and administrative skill and abilities were qualities to be desired in addition to the usual requirements of judicial competence and integrity."[17]

He had used his first appointment to make Earl Warren chief justice following Fred Vinson's unexpected death from a heart attack in 1953. Burly, white-haired, and a devout Baptist, Warren was, at the age of sixty-two, grandfatherly and mild-mannered. A three-term California governor who ran for vice president with Republican presidential nominee Thomas E. Dewey in 1948, he was instrumental in securing the Republican nomination for Eisenhower four years later.[18] Ike was grateful. And he liked Warren's friendliness.[19]

He also "noted approvingly Governor Warren's reputation for running a nonpartisan administration in California."[20] According to Brownell, Ike "emphasized that partisan politics should have no place in the selection of a member of the Supreme Court."[21]

For all his appealing qualities, however, there were aspects of Warren's past that were troubling. He had belonged to an anti-Asian organization, the white supremacist Native Sons of the Golden West, and, as governor, had instigated the internment of some 110,000 Japanese-Americans on the West Coast during World War II.[22] In 1943 he had told a national governors' convention in Columbus, Ohio, "If the Japs are released no one will be able to tell a saboteur from any other Jap."[23] He had warned, "We don't want to have a second Pearl Harbor in California."[24]

Warren had since come to regret his position and to moderate his views. He said some years later, "Now that society is so much more aware of civil rights, interning them seems like a terribly cruel thing to do, and it *was* a cruel thing, especially uprooting the children from their schools, their communities and friends, and having whole families transferred out to a strange environment and a less desirable environment."[25]

He had also become an outspoken advocate on behalf of African Americans. During the 1948 presidential campaign, he called on Congress to enact voting rights and antilynching legislation.[26] And in 1952, he told *The Pittsburgh Courier*, which was the widest-circulating national African American newspaper, "I am for a sweeping civil rights program, beginning with a fair employment practices act. I insist upon one law for all men."[27]

Brownell recalled that Warren "had a solid reputation as an internationalist and as a supporter of the United Nations, and in domestic affairs he was considered a progressive who supported legislation for fair-employment practices for black citizens."[28] Ike was satisfied that Warren was "a man of high ideals and common sense."[29]

He was, therefore, selected from among a handful of leading candidates that included Arthur Vanderbilt, chief justice of the New Jersey state supreme court and Brennan's mentor.[30] When it came to light that Vanderbilt had recently suffered a stroke, misgivings about his longevity virtually sealed Warren's nomination.[31]

Ike's second appointment was of John M. Harlan II to replace Associate Justice Robert H. Jackson, who died in October 1954. Born the scion of a well-connected Chicago family in 1899, Harlan's demeanor on the bench was once described as that of a "patrician patiently enduring a proletarian rite and wondering if the steward of his club hadn't been tapping his private stock of perfectly aged Camembert lately."[32]

Harlan had graduated from Princeton in 1920; attended Oxford University, where he studied jurisprudence on a Rhodes Scholarship; then acquired his grounding in American law at New York Law School. He finished his legal studies in a year and gained admission to the New York bar in 1924.

His namesake grandfather John Marshall Harlan had served on the Court as an associate justice from 1877 to 1911. In 1896, he had written the lone prophetic dissent in *Plessy v. Ferguson,*[33] which established the separate-but-equal doctrine that formalized racial segregation in America. "Our Constitution is color-blind," the maverick elder Harlan had protested, "and neither knows nor tolerates classes among its citizens."[34]

He went on, "In respect to civil rights, all citizens are equal before the law. The humblest is the peer of the most powerful. The law regards man as man, and takes no account of his surroundings or of his color when his civil rights as guaranteed by the supreme law of the land are involved."[35]

In contrast to his grandfather, whom history would remember for his grandiosity and visionary eloquence, Harlan II had a reputation of being a "lawyer's lawyer,"[36] a master of mundane legal technique who was exhaustively attentive to detail. After decades of successful practice both on Wall Street and as a prosecutor, he was by the early 1950s regarded as "one of the nation's foremost litigators in antitrust and related actions."[37] His corporate clientele included the Du Ponts, and he counted among his friends New York Governor Thomas E. Dewey, whom he had served as chief counsel to the New York crime commission.[38]

Through his association with Dewey, Harlan had rekindled his acquaintance with Brownell, one of Dewey's key advisers and manager of the governor's 1948 presidential campaign. Brownell had originally met Harlan during the 1920s when the two had worked together at the New York corporate firm of Root, Clark, Buckner, Howland & Ballantine.[39]

As attorney general, Brownell was credited with getting Harlan appointed to the U.S. Court of Appeals for the Second Circuit, and to the Supreme Court a short time later.[40] Ike had been especially impressed with Harlan's anticommunist credentials.[41] During his brief tenure as an appellate judge, Harlan had upheld the convictions of twelve communists under the Smith Act, writing a majority opinion in *United States v. Flynn*[42] in 1954 that was extraordinarily deferential to the government.

One critic of the opinion claimed that Harlan's willingness to allow criminal punishment of free speech took the country back to "the law of constructive treason under the worst days of the English common law."[43] Another claimed that under Harlan's ruling in

Flynn, "the danger need not be either 'clear' or 'present' but only 'potential' to warrant Congress' interfering with free speech and press."[44]

Harlan's Senate confirmation had been delayed for about five months by conservative Republicans who joined forces with segregationist Southern democrats.[45] Ostensibly, opposition was based on concern over Harlan's role as an adviser to the Atlantic Union Committee, "an organization established to forge closer relations among the nations of the Atlantic community."[46] Detractors labeled him a "one worlder," asserting that his views represented a threat to American sovereignty.[47]

Ironically, an investigator for the Senate Judiciary Committee even went so far as to accuse Harlan of being a communist sympathizer.[48] As it turned out, however, "the committee investigator had been investigating the wrong John Harlan—an unknown gentleman from Baltimore."[49]

In reality, the obstruction of the confirmation process was in response to the Supreme Court's ongoing consideration of the school desegregation cases consolidated under the heading *Brown v. Board of Education of Topeka.*[50] Southern senators and their allies clearly feared that Harlan II "would follow his grandfather's (in their view improper) interpretation of the Fourteenth Amendment" and vote to outlaw segregation.[51] Eventually the Senate approved the nomination by a vote of 71 to 11, with fourteen abstentions.[52]

A number of prominent names surfaced in the press as potential replacements for Minton, including Thomas Dewey, Secretary of State John Foster Dulles, and Brownell, who never really considered himself at that time a serious candidate.[53] As he put it, whenever there is a vacancy on the Court, "the name of the incumbent attorney general is always mentioned for the post in speculative press stories."[54]

Also mentioned as a potential nominee was William H. Hastie, a friend and associate of Thurgood Marshall, who would have become the first African American nominated for the Supreme Court.[55] Hastie, fifty-one, was a graduate of Harvard Law School. He had served as governor of the Virgin Islands from 1946 to 1949, when President Truman appointed him to the U.S. Court of Appeals for the Third Circuit.[56]

All were eminently qualified. So was William Brennan of New

Jersey. According to Brownell, "Brennan's name was among those submitted to the president for consideration."[57]

Brennan easily satisfied Ike's four basic criteria. At the age of fifty, he would be the youngest justice. The ABA reported favorably on him, as did the FBI.[58] And Vanderbilt, his state's chief judicial officer, who was highly thought of within the administration, offered his enthusiastic endorsement. Indeed, according to Eisenhower, Vanderbilt told him that Brennan possessed "the finest legal mind that he had ever known."[59]

He was desirable for several other reasons, as well. Brownell recalled, "Eisenhower had told me he wanted to appoint a Democrat to the Court should the opportunity arise. His previous nominees had been Republicans, and he wanted to demonstrate to the public that partisan politics was not the major consideration in his judicial appointments."[60] Brennan, a lifelong Democrat, would add a measure of bipartisanship to the Court.

Moreover, according to Brownell, "The Conference of Chief Justices of the State Courts claimed that the existing Court was weakened because none of the sitting justices had had experience on a state court. As a result they pointed out, proper recognition of the position of the states in determining federal-state relationships was missing from the Court."[61] Brennan was a state judge with considerable experience at both the trial and appellate levels, and his appointment would address their concerns.

Another factor was that, contrary to tradition, none of the sitting justices was Catholic, a fact that had not escaped the notice of the Conference of Catholic Bishops.[62] This created a situation in which, in contrast to many of his personal experiences, Brennan's faith worked to his advantage. With the presidential election looming, Brennan's appointment could gain the Republican Party support among Catholic voters, especially in the northeastern United States, from which Brennan hailed.

Finally, the administration had recognized a need "to expedite judicial procedures and to eliminate backlogs in court calendars" within the federal judiciary.[63] Obviously this made Brennan's court-reform credentials appealing.

In this last regard, however, his selection was something of a fluke. Brownell was impressed with a speech Brennan had delivered at a conference Brownell had sponsored on judicial administration in the spring of 1956.[64] According to Brownell, "Brennan's address made our conference a success."[65] He recalled, "He and I struck up a friendship at that time."[66]

Ironically, Vanderbilt later claimed that the speech was not Brennan's. "It was mine," he said.[67] "I was ill and he read it in my place."[68]

Brennan said, however, that the "speech" was in fact his. He told interviewer Nat Hentoff in 1990, "For some years, the No. 1 figure in the [court-reform] movement had been Arthur Vanderbilt. He became ill two days before the meeting, and I was pushed in to substitute for him. Having had so little time to prepare a speech, I spoke mostly off the cuff, for close to an hour."[69]

Brennan recounted his appointment to the Court in an interview with Donna Haupt of *Constitution* magazine in 1989. He began, "You have to go back to the 28th of September, a Friday night in the fall of 1956. I was in New Jersey about to move into a new set of chambers, and my clerk and I were busy transferring my library when the phone rang. It was Attorney General Brownell and he said, 'The President would like to see you tomorrow morning at 9 o'clock.'"[70]

He went on, "Well, I demurred that I really had so much to do and I didn't really know how I could. But Brownell, without telling me why, simply said, 'You can't say no to the President of the United States.' And I agreed, I suppose I couldn't. We lived in Rumson at that time, outside of Red Bank, New Jersey, and I was able to catch the 1 A.M. sleeper to Washington, getting in about 5:30 the next morning."[71]

His wife, Marjorie, had a somewhat different recollection of the same events. In October 1956, she told *Time* magazine, "On Friday afternoon my husband called me from the office and said there was a telegram from the Attorney General. It said something about 'Come down and have breakfast with me and then we'll see the President.' It was such a surprise that we even had to borrow a suitcase from a neighbor, so that we could get him off in time to make the train."[72]

Brownell met Brennan at Union Station on Saturday morning. "As I approached the gates to go out," Brennan told Haupt, "there was standing the Attorney General, and he greeted me and said, 'We're going to have breakfast at our house.' So I shrugged and said fine, and we got into his chauffeured limousine. I still had no idea, mind you, why I was there.''[73]

He continued, "Well, we hadn't gone but a few blocks when Brownell said, 'You know why the President wants to see you, don't you?' and I said, 'If it has to do with that follow-up conference I don't see…' He interrupted me and said 'No, no, no. He wants to ask you if you'll take the seat vacated by Justice Sherman Minton.'"[74]

Brennan was floored. "Well, I knew we got to his house, and I knew we had breakfast, but I was utterly in a daze," he recalled.[75] "Anyone would be. I had absolutely no expectation about a thing like that. I'm sure the papers at the time had been full of possible successors to Justice Minton. For example, John Foster Dulles, who was Secretary of State at that time, or any number of people very prominent in the administration were mentioned. It never dawned on me at the time that my name would be suggested, none whatsoever.[76]

"In any event," he went on, "we got to the White House and I was taken to the Oval Office."[77] He told *Life* magazine, "I thought there'd be other people, but suddenly I found myself alone in the room with him, not a soul but me and the President. It was something!"[78] It was there in the Oval Office that the president informed him that he would in fact be appointed.

Frederick Hall has remarked, "It is curious that it was thought by some that the President was naming a 'conservative' when he appointed him [Brennan]; obviously those people had not done their homework."[79] Yet years later, after Brennan manifested his liberal judicial philosophy on the Court, Ike reportedly lamented the appointment as "the second biggest mistake I ever made," the choice of progressive-thinking Earl Warren as chief justice having been the biggest.[80]

According to Fred Friendly, former president of CBS News and Edward R. Murrow Professor Emeritus of the Columbia University Graduate School of Journalism, Ike made disparaging remarks about both appointees when Friendly and Walter Cronkite interviewed the retired president at his home in Gettysburg, Pennsylvania, in early 1961. In an interview with the *Legal Times* in September 1990, Friendly recalled, "We were having lunch, and I was just making small talk. I don't know why, but I brought up Earl Warren," whose appointment, Friendly suggested, was something for which Ike would be remembered favorably.[81]

He went on, "As I spoke, a cloud began to form on his forehead, and it was massive. He said, 'I'm surprised to hear you say that. I made two mistakes as President and they are both sitting on the Supreme Court.'"[82]

Referring to his advisers who were involved in the selections, Eisenhower concluded, "We learned a terrible lesson. He [Warren] and Brennan."[83]

Friendly insisted that Ike made the remarks. "There is no doubt in my mind," he contended.[84] But the comments were not part of the taped interview and so do not exist as part of any public record.[85]

Brownell addressed the controversy in his memoirs. "When Justice William Brennan resigned from the Supreme Court" in 1990, he wrote, "the media reported that Eisenhower 'is said to have said' that Brennan's appointment to the Court was one of the worst political mistakes he had ever made. No published basis whatsoever exists for that report so far as I know, and it heightens my belief that the stories are apocryphal or at least do not represent Eisenhower's overall assessment."[86]

Brennan's elder son, William III, reportedly told the *Legal Times* that Eisenhower once wrote to his father denying the remarks and apologizing for any misunderstanding.[87]

For his own part, Brennan said that he hoped Eisenhower had no regrets about his appointment. About a month before his retirement from the Court in 1990, he told Sean O Murchu that if Ike did, "He certainly never said so to me."[88] He conceded, "I have heard it said that he thought that both Chief Justice Warren and I were his mistakes. But as far as I know, that's just a story."[89]

As for how thoroughly he did his homework into Brennan's background, Brownell has insisted that he "read all his [Brennan's] published opinions," finding them to be "well reasoned and well written."[90] This is consistent with Brennan's recollection of his Oval Office meeting with Ike. According to Brennan, "The President had been well briefed on everything I'd ever done and talked to me about it for a while."[91]

Brennan recalled that during their conversation, the president "asked me particularly about the health of Chief Justice Vanderbilt, who had previously suffered a stroke. President Eisenhower knew him well and felt bad because he wasn't able to appoint him to the Court, due to his poor health."[92]

He added, "I don't know that I was his second choice. I imagine that I was, but the President didn't say that."[93]

After their discussion, Ike advised him to call his wife and mother with the good news. Marjorie was too excited to remember much of that conversation. She explained, "[H]e called and told me what the President told him about the appointment—but I've been so excited about it that what he said has gone out of my mind."[94]

When he called his seventy-eight-year-old mother, Agnes, he told her first, "Now just sit down."[95] Afterward, he said, "All she could say was 'Wh-wh-what?'"[96] Her recollection of the conversation was that she responded by telling him, "God bless you, my son," over and over again. "God bless you."[97]

At first, Eisenhower instructed Brennan to inform no one outside his immediate family until the president had a chance to notify the senators from New Jersey.[98] But as soon as he had finished talking to his wife and mother, he recalled, "the Attorney General rushed in and said the President would like me to come back. I thought to myself 'Oh no! He's changed his mind.'"[99]

Instead, Ike had decided to announce the appointment on the spot.[100] He introduced the justice-designate to the White House press corps.[101]

Reaction to the nomination was generally favorable. *U.S. News & World Report* was tepid in its endorsement, stating simply that Brennan had "compiled a record—both as a lawyer and as a judge—of solid rather than spectacular achievement."[102] But Time, Inc., publications were more laudatory. *Time* magazine described him as "a jurist of solid experience and reputation,"[103] his mind "quick and sharp,"[104] and *Life* assured its readers that Brennan would bring to the Court "one of the keenest, quickest judicial minds in the country."[105]

The *New York Times*, for its part, was ebullient. A *Times* editorial called Brennan "a man of high repute and recognized achievement [who] may go to his new post with the knowledge that he owes no service to anything but his conscience. His record, even his comparative obscurity, promises well."[106] The newspaper called him "a foe of the law's delays"[107] and a "defender of civil rights."[108]

Arthur Krock, a *Times* columnist, touted him as "an outstanding trial lawyer" and "an experienced judge whose work has been generally applauded by the bar."[109] He added, "[I]t is also an important proof of democracy when a Supreme Court justice is representative of what an American can, with honor and industry, achieve without the birthright of social and economic privilege."[110]

As a man, Brennan was introduced to the American public in various ways. Jack Alexander wrote of him in the *Saturday Evening Post*, "His face is that of a combative cherub, and the cherubic effect is heightened by a frame of only five feet, eight and a half inches onto which Nature has compacted 167 pounds."[111] He added, "He has a prodigious capacity for sustained work and a brand of self-discipline that is awesome."[112]

Time described him to its readers as an "affable, storytelling Irishman."[113] It went on, "Brennan has been called jaunty, dapper, lacking the austere aspect commonly associated with Justices. A much-sought after-dinner speaker, he also plays duffer golf (low 100s), likes to read American history, Plato, dime novels."[114]

Life called him "a lifelong, city-bred Democrat, a genial, outgoing, even garrulous man, much more like a successful toastmaster than a sobersided jurist."[115]

Inside Washington, D.C., the Sunday edition of the influential *Evening Star* portrayed him as "a man who enjoys and is fascinated by his work to the exclusion of hobbies, a man with a delightful sense of humor and a zest for the law."[116]

A friend, presidential appointments secretary Bernard Shanley, praised him unreservedly. "They don't come like this guy," he told reporters.[117] "He is extraordinarily brilliant; he has a tremendous personality; and he is genuine from top to toe."[118]

The *New York Times* credited Shanley and Secretary of Labor James Mitchell with "having brought the new justice to the attention of the President and Attorney General Brownell and pressed the numerous good arguments for his choice."[119] Brennan had worked for Mitchell, a fellow New Jerseyan, while Mitchell was chief of the industrial personnel division of the army service forces during World War II.[120] Apparently, Mitchell also knew Brennan from having done labor-relations work for Western Electric.[121]

Brennan, for his part, attributed his appointment to "the accomplishments of the New Jersey court system," which, he said, "have attracted widespread attention in this country and, indeed, in other lands as well."[122] He also thanked Shanley for his help, but Shanley told him, "I have done nothing for you."[123] Still, having an admiring friend so close to the president could not have hurt his chances.

Meanwhile, commentators indulged in the inevitable speculation about the kind of justice Brennan was likely to become. *U.S. News & World Report* predicted, "A close study of the career of the new appointee to the Court indicates that he cannot be counted on to join either a 'liberal' or 'conservative' bloc on the nation's highest tribunal."[124]

The magazine's conclusion was based on a source identified only as an "administration official who has known Justice Brennan for many years."[125] Such an official might well have been Shanley. The source was quoted as having called Brennan "a man with a lot of progressive ideas," adding, however, "I would say that Mr. Brennan's beliefs are very close to President Eisenhower's on many issues. I would call him a middle-of-the-roader."[126]

Life concurred, calling the opinions Brennan wrote as a New Jersey justice "clear, forceful, and middle-of-the-road."[127] *Time* called them "clear, forceful, and moderate."[128] Washington's *Evening Star* described him as "closest in legal background and judicial attitudes to Justice Harlan than to any of the other members of the high court."[129] It went on, "One prominent jurist rated him more conservative than Chief Justice Warren and Associate Justice Black and less conservative than the other associate justices."[130]

Back home in New Jersey, however, those who knew him had a more accurate idea of what to expect. Democratic governor Robert Meyner called Brennan "a sound liberal of the highest personal character and with great intellectual drive." He added, "He is only a nominal Democrat in that he has never been active in party politics. But I suspect his opinions will not be quite as 'middle-of-the-road' as some Republicans seem to think."[131]

Most prescient of all, however, was J. L. Bernstein, former editor of *The Reporter*, a publication of the Passaic County, New Jersey, bar association. In an article entitled, "The Philosophy of Mr. Justice Brennan," which appeared in *The Reporter*'s November 1956 edition, he wrote: "Justice Brennan, it would appear, has broad, liberal, humane views. Implicit in his writings one discerns a 'great sense of fairness,' indeed sometimes to the point of being unrealis-tic....But he can also be very realistic as well as being idealistic, giving the impression at all times of seeking to be scrupulously fair and objective."

Bernstein concluded, "We have a 'hunch' that Justice Brennan will be heard from more and more in a way to gratify liberal sentiment in this country."

A few days after his meeting with Eisenhower, Brennan went to pay a call on Chief Justice Warren at the Supreme Court. Minton's resignation was to become effective October 15, 1956.[132] Eisenhower gave Brennan a recess appointment effective as of that date because Congress was out of session until the new year. Under Article II, section 2 of the Constitution, the president has the power to make temporary appointments to the Court to fill vacancies that occur while the Senate is in recess. Upon Congress's return, the Senate would take up the matter of Brennan's formal confirmation.

In a 1987 interview with National Public Radio, Brennan said that Warren took him up to the third floor of the building, where, he recalled, "In a small room, my seven new colleagues were sitting around a table having sandwiches. The room was dark, and he put on the light, and there they all were, watching the opening game of the 1956 World Series" between the New York Yankees and the Brooklyn Dodgers.[133] Brennan was an avid Dodgers fan.

He went on, "I was introduced by the Chief to each of them, and someone said, 'Put out the light.' They put out the light, and they went on watching the game."[134]

That made it official: William Brennan was a member of the Supreme Court.[135]

CHAPTER 10

Life in Georgetown

Tiny fenced-off patches of ground at the rear, recently littered with rubbish, again turned into gardens and patios with lilac bushes and crape myrtle nursed back to vigor by pruning and feeding. Every rejuvenated spot inspired the redemption of others, while real estate brokers hastily played down their decades-old argument that once a neighborhood had become part-Negro, it deteriorated with inexorable rapidity.

—Historian Constance McLaughlin Green on the revitalization of Georgetown in the 1950s

HER HUSBAND'S ELEVATION to the U.S. Supreme Court thrilled and flustered Marjorie so much that she forgot guests were coming for dinner on the Saturday that Bill gave her the news. That evening, she was an uncharacteristically inattentive hostess. Distracted by the day's events, she hadn't cooked enough food. By the time she served it, it was cold. And she was called away from the dining room table every five minutes to answer some reporter's phone call.

She was elated at the prospect of returning to Washington. But there were so many things to think about and plan. Not least among them was where to live once they got there.

When Bill served in the army during World War II, they had lived in Chevy Chase, Maryland, just across the District of Columbia's northwestern boundary.[1] WASPy and affluent, Chevy Chase was "a much older, sophisticated region of roomy houses built on large lots in the vicinity of the country club"[2] that was the oldest in the nation's capital, founded at around the turn of the century.[3] Bill III and Hugh had attended Chevy Chase Elementary School.[4] What a coincidence it would be for daughter Nancy, now age seven, to wind up there.

Marjorie knew she would miss being close to Hugh, who was working for a construction company during the day and taking night classes at nearby Monmouth College.[5] At the same time, she was heartened by the thought of seeing more of Bill III, who was a second lieutenant in the marines, stationed at Quantico, Virginia, about thirty-five miles southwest of D.C.[6]

When her husband proposed that they live in Georgetown, she was doubly excited, for she loved that historic area. She imagined herself window shopping the multitude of specialty stores, or dining in quaint, haute cuisine restaurants with her husband, the Supreme Court justice. She pictured Georgetown's regal townhouses fronted by wrought-iron steps and fences. She envisioned the verdurous cobblestone streets that echoed to the footsteps of passersby.

The Brennans may not have realized it, but they could not have chosen a smarter place to live. Originally one of the three separate cities that made up the District of Columbia—the others were the City of Washington and the City of Alexandria—Georgetown had many stately and elegant colonial-style townhouses that had fallen into disrepair between the founding of the Republic and the mid-twentieth century. But by the mid-1950s, the area was making a comeback.

According to Pulitzer Prize–winning historian Constance McLaughlin Green, "In 1930 about half her [Georgetown's] inhabitants were poverty-stricken Negroes, most of them occupying substandard dwellings, some without running water or electricity. Yet the convenience of the location and the yeast of the abiding charm of the shabby little village had begun to work in the late 1920's."[7]

She explained, "The remodeling started then had proceeded slowly during the depths of the depression but about 1934 suddenly gained momentum. Impecunious young New Dealers moved into the cramped restored little houses. Tiny fenced-off patches of ground at the rear, recently littered with rubbish, again turned into gardens and patios with lilac bushes and crape myrtle nursed back to vigor by pruning and feeding. Every rejuvenated spot inspired the redemption of others, while real estate brokers hastily played down their decades-old argument that once a neighborhood had become part-Negro, it deteriorated with inexorable rapidity."[8]

As Green portrayed it, "Colored families usually were unable to resist the prices white dealers offered for Georgetown property or else could not afford the higher rentals caused by improvements to adjoining property."[9] Hence, by the mid-1950s the "decoloration" of Georgetown was complete.[10] The African Americans had moved out. In came "yuppies" like the Brennans.

Other newcomers included Justice and Mrs. John and Ethel Harlan, who moved to 1677 31st Street, N.W., not far from where the Brennans would take up residence.[11] At first, Ethel Harlan had misgivings about leaving the pastoral Weston, Connecticut, country-side for urban Washington.[12] But in April 1955, she wrote to Marion Frankfurter, wife of Justice Felix Frankfurter, "Georgetown and our own house have done a lot to make me feel better."[13]

She explained, "We have so many small amusements along our street and pleasant experiences getting settled that the first rather alarming impact of Washington has worn off. People have, as you said, been kind and cordial, and I am feeling much gayer."[14]

The Frankfurters, for their part, had been Georgetowners for some time. In fact, it was Frankfurter, Brennan's law professor at Harvard, who arranged for the Brennans, as he had for the Harlans, to move into the neighborhood. The house the Brennans eventually chose was across the street from the Frankfurters in the 3000 block of Dumbarton Avenue, now Dumbarton Street. In the meantime, however, the newest justice took up residence in the Brighton Hotel at 2123 California Street, N.W.,[15] north of another fashionable neighborhood, Dupont Circle, and prepared for his first day of work.

He returned home to Rumson to tie up loose ends and settle affairs as much as he could in the short time available. The Supreme Court opens each term on the first Monday in October, and he wanted to be ensconced as close to that date as possible.

He was lauded by the state bar as a conquering hero. Vanderbilt closed court for a day in his honor. Meanwhile Bill and Marjorie packed and made arrangements for their move. Finally, he said goodbye to his home on Conover Lane and walked out into the front yard carrying three judicial robes.[16]

"The oldest I got eight years ago," he explained to a *Life* reporter, there to record his New Jersey farewell for a feature story that ran in the magazine's October 29, 1956, edition.[17] "I wore it as a trial judge in Hudson County, on the Appellate Division in Newark, on the Supreme Court in Trenton. I guess it's still got a lot of life left in it."[18]

On Tuesday, October 16, 1956, a couple of weeks into the Court's 1956–57 term, Marjorie helped him don that robe in the conference room of the Supreme Court of the United States for his swearing in as an associate justice.[19] His mother, Agnes, his daughter, Nancy, both sons, and his daughter-in-law were in attendance.[20] When questioned how she felt, his mother asked reporters, "Do you blame me for being grateful?"[21]

The chief justice sits in the middle of the bench. The associate justice most senior in length of service on the Court sits to his immediate right. The second most senior justice sits to the chief's immediate left, the third most senior one removed on the right, the fourth one removed on the left, and so on, so that Brennan as the junior member sat farthest to the left of Warren.

The Court he joined was hard-pressed on account of both its workload—a backlog of some 450 cases—and the monumentally complex and controversial nature of the issues that it faced. The Red Scare—like Senator Joe McCarthy, who personified it—was waning but not dead. The justices had before them a number of cases challenging the intrusions on civil liberties that were all too common during the era.

In addition, the federal judiciary in general and the Supreme Court in particular were confronted with "massive resistance" to school desegregation, which the Court had initiated with its unanimous decision in Brown v. Board of Education in May 1954, nearly two years before.

On March 12, 1956, just a few short months before Brennan's recess appointment, nineteen senators and sixty-three members of Congress, all from the South, signed the so-called "Southern Manifesto." That document called the ruling in Brown an "unwarranted exercise of power by the Court" and declared, "We pledge ourselves to use all lawful means to bring about a reversal of this decision which is contrary to the Constitution and to prevent the use of force in its implementation."[22]

The Manifesto spawned the formation of groups "which in

many cases condoned and even encouraged rioting to resist desegre-gation of the public schools."[23]

Beyond the scope of school desegregation was the question of private discrimination. The ruling in *Brown* was momentous, with far-reaching implications. But its explicit application was limited to the public schools; the Court had not outlawed race discrimination across the broader spectrum of American society. In fact, given the opposition to *Brown*, the justices seemed reluctant to "look behind" state laws and municipal ordinances that were racially neutral on their face but discriminatory in practice.

Another explosive issue, fundamental to the federal system of government, was the extent to which the federal Bill of Rights should apply to the states. As Brennan years later explained, "In the decades between 1868, when the fourteenth amendment was adopted, and 1897, the Court decided in case after case that the amendment did not apply various specific restraints in the Bill of Rights to state action."[24]

He went on, "The break-through came in 1897 when the [Fifth Amendment] prohibition against taking property for public use without payment of just compensation was held embodied in the fourteenth amendment's proscription, 'nor shall any state deprive any person of...property, without due process of law.' But extension of the rest of the specific restraints was slow in coming. It was 1925 before it was suggested that perhaps the restraints of the first amendment applied to state action. Then in 1949 the fourth amendment's prohibition of unreasonable searches and seizures was extended...."[25]

By the 1956–1957 term, the kinds of questions that had begun to percolate up from the lower courts included whether the Bill of Rights entitled an indigent criminal defendant to be given a lawyer paid for by the state; whether there was a right to appeal a criminal conviction at the state's expense; and whether the Fourth and Fifth amendments prohibited the states from convicting criminal suspects using illegally seized evidence or forced confessions.

There were also issues related to the right to vote. The nation's state legislatures were clearly malapportioned with rural areas overrepresented to the disadvantage of suburbanites and city dwellers. Did the federal courts have the power to overrule the way states apportioned their legislatures?

The justices were split and contentious over most of these issues, except desegregation. On that question, they spoke as one, though they often disagreed as to the most effective method for bringing about the desired goal. On the other matters, however, they were divided even as to the proper role of the Court.

The intellectual leader of the "liberal" end of the Court's spectrum was Hugo Black, seventy, appointed by President Franklin Roosevelt in August 1937. Black was FDR's first appointment to the Court.[26] At the other end of the spectrum were the proponents of "judicial restraint" whose intellectual leader was Felix Frank-furter, seventy-three, erstwhile Harvard law professor and political gadfly, like Black a Roosevelt New Dealer, appointed by FDR in 1939.[27]

The Court that Brennan joined in October 1956 was evenly divided 4 to 4 between "liberals" and "conservatives." Chief Justice Warren, sixty-five, and Associate Justices William O. Douglas, fifty-eight, and Wiley B. Rutledge, sixty-two, were generally regarded as being in Black's liberal camp. Frankfurter, together with Harold H. Burton, sixty-eight; Tom C. Clark, fifty-seven;, and John M. Harlan, fifty-seven, represented the Court's conservative bloc.

The youngest of eight children, Hugo Lafayette Black was born in Ashland in rural Clay County, Alabama, in 1886. His mother, Martha, named him after the French writer Victor Hugo because when she went into labor with him she was reading *Les Miserables*, Hugo's sympathetic novel of the French Revolution.[28]

A self-described "backward country fellow,"[29] young Hugo managed through sheer determination and intelligence to rise above his humble circumstances and make his mark as a clever if un-scrupulous trial lawyer and wily, populist politician. He completed the two-year undergraduate law program at the University of Alabama and for a time served as a police court judge.[30] In the early 1920s, he ran for the U.S. Senate and was elected twice.[31] As a senator, he "applauded FDR's New Deal and voted for virtually every measure that the administration sponsored."[32]

Indeed, his zealous commitment to the New Deal "alarmed even the President with his attacks on privilege and his support for the thirty-hour workweek."[33] Black believed the shorter workweek was needed during the Depression to spread jobs around without reducing the income of individual workers.

His proposal for a reduced workweek failed, in part because it was not backed by the administration, which pushed through its own Fair Labor Standards Act with guaranteed minimum wages and maximum hours. Nonetheless, "FDR made it a point to assure him that his ideas had been instrumental in advancing the administration's own thinking and that the final legislation was a product in large part of the Alabama Senator's efforts."[34]

Black was also an enthusiastic supporter of FDR's Court-packing plan. Frustrated by Supreme Court rulings that struck down as unconstitutional a number of key laws that went to the heart of his New Deal social agenda, Roosevelt in 1937 proposed increasing the number of justices from nine to fifteen.

As Rodell described it, "Though obviously aimed at the intransigent Nine, or Five-out-of-Nine, the plan, on its literal terms, dealt with the entire federal judiciary. What the President asked was that, whenever a federal judge reached the age of seventy and failed to retire, another judge would be appointed to supplement, not to replace, the old fellow—with the total number of new judges who could be so named not to exceed fifty, and with the Supreme Court held to a top membership of fifteen justices."[35]

At the time, six of the nine sitting justices were beyond the age of seventy, including the so-called "Four Horsemen" who made up the Court's conservative core. Thus the Court-packing plan would have enabled FDR immediately to appoint six new justices.

The original Supreme Court was comprised of six justices, as provided under the Judiciary Act of 1789.[36] In 1801, Congress reduced the Court's membership to five.[37] A year later, it was restored to six.[38] A seventh justice was added in 1807, and the eighth and ninth were added in 1837.[39] Membership was enlarged to ten justices in 1863.[40]

At first, the number of justices was linked loosely to the number of federal judicial circuits, which increased as the nation expanded westward.[41] The addition of a tenth justice in 1863 was, however, intended to secure a majority for President Abraham Lincoln's Civil War policies.[42]

Subsequently, "antagonism toward President Andrew Johnson's Reconstruction program combined with dissatisfaction over the unwieldy number of members resulted in an 1866 statute reducing court size by attrition to seven."[43] After that, the Judiciary Act of

1869 fixed the number once again at nine,[44] where it stood at the time of FDR's Court-packing proposal and where it has remained since.

According to Rodell, "The beauty of the [FDR Court-packing] plan was its simplicity; the size of the Court had been varied several times before and the three post–Civil War shifts had been for strictly political purposes; nor was there any slightest doubt of the plan's constitutionality, since the Constitution left the size of the Court entirely up to Congress."[45]

Black endorsed the Court-packing proposal in a radio address to the nation, insisting, "Neither the people who wrote nor the people who approved the Constitution ever contemplated that the Supreme Court should become all powerful and omnipotent."[46] He went on, "The time has arrived when those who favor fitting laws to modern needs in order to correct and cure social and industrial injustice must face the problems squarely and fairly."[47]

He concluded, "Everybody knows that Supreme Court decisions by a bare majority have for years been thrown as impassable barriers in the way of the solemn and well-matured legislative plans supported by the people."[48]

Despite Black's efforts on the president's behalf, however, the Court-packing scheme was rejected. "Indeed the simplicity of the plan was part of its eventual undoing; it was so simple that it seemed to many diabolically clever—no amending of the Constitution, no curbing of the Court's power, merely (as FDR put it) the 'infusion of new blood' into the otherwise untouched federal judiciary."[49]

Where Black was able to effectively serve the president, however, was by undertaking congressional investigations of major corporate groups, such as private shipping operators, the commercial airlines, and the behemoth utility holding companies. Applying his skillful trial lawyer techniques, he was able to use investigative hearings as forums for exposing corrupt practices and price fixing by big business interests.

But his tactics, including his relentless questioning of witnesses and his self-righteousness, aroused suspicion. After seeing him in action, one member of the Washington press corps wrote, "My impression of the man is that he is essentially cheap. He is smart as the devil. He has one of the shrewdest minds in the Senate. But I wouldn't trust him farther than I could throw a cow by the tail. His orbit is that of a small town lawyer, more aptly, a small town prosecutor."[50]

His nomination to the high court was almost sabotaged when it was revealed that he had been a member of the Ku Klux Klan from 1923 to 1926.[51] Although he had resigned from the organization on the eve of his first Senate campaign, he had won his Senate seat with Klan support.[52]

Poor, resentful, and suspicious of the outside world, the kind of dirt-poor Clay County residents who joined the Klan were inspired by Black's fiery, populist rhetoric. On March 20, 1926, he addressed a campaign rally near Ashland, asking rhetorically, "Shall we return to the old shackles, cut from our people by sacrifice and blood, and say that the great common people of America can only be represented by the sons of distinguished fathers?"[53]

He made clear that Hugo Black, of humble origins, the son of a rural storekeeper, was a spokesman for the common man. He was one of them, and proud of it. He knew how to speak their language.

Much of that language was the nomenclature of racism, which he exploited by appealing to their white supremacist, "America first" sentiments. He declared, "The melting pot idea is dangerous to our national inheritance. I oppose further immigration, and believe our nation would be greatly benefited by closing the gates until we can educate and Americanize those already here."[54]

Three thousand hooded Klansmen celebrated his victory in the state's Democratic primary in 1926 with a rally in downtown Birmingham.[55] Black was presented with a Klan passport, which he accepted with flowery praise for the Klan's commitment to "American manhood and womanhood"[56] and for "revering virtue of the mother race [and] loving the pride of Anglo-Saxon spirit."[57]

He pledged the Klansmen "my faith from the bottom of a heart that is yours."[58]

Despite the controversy that his Klan connection ignited, "Black rode out the storm with the help of a radio talk, in which he accurately assured the country that there was no iota of intolerance in his record or in his bones, and his new brethren greeted him to the Court in the fall" of 1937.

Years later he explained that as a struggling young trial lawyer, joining the "Invisible Empire" was an act of professional and political expediency. His Robert E. Lee Klan chapter "counted among its members many of Birmingham's lawyers as well as hundreds of miners and other laborers who comprised Black's clientele and juries."[59]

After joining the Court, Black formulated the theory of "total incorporation" that was the linchpin of his jurisprudence. Based on his reading of the Fourteenth Amendment's history, he had come to the conclusion that the entire Bill of Rights, the full gamut of protections embodied in the Constitution's first eight amendments, was meant to apply to the states. Belying his southern roots, Black believed firmly that the North's victory in the Civil War subordinated states' rights to the individual rights guaranteed by the Constitution. In 1947, he put forward his theory and the historical bases for it in an eloquent dissent in *Adamson v. California*.[60]

The facts of *Adamson* were straightforward enough. As James F. Simon, former dean and professor of law at New York Law School, has recounted sardonically, "The most impressive official fact about Admiral Dewey Adamson was his name. Otherwise he did not seem very different from other poor, ignorant blacks whose records revealed too many run-ins with the law."[61]

Adamson had served two prison terms: one for burglary in 1920, the other for robbery seven years later.[62] He had been out of jail for 17 years when he was arrested and charged with the murder of a sixty-four-year-old white Los Angeles woman, Stella Blauvelt.[63] According to police, Adamson's fingerprints were found at the scene of the crime.[64]

At his trial, Adamson's lawyer was concerned that if his client testified in his own defense, the prosecutor would impeach his testimony with questions about his past.[65] He was convinced that if the jury found out Adamson was an ex-convict, a guilty verdict in the Blauvelt murder was all but certain.[66]

The Fifth Amendment to the U.S. Constitution provides that no person "shall be compelled in any criminal case to be a witness against himself." But when Adamson refused to take the stand, the state "suggested to the jury that this was definitive proof of his guilt."[67] Under California law, guilt could be inferred from a defendant's failure or refusal to testify in his own behalf. The prosecutor asserted in his summation that if Adamson had been innocent, it would have taken "twenty or fifty horses" to keep him off the witness stand.[68] Adamson was found guilty.

Adamson's Supreme Court appeal challenged the California law as a violation of his Fifth Amendment rights, which he claimed applied to the states through the Fourteenth Amendment's due process clause. The argument, in essence, was that "[c]omment on a defendant's failure to testify was as bad as forcing a defendant to take the stand" and as such undermined due process.[69]

The Court had addressed the issue squarely at least once before. In the case of *Twining v. New Jersey*[70] in 1908, the Court had ruled that "the exemption from compulsory self-incrimination is not a privilege or immunity of National citizenship guaranteed by this [due process] clause of the Fourteenth Amendment against abridg- ment by the States."[71] In other words, the guarantee against self- incrimination applied only to the federal government. Brennan had followed the *Twining* precedent as a New Jersey trial judge, recognizing in *In re Pillo*[72] that the Fifth Amendment privilege did not apply to the states.

In *Adamson*, the justices reaffirmed their earlier ruling in *Twining*. In so doing they relied in large part on another previous case, *Palko v. Connecticut*,[73] decided in 1937, in which Black had joined the majority as a freshman justice. Writing for the majority in *Palko*, Justice Benjamin Cardozo had put forward his own theory regarding the extent to which the federal Bill of Rights applied to the states. According to Cardozo, the states were bound only by those parts of the U.S. Bill of Rights that were "fundamental principles of liberty and justice which lie at the base of all our social and political institutions,"[74] such as the First Amendment's guaran- tee of free speech.

The problem, as Felix Frankfurter conceded in his own, sepa- rate concurrence in *Adamson*, was that under Cardozo's *Palko* doctrine, some rights "are in and some are out, but we are left in the dark as to which are in and which are out. Nor are we given the calculus for determining which go in and which stay out."[75]

He went on, "If the basis for selection is merely that those provisions of the first eight Amendments are incorporated which commend themselves to individual justices as indispensable to the dignity and happiness of a free man, we are thrown back to a merely subjective test."[76]

In his *Adamson* dissent, Black stated, "If the choice must be between the selective process of the *Palko* decision applying some of the Bill of Rights to the States, or...applying none of them, I would choose the *Palko* selective process. But rather than accept either of these choices, I would follow what I believe was the original purpose of the Fourteenth Amendment—to extend to all the people of the nation the complete protection of the Bill of Rights."[77]

He concluded, "To hold that this Court can determine what, if any, provisions of the Bill of Rights will be enforced, and if so to what degree, is to frustrate the great design of a written Constitution."[78]

In addition to his overall view of the Bill of Rights, Black had come to believe in the primacy of the First Amendment. Without freedom of speech and of the press, he believed, the other rights granted under the Constitution would be meaningless. For him, free speech was the fountain from which the other rights flowed. He therefore promoted an "absolutist," or "literalist," interpretation of the First Amendment.

The First Amendment provides, "Congress shall make *no law* respecting an establishment of religion, or prohibiting the free exercise thereof; or abridging the freedom of speech, or of the press; or the right of the people peaceably to assemble, and to petition the Government for a redress of grievances." (Emphasis added.) For Black, "no law" meant *no* law. Therefore, he "opposed controls over obscenity, libel, and 'subversive' speech as well as the clear and present danger test, balancing and other nonabsolutist measures of governmental authority."[79]

He once wrote, "Neither as offered nor as adopted is the language of this Amendment anything less than absolute."[80] He went on, "To my way of thinking, at least, the history and the language of the Constitution and the Bill of Rights...make it plain that one of the primary purposes of the Constitution with its amendments was to withdraw from the Government all power to act in certain areas—whatever the scope of those areas may be. If I am right in this then there is, at least in those areas, no justification whatever for 'balancing' a particular right against some expressly granted power of Congress. If the Constitution withdraws from Government all power over subject matter in an area, such as religion, speech, assembly, and petition, there is nothing over which authority may be exerted."[81]

Meanwhile, his civil rights record put to rest concerns about his past. Hugo Black became one of the staunchest defenders of the rights of African Americans ever to sit on the high court. He never forgot his southern roots. He simply saw racial progress as the only way for the South to become part of the vast American mainstream, instead of an isolated, conquered region with peculiar and indefensible institutions and interests.

As both a man and a constitutional theorist, Felix Frankfurter was very different from Hugo Black. A Jew who was born in Vienna, Austria, in 1882, Frankfurter emigrated to the United States with his parents at the age of twelve.[82] He rose above his circumstances, like Black, through hard work and sheer intelligence. He spoke both Hebrew and Yiddish before he could speak English.[83] His academic performance at City College of New York gained him admission to Harvard Law School, from which he was graduated first in his class.[84]

He taught law off and on at Harvard from 1913 until 1939, when he was appointed to the Court, revering that academic institution as "the most egalitarian place on earth—an aristocracy of talent and intellect."[85] In addition to teaching, he served as a labor troubleshooter for President Woodrow Wilson from 1916 to 1918, and in various capacities for, among others, such mentors as justices Oliver Wendell Holmes and Louis Brandeis throughout the 1920s and 1930s.[86]

Frankfurter rejected Black's total incorporation theory as well as Black's view as to the role of the Court. He was, on the one hand, a civil libertarian who had devoted much of his life to defending the powerless and persecuted against the excesses of the state. Early in his career, for example, he had been a legal adviser to the American Civil Liberties Union (ACLU).[87] He had also served on the legal committee of the National Association for the Advancement of Colored People (NAACP), helping to develop the litigation strategies that ultimately evolved into *Brown v. Board of Education*.[88]

Moreover, he had worked tirelessly to save the lives of Nicola Sacco and Bartolomeo Vanzetti, sentenced to die for robbery and murder in South Braintree, Massachusetts, in 1920. At the time, the nation was in the throes of its first Red Scare, and Sacco and Venzetti, "both Italian immigrants with well-documented records of draft resistance and anarchist politics, served as ripe targets for those in and out of government who wanted to cleanse the country of subversive influence."[89]

Like Black he was a passionate New Dealer and, while teaching at Harvard, had been active as a behind-the-scenes adviser to FDR, assisting in the formulation of the New Deal's economic and social agenda. For example, in 1933 Frankfurter "engineered John Maynard Keynes' open letter to Franklin D. Roosevelt in the *New York Times*, urging the President to forsake balancing the budget and adopt deficit spending to spark the economy."[90] In addition, "Frankfurter used the Harvard Law Review to lend credibility to New Deal legislation instigated by his mentor," Justice Louis Brandeis.[91]

Indeed, Frankfurter's involvement in liberal and unpopular causes, together with his foreign origins, explained in part why he became "the first nominee in the 150-year history of the Supreme Court to be subjected to a full inquiry by a Senate committee."[92]

Prior to Frankfurter's nomination, presidents had been accorded such deference in the selection of justices that only one nominee, Harlan Fiske Stone in 1925, had appeared before the Judiciary Committee in person. In some quarters, Frankfurter was regarded as a dangerous radical. At his confirmation hearings in 1939, for example, Senator Patrick McCarran accused him of being "a friend of known communists."[93]

Even after he joined the Court, he remained active politically. "He spoke to the President [FDR] often and sent scores of notes and letters to him covering a wide range of major domestic and foreign policy issues. Beyond mere advice, Frankfurter drafted new legislation, delivered advisory opinions on the legality of existing laws, wrote first drafts of campaign speeches for the President and made specific recommendations for Cabinet-level positions, then lobbied for his choices."[94]

Nevertheless, disappointed admirers of his civil liberties record claimed that he changed after he reached the high court. Outwardly, he had. Unlike Black, who believed that the Court's primary role was "to protect the individual liberties guaranteed in the Bill of Rights,"[95] Justice Frankfurter insisted that the Court "must not squander its always limited and precious reserve of political influence by entering into political questions."[96]

In his personal diary he reflected on what he regarded as the inherent evil of using the Court as a base from which to pursue political goals. "When a priest enters a monastery," he wrote, "he must leave...all sorts of worldly desires behind him. And this court has no excuse for being unless it's a monastery."[97]

For him in his role as a justice, this meant according broad deference to legislators and other elected officials in the formulation and conduct of policy. As one biographer put it, "Frankfurter continued to express concern for civil liberties, but in the final analysis he relied on the legislative branch for guidance."[98]

He was, in other words, a man of irreconcilable contradictions. He advocated judicial restraint, but he adhered to the selective incorporation doctrine that gave judges wide latitude in interpreting the Bill of Rights.[99] He abjured political activism by the Court yet remained an influential behind-the-scenes player even after his own appointment. He was sensitive to the plight of minorities and those who held unpopular or disfavored views. Yet he rejected Black's absolutist view of the First Amendment. Instead he was a "balancer," willing to subordinate free speech to the government's desire under certain circumstances to suppress it.

At the age of fifty, Brennan became the Court's youngest member. He was, in addition, the first Catholic justice since Frank Murphy's death in 1949; the first former state supreme court justice since Benjamin Cardozo (1932–38); and the first New Jersey native since Mahlon Pitney (1912–22).

Characteristically, he threw himself into his work. As always his self-discipline was monumental, his hours of work incalculable. The result was a Catch-22 situation. The harder he worked, the more his home life suffered, but time with his family compromised his work. From the time she was a girl, his daughter, Nancy, saw her father's life as "a knitting of compromised work and compromised family."[100]

She told Donna Haupt in 1989, "Dad would come in every night with a full briefcase and spend the time before dinner talking with my mother and listening to the news. We almost invariably ate between 6 and 6:30 and then one of two things happened. Either he'd go up to the den and sit at his old desk that was falling apart. Or, more commonly he set up a green card table in the middle of the living room and spread all these piles of papers within arm's reach on the rug. He'd work until he was just too tired, until 9:30 or 10."[101]

On Saturday and Sunday mornings, she recalled, he would usually "be at the card table by 8:30 or 9, working through most of the day."

Brennan admitted to having no hobbies or diversions, telling *Life* in October 1956, "I won't be so corny as to say my work is my hobby. My work is my work, and I love every minute of it."[102]

Daughter Nancy agreed. Reflecting on her father's life and career, she told Haupt, "I think his energy is simply explained by the love of what he does. Even when things are not going to be easy during the day, he gets up with a true enthusiasm for what he is spending his life doing. If you ask why he's so positive he'd probably tell you that the world is going to hell in a handbasket. But that totally belies the attitude he takes toward everything—to other human beings, to what he does, to his interactions with strangers."[103]

She went on, "He really *is* a very positive person and that's infectious. I think it energizes other people around him and it's one of his greatest assets."[104]

The way he handled the traffic accident he was involved in shortly after he joined the Court exemplified his good nature.

During the nineteenth century, members of Congress, senators, and justices who loved living in Georgetown invariably lamented the time-consuming three-mile horse ride to and from the Capitol. Modern automobiles meant, however, that Bill Brennan was only a fifteen-minute drive from his office at the Court.

Unlike Attorney General Brownell, who had greeted him at Union Station for his interview with the president in a chauffeured limousine, and other cabinet officers, justices were not provided with drivers and government cars. So Brennan who, like his father, was not particularly adept behind the wheel, drove himself to and from work each day like any other working person.

One rainy morning in March 1957, he stopped for a traffic light that seemed to go too quickly from green to red. The city bus that was following him skidded, could not stop in time, and smashed into the back of his new, medium-priced car. Brennan and the driver got out to inspect the damage, which was "grievous but purely cosmetic."[105] Then Brennan invited the driver, who was an African American, into his car and out of the rain to exchange names, phone numbers, and addresses.

The driver was apologetic and naturally concerned about how his superiors would react to the mishap. Brennan assured him, "Don't worry about this thing. It happens every time there's a rain, and it's nobody's fault at all."[106]

The driver got back on his bus, extolling the nice guy he had just met. He had no idea that Brennan was a Supreme Court justice. Nor did any of his passengers, except one: Edward F. Woods, Supreme Court correspondent for the *St. Louis Post-Dispatch*. Woods wrote a story about the accident that was picked up by the wire services and appeared in newspapers across the country.

Despite his rigorous work schedule, Bill and Marjorie managed to have an enjoyable social life once ensconced in their new home. They ended up renting a semidetached house on Dumbarton Avenue. Georgetown was too rich for their blood; they could not afford to buy a place on the justice's $35,000 annual salary. Also, they had no down payment from Conover Lane in Rumson; instead of selling that property they had decided to let their son Hugh live in it.

The *Saturday Evening Post* profiled the Brennans as being "popular socially in a non-society-page way."[107] They joined the Chevy Chase Country Club and golfed occasionally. Also, a friendship with Earl Warren blossomed, nurtured by a mutual love of baseball. Brennan joined the chief justice for Washington Senators games at Griffith Park. The perennial cellar dwellers lived up to the adage "Washington, first in war, first in peace, and last in the American League."

Some Friday nights, the justice and his wife hosted dinner parties—informal buffets—for friends and neighbors that were sparkling, congenial affairs. On such occasions, one might see justices "Johnny" Harlan and "Wild Bill" Douglas huddled in a discussion of social policy over cocktails. Warren, Douglas, Harlan, and their wives became the Brennans' very good friends.

Like Frankfurter, Douglas had been a Georgetown resident for some time. In fact, he had become a prominent community activist. A lover of the outdoors, he had organized a "crusade" to save the C & O (Chesapeake & Ohio) Canal, which runs through Georgetown from Washington to Cumberland, Maryland, after plans were announced to convert the abandoned aqueduct into a freeway. The threatened area was treasured by hikers, bicyclists, bird watchers, and naturalists. Douglas described it as "a refuge, a place of retreat, a long stretch of quiet and peace at the Capitol's back door."[108]

In 1954, he had led conservationists, fellow "crusaders," in a much-publicized protest hike through the area. His efforts were successful in persuading Congress to designate the C & O a national park that is now dedicated to Douglas's memory.

Brennan always invited his law clerks to the dinner parties. Daniel O'Hern, who clerked for Brennan during the 1956–57 term and went on to become a New Jersey state supreme court judge, remembers stopping by Dixie Liquors on Georgetown's M Street to pick up "provisions" for those relaxed but at the same time stimulating evenings.

Meanwhile, Brennan's relationship with Frankfurter, almost a quarter-century his senior, remained cordial. Upon Brennan's appointment, Frankfurter wrote to a friend, "It makes me feel like an old man to think of having a former student on the Court and, of course, it gives me great pleasure to find myself on the Court with a former student."[109] Yet if Frankfurter expected Brennan to remain under his beneficent tutelage, he was sorely mistaken.

There was, however, no reason to believe that philosophy alone stood between Brennan and Frankfurter personally. Harlan abjured judicial activism every bit as much as Frankfurter did, but whatever philosophical differences he may have had with Brennan at the time did not keep the two men from evolving into close friends.

Instead what Brennan found difficult to take was Frankfurter's style. Discussions with him were more like lectures from his former professor than a collegial exchange of ideas. It was nothing personal—Frankfurter was like that with everybody. He "always treated his colleagues on the Court as if they were his students."[110]

But what particularly irked Brennan was Frankfurter's disingenuousness. He recalled, "I looked to Felix to help a novice get his feet wet. And Felix went out of his way, but he did that for everybody. After a while, I realized it was not just out of kindness."[111]

What Frankfurter was looking for was an ally in his ideological struggle with Black for the Court's soul. But by patronizing Brennan, he antagonized him, much as he had alienated Warren after the chief justice joined the Court in 1953.[112]

"After I came on the Court, I was treated as one of Felix's

students—and not a favorite one either," Brennan recalled.[113] "When Felix didn't get his way, he was like a child."[114]

He could be even more condescending behind Brennan's back than he was to his face. After losing Brennan's vote in a case he regarded as crucial, he wrote to Harlan expressing disappointment in his former student.

"I wish he [Brennan] was less shallow and thereby less cock-sure," he stated, allowing, "but his honesty cheers me much and gives me considerable hope. To me it is a constant puzzle why men like him can't read or rather reflect on what they read."[115]

On another occasion he quipped, "I always encouraged my students to think for themselves, but Brennan goes too far!"[116]

Meanwhile, Brennan developed an admiration for Black, who was plainspoken and straightforward, and who cut right through to the heart of matters with his incisive mind and piercing blue eyes. Black and his second wife, Elizabeth, had the Brennans out to their country club in Virginia on occasion. And the couples shared other relaxed times.

Like Frankfurter, Black was not the most appealing personality. His blunt manner was very much borne of his absolutism. Insofar as the Constitution was concerned, he was convinced that he was right. He was stubborn, inflexible, reluctant to compromise, wrapped up in himself, though not in a selfish way.

Nevertheless, Brennan found him compelling. He recalled that in conference, "Hugo would sneer 'How can you think *that*?' But he was usually brief, except in 5-4 votes when he could make quite a stump speech. More often than not, the speech was brief and to the point."[117]

He went on, "Felix, on the other hand, argued at a high decibel level, running around in conference grabbing books off the shelves. He would go to Volume 360 [of the Court's opinions in *U.S. Reports*] and quote page and paragraph ad nauseam. When he felt strongly about something, he could be a pain in the neck."[118]

Ultimately, Brennan would settle into neither Black's nor Frankfurter's "camp." He would instead cultivate his own result-oriented jurisprudence based on consensus. In the meantime, he would first have to finalize his appointment to the Court by winning formal Senate confirmation.

CHAPTER 11

Justice Brennan Versus Senator McCarthy

The appearance of a Justice of the U.S. Supreme Court before a committee dominated by Joe McCarthy was unfortunate, and a concession to what Bruce Catton, in *This Hallowed Ground*, calls the "rowdy strain in American life."

> —J. L. Bernstein in *The Reporter*,
> a publication of the Passaic County,
> New Jersey, bar association

B Y THE TIME CONGRESS RETURNED to session in Washington in January 1957, William Brennan had not been on the Supreme Court long enough to make enemies. Because he was regarded in some circles as a middle-of-the-roader or even a conservative, there had been some speculation as to whether liberal Adlai Stevenson would have submitted his name to the Senate for confirmation if he had managed to defeat Eisenhower in the November 1956 presidential election. Ike's recess appointment of Brennan would not have bound Stevenson to do so. But as it turned out, his nomination was never in jeopardy. The year 1956 belonged to Ike by a landslide.

There were, however, those who were skeptical as to who Brennan was and suspicious of his motives. Senator Olin D. Johnston of South Carolina was one. A segregationist jittery over where the Court was headed in the aftermath of *Brown*, he called upon the Senate to "take a close look" at Brennan's beliefs and background.[1]

Senator Joseph McCarthy was another. Angered by Brennan's St. Patrick's Day speech in 1954 and by his remarks to the Monmouth Rotary Club the following year that reveled in McCarthy's Senate censure, he lay in wait, determined to turn the Senate Judiciary Committee's hearings on the nomination into an inquisition.

Actually, McCarthy was not even a member of the Judiciary Committee. But he requested and was granted special permission to participate in the hearings.

"He knew about me," Brennan recalled in his interview with Nat Hentoff in 1990.[2] "Hell, when I made those speeches I had no idea I would ever get to sit on the Supreme Court.

"And," he added, "those weren't the only times I paid my respects to Senator McCarthy. I made speeches calling him all sorts of names before other groups around Monmouth County. So when Eisenhower announced he was going to appoint me, McCarthy issued a statement saying that I was supremely unfit for the Supreme Court. And, though he wasn't on the Judiciary Committee, he asked to sit with that committee, so that he could interrogate me.

"At first, there was resistance to McCarthy's sitting in on the committee," Brennan explained.[3] "He was in decline. He had already been censured, and he died not long after my hearings."[4]

Nevertheless, looking back he reflected, "I thought those who were against his sitting with the committee were wrong. There's absolutely nothing in the Constitution which limits the advice-and-consent function of the Senate. Nothing. And, because each senator has to cast his own vote on the matter, he should be able to interrogate the nominee if he wants to. And any senator, furthermore, is entitled to ask any damn question he wants—about ideology or whatever the hell it may be."[5]

According to Brennan, McCarthy inquired into "Oh, just the craziest things."[6] In recollecting the kinds of questions McCarthy asked, he imitated what Hentoff described as the Wisconsin senator's "heavy cadences" and "ominous pauses."[7] For example, " 'Do you mean to tell me you don't think the most *important* thing we can possibly do is rout out Communists, wherever they are?'"[8]

Brennan concluded, "I gather that those who heard the ex-changes between us all that day did not think it was one of Senator McCarthy's finest hours."[9]

It was not one of Justice Brennan's finest hours, either. In fact, when confronted by McCarthy during the hearings on February 26, 1957, he soft-pedaled his New Jersey rhetoric.

In his St. Patrick's Day speech, for example, he had likened the proceedings of the Committee on Un-American Activities and other aspects of the Red Scare to the Salem witch hunts of the seventeenth century. Such statements prompted McCarthy to demand of him, "Do you approve of congressional investigations and exposure of the Communist conspiracy set up?"[10]

Brennan's response was ingratiating. "Not only do I approve, Senator," he declared, "but personally I cannot think of a more vital function of the Congress than the investigatory function of its committees, and I can't think of a more important or vital objective of any committee investigation than that of rooting out subversives in Government."[11]

At other times, he double-talked like a nervous schoolboy. McCarthy demanded, "Have you ever approved an investigation of the Communist exposure? If you will think back, and you have made speeches saying you are against communism—have made some fine high-sounding speeches along that line—while you have been making those speeches against communism generally, can you tell us where you have approved a single investigation of the same Commu-nists you were talking about?"[12]

Brennan replied, "Senator, I don't know quite what you mean where I have approved. I say and I say again that I think that we cannot do enough to make certain that this fight is won. We can't do enough to see that anything like it within or out of Government is exposed."[13]

He muddled on, "What I was talking to was a premonition I felt that unless it were approached differently than it was being approached, we would lose our eyes—would get our eyes off the target and on other things which would dissipate our energies to do it. That's what I was talking about."[14]

McCarthy would not let him off the hook so easily. He proceeded sarcastically, "We will get back to that different approach that you have in mind in a minute, if the Chair will bear with me. In the meantime, I may say, I have a rather long memory, I think at least 3 minutes, I recall the question I asked you.

"The question is, Have you ever approved an investigation of the Communist exposure? If you will just think back in any of these speeches, have you ever approved by one little word the exposure of Communists, either by the Internal Security Committee, the House committee, by the Investigating committee, any other committee?"[15]

Forced into the awkward position of having to defend some-thing he had not said, Brennan responded obliquely and tentatively. "I had no occasion in either of these speeches. I don't recall I have had any other occasions when I affirmatively in public, Senator, got up to say what I just said now. I can only say that if I ever had I would have said precisely what I said now: That I was very much for it, very, very much for it. I just want to be certain that we don't, as I put it before, dissipate our energies by not doing it as effectively as we could."[16]

A short time later, when asked to defend a specific charge he had leveled in his Monmouth Rotary Club address, he backed down completely. In that speech he had eloquently defended those who invoked the Fifth Amendment's privilege against self-incrimination in response to intrusive congressional investigations.

Brennan had stated, "Frankness with ourselves must compel the acknowledgment that our resentment toward those who invoked its [the Fifth Amendment's] protection led us into a toleration of some of the very abuses which brought the privilege into being so many centuries ago. The abuses took on modern dress it is true—not the rack and the screw, but the distorted version of the happenings at secret hearings released to the press, the shouted epithet at the hapless and helpless witness."[17]

Now McCarthy moved in for the kill. "You talked about the epithets hurled at hapless and helpless witnesses," he said. "Could you give us one example of such epithets?"[18]

Brennan was disarmed. "No," he replied, "these, Senator, were honestly illustrations, a little artist's license, if you please, of what it was I was getting at."[19]

He babbled on, "I can't tell you exactly now what it was I had in mind, but I know that there was certainly an impression abroad—and, believe me, I think actually the appearance for this purpose is as bad or almost as bad as the actuality—that witnesses in some of these instances were not treated as I am presently being treated, for example."[20]

McCarthy turned the knife with great, rhetorical flair and relish. "While you were talking about the epithets that are being hurled at hapless and helpless victims, when you were talking about Communist investigations, you did not have in mind any single incident; is that right?"[21]

Brennan struggled with all his worst fears. Even if he managed to hold his seat on the Court, he might come out of this so damaged as to undermine his credibility, or as a laughingstock. Clearly he had lost control of the situation. Now the lights felt hot. He took out his handkerchief and dabbed beaded perspiration from his forehead. His mouth was dry; he drank some water. He knew he was squirming.

His response was jumbled. "If you get back to those days," he began, "you will recall—it is hard completely to recapture them— that there was a great deal written and said on this subject. I don't suppose there was a community in the country where this whole business was not very widely discussed."[22]

He stammered on, "I know I had the impression and I think many others did that there were witnesses at whom epithets were shouted, that there were distorted versions of the happenings at secret hearings released to the press. We certainly had the impres- sion, and I can't tell you from any actual knowledge but, as I said before, I think the appearance of that kind of thing in our concept of it in America is as bad in its ultimate result as is the actuality."[23]

Republican Senator William E. Jenner of Indiana, a McCarthy ally, broke in, "May I interrupt?"[24] He asked Brennan, "Did you ever hear any of the epithets that were hurled at the committee members?"[25]

"No, sir," Brennan replied.[26]

"Some of those were pretty bad, too."

Jenner's comment drew a smattering of laughter from the audience gathered in Room 424 of the Senate Office Building.[27] But the levity was lost on McCarthy, who was determined now to settle for nothing less than abject surrender.

He insisted, "People were entitled to think when you made a statement that you were basing it on fact. Do I understand now that when you talked about epithets being hurled at hapless and helpless victims you had no incident in mind, that you were merely speaking from what you thought might have been an impression created?"[28]

Brennan all but gave in. "No," he admitted, "I probably did, but I don't now remember. Certainly that was a general impression."[29]

From then on, McCarthy grandstanded in the style he had made famous, hectoring Brennan, vilifying him, impugning his patriotism.

He asked the hapless witness whether he read the *Daily Worker*, the official newspaper of the American Communist Party. When Brennan replied, "No, I have never read a copy of it," McCarthy pounced on him.[30]

"I do," the senator proclaimed.[31] "I read it. I have been reading in every left-wing paper, the same type of gobbledygook that I find in your speeches talking about the barbarism of committees, the same Salem witch hunts. I just wonder if a Supreme Court Justice can hide behind his robes and conduct a guerrilla warfare against investigating committees and you talked about barbaric procedures."[32]

Moments later, committee chairman James O. Eastland mercifully recessed the proceedings until the following morning.[33]

The next day, Wednesday, February 27, 1957, William Brennan was reprieved. McCarthy, an alcoholic who would be dead in two months' time from liver disease, failed to show up for the hearing. Instead he submitted a letter that Chairman Eastland read into the record, attacking Brennan for being soft on communism.

It read, "I am convinced after yesterday's session that there is no further doubt about the accuracy of my initial conclusions. I believe that the written record of the committee now confirms [that] Justice Brennan harbors an underlying hostility to congressional attempts to investigate and expose the Communist conspiracy and I am doubtful that further questioning on the subject would serve any useful purpose."[34]

With McCarthy out of the picture, the worst was over. But William Brennan's ordeal was not quite ended. He was called upon to explain and defend his Catholicism.

There was no reason to suspect that Brennan's religious convictions would unduly influence his decision making on the Court. Those who knew him realized that although he was a decent person and God-fearing, he was not a zealously religious man. He was a catholic with a small "c." He and Marjorie had belonged to the Church of the Nativity in Fair Haven, New Jersey. When they moved to Washington, he attended Mass at Holy Trinity Church in Georgetown, and on Holy Days of obligation he usually went to St. Peter's Church on Capitol Hill, not far from the Supreme Court.

Democratic Senator Joseph C. O'Mahoney of Wyoming, him-self an Irish Catholic, nonetheless felt compelled to question Brennan about his religious beliefs. There was still enough distrust of Catholics in high office to warrant a full discussion of the issue for the record.

O'Mahoney proposed putting to Brennan a question that had been suggested by Charles Smith, a representative of the National Liberal League and editor of a publication called *The Truth Seeker*, ostensibly dedicated to the cause of separation of church and state. The question read:

"You are bound by your religion to follow the pronouncements of the Pope on all matters of faith and morals. There may be some controversies which involve matters of faith and morals and also matters of law and justice. But in matters of law and justice, you are bound by your oath to follow not papal decrees or doctrines, but the laws and precedents of this Nation. If you should be faced with such a mixed issue, would you be able to follow the requirements of your oath or would you be bound by your religious obligations?"[35]

Democratic Senator Estes Kefauver of Tennessee objected to the question. "Let me say that the very basis of our country is that one's religion and politics and thoughts are supposed to have freedom in connection with them. I would hate for this precedent to start a wave of religious considerations pro and con in connection with issues or with nominees to various positions."[36]

He went on, "I hope that—of course, I recognize the prerogative of the Senator asking the question he wants, but I just hope that the public won't feel that this is the kind of issue that we think has any relevance here."[37]

What followed was a parliamentary shell game. The members of the committee all agreed that the question was inappropriate and irrelevant but that O'Mahoney had a right to ask it. And so the inquiry was in fact put to Brennan, who stated clearly that his secular obligation was single and paramount.

He replied, "[M]y answer to the question is categorically that in everything I have ever done, in every office I have held in my life or that I shall ever do in the future, what shall control me is the oath that I took to support the Constitution of the United States and so act upon the cases that come before me for decision that it is that oath and that alone which governs."[38]

Brennan's declaration was apocalyptic, for as a Supreme Court justice he would be instrumental in defining the proper relationship between church and state.

Outside Congress, reactions to Brennan's committee perform-ance were predictably mixed. According to Brennan, some Cathol-ics were angered by his subordination of his religious views to the dictates of the Constitution. "The Catholic publication in Brooklyn demanded that I be strung from the nearest flagpole," he told Sean O Murchu in 1990.[39]

"Well," he went on, "at the time the Archbishop of Washington was Archbishop O'Boyle—he wasn't yet a cardinal—and he had a young assistant, who's now the Archbishop of New Orleans [Archbishop Phillip Hannan], come over to see me. He said, 'Now look, the *Register,* our local Catholic paper, will take care of that,' and they backed me up solidly."

As for his exchanges with McCarthy, Brennan, in an April 17, 1957, conversation with Daniel M. Berman, who was an acting professor of political science at the State University of New York at Fredonia, insisted that he patronized the Wisconsin senator throughout the hearing. As Berman put it, "Brennan was influ-enced by the fact that, having received a recess appointment, he was a sitting Justice and had no desire to embarrass the Court by 'going to the mat'" with McCarthy.[40] He refused, in Berman's words, to "dignify McCarthy by engaging in combat with him."[41]

There was, however, at least one critic who was contemptuous of the way Brennan handled himself. According to Brennan biogra-pher Kim Isaac Eisler, "Liberal columnist Murray Kempton de-scribed Brennan as 'too soggy for sympathy!' Instead of rising to the challenge like a man, Kempton wrote, 'Brennan assumed a bearing that my own inflamed sensibilities could only take for abjection.'"[42]

Back home in New Jersey, Brennan was defended by J. L. Bernstein in the March 1957 edition of *The Reporter.* "The appearance of a Justice of the U.S. Supreme Court before a committee dominated by Joe McCarthy was unfortunate," Bernstein lamented, "and a concession to what Bruce Catton, in *This Hallowed Ground*, calls the 'rowdy strain in American life.'"[43]

Bernstein went on to assail the U.S. Senate for being "perhaps the weakest link in the American system of government."[44] He wrote, "One recalls its long tolerance of McCarthyism, its curious introverted scheme of values in disciplining members, its perennial role as the grave digger of civil rights, its mediocre membership, its weak leadership, its antiquated and undemocratic procedures, its irresponsible investigations of 'subversive' activities, its impervious resistance to proposed improvements in its internal processes, and its prolonged operation as an agency of minority rule and as a battleground for the politics of sectional interest."[45]

Eisenhower's former attorney general Herbert Brownell has insisted that despite McCarthy's theatrics, Brennan's nomination was never in peril. Dismissing McCarthy's negligible influence, he stated simply in his memoirs that "there was no controversy at [Brennan's] confirmation hearings."[46]

In fact, Brennan was confirmed by the full Senate on March 19, 1957, along with Charles Evans Whittaker, an eighth circuit federal appeals court judge who had been nominated by Ike two weeks earlier to replace retiring Associate Justice Stanley F. Reed. Whittaker, a Missouri native, was approved unanimously.

Not quite so with Brennan. When the vote on him was called, the Senate chamber reverberated with Joe McCarthy's lone, angry "No!"

CHAPTER 12

"An Incredibly
Buoyant Person"

The relationship between Earl Warren and William Brennan was one of the most extraordinary relationships between two colleagues that I have ever known; surely, it must be one of the most famous in the law.

—Owen Fiss, Yale law professor
and former Brennan law clerk

AT THE END OF *Man's Fate*, André Malraux's epic novel of the Chinese revolution, Old Gisors, an elderly Marxist professor of sociology at the University of Peking, is disconsolate over the death of his son Kyo, killed in the struggle against anticommunist forces loyal to Chiang Kai-shek. Gisors tells Kyo's widow, his grieving Russian daughter-in-law May, "You know the phrase: 'It takes nine months to make a man, and a single day to kill him.' We both know this as well as one can know it.... May, listen, it does not take nine months, it takes fifty years to make a man, fifty years of sacrifice, of will...of so many things!"[1]

At the age of fifty, Bill Brennan was finally made of all those many things: his Irish immigrant father's struggle up from the bowels of the Ballantine brewery; his mother's selfless devotion to husband and family; Harvard Law School; his brother's death at

113

Leyte Bay; his own trials and tribulations making a living for himself and his family in a difficult world. He was, in other words, tempered by knowledge and experience.

How ironic then that at this age, this time of life when wisdom and power coincided for him, he was forced to confront his mortality. In the spring of 1957, he was diagnosed with an irregular heartbeat by the doctors at Bethesda Naval Hospital.

He had smoked all his adult life, before the dangers of tobacco were documented. To his father, who smoked pipes and collected them for a hobby, cigarettes were loathsome, degrading. But Bill Jr. told the *Saturday Evening Post* in the fall of 1957, "That was one battle he lost. All of us, the girls included, took up cigarettes. But," he went on, "his crochet about cigarettes still influences me to a certain extent. I don't know how it is with the others, but I smoke less than half a pack a day. The rest of the time I use a pipe."[2]

He was advised by his doctors to exercise, so he began each day, rain or shine, with a brisk walk. Rising at 5:00 A.M., he would strike off into the predawn darkness. His route took him east on Dumbarton to 27th Street, where he turned left and went over to Q Street. From there he crossed over the Q Street bridge above the Rock Creek and Potomac Parkway and would wend his way through the smaller streets to Sheridan Circle. He followed Massachusetts Avenue off the circle north toward the National Cathedral and the intersection of Massachusetts and Wisconsin avenues. From there he traveled south down Wisconsin back to Dumbarton.

His doctors had recommended walking two miles a day. The route he settled on was closer to four.

By the time he got home, the morning newspapers had been delivered. He read the *Washington Post*, the *New York Times*, and the *Wall Street Journal* religiously from front to back, everything from sports to the latest confrontation with the Soviet Union. Then he made breakfast for himself, Marjorie, and Nancy. He would eat his own food and leave theirs on the stove. When they rose, he jumped into the bathroom to shave and shower.

He had decided to give up driving after the bus mishap, so one or the other of his law clerks picked him up each day at 8:15 A.M. This did not, however, mean that his short commute always went smoothly. One morning when Daniel O'Hern was driving they ran out of gas not far from the White House on Pennsylvania Avenue.

O'Hern was humiliated over his thoughtlessness, not having stopped to fill the tank. But Brennan good-naturedly forgave the oversight. He got out, loosened his collar, rolled up his sleeves, and helped his law clerk push the car over to the curb.

"He was an incredibly buoyant person," O'Hern recalled. "[A]n early riser, he literally breezed into the office to start work" at about 8:45 A.M. This despite being slowed, to his consternation, by the low-cholesterol diet prescribed for him at Bethesda, to which he was struggling to adjust.

At work, as Yale law professor Owen Fiss has written, "Justice Brennan's contribution to the ensemble known as the Warren Court had many dimensions. He was devoted to the values we identify with the Warren Court—equality, procedural fairness, freedom of speech, and religious liberty—and he was prepared to act on them."[3]

Fiss went on, "The overall design of the Court's position may have been the work of several minds, fully reflecting the contributions of such historic figures as Black, Douglas, and Warren, but it was Brennan who by and large formulated the principle, analyzed the precedents, and chose the words that transformed the ideal into law. Like any master craftsman, he left his distinctive imprint on the finished product."[4]

His relationship with Warren was pivotal. Fiss has written, "Warren and Brennan were invariably on the same side in the great constitutional cases of the day. They served together for thirteen terms and agreed in 89% of the more than 1400 cases they decided. Indeed, it is hard to think of a case of any import where they differed."[5]

He went on, "In part, this reflected the unusual personal tie that developed between the two. The Chief—as Justice Brennan always called him—visited Brennan's chambers frequently, and each visit was an important occasion for the chambers as a whole and for Justice Brennan in particular. One could see at a glance the admiration and affection that each felt for the other."[6]

He concluded, "The relationship between Earl Warren and William Brennan was one of the most extraordinary relationships between two colleagues that I have ever known; surely, it must be one of the most famous in the law."[7]

Abraham Sofaer, a former legal adviser to the U.S. State

Department who clerked for Brennan in 1966, recalled the Chief's friendship with his old boss. "The two of them were in the majority then and their friendship was very close," Sofaer told Donna Haupt in 1989.[8] "Warren was a wonderfully friendly and disarming man who would plop himself down in a chair in our clerks' office whenever he couldn't find Justice Brennan and he'd chat with us. They had a very close personal relationship and it made them both more effective at what they wanted to accomplish."[9]

Warren biographer Bernard Schwartz has written that soon after his appointment, "Brennan...became Warren's closest colleague. The two were completely dissimilar in appearance: the new Justice small and feisty—almost leprechaun-like in appearance. Yet he had the same hearty bluffness and ability to put people at ease that characterized the Chief. On a personal basis, Warren was more comfortable with Brennan than with any of the other Justices, and an intimacy developed between them of a type that never took place between Warren and Black or Warren and Douglas, however close the latters' views may have been to his."[10]

According to Schwartz, "The Chief would turn to Brennan when he wanted to discuss a case or some other matter on which he wanted an exchange of views. The two would usually meet on Thursday, when Warren would come to Brennan's chambers to go over the cases that were to be discussed at the Friday conference."[11]

At those weekly Friday conferences, the justices gathered as a group in the conference room adjacent to the chief justice's chambers to discuss and vote on the cases that had recently been argued before them. It was the Chief's prerogative when he voted with the majority on a given matter to assign the writing of the opinion. Time and again Warren used this power to make Brennan "the justice primarily assigned to speak for the Court,"[12] despite his status as a newcomer.

Fiss has observed, "Sometimes where he felt the need for the imprimatur of his office, or where the issue was especially close to his heart, Warren wrote the opinion. But generally he turned to Justice Brennan."[13]

According to Fiss, "Brennan could be trusted to choose his words in a way that would minimize the disagreement among the justices and those silly squabbles that might interfere with the smooth functioning of a collegial institution, as the Court most

William Joseph Brennan Sr., the Supreme Court justice's father, arrived in New Jersey from his native County Roscommon, Ireland, in 1893 at the age of twenty. He shoveled coal in the Ballantine brewery in Newark and was active in the union movement. In 1917, he was elected public safety commissioner, becoming in effect the most powerful public official in Newark. (SCUS)

Photographs from the Collection of the Supreme Court of the United States are credited SCUS.

William Joseph Brennan Jr. as a college senior. Bill Jr. attended the University of Pennsylvania's undergraduate Wharton School of Finance and Commerce. Wharton was a sensible choice: A lawyer who might one day be in practice for himself needed to develop a good business sense. (SCUS)

Brennan was named chief of the army ordnance department's civilian personnel division in 1943 and rose to the rank of full colonel by the end of World War II. He was awarded the Legion of Merit for his contributions to the military's procurement programs. (SCUS)

Attorney William Joseph Brennan Jr. with his elder son, William Joseph III, at 2 Brookwood Road in South Orange. An opponent recalled that Brennan "looked like one of the bluebloods from Essex County." (SCUS)

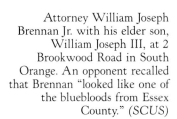

During his third year at Harvard Law School, Bill Brennan *(front row, far left)* posed with the other members of the Harvard Legal Aid Society. Working with this group gave Brennan a taste of the real world and a chance to deal with people's problems firsthand. *(Photo by Stolmarf Studios; SCUS)*

A labor law specialist, Brennan found his talents in great demand after the war. He was made a name partner in a prestigious Newark law firm and lived with his family in this spacious home in South Orange, New Jersey. *(Photo by George Biggs, Inc.; SCUS)*

New Jersey governor Alfred Driscoll appointed Brennan to a superior court judgeship in 1949. The strains of private practice had become so great that Brennan's family feared he was on the verge of a nervous breakdown. *(Photo by Harry B. Hawes, Paterson Evening News)*

Brennan delivered the keynote address at the Charitable Irish Society's St. Patrick's Day Dinner in Boston in 1954. Notables there included George O'Neill, CIS president; Ambassador Henry Cabot Lodge; Massachusetts governor Christian Herter; Boston mayor John B. Hynes; and Massachusetts senator Leverett Saltonstall *(far right)*. *(John J. Burns Library, Boston College)*

Marjorie Leonard was William Brennan's first wife. They were married a month before his college graduation, and she supported him through law school. The marriage produced three children—William Joseph III (*pictured here*), Hugh Leonard, and Nancy—and lasted some fifty-four years, until her death in 1982. Nancy said her dad "really did a nosedive after Mother died." (*Photo by Underwood & Underwood; SCUS*)

Justice Sherman "Shay" Minton was Brennan's predecessor on the Supreme Court. Considered a liberal when President Truman appointed him in 1949, Minton later embraced the conservative philosophy of judicial restraint. Pernicious anemia forced him to retire in September 1956. (*Photo by Harris & Ewing; SCUS*)

President Eisenhower with Brennan in the White House shortly after announcing Brennan's appointment to the Court in October 1956. Years later, Ike reportedly lamented the appointment as "the second biggest mistake I ever made"—second, that is, to choosing Earl Warren as chief justice. (UPI/Bettmann)

Agnes McDermott with her son on the eve of his investiture in October 1956. Agnes outlived her domineering husband, William Brennan Sr., by thirty-five years. *(Photo by Robert Striar; SCUS)*

Justice Brennan with New York governor Thomas E. Dewey under a portrait of Arthur T. Vanderbilt at a memorial service for Vanderbilt in 1957. As chief justice of the New Jersey state supreme court, Vanderbilt shepherded Brennan's rise through the judicial ranks. *(Photo by William R. Simmons; SCUS)*

Frank *(left)* and Tom Brennan with their mother, Agnes, and brother, Bill, in the Sheraton Park Plaza Hotel in Washington, D.C., the night before the swearing in. *(Photo by Robert Striar; SCUS)*

The Brennan clan: sons, Hugh Leonard and William Joseph III, then a marine lieutenant; wife, Marjorie; and daughter, Nancy, on October 16, 1956, the day William Brennan was sworn in as an associate justice of the Supreme Court. (*Newark News Photo; SCUS*)

Justice Brennan heads home after his first day at the Court. Usually, one of his law clerks drove him to and from work. Like his father, he was not very adept behind the wheel. He gave up driving himself to work after a city bus rear-ended him on a slick street during a rainy morning rush hour. (*Newark News Photo; SCUS*)

certainly is, but also to produce a majority opinion and strengthen the force of what the Court had to say. Only five votes are needed for a decision to become law, but the stronger the majority and broader the consensus, the more plausible is its claim for authority."[14]

As Fiss explained, "Aside from a proper regard for institutional needs, a successful opinion requires a mastery of legal craft, which Warren also found in Brennan. Justice Brennan was as much the law-yer as the statesman. Law is a blend of the theoretical and the technical, and though there were others as gifted as Brennan in the formulation of the theoretical principle, there was no one in the ruling coalition...who had either the patience or the ability to master the technical detail that is also the law. Everyone on the Court, law clerk and justice alike, admired Brennan's command of vast bodies of learning, ancient and modern. He knew the cases and the statutes, and how they interacted, and understood how the legal system worked and how it might be made to work better. Among the majority, he was the lawyer's judge."[15]

Warren acknowledged years later in an article for the *Harvard Law Review*, "In the entire history of the Court, it would be difficult to name another Justice who wrote more important opinions in his first ten years than [Brennan]."[16]

Warren was unquestionably a strong leader. As the late Justice Potter Stewart, who joined the Court in 1958, observed, "Warren's great strength was his simple belief in the things we now laugh at: motherhood, marriage, family, flag, and the like."[17] Stewart called these the "eternal, rather bromidic, platitudes in which he [Warren] sincerely believed."[18]

According to Schwartz, "When we add to this Warren's bluff masculine bonhomie, his love of sports and the outdoors, and his lack of intellectual interests or pretensions, we end up with a typical representative of the Middle America of his day. Except for one thing—Warren's leadership abilities."[19] In Justice Stewart's view, Warren "had instinctive qualities of leadership."[20]

But Brennan was smarter, and Warren saw this. He knew he lacked his new protégé's intellectual firepower and resolve. "Bren-nan's twinkling eyes and unassuming manner masked a keen intelligence."[21] In addition, Brennan "was probably the hardest worker among the Brethren."[22]

Instead of resenting him for his intellectual gifts and remarkable qualities, his "ability and affability," which even Frankfurter was forced to concede,[23] Warren used him to full advantage. He counted on Brennan to give forceful, eloquent shape to the goals and principles they both shared in a way that Warren himself never could, indeed as no one else could, or would.

For example, by the 1956–57 term, Warren had become "a wholehearted advocate of judicial activism, finally rejecting the Frankfurter philosophy of judicial restraint."[24] Yet he was uncomfortable with the absolutism of both Black and Douglas. For them, in Warren's view, their own peculiar judicial philosophy took precedence. They seemed all too willing to go their own way, even when doing so left them in dissent.

By contrast, Brennan was a pragmatist. He knew the overriding importance of winning five votes. He understood that he was doing more than writing constitutional doctrine; he was affecting people's lives. To an extent this resulted from his father's background as a labor leader, and his own as a labor lawyer. So much of labor law had less to do with doctrine than with bridging differences between divergent viewpoints and competing interests.

According to Fiss, "Brennan was, in the highest and best sense of the word, a statesman: not a person who tempers principle with prudence, but rather someone who is capable of grasping a multiplicity of conflicting principles, some of which relate to the well-being of the institution and remind the judge that his duty is not just to speak the law but also to see to it that it becomes an actuality."[25]

Brennan wrote several major opinions during his first term. In *United States v. E. I. du Pont de Nemours & Co.*,[26] delivered on June 3, 1957, he enraged big-business interests by ruling that federal antitrust laws applied to "vertical" as well as "horizontal" stock purchases. In other words, "he ruled that the acquisition of the stock of a customer corporation may be just as violative of anti-trust laws as the acquisition of the stock of a competing corporation."[27]

At issue in *du Pont* was "whether the 'commanding position' which du Pont occupied as the supplier of automotive fabrics and finishes to General Motors Corporation was gained because of its competitive merit or through its ownership of twenty-three percent of General Motors' stock."[28] Du Pont had been accused of using its leverage as a principal stockholder "to channel General Motors' purchases to du Pont."[29]

In a 4-to-2 decision in which he was joined by Warren, Black, and Douglas, Brennan concluded, "The fact that sticks out in this voluminous record is that the bulk of du Pont's production has always supplied the largest part of the requirements of the one customer in the automobile industry connected to du Pont by a stock interest. The inference is overwhelming that du Pont's commanding position was prompted by its stock interest and was not gained solely on competitive merit."[30]

Justices Frankfurter and Burton dissented. Justices Clark, Harlan, and Whittaker took no part in the decision. Harlan was forced to recuse himself because he had represented du Pont in the case, winning at the district court level on the company's behalf. He was angered by his new friend Brennan's ruling.

In fact, while Brennan was summarizing his opinion from the bench, Harlan wrote an angry note to Frankfurter, complaining, "Now that my lips are no longer sealed, if there was ever a more *superficial* understanding of a really impressive record, than Bill's opinion in *du Pont*—I would like to see it. I hardly recognize the case as I listen to him speak. Harold's [Burton's] and your dissent at least puts on the Court's record something towards redeeming what (between you and me) for me has been the most disillusioning blot on the Court's processes."[31]

Big business was angered as well. Henry Luce's Time, Inc., publishing empire, which had so enthusiastically endorsed Brennan's appointment, changed its tone, assailing Brennan's philosophy of "Anti-Bigness." The July 1957 edition of *Fortune* magazine, which hit the newsstands within a month of the opinion, reported, "Justice Brennan's sweeping assertion of the government's right to outlaw intercorporate relationships of long standing—even where no monopoly exists and where none is alleged—immensely strengthened the Clayton Act. Indeed, it is difficult to see why the Justice Department should henceforth trouble to prove monopoly or restraint as required under the Sherman Act when it can achieve the same end simply by showing the possibility of restraint under the newly interpreted Clayton Act. As New Deal brain-truster Adolf Berle puts it, 'The Supreme Court has made new law.'"[32]

The magazine went on, "The Brennan 'law'...is basically an anti-bigness law. Professor S. Chesterfield Oppenheim, co-chairman of the Attorney General's Committee to Study the Anti-Trust

Laws, says: 'The implications are far-reaching and seem to imply a philosophical issue: anti-bigness.'"[33]

Even more controversial than his ruling in *du Pont*, however, was Brennan's decision in *Jencks v. United States*,[34] handed down the same day, aimed at curtailing FBI Red Scare tactics used to expose suspected subversives. In that case, the Court overturned by a 7-to-1 vote the conviction of Clinton E. Jencks, a New Mexico labor leader who had been convicted of stating falsely on a Taft-Hartley Act affidavit that he was not a communist.

Justice Brennan wrote the opinion of the Court. Justice Burton, joined by Justice Harlan, filed a separate concurrence. Justice Clark dissented. Justice Whittaker was appointed after the Court had heard oral arguments and so took no part in this consideration of the case.

Jencks's conviction was based in large part on the testimony of two government witnesses, Harvey Matusow and J. W. Ford, former members of the Communist Party who were paid FBI informers. Matusow and Ford claimed that they had known Jencks to be a Communist Party official, and that contrary to his sworn affidavit he had engaged in communist activities.

Jencks claimed the right to use in his defense oral and written reports submitted to the FBI by Matusow and Ford. But the government claimed a "legitimate interest" in "safeguarding the privacy of its files, particularly where the documents in question were obtained in confidence."[35] Jencks asserted that he had no idea what specific charges were contained in the FBI papers. Nor did Matusow, for that matter. In fact, Matusow had even admitted, "I don't know what I put in my reports two or three years ago."[36] Jencks asked that, at the very least, the trial judge be allowed to examine the documents to determine their relevancy.

Jencks's request was denied by the trial judge, whose ruling was upheld by the U.S. Court of Appeals for the Fifth Circuit. Writing for the Court, Brennan overruled the lower courts and reversed Jencks's conviction. He declared, "We now hold that the petitioner was entitled to an order directing the Government to produce for inspection all reports of Matusow and Ford in its possession, written and, when orally made, as recorded by the F.B.I., touching the events and activities as to which they testified at the trial."[37]

He went on, "We hold, further, that the petitioner is entitled to inspect the reports to decide whether to use them in his defense. Because only the defense is adequately equipped to determine the effective use for purpose of discrediting the Government's witness and thereby furthering the accused's defense, the defense must initially be entitled to see them to determine what use may be made of them."[38]

He declared, "Justice requires no less," adding, "The practice of producing government documents to the trial judge for his determination of relevancy and materiality, without hearing the accused, is disapproved."[39]

Citing established precedent, he ordered Jencks's release. The government, he explained, "can invoke its evidentiary privileges only at the price of letting the defendant go free. The rationale of the criminal cases is that, since the Government which prosecutes an accused also has the duty to see that justice is done, it is unconscionable to allow it to undertake prosecution and then invoke its governmental privileges to deprive the accused of anything which might be material to his defense."[40]

Justice Tom C. Clark filed a lone, strongly worded dissent. An independent-minded Texan, an affable hail-fellow-well-met who got along well with Brennan personally, Clark had become Harry Truman's attorney general in 1945. When Truman appointed him to the Supreme Court after Frank Murphy's death in 1949, "criticism of his zeal for national security from civil liberties groups helped fuel three days of Senate debate prior to his confirmation by a vote of 73 to 8."[41]

That same zeal now inspired his attack on the Court's ruling in *Jencks*. He warned, "Unless the Congress changes the rule announced by the Court today, those intelligence agencies of our Government engaged in law enforcement may as well close up shop, for the Court has opened their files to the criminal and thus afforded him a Roman holiday for rummaging through confidential information as well as vital national secrets."[42]

Implying that Brennan, a former state court judge, was naïve to the more sophisticated concerns of the national government, he complained, "This may well be a reasonable rule in state prosecutions where none of the problems of foreign relations, espionage, sabotage, subversive activities, counterfeiting, internal security, national defense, and the like exist, but any person conversant with federal government activities and problems will quickly recognize that it opens up a veritable Pandora's box of troubles. And all in the name of justice."[43]

The White House, for its part, apparently felt that Clark's fears were overstated. The *New York Times* reported "guarded acknowl-edgments that the situation might not be too bad"[44] from within the Eisenhower administration. As the *Times* observed dryly, "There were no indications that the FBI [and] other investigative agencies of the government were planning to 'close up shop.'"[45]

Nevertheless, the president backed and signed a bill rushed through Congress that modified the effects of the decision. Popu-larly known as the "Jencks Act," the legislation modified Brennan's ruling in at least two significant ways. First, trial judges were authorized to inspect privileged documents and select which were relevant to the accused's defense, if any.[46] This addressed Clark's concern about criminals "rummaging" through secret files.

Second, judges were empowered to order a mistrial in cases where the government refused to make privileged material available, rather than dismiss the charges against the accused altogether.[47]

Eisenhower expressed in private his personal displeasure with the ruling. He told dinner guests, "I've never been as mad in my life" as at what he called the Court's decision to "open secret FBI files to accused subversives."[48]

Meanwhile, conservatives in Congress had a field day. Senator Olin Johnston of South Carolina declared, "Red spies will not be brought to trial because the Justice Department will not risk giving up files to the Communist defendant's lawyer."[49] And Republican Senator Everett Dirksen of Illinois announced, "We hold up our hands in Holy Horror. Something has to be done. The government is about to topple."[50]

According to biographer Kim Isaac Eisler, Brennan was shaken by the controversy his decision aroused. He wrote in a private note to Frankfurter, "I confess to considerable concern...that I may have been the instrument (and in my first year) for demeaning the standing of the Court."[51] Eisler writes, "Brennan, normally full of jolly self-confidence and rarely given to introspection, revealed a side of himself that even his clerks say surprised them."[52]

But according to Daniel O'Hern, one of Brennan's two law clerks during the 1956–57 term, the justice was "far from shell-shocked" by the events.[53] In fact, Brennan was "amused that the public thought *Jencks* was so important."[54] After all, as O'Hern pointed out in a 1993 interview with the author, *Jencks* "merely accorded suspects the same kind of discovery we now find commonplace in our state courts."[55]

As one commentator observed, "It was as though Brennan had enunciated a new and outlandish rule of law instead of merely reaffirming the salutary principle that each side in a case should have access to relevant information in the possession of the other."[56]

In this regard, Brennan's opinion in *Jencks* was consistent with his dissent in *State v. Tune*[57] some years before. In that case, the New Jersey supreme court ruled that a defendant in a murder trial had no right to inspect for use in his defense at trial a confession that he had earlier given to police. Brennan had complained bitterly that the majority decision "shocks my sense of justice."[58]

Moreover, *Jencks* was hardly the only ruling for which the Court came under attack from the far right, the zealous, anticommunist remnants of McCarthyism. During the 1956–57 term, the justices dealt a number of serious setbacks to the witch hunters.

For example, in *Grunewald v. United States,*[59] decided May 27, 1957, the Court by a 5-to-4 vote bolstered the Fifth Amendment privilege against self-incrimination by holding that a defendant's refusal to testify before a grand jury could not be used to impeach his later testimony at trial. The defendants in *Grunewald* were charged with and convicted of tax evasion, not subversive activity. But the implications for other cases involving charges or suspicions of subversion were clear.

Harlan and Brennan joined with liberals Warren, Black, and Douglas to form the *Grunewald* majority. But Harlan would do so only if allowed to write the majority opinion, narrowing its holding to the facts of the specific case. Warren agreed, and in writing for the Court Harlan emphasized the "special circumstances" and legal technicalities upon which his decision was based.

Black wrote an expansive concurrence in which he was joined by Brennan, Warren, and Douglas. He used Harlan's opinion as a point of departure for a broader assertion of Fifth Amendment protection. As Black recounted the facts of the case, a man named Halperin, who was one of the accused, refused to answer certain questions when subpoenaed to testify before a grand jury, asserting his Fifth Amendment privilege. "Later, at his trial," Black wrote, "Halperin took the stand to testify in his own behalf. On cross-examination the prosecuting attorney asked him the same questions that he had refused to answer before the grand jury.

"This time Halperin answered the questions; his answers tended to show that he was innocent of any wrong-doing. The Government was then permitted over objection to draw from him the fact that he had previously refused to answer these questions before the grand jury on the ground that his answers might tend to incriminate him."[60]

The problem, as Black saw it, was that "[a]t the conclusion of the trial the judge instructed the jury that Halperin's claim of his constitutional privilege not to be a witness against himself could be considered in determining what weight should be given to his testimony—in other words, whether Halperin was a truthful and trustworthy witness."[61]

He declared, "I agree with the Court that use of this claim of constitutional privilege to reflect upon Halperin's credibility was error, but I do not, like the Court, rest my conclusion on the special circumstances of this case."

Instead, he went on, "I can think of no special circumstances that would justify use of a constitutional privilege to discredit or convict a person who asserts it. The value of constitutional privileges is largely destroyed if persons can be penalized for relying on them."

He continued, "It seems peculiarly incongruous and indefensible for courts which exist and act only under the Constitution to draw inferences of lack of honesty from invocation of a privilege deemed worthy of enshrinement in the Constitution."

Brennan's decision to join Black's concurrence in *Grunewald* reflected an evolution in his thinking. As a New Jersey state supreme court justice, he had in *State v. Fary*[62] recognized the privilege against self-incrimination as "precious to free men as a restraint against high-handed and arrogant inquisitorial practices."[63] But he had taken a dim view of a witness's refusal to testify before a grand jury in that case. The same refusal seemed to trouble him less, if at all, in *Grunewald*. Instead his overriding concern was with strengthening the Fifth Amendment.

A few weeks later, on June 17, 1957, a date which will live in infamy among the Court's critics as "Red Monday," the Court issued three far-reaching decisions that, taken together, all but doomed whatever was left of McCarthyism: *Yates v. United States*,[64] *Watkins v. United States*,[65] and *Sweezy v. New Hampshire*.[66]

In *Yates*, the Court ordered new trials for a number of communists convicted under the Smith Act. The decision "seemed to set standards for 'political' prosecutions that could rarely if ever be met, and it was popularly assumed that no conviction of Communist Party members could again survive a first amendment challenge."[67]

Again, Justice Harlan wrote for the Court, narrowly focusing the decision on legal technicalities and a pivotal distinction between mere advocacy and imminently threatening activity.[68] His majority opinion was joined by Warren and Frankfurter, with Justice Burton concurring in the result. Black, joined by Douglas, concurred in part and dissented in part. Brennan and Whittaker, the newcomers, arrived after the oral arguments had been presented and so took no part in the consideration of the case. Clark dissented.

Black used his separate opinion to label Smith Act prosecutions as nothing more than political trials that violated the Constitution. Reiterating his and Douglas's dissents in *Dennis v. United States*[69] and *American Communications Association v. Douds*,[70] he wrote, "I would reverse every one of these convictions and direct that all the defendants be acquitted. In my judgment the statutory provisions on which these prosecutions are based abridge freedom of speech, press and assembly in violation of the First Amendment to the United States Constitution."[71]

He went on, "The kind of trials conducted here are wholly dissimilar to normal criminal trials. Ordinarily these 'Smith Act' trials are prolonged affairs lasting for months. In part this is attributable to the routine introduction in evidence of massive collections of books, tracts, pamphlets, newspapers, and manifestoes discussing Communism, Socialism, Capitalism, Feudalism and governmental institutions in general, which, it is not too much to say, are turgid, diffuse, abstruse, and just plain dull. Of course, no juror can or is expected to plow his way through this jungle of verbiage. The testimony of witnesses is comparatively insignificant. Guilt or innocence may turn on what Marx or Engels or someone else wrote or advocated as much as a hundred or more years ago. Elaborate, refined distinctions are drawn between 'Communism,' 'Marxism,' 'Leninism,' 'Trotskyism,' and 'Stalinism.' When the propriety of obnoxious or unorthodox views about government is in reality made the crucial issue, as it must be in cases of this kind, prejudice makes conviction inevitable except in the rarest circumstances."[72]

Brennan's participation in *Yates* would not have affected the outcome. Of the seven justices who took part in the case, Black and Douglas would have gone even further to undermine Smith Act prosecutions than the majority; only Clark dissented from the result. Nevertheless it is worth noting that as a New Jersey state supreme court justice, Brennan had concurred in a unanimous ruling that the New Jersey Communist Control Act of 1954 was constitutional.[73]

In *Watkins*, the Court overturned the contempt-of-Congress conviction of a labor leader who had refused to answer questions put to him by a subcommittee of the House Committee on Un-American Activities. The defendant did not plead his Fifth Amendment privilege against self-incrimination. Instead he based his refusal to answer on the assertion that the questions asked of him were not legitimate matters of congressional inquiry under the law. The legal issues raised in the case went to the very heart of the McCarthy-style congressional inquisitions of suspected subversives.

Chief Justice Warren wrote the opinion of the Court. He was joined by Black, Douglas, Brennan, and Harlan. Frankfurter wrote a separate concurrence. Whittaker and Burton took no part in the case. Clark again found himself in lone dissent.

Warren began by noting that the "power of the Congress to conduct investigations is inherent in the legislative process" and that that power is "broad."[74] But, he cautioned, "No inquiry is an end in itself; it must be related to, and in furtherance of, a legitimate task of the Congress. Investigations conducted solely for the aggrandizement of the investigators or to 'punish' those investigated are indefensible."[75]

With that said, he observed, "In the decade following World War II, there appeared a new kind of congressional inquiry unknown in prior periods of American history. Principally this was the result of the various investigations into the threat of subversion of the United States Government, but other subjects of congressional interest also contributed to the changed scene. This new phase of legislative inquiry involved a broad-scale intrusion into the lives and affairs of private citizens."[76]

He went on to decry the "[a]buses of the investigative process"[77] that had characterized the McCarthy era. These abuses, he wrote, "may imperceptibly lead to abridgment of protected freedoms. The mere summoning of a witness and compelling him to testify, against his will, about his beliefs, expressions or associations is a measure of governmental interference. And when those forced revelations concern matters that are unorthodox, unpopular, or even hateful to the general public, the reaction in the life of the witness may be disastrous. This effect is even more harsh when it is past beliefs, expressions or associations that are disclosed and judged by current standards rather than those contemporary with the matters exposed."[78]

He continued, "Nor does the witness alone suffer the consequences. Those who are identified by witnesses and thereby placed in the same glare of publicity are equally subject to public stigma, scorn and obloquy. Beyond that, there is the more subtle and immeasurable effect upon those who tend to adhere to the most orthodox and uncontroversial views and associations in order to avoid a similar fate at some future time. That this impact is partly the result of non-governmental activity by private persons cannot relieve the investigators of their responsibility for initiating the reaction."[79]

Declaring that "there is no congressional power to expose for the sake of exposure,"[80] the opinion was "full of language suggesting that the Court might consider the legitimacy of the Committee on Un-American Activities."[81] At one point, Warren asked rhetorically, "Who can define the meaning of 'un-American'?"[82]

According to University of Texas law professor Michael F. Tigar, Warren's words "were all the more welcome because by this time [1957] the Committee, and its stepbrother the Senate Internal Security Committee, frequently entered communities at the behest of local reactionary politicians [and conducted hearings on site] in order to pillory members of various professions and trade unions."[83]

Moreover, abusive congressional investigative practices were being copied by the states. In Sweezy, the third of the blockbuster Red Monday decisions, the Court extended the limitations on legislative inquiries imposed under its Watkins ruling beyond the houses of Congress to the states.

Sweezy was a visiting Marxist professor of economics at the

University of New Hampshire. He had been summoned to appear before the state attorney general on two occasions—January 5, 1954, and again on June 3, 1954—to answer questions regarding, among other things, his political views and prior contacts with suspected communists. He was also questioned concerning the beliefs and associations of others, including his wife, Nancy.

The interrogations were conducted under the authority of the "Joint Resolution Relating to the Investigation of Subversive Activities"[84] passed by the New Hampshire legislature in 1953. As interpreted by the state courts, the resolution in effect authorized the state attorney general to act as "a one-man legislative committee"[85] to root out communists in accordance with the New Hampshire Subversive Activities Act of 1951.[86] Although the attorney general did not have power to hold witnesses in contempt, he was empowered to "invoke the aid of a State Superior Court which could find recalcitrant witnesses in contempt of court."[87]

Sweezy refused to answer those questions that he claimed were "not pertinent to the subject under inquiry as well as those which transgress[ed] the limitations of the First Amendment."[88] He was subsequently adjudged in contempt of court.

Chief Justice Warren, in a decision joined by Black, Douglas, and Brennan, overturned Sweezy's contempt citation. "The plurality opinion upholding his [Sweezy's] refusal [to testify] stressed the first amendment values inherent in the concept of academic freedom."[89]

Frankfurter, joined by Harlan, concurred in the result. Clark was joined this time by Burton in dissent. Whittaker took no part in the decision.

With these rulings, in which Brennan, when he took part, joined liberals Warren, Black, and Douglas, the heyday of the Warren Court had dawned; the resurrection and expansion of the Bill of Rights had begun. By replacing Minton with Brennan, Eisenhower, wittingly or not, had clearly liberalized the Court.

But before the Warren Court could proceed with recapturing the full range of liberties eroded by the Red Scare and with widening the reach of the Bill of Rights, it would be challenged to hold its ground on the question of racial equality. William Brennan was about to emerge as the spearhead of that effort.

CHAPTER 13

Faubus, Little Rock, and Justice Brennan

Almighty God, we make our earnest prayer that Thou wilt keep the United States in Thy holy protection, that Thou wilt incline the hearts of the citizens to cultivate a spirit of subordination and obedience to government, and entertain a brotherly affection and love for one another and for their fellow-citizens of the United States at large.

— George Washington's
Prayer for the Nation

SOMEWHERE IN HIS CLASSIC, nineteenth-century tome *Democracy in America* French political philosopher Alexis de Tocqueville observed that there is hardly a political issue which arises in the United States that is not resolved sooner or later into a judicial question. Tocqueville considered the American proclivity for letting judges settle not just legal but also key social, political, and moral matters unique in the annals of history. He attributed the propensity to America's unusual constitution.

On the one hand, the U.S. Constitution makes the judiciary the weakest—in Alexander Hamilton's words, the "least dangerous"[1]— of the three branches of government. The judiciary "has no influence over either the sword or the purse; no direction either of the strength or of the wealth of the society; and can take no active resolution whatever," having no enforcement power.[2] The courts "may truly be said to have neither FORCE nor WILL, but merely judgment; and must ultimately depend upon the aid of the executive arm for the efficacious exercise even of this faculty."[3]

At the same time, however, the Constitution insulates the judiciary from direct political pressure. Supreme Court justices hold office for life during "good behavior," which creates the public perception that they are free to be impartial. This perceived impartiality makes the Court a powerful and desirable forum for resolving all kinds of disputes that have far-reaching implications. As Hamilton put it, "nothing can contribute so much to its [the judiciary's] firmness and independence as PERMANENCY IN OFFICE, this quality may therefore be justly regarded as an indispensable ingredient in its constitution; and, in a great measure, as the CITADEL of the public justice and the public security."[4]

Yet how best to use their independence, power, and credibility to adjudicate legal, social, and political issues has perplexed jurists since the founding of the republic. Judges are typically trained as lawyers, not as economists, social scientists, historians, theologians, moralists, or philosophers.

Traditional legal scholars like to think that by emphasizing objectivity and adherence to precedent, the law can be made more rational and predictable and hence more just, less prone to subjective value judgments and caprice. But Justice William O. Douglas was fond of pointing out that those who sit on the Supreme Court, like anybody else, have "predilections" which color their thinking and are based on a host of intangibles, including their personal experiences, individual backgrounds, and prejudices.

As Yale law professor Fred Rodell once wrote, "Only a dull-witted justice would suppose, and only an intellectually dishonest one would pretend—and the Court has been manned by far too many of both—that he could ever purge his thinking processes, for the purpose of making decisions, of all his personal predilections even of a conscious kind, much less the unconscious and unrecognized."[5]

If this is so, then perhaps the best the American people can hope for, and the very least to which they are entitled, is some understanding of a justice's predilections. That knowledge may provide some basis for understanding and assessing the validity of the justice's point of view.

By the late 1950s, William Brennan's judicial philosophy was still evolving. It would be years before he would manifest fully his own unique judicial temperament. But in a speech entitled "Law and Social Sciences Today," delivered to students and faculty at the annual Gaston Lecture at Georgetown Law Center on November 25, 1957, he provided a number of insights into his thinking about law and society, and the relationship among the academic disciplines.

Brennan's underlying premise, as he stated it, was that the law "is not an end in itself, nor does it provide ends."[6] Instead, he asserted, "It is preeminently a means to serve what we think is right."[7] He declared, "Law is here to serve! To serve what? To serve...the realization of man's ends, ultimate and mediate."[8]

He defined those ends as the realization of human dignity through full opportunity and the eradication of bias. Quoting from an article that Professors Harold D. Lasswell and Myres S. McDougal had written for the *Yale Law Journal* in 1943,[9] he stated, "The supreme value of democracy is the dignity and worth of the individual; hence a democratic society is a commonwealth of mutual deference—a commonwealth where there is full opportunity to mature talent into socially creative skill, free from discrimination on grounds of religion, culture or class."[10]

Brennan rejected the idea that law can somehow isolate itself and yet still achieve "greater perfection in the study of the human condition."[11] He quoted his mentor Arthur T. Vanderbilt, who once said, "[I]t can no longer be maintained that the law can be isolated from the other social sciences or understood without them."[12]

He added to Vanderbilt's thoughts an addendum from the writings of another state supreme court judge, the late Justice Roger J. Traynor of California, who offered that "human relations are infinitely complex, and subtlety and depth of spirit must enter into their regulation."[13]

Brennan went on, "In the workaday life of the lawyer, what Plato called the 'taint of the shop' little appears because the march of events is undermining the old adage that 'law sharpens the mind by narrowing it.' He is an unwise lawyer who rejects what can be learned from history and sociology and psychology."[14]

He continued, "[T]he legal scholar's role is, par excellence, a creative one. He is more likely to have the leisure and range of thought necessary to reach across the arbitrary divisions between disciplines in the academic world and sense values that the law may properly serve and techniques it may profitably use. The mind of the layman unfamiliar with the judicial process supposes it to exist in the air, as a self-justifying and wholly independent process. The opposite is of course true, that judicial decision must be nourished by all the insights that scholarship can furnish and legal scholarship must in turn be nourished by all the disciplines that comprehend the totality of human experience."[15]

Francis P. McQuade, an assistant professor of philosophy at Fordham University School of Education, and Alexander T. Kardos, who worked for the general counsel's office at Brennan's former client Johnson & Johnson, analyzed the new justice's Georgetown lecture in the May 1958 edition of *The Notre Dame Lawyer*, a scholarly journal.[16] They wrote, "At present, Mr. Justice Brennan's juristic philosophy cannot be absolutely categorized. His flexibility and complexity render each of his decisions forceful and exciting. When one attempts to reconcile his various decisions, and thus piece out his philosophy inconsistencies appear. But this is no doubt due to his insistence upon giving paramount importance to the facts of each individual case."[17]

They went on, "He defends the use by lawyers and the courts of truth wherever it can be found, even in the findings of social sciences such as economics, sociology, and even social psychology."[18] They added, "Mr. Justice Brennan would urge lawyers to 'turn their minds to the knowledge and experience of the other disciplines, and in particular those disciplines that investigate and report on the functioning and nature of society.'"[19]

The authors struck a note of caution, warning, "In the search to solve the great problems of our day, *viz.*, the reconciliation of freedom with responsibility, of the desires of the individual with the good of the community, of the interests of the nation with the requirement of international amity, and, in general, the balancing of personal ambition with the moral demands of human nature, a lawyer and certainly a jurist may not rely solely upon the descriptive social sciences, as helpful as they are. Rather, one must supplement his factual, positivistic knowledge with interpretative and principled learning."[20]

They predicted, "Mr. Justice Brennan undoubtedly recognizes this. When he actually accomplishes it, he will become, with his great legal potential, one of America's outstanding jurists."[21]

According to McQuade and Kardos, Brennan's Gaston lecture at Georgetown was an implicit defense of Chief Justice Earl Warren's citation of "non-legal works"[22] in *Brown v. Board of Education*[23] in 1954. As two other noted scholars had observed, "A revolutionary judicial technique—one which will govern the course of decision in many fields of the law—was evolved for the first time in Chief Justice Warren's unanimous opinion [in *Brown*]. It was a technique giving increased importance to the utilization of nonlegal data and developing a new use for such materials as a means of informing and guiding the judicial mind."[24]

In his Georgetown speech, Brennan had quoted Vanderbilt, who named Harvard Law School dean Roscoe Pound as the "exponent" of the "sociological school of jurisprudence."[25] Vanderbilt had also stated that it "was Louis D. Brandeis, the lawyer...who was the pioneer in the use of social facts in litigation, insisting that 'Out of the facts grows the law,' a theme that was to find later utterance in his judicial opinions, and that will doubtless increasingly influence the course of our judicial decisions in the future."[26]

Early in the century, Brandeis had incorporated into his Supreme Court brief in the case of *Muller v. Oregon*[27] a wealth of sociological data. As lawyer for the state in that case, Brandeis had used the information to show that there was at least a *rational basis* for an Oregon law that limited the number of hours that women were permitted to work each week, whether one agreed with the imposition of the limitation or not. The justices were persuaded and let the Oregon law stand.

By the late 1950s, however, the tenets of the so-called "sociological," or interdisciplinary, school of jurisprudence were most ably applied by Thurgood Marshall, the future Supreme Court justice. As director of the NAACP Legal Defense and Educational Fund, Marshall had made extensive use of sociological, historical, and psychological evidence to win *Brown v. Board of Education*.

In *Brown*, the Court rejected the "separate but equal" doctrine that it had established in *Plessy v. Ferguson*[28] a half-century earlier and ordered the desegregation of the nation's public schools. Sources offered by Marshall that were relied on by the Court and cited by Warren in the *Brown* opinion included, among others, psychologist Kenneth B. Clark's *Effect of Prejudice and Discrimination on Personality Development* (Midcentury White House Conference on Children and Youth, 1950) and Swedish economist Gunnar Myrdal's *An American Dilemma: The Negro Problem in Modern Democracy* (1944).

The opinion in *Brown* was intentionally written to be moralistic in tone, yet nonaggressive, nonaccusatory, and easily understandable to lay people. Yet from its inception critics attacked it from a theoretical perspective. It lacks, some have said, the proper grounding in hard legality that would have lent greater force and weight to the result.

For example, in an article for the *Howard Law Journal* in 1987, future Supreme Court justice Clarence Thomas wrote, "The great flaw in *Brown* is that it did not rely on Justice Harlan's great dissent in *Plessy*, which understood well that the fundamental issue of guidance by the Founders' constitutional principles lay at the heart of the segregation issue. On the contrary, Chief Justice Warren, writing *Brown*, made sensitivity the paramount issue."[29]

Thomas explained, "Note his [Warren's] decisive reason for declaring segregated schools a violation of the fourteenth amendment's equal protection clause: 'To separate [black] children from others of similar age and qualifications solely because of their race generates a feeling of inferiority as to their status in a community that may affect their hearts and minds in a way unlikely ever to be undone.'"[30]

Thomas went on, "Warren then cites a passage from [psychologist] Kenneth Clark: 'A sense of inferiority affects the motivation of a child to learn. Segregation with the sanction of law, therefore, has a tendency to [retard] the educational and mental development of negro children and to deprive them of some of the benefits they would receive in a racial[ly] integrated school system.' Warren goes on to declare that 'whatever may have been the extent of psychological knowledge at the time of *Plessy v. Ferguson*, this finding is amply supported by modern authority. Any language in *Plessy v. Ferguson* contrary to this finding is rejected.'"[31]

According to Thomas, "The *Brown* psychology makes the legal and social environment all-controlling: 'the feeling of inferiority' or 'the sense of inferiority' is the problem."[32]

"Thus," Thomas wrote, "the *Brown* focus on environment overlooks the real problem with segregation, its origin in slavery, which was at fundamental odds with the founding principles [of this nation]. Had *Brown* done so, it would have been forced to talk about slavery, which it never mentions."[33]

Thomas's conclusion: "*Brown* was a missed opportunity."[34]

Others have attacked the decision from a more practical standpoint, arguing that the Court left too much room for maneuver and evasion by segregationists who sought to avoid desegregation. The Court's reliance on sociological data was indeed unique. "Of even greater legal significance," however, "was the precedent-making manifestation of judicial flexibility evidenced in the manner in which the decision was implemented. Virtually no judicial decisions are handed down in two parts, first setting forth the nature of the right and then providing the remedy which would effectuate that right."[35] Yet this was precisely what the Court did in *Brown.*

The decision that became popularly known as *Brown* was in fact two rulings. The first, issued on May 17, 1954, outlawed segregation in the public schools. It also ordered further arguments in the case in order to determine an appropriate remedy. The result a year later was *Brown II,*[36] an enforcement decree, announced on May 31, 1955. *Brown II* established that the desegregation ordered under the first ruling must occur "*with all deliberate speed.*"[37]

According to Justice William O. Douglas's autobiography, *The Court Years (1939–1975)*, the phrase "with all deliberate speed" was added to the opinion "because of Frankfurter's persuasion."[38] Douglas wrote, "He [Frankfurter] pointed out that it was an old equity expression, that [Oliver Wendell] Holmes as a state judge had used it, that it expressed the tolerance and yet firmness which was required. (I later did research on the use of that phrase and I think Frankfurter overstated its history.) Some, including Black and me, were opposed, but everyone eventually acquiesced."[39]

Thurgood Marshall is said to have commented, "I was terribly disappointed that the Court did not set a firm date for desegregation in the fall of 1955, or at worst of 1956."[40] Never a man to mince words, he reportedly asked journalist Carl Rowan, "How the fuck do you have all deliberate speed?"[41]

Another critic of *Brown II*, history professor Laura Kalman of the University of California at Santa Barbara, who has written extensively about the Supreme Court, has asserted that "the Supreme Court's decree implementing *Brown* 'with all deliberate speed' instead of setting a definite date delayed the pace of desegregation."[42]

But as a practical matter, the justices had little choice. As journalist Nicholas Lemann has astutely observed, "In the short run, even the Supreme Court, with its immense power of fiat, pushes up against the limits of public consent, especially on racial issues."[43]

A case in point, Lemann has written, "is the Court's rehearing of the *Brown* case, resulting in the order that the South proceed on school integration 'with all deliberate speed'…which surely was motivated in part by a fear that if the order had said 'immediately' it would have been openly flouted and the legitimacy of the Court undermined."[44]

As Douglas wrote, " 'All deliberate speed' was used to drag feet, but even without that phrase the progress would have been slow, for the spirit of revolt against the Court's decision ran high. Legislators, governors and others running for public office thought up ingenious as well as ingenuous plans to forestall such programs."[45]

Besides, critics who have seized on the single phrase "with all deliberate speed" overlook the other operative language in the opinion. What *Brown II* in fact did was establish a framework for adjudicating desegregation compliance at the district court level.

During the summer of 1958, just a few short months after Brennan's defense of *Brown* at Georgetown, the justices were confronted with the situation that had developed in and around Central High School in Little Rock, Arkansas. Brennan's opinion in that case, *Cooper v. Aaron*,[46] would become the Court's first major desegregation ruling since *Brown*.

The Court usually goes into recess in May or June and resumes business on the first Monday of the following October. But in August 1958, Warren called the justices into a special session to consider the situation in Little Rock. By that time, the federal government had withdrawn elements of the U.S. Army's elite 101st Airborne Division that had been dispatched to Central High by President Eisenhower in September 1957 to restore order. But the situation was still dangerous, and the National Guard was required to protect the "Little Rock Nine," the nine black students who had desegregated the school in the fall of 1957.

At first, Little Rock's schools were to be desegregated under the school board's "Blossom Plan," named for Little Rock school superintendent Virgil T. Blossom. Adopted a week before *Brown II* was handed down, the plan "provided for desegregation at the senior high school level (grades 10 through 12) as the first stage. Desegregation at the junior high and elementary levels was to follow. It was contemplated that desegregation at the high school level would commence in the fall of 1957, and the expectation was that complete desegregation of the school system would be accomplished by 1963."[47]

The Little Rock board "wanted to integrate first at the high school level, with the oldest and therefore most mature students, then use that experience as a guide for implementing desegregation at the lower levels. By so doing, the board explained, it would have 'the opportunity to benefit from our own experience as we move through each phase of this plan, thus avoiding as many mistakes as possible.'"[48]

Thurgood Marshall and the NAACP challenged the Blossom Plan because it would not result in complete desegregation for almost a decade. But the plan was upheld by the eighth circuit court of appeals, and Marshall did not pursue the matter further, fearing that a U.S. Supreme Court ruling that affirmed Little Rock's incremental approach would make it a model for other school systems in the nation, some of which might otherwise desegregate faster.[49]

The Blossom Plan was undermined by Governor Orval Faubus. At Faubus's instigation, Arkansas placed itself in open defiance of the Supreme Court. In November 1956, the state constitution was amended to command the state legislature to oppose "in every Constitutional manner the Un-constitutional desegregation decisions"[50] in *Brown I* and *Brown II*. In accordance with this dictate, a law was passed that relieved children from compulsory attendance at racially mixed schools.[51] Subsequently, on September 2, 1957, the day before school opened, Faubus "dispatched units of the Arkansas National Guard to the Central High School grounds and placed the school 'off limits' to colored students."[52]

Meanwhile, the home of Daisy Bates, president of the Arkansas NAACP, who had organized the nine black students in their desegregation effort, had been attacked and her life threatened. A brick was thrown through her living room window with a note attached: "Stone this time. Dynamite next."[53]

When school opened the first week of September 1957, angry whites came close to lynching one of the black students, Elizabeth Eckford.[54] In an ugly confrontation outside Central High on September 4, she was told, "No nigger bitch is going to get into our school. Get out of here!"[55] Eckford recalled, "I tried to see a friendly face somewhere in the mob. I looked into the face of a old woman, and it seemed a kind face, but when I looked at her again, she spat on me."[56]

Desperate and frightened, Eckford turned for protection to the National Guardsmen deployed by Faubus, but one of them who had let white students pass through the ranks and into the school blocked her path.[57] Other guardsmen moved toward her with raised bayonets.[58] She heard cries of "Lynch her! Lynch her!"[59] When she ran toward the bus stop she heard someone shout, "Drag her over to the tree."[60] Fortunately, two white strangers, one a *New York Times* reporter named Benjamin Fine who was covering the events, intervened and escorted her to safety.[61]

Eisenhower's efforts to negotiate Faubus's compliance with the *Brown* decisions failed, and the paratroopers of the 101st Airborne were moved into place by the end of September 1957. Within two months, the army troops had returned to their base at Fort Campbell, Kentucky.[62] But while the situation outside the high school was under control, the overall situation remained extremely tense.

According to Ernest Green, managing director of the Shearson Lehman Brothers investment firm in Washington, D.C., who was one of the Little Rock Nine, the black students were subjected to taunts and petty acts of cruelty and violence inside the school after the federal forces left. He recalled, "The problems with our lockers being constantly broken into, the [threatening] phone calls in the middle of the night to our homes, the taunts when we would drive up or the remarks made in the hallway when we were changing classes, the attempts at physical abuse in our physical education classes—all of this was constant, it was like being in a war zone, and it just didn't let up."[63]

In addition, he revealed, "We were barred physically by the school board from participating in any extracurricular activities—that was one of the conditions of our going to school there—so that I played in the band [in junior high school] but wasn't allowed to play in the band at Central. We were not allowed to attend the dances or do any of that. This was all a big taboo."[64]

Green concluded, "These were the ground rules set when we first decided that we were going to go to Central—that we would not be allowed to participate in any extracurricular activities."[65]

On February 20, 1958, the school board and superintendent went into U.S. District Court and sought postponement of their own desegregation program. "Their position in essence was that because of extreme public hostility, which they stated had been engendered largely by the official attitudes and actions of the Governor and the Legislature, the maintenance of a sound educational program at Central High School, with the Negro students in attendance, would be impossible. The Board therefore proposed that the Negro students already admitted to the school be withdrawn and sent to segregated schools, and that all further steps to carry out the Board's desegregation program be postponed for a period later suggested by the Board to be two and one-half years."[66]

The district court granted the school board's petition, finding that the continuous "chaos, bedlam and turmoil" made the situation at Central High "intolerable."[67] But the eighth circuit appeals court reversed the lower court's ruling while at the same time deferring the entire matter to the U.S. Supreme Court.

After hearing oral arguments and considering the situation at its special session in August 1958, the justices issued on September 12, 1958, a *per curiam* order, a simple ruling unaccompanied by a discussion of the legal issues raised in the case, timed to coincide with the opening of the 1958–59 school year. The *per curiam* in effect ordered that desegregation should proceed as originally planned despite the threat of violence. A full opinion with a thoroughgoing discussion of the relevant legal issues was promised "in due course."[68]

The justices were in unanimous agreement that Little Rock should proceed with desegregation notwithstanding white opposition. Clearly there were governing decisions of the Court, *Brown I* and *Brown II*. In this regard, the case was not difficult. *Brown II* had accorded local school boards a certain amount of latitude in implementing desegregation. "Traditionally," the Court had stated, "equity has been characterized by a practical flexibility in shaping remedies and by a facility for adjusting and reconciling public and private needs."[69]

For example, in considering the adequacy or sufficiency of a desegregation plan, district court judges were free to consider "the public interest."[70] The justices understood that "[o]nce a start has been made, the courts may find that additional time is necessary to carry out the ruling in an effective manner."[71]

Even Thurgood Marshall recognized as much. He conceded in an interview shortly after *Brown II* was handed down, "Some states will take longer than others. The length of time, I wouldn't predict. Mississippi, Alabama, South Carolina and Georgia will take quite a while. I don't think Virginia will take long."[72]

"But," the Court had plainly warned, "it should go without saying that the vitality of these constitutional principles cannot be allowed to yield simply because of disagreement with them."[73]

The problem, therefore, was political. The challenge would be to somehow take into account the practical limitations that confronted the Court and yet somehow word the opinion in such a way as to make it powerful and command respect.

From this perspective, the risks were as clear as the legalities, for the nation's political leadership was not in step with the Court on *Brown*. President Eisenhower had commanded a racially segregated army during World War II. Also, his West Point education did not especially lend itself to questioning the status quo, and segregation, not integration, represented the established social order, especially in the South. Evidently, the president had even gone so far as to tell a group of southern governors, "I personally think the decision [*Brown*] was wrong."[74] According to Douglas, "It was common knowledge in Washington that such were Ike's views."[75]

"There was tragedy in [Eisenhower's] attitude," Douglas wrote in his autobiography a quarter-century later, "for if he had gone to the nation on television and radio telling the people to obey the law and fall into line, the cause of desegregation would have been accelerated. Ike was a hero and he was worshipped. Some of his political capital spent on the racial cause would have brought the nation closer to the constitutional standards. Ike's ominous silence on our 1954 decision gave courage to the racists who decided to resist the decision ward by ward, precinct by precinct, town by town, and county by county."[76]

At the state level, meanwhile, what Douglas called the "racial cause" was grist for the demagogues' mill. Faubus, for example, had exploited the issue successfully. Ernest Green recalled, "Arkansas was generally regarded as a moderate southern state. The City of Little Rock had desegregated its buses without incident, had desegregated libraries and parks. The University of Arkansas had admitted a few black students to medical school and to the law school. So there was what we regarded as a general level of tolerance. That's why there was an expectation that our entrance into Central would go rather smoothly, that there wouldn't be a great deal of difficulty. So it was unexpected when Faubus called out the National Guard to prevent us from going there."

According to Green, Faubus's attitude toward African Americans had been perceived as fairly moderate. "He had been elected with a large black vote," Green explained. Moreover, Faubus "came from northern Arkansas, and the way the state is divided, the topography, is that northern Arkansas had few blacks. As you got closer to the [Mississippi River] Delta, which is Mississippi and Louisiana, you had a larger black population, and the center of the state is Little Rock, the state capital, the government—more college and university people with middle class kinds of white collar jobs. Little Rock as compared to say Jackson, Mississippi, or Birmingham, Alabama, was a fairly progressive southern city."

The problem, according to Green, was that Faubus "was being challenged in his bid for another term by a right wing segregationist. This candidate [Jim Johnson] was one that was appealing to the eastern Arkansas crowd—the planters, the farmers, the big agricultural interests that depended a lot upon fairly servile black help.

"Faubus thought he had to somehow appear to be a bigger segregationist than his opponent and that he had to hold on to a large enough white vote, which he believed was opposed to desegregation, and in that way be able to go forward as somebody who represented white concerns."

Green continued, "The numbers in Arkansas were such that the black population of the state was no more than maybe 10 percent. Arkansas has never had huge numbers of blacks. I believe it was partly the smallness of these numbers that made the Little Rock school board believe it could go forward with a fairly reasonable plan for desegregation and that it would go fairly quietly."

He went on, "The rest was a simple matter of race and racism in a southern state. Some whites saw desegregation as the doom of their lives. Plus the two Arkansas senators, both Fulbright and McClellan, signed the Southern Manifesto, so that the leadership was either silent or was vocally opposed to desegregation. There were maybe some church leaders who spoke out in favor of going ahead with it. But for the most part, all the leadership, economic as well as political, was either silent, or they were opposed."

Elsewhere, school desegregation efforts were producing mixed results. In Missouri, it proceeded almost without incident. The same could be said of West Virginia and such cities as Baltimore and Washington, D.C. But there was unrest or disturbance throughout the states that made up the Old Confederacy.

Even the army that had been sent to Little Rock was divided beneath the surface along racial lines, a reflection of society at large. Although the armed forces had been formally desegregated during the Truman administration, the soldiers of the 101st Airborne in Fort Campbell, Kentucky, some ten to 12 percent of whom were African American, rarely socialized interracially at anything other than official functions. Whites and African Americans had separate intramural athletic teams, and separate bathroom facilities existed on the base although they were no longer designated as such.

Era editions of the base newspaper, *The Screaming Eagle*, also reveal that Fort Campbell personnel routinely participated in such activities as a Hopkinsville, Kentucky, Kiwanis minstrel show at a local high school, where white singers and dancers performed in mocking blackface.

But whatever the soldiers' personal feelings or values might have been, the men and women of the 101st performed admirably in Little Rock. They did their jobs when called upon, as did the president who overcame his own reservations and sent them there to enforce the Court's order. On the night of Tuesday, September 24, 1957, the day he dispatched the troops, Eisenhower addressed the nation on television from the Oval Office to express his "sadness" over the action he was forced to take, but also the firmness of his intentions.

He declared, "In [Little Rock], under the leadership of demagogic extremists, disorderly mobs have deliberately prevented the carrying out of proper orders from a federal court....Whenever normal agencies prove inadequate to the task...the President's responsibility is inescapable....Our personal opinions about the [*Brown*] decision have no bearing on the matter of enforcement....Mob rule cannot be allowed to override the decisions of our courts....The foundation of the American way of life is our national respect for law."

During the day, the 101st kept the white rabble at bay with an overwhelming display of power and purpose, poise, discipline, and reserve. To minimize community hostility, black troops from the 101st were kept away from Central High and instead stationed at nearby Fort Chafee. To further defuse tension and resentment, the white soldiers engaged in charitable activities, such as a Halloween party sponsored by the unit for the orphans in Little Rock's St. Joseph's Orphanage.

The paratroopers' attitudes were illustrated by the Saturday morning in October when the division's 327th Airborne battle group joined in a call to prayer for guidance in fulfilling their mission in Little Rock. The October 16, 1957, edition of *The Screaming Eagle* reported that they heard Chaplain (Major) Chester Lindsey read George Washington's Prayer for the Nation, "so enduring in its appeal," as the newspaper described it, that "it might well have been written with the present crisis in mind:

'Almighty God, we make our earnest prayer that Thou wilt keep the United States in Thy holy protection, that Thou wilt incline the hearts of the citizens to cultivate a spirit of subordination and obedience to government, and entertain a brotherly affection and love for one another and for their fellow-citizens of the United States at large.'"

No one on the Court wanted a second civil war, followed by another reconstruction, during which the federal government would have to move the army in to run the South. Yet not only would backing down have been wrong, it would have reduced the Court forever to a second- or third-rate arm of government. Serious issues had been raised that ran to the very heart of the federal system. The states could not be given the power to defy the Constitution. The justices were in unanimous agreement about what needed to be done.

Warren chose not to write the opinion himself, perhaps because he wanted to demonstrate broad, continuing support for *Brown* among the other justices. Instead, he asked Brennan to write it. Given Brennan's relative inexperience, the fact that he had not been on the Court during *Brown*, and the fact that he had no particular background in civil rights or constitutional law, the assignment demonstrated the Chief's extraordinary trust in and respect for his new colleague.

Frankfurter might have been a better choice, to show solidarity among conservatives as well as liberals on the desegregation question. Black, as a southerner, might have soothed concerns that the South was somehow being singled out as a matter of regional prejudice. But whatever the reasons for the assignment, or the wisdom of it, which would be demonstrated only over time, Brennan set to work at once with the assistance of his two law clerks. One was Peter M. Fishbein, who went on to become a managing partner with the prestigious New York law firm of Kaye, Scholer, Fierman, Hays & Handler. The other was Dennis G. Lyons, later a senior partner with Arnold & Porter in Washington, D.C. Both were graduates of their boss's alma mater, Harvard Law School.

Lyons set to work compiling and recounting the procedural history of the case, which was tangled and complex, involving a host of both federal and state court rulings and numerous actions taken by state and local political entities. Fishbein devoted himself to the substantive issues. In an undated memorandum to Brennan, carefully researched but hastily written and full of typographical errors and informalities, Fishbein elaborated upon the issues as he saw them and offered a keen analysis of a range of questions.

He began by suggesting that the time might be right for the Court to revisit *Brown II* and clarify that enforcement decree's ambiguities. He wrote, "As I read the opinion in the second *Brown* case, three separate things are required of the local authorities, presumably the school boards, upon whom is [sic] placed the 'primary responsibility' for initiating and implementing integration in the local schools. They must (1) act in good faith in (2) making a 'prompt and reasonable start' toward (3) bringing about total integration with 'all deliberate speed.'"

He speculated, "I would guess that over 40 cases have been

decided in the lower federal courts since the *Brown* decision, dealing with various aspects of the integration problem. The fact that there are so many precedents and fact situations to draw upon plus the fact that the lower courts and the school boards are obviously uncertain as to what the requirements laid down in *Brown* really mean may indicate that the time has come for a further clarification of those requirements."

He reasoned, "If this could be successfully done at this time it would undoubtedly aid the lower courts as well as the many school boards which seem to honestly intend to comply with the law. This case may be an appropriate vehicle for the Court to promulgate a major opinion dealing with the problem."

Fishbein went on to discuss the problem of community resistance. He wrote, "There is language in *Brown* which indicates that local hostility is not to be considered a relevant factor in formulating a plan." He explained, "If such disagreement or hostility or community attitude is not a relevant factor, then all deliberate speed is not hard to define. If the only excuse for not effecting immediate and complete integration are [sic] such administrative ones as building facilities, transport, etc., then there is no reason why such total integration should not be completed within a few years."

He continued, "Therefore, if community hostility is not a relevant factor, a maximum limit of two or three years from the date the school board is ordered to present a [desegregation] plan would certainly be reasonable; indeed a one year delay is probably all that is necessary for this purpose."

At the same time, however, Fishbein recognized that as a practical matter, community hostility posed an inescapable stumbling block to integration. He wrote, "I think that community hostility must be considered a relevant factor in determining whether any particular plan meets the test of all deliberate speed. Otherwise many integration programs will be practically unworkable with the consequent disruptions that would come from ramming the plan down the throats of a populace that is not yet prepared to accept it."

He went on, "I don't see any reason why the process of integration should not be as slow as necessary in each area. I think the [Little Rock] school board's argument in this case [*Cooper v. Aaron*] that unduly precipitate action will ruin the educational system and leave scars and ill feelings that will delay successful integration far beyond the time that a more gradual program would take has a great deal of merit to it."

On the one hand, he asserted, "I don't see how an intelligent plan with a fair chance for success can be formulated without considering the attitude of the community." At the same time, he realized that "the great danger in recognizing community hostility as a valid reason for delaying integration is that this might encourage overt manifestations of that hostility."

He added, "This is an especially serious problem in the present case, since any delay might be interpreted as giving in to violence."

The problem for the Court then, as Fishbein saw it, was how to take community hostility or the potential for violence into account without appearing to surrender to it. His answer was to distinguish between desegregation plans at their initial stage of formulation and their subsequent stages of implementation. As he put it, "[T]aking community hostility into account when a plan is initially formulated and approved doesn't seem to encourage continued hostility as would postponing the timetable of a previously accepted plan."

The Little Rock case provided a perfect example of what Fishbein was writing about. The school board had, implicitly, taken community resistance into consideration when it formulated a plan that was to be implemented gradually. Fishbein reminded Brennan, "The Little Rock plan itself wasn't scheduled to bring about total integration until 1963 and it was approved by the district court and the court of appeals."

Even if they did not explicitly say so, he insisted, "These courts must have accepted the need to overcome community hostility as a valid reason for delaying integration, for there seems to be no other justification for the delays involved."

Fishbein saw some degree of ambiguity as beneficial. He explained, "Thus even if it is necessary to order integration at Central High School at once so as not to encourage resistance to integration, an opinion could and I believe should still state that community attitudes are relevant in the initial formulation of a plan. This would...make it impossible to define all deliberate speed with any precision. However, if the opinion made it clear that integration was to proceed as quickly as practicable and that school boards had to formulate definate [sic] plans at once with set timetables for future integration, I doubt that the process would proceed any slower than it would if hostility is not considered a relevant factor."

He concluded, "The fact must be faced that integration in some areas will not become a reality for some time no matter what this Court says, and the less friction of the kind that took place in Little Rock that develops in the process, the faster successful integration will be achieved."

Brennan took Fishbein's memorandum into consideration. Community resistance would have to be, and in fact already had been, taken into account in Little Rock and elsewhere in planning desegregation. But Brennan saw no need to make that fact explicit. The Court would sound forceful if it demanded implementation of the Little Rock school board's original Blossom Plan *now*. The fact that the plan called for gradual, rather than immediate, desegregation would at this point probably pass without notice.

Besides, Brennan could emphasize that in this particular case, the community resistance was instigated by state action. He would blame Arkansas state government officials, and rightly so, not the local school board or even the local citizenry for the delays and obstruction.

By so doing, he could write in such as way as to minimize the racial aspects of the problem, insofar as that was conceivably possible. He would frame the issues instead as a test of federal versus state power, of constitutional authority and the need to reaffirm the rule of law. To the extent that race needed to be touched on directly, he would discuss only "desegregation," not "integration," a subtle yet significant distinction in the minds of white southerners.

The property the Brennans had moved into on Dumbarton Avenue was owned by NBC news correspondent Richard Harkness, who lived in the adjacent semidetached house. One evening when Brennan was in the process of drafting his *Cooper* opinion, he had a friendly conversation with Harkness on the front porch. Harkness shared with Brennan some thoughts on his recent travels through the South. He explained to the Irish Catholic justice from New Jersey that to southerners, "desegregation" meant no longer excluding African Americans, while "integration" implied forced race-mixing, which had more unsettling connotations.

Brennan circulated a first draft of eight single-spaced pages on
September 17, 1958, prepared by the Court's print shop. Five other
drafts followed, incorporating numerous suggestions and revisions
requested by the other justices. Black, for example, considered
Brennan's original opening too flat, a dry recitation of the case's
complex legal history. He offered his own opening which he
scrawled extemporaneously in his bold and inimitable, almost
indecipherable, longhand.

Black was a powerful writer, and the passage he offered was
gripping and immediate. Brennan incorporated it almost verbatim
into the opinion, which now began, "As this case reaches us it raises
questions of the highest importance to the maintenance of our
federal system of government. It necessarily involves a claim by the
Governor and Legislature of a State that there is no duty on state
officials to obey federal court orders resting on this Court's
considered interpretation of the United States Constitution."[77]

The opening paragraph concluded, "We are urged to uphold a
suspension of the Little Rock School Board's plan to do away with
segregated public schools in Little Rock until state laws and efforts
to upset or nullify our holding in *Brown v. Board of Education* have
been further challenged and tested in the courts. We reject these
contentions."[78]

The extensive history of the case followed, punctuated with
relevant quotations from the Court's rulings in *Brown*. Then
Brennan turned to a discussion of the events in Little Rock,
declaring, "The constitutional rights of [black] respondents are not
to be sacrificed or yielded to the violence and disorder which have
followed upon the actions of the Governor and Legislature."[79]

He went on to place the blame for the disorders squarely at the
feet of state officials. He wrote, "The record before us clearly
establishes that the growth of the [School] Board's difficulties to a
magnitude beyond its unaided power to control is the product of
state action."[80]

"A State," he explained, "acts by its legislative, its executive, or
its judicial authorities. It can act in no other way. The constitutional
provision, therefore, must mean that no agency of the State, or of the
officers or agents by whom its powers are exerted, shall deny to any
person within its jurisdiction the equal protection of the laws."[81]

"In short," he went on, "the constitutional rights of children not to be discriminated against in school admissions on grounds of race or color declared by this Court in the *Brown* case can neither be nullified openly and directly by state legislators or state executive or judicial officers, nor nullified indirectly by them through evasive schemes for segregation whether attempted 'ingeniously or ingenuously.'"[82]

He equated the actions of Faubus and other Arkansas officials with treason: "No state legislator or executive or judicial officer can war against the Constitution without violating his undertaking to support it."[83]

Harlan suggested language to emphasize that justices who had recently joined the Court were as committed to *Brown* as their predecessors. Brennan at first thought that Harlan's sentiments should go without saying but eventually agreed to include the language in the final opinion. The passage read, "Since the first *Brown* opinion, three new Justices have come to the Court. They are at one with the Justices still on the Court who participated in the basic decision as to its correctness, and that decision is now unanimously reaffirmed."[84]

Brennan concluded with regard to *Brown*, "The principles announced in that decision and the obedience of the States to them, according to the command of the Constitution, are indispensable for the protection of the freedoms guaranteed by our fundamental charter for all of us. Our constitutional ideal of equal justice under law is thus made a living truth."[85]

Brennan agreed to numerous other changes as well, most of which were minor or stylistic. But overall the language was distinctly his. Frankfurter suggested, however, that all nine justices sign the opinion, instead of having just one justice speak for the entire Court. It was an unprecedented gesture, designed to lend the decision force and weight. All but Douglas agreed to it. Eventually, however, he joined with the others in what was on September 29, 1958, announced from the bench by Chief Justice Warren as the opinion of all nine men.

There would be more evasion and obstruction by Faubus and other state officials before the desegregation of Little Rock's schools would be allowed to proceed smoothly and peaceably as it eventually did. But *Cooper* was the turning point in stemming the tide of massive resistance to *Brown*. Yet it was still, to borrow another phrase from Churchill, only the beginning of the end of racial inequality.

Few were even cognizant of the extent to which racism and its effects, blatant or subtle, were entrenched in their immediate surroundings. No one even remarked on the irony of segregation at the Court itself while the Court was embroiled in desegregating the nation. During the late 1950s, African Americans who worked at the Court held only menial positions as cafeteria workers, janitors, elevator operators, or messengers who were more like the justices' personal valets. There were no black justices, law clerks, secretaries, librarians, or even guards. It was a situation that would change little until the 1970s.

But Bill Brennan at least thought about it. One evening as he left work for home he paused contemplatively in the Court's Great Hall, where an army of black maintenance people were polishing brass appointments and scrubbing the imposing marble walls. He thought of them and their lives and families in Washington, which was one of the most prejudiced and segregated cities in the United States. He hated the unfairness of their struggle.

He shrugged it off with a weary sigh, turned to Dennis Lyons, the law clerk who was about to drive him home that evening, and said under his breath, "You know, I always wonder how these people take it as well as they do."

CHAPTER 14

Outwitting the Conservatives

Judicial self-restraint which defers too much to the sovereign powers of the states and reserves judicial intervention for only the most revolting cases will not serve to enhance [James] Madison's priceless gift of "the great rights of mankind secured under this Constitution."

—Justice William J. Brennan Jr.,
The James Madison Lecture (1961)

FELIX FRANKFURTER HAD INSISTED that the *Cooper* decision be delivered in the names of all nine justices to emphasize their continued, unanimous support for desegregation. After they had agreed to do so, however, he announced that he would file his own separate concurrence in the case. According to Chief Justice Warren, Frankfurter's announcement "caused quite a sensation on the Court."[1] Justice Burton wrote in his diary that efforts by the other justices to dissuade Frankfurter proved futile. Although he "agreed not to file his separate opinion until a week or so after the Court opinion [was] filed," Frankfurter was determined to "say something more."[2]

No one understood what additional comments were needed, or why the senior justice had taken it upon himself to make them. All

151

Frankfurter offered later by way of explanation was that his opinion, "by its content and its atmosphere, was directed to a particular audience, to wit: the lawyers and the law professors of the South, and that is an audience which I was in a peculiarly qualified position to address in view of my rather extensive association, by virtue of my twenty-five years at the Harvard Law School, with a good many Southern lawyers and law professors."[3]

Brennan and Black were understandably furious. They feared that any separate opinion would undercut the solidarity the justices had gone to unprecedented lengths to project. Black drafted a short separate opinion that he and Brennan threatened to issue if Frankfurter went ahead as planned. It read, "Justices Black and Brennan believe that the joint opinion of all the Justices handed down on September 29, 1958 adequately expresses the views of this Court, and they stand by that opinion as delivered. They desire that it be fully understood that the concurring opinion filed this day by Justice Frankfurter must not be accepted as any dilution or interpretation of the views expressed in the Court's joint opinion."[4]

The chief justice, for his part, wanted Frankfurter to be ignored. According to Warren biographer Bernard Schwartz, Warren "felt that it would be unwise to issue still another opinion, particularly one that would make public the animosity toward the Frankfurter opinion."[5] The other justices agreed.[6] But Brennan and Black were determined to proceed until Harlan defused the situation with his own satirical concurrence.[7]

Harlan's satire read, "MR. JUSTICE HARLAN concurring in part, expressing a *dubitante* in part, and dissenting in part.

"I concur in the Court's opinion, filed September 29, 1958, in which I have already concurred. I doubt the wisdom of my Brother FRANKFURTER filing his separate opinion, but since I am unable to find any material difference between that opinion and the Court's opinion—and am confirmed in my reading of the former by my Brother FRANKFURTER'S express reaffirmation of the latter—I am content to leave his course of action to his own good judgment. I dissent from the action of my other Brethren in filing their separate opinion, believing that it is always a mistake to make a mountain out of a molehill. *Requiescat in pace.*"[8]

No more was said. Frankfurter's concurrence was the only separate opinion filed. Nevertheless, his decision to go forward with it marked the beginning of the decline of his influence. According to Schwartz, "Warren saw in Frankfurter's persistence in issuing the separate *Cooper v. Aaron* opinion a confirmation of an increasingly negative attitude. Until Frankfurter's retirement in 1962, the Chief displayed what even some of his law clerks characterized as 'a mild paranoia' about Frankfurter."[9]

Schwartz goes on, "Warren was, for instance, most insistent that there be a minimum of contacts between his clerks and Frankfurter, or even Frankfurter's clerks. It was more than a quip when Frankfurter asked one of Warren's clerks to come to his office, unless, of course, he was 'quarantined.'"[10]

What Brennan felt went beyond anger. He was embittered. In his view, the actions of his former law professor had done more than undermine the Court's solidarity; Frankfurter, albeit unwittingly, had given aid and comfort to the segregationists.

As might have been expected, the justices had received a lot of hate mail since the 1954 decision in *Brown.* A number of them had even had crosses burned in front of their Washington residences.[11] Since *Cooper,* Brennan had received his share of hate mail, too. One was a letter from a man named Carleton Putnam, a self-described northerner who had spent a large part of his life as a businessman in the South. Putnam claimed to have a law degree, but to be engaged in historical writing. The letter sent to Brennan, dated October 13, 1958, was reprinted in various forms in newspapers throughout the South.

Putnam seized on some of the language in Frankfurter's concurrence to attack the notion that African Americans were entitled to equal treatment under the law. For example, in addressing himself to the practice of racial segregation, Frankfurter had written, "Local customs, however hardened by time, are not decreed in heaven. Habits and feelings they engender may be counteracted and moderated. Experience attests that such local habits and feelings will yield, gradually though this be, to law and education."[12]

Putnam's response was that "the local customs in this case 'hardened by time' for a very good reason, and that while they may not, as Frankfurter says, have been decreed in heaven, they come closer to it than the current view of the Supreme Court."[13]

Putnam went on to assert the "natural inferiority" of blacks. He wrote that "the crux of this issue would seem obvious: social status has to be earned. Or, to put it another way, equality of association has to be mutually agreed to and mutually desired. It cannot be achieved by legal fiat."[14]

He went on, "Personally, I feel nothing but affection for the Negro. But there are facts that have to be faced. Any man with two eyes in his head can observe a Negro settlement in the Congo, can study the pure-blooded African in his native habitat as he exists when left on his own resources, can compare this settlement with London or Paris, and can draw his own conclusions regarding relative levels of character and intelligence or that combination of character and intelligence which is civilization. Finally he can inquire as to the number of pure-blooded blacks who have made contributions to great literature or engineering or medicine or philosophy or abstract science. (I do not include singing or athletics as these are not primarily matters of character and intelligence)."[15]

He concluded, "Nor is there any validity to the argument that the Negro 'hasn't been given a chance.' We were all in caves or trees originally. The progress which the pure-blooded black has made when left to himself, with a minimum of white help or hindrance, genetically or otherwise, can be measured today in the Congo."[16]

According to Fishbein, much of Brennan's hate mail was from "just sick people."[17] The justice, he said, would not read the letters, but his law clerks would.[18] Abraham Sofaer, another of Brennan's former clerks, recalled, however, that when he received hate letters, Brennan "would look at every one of them and, I guess, suffer."[19] This was an apt description of his reaction to Putnam's correspondence.

At the same time, however, Putnam's letter reassured him that his approach to *Cooper* had been the correct one, for it left no room for rebuttal or maneuver. He saw for the first time that there was no way to reason with white supremacists. He had been right to approach the matter as a test of will and power. He filed Putnam's letter so that he could refer to it from time to time and thereby be reminded of the un-Reconstructed nature of the enemy.

By the early 1960s, William Brennan was convinced of the need for what he called "the face of the law"[20] to change. On February 17, 1960, Hugo Black had delivered the first James Madison Lecture at New York University, named after the Founding Father who had been the principal author of the Bill of Rights. Black had used the forum to expound upon his absolutist view of the First Amendment and his belief that the Bill of Rights should apply in its entirety to the states,[21] the theory of total incorporation that he had first advanced in his dissent in *Adamson v. California*[22] in 1947.

A year later, on February 15, 1961, Brennan delivered the second James Madison Lecture.[23] His remarks reflected his maturing judicial philosophy and revealed many of the goals he had been working toward during his first five years on the Court. He was not prepared to embrace Black's absolutist First Amendment views. But his thinking was more expansive than Black's on the question of total incorporation. Not only did Brennan believe that the entire Bill of Rights should apply to the states, he felt that the states should be bound to protect freedoms beyond those enumerated in the Constitution's first eight amendments.

The due process clause of the Fourteenth Amendment to the U.S. Constitution provides that no state shall "deprive any person of life, liberty, or property, without *due process* of law." Black and Douglas defined "due process" as those rights enumerated in the Bill of Rights. But Brennan seized on a passage from Justice Frank Murphy's dissent in *Adamson* which "indicated that the door may be opened to still more"[24] rights under the due process clause.

Murphy, whose dissent had been joined by Justice Wiley Rutledge, had written, "I agree that the specific guarantees of the Bill of Rights should be carried over intact into the first section of the Fourteenth Amendment. But I am not prepared to say that the latter is entirely and necessarily limited by the Bill of Rights. Occasions may arise where a proceeding falls so far short of conforming to fundamental standards of procedure as to warrant constitutional condemnation in terms of a lack of due process despite the absence of a specific provision in the Bill of Rights."[25]

In his James Madison Lecture, Brennan asserted that the Court should apply the due process clause in accordance with Murphy's view. He allowed, "It is reason for deep satisfaction that many of the states effectively enforce the counterparts in the state constitutions of the specifics of the Bill of Rights. Indeed, some have been applied by states to an extent beyond that required of the national government by the corresponding federal guarantee."[26]

Nevertheless, he complained that "too many state practices fall far short. Far too many cases come from the states to the Supreme

Court presenting dismal pictures of official lawlessness, of illegal
searches and seizures, illegal detentions attended by prolonged
interrogation and coerced admissions of guilt, of the denial of
counsel, and downright brutality."[27]

He declared, "Judicial self-restraint which defers too much to
the sovereign powers of the states and reserves judicial intervention
for only the most revolting cases will not serve to enhance
Madison's priceless gift of 'the great rights of mankind secured
under this Constitution.' For these secure the only climate in which
the law of freedom can exist."[28]

Over the next few years, the Court moved forward with the
Bill of Rights' total incorporation. As Brennan explained years later
in an article for the *Harvard Law Review*, "It was in the years from
1962 to 1969 that the face of the law changed. Those years
witnessed the extension to the states of nine of the specifics of the
Bill of Rights; decisions which have had a profound impact on
American life, requiring the deep involvement of state courts in the
application of federal law."[29]

Brennan wrote, "The thread of this series of Bill of Rights
holdings reflects a conclusion—arrived at only after a long series of
decisions grappling with the pros and cons of the question—that
there exists in modern America the necessity for protecting all of us
from arbitrary action by governments more powerful and more
pervasive than any in our ancestors' time."[30] He called the rulings
that applied the Bill of Rights to the states "the most important of
the Warren era."[31]

By name these rulings included *Mapp v. Ohio* (1961),[32] which
applied to the states the Fourth Amendment prohibition on unreasonable searches and seizures and established the "exclusionary
rule," under which illegally seized evidence cannot be used in the
prosecution of a criminal defendant; *Robinson v. California* (1962),[33]
extending to the states the Eighth Amendment prohibition on cruel
and unusual punishment; *Gideon v. Wainwright* (1963),[34] which
required the states to provide court-appointed attorneys for indi-
gents in all criminal trials because the Sixth Amendment extends to
all criminal defendants the right to have assistance of counsel;
Malloy v. Hogan (1964),[35] binding the states to the Fifth Amendment privilege against self-incrimination; *Pointer v. Texas* (1965),[36]
which held that the Sixth Amendment right of a criminal defendant

to be confronted by the witnesses against him applied to the states; *Klopfer v. North Carolina* (1967),[37] another Sixth Amendment case, which extended to the states the right of a criminal defendant to a speedy trial; *Duncan v. Louisiana* (1968),[38] which extended to the states criminal defendants' Sixth Amendment right to a jury trial; and *Benton v. Maryland* (1969),[39] which held that the Fifth Amendment's protection against "double jeopardy" barred the states from prosecuting a criminal defendant more than once for the same crime.

Of these, *Malloy v. Hogan*[40] was written by Brennan. Delivered in 1964, *Malloy* extended to the states the Fifth Amendment's privilege against self-incrimination, overturning *Twining v. New Jersey*,[41] which had been decided in 1908. In *Twining*, the Court had held that a criminal defendant's refusal to testify in his own behalf could be used against him to infer guilt.

In *Malloy*, the state of Connecticut insisted that it was lawful to jail a suspect who refused to answer questions concerning illegal gambling in Hartford because those questions were asked in connection with a legislative inquiry, not a criminal prosecution. The defendant asserted, however, that the answers might eventually have been used to prosecute him criminally. He also pointed out that if the legislative inquiry had been conducted at the federal level, the Fifth Amendment privilege would have been available to him.

As Brennan saw it, the state's claim was that "only the core of the Self-Incrimination Clause, that is, the prohibition against use of physically coerced confessions, applied to the states, not the full clause or all of the procedural refinements applicable in federal proceedings."[42] Writing for a five-member majority, he rejected Connecticut's "watered-down"[43] version of the Fifth Amendment.

Brennan was particularly proud of *Malloy* because it represented the first time the Court had decided a case "by speaking in explicitly incorporationist terms."[44] He wrote that the "explicit articulation of the incorporation theory [in *Malloy*] clarified the reasoning of the Court's earlier decisions and advanced significantly the progress toward full nationalization [of rights]."[45] As he put it, "the Court's opinion in *Malloy* made clear that the rights and prohibitions nationalized in the past were now considered to apply to the states with full federal regalia intact."[46]

Malloy also "held profound significance for the future."[47] It laid the groundwork for the Court's subsequent landmark ruling in

Miranda v. Arizona[48] in 1966, requiring police to read apprehended suspects their rights, including their rights to remain silent or to be represented by an attorney, thereby putting an end to "decades of police coercion, by means ranging from torture to trickery."[49]

Meanwhile, Brennan pursued his effort to apply to the states rights beyond those specifically enumerated in the Bill of Rights. For example, he proceeded with patience and cunning to expand and liberalize the exercise of *habeas corpus* power by the federal courts.

"*Habeas corpus*" refers to a writ that may be issued by a court to force the release of a person from unlawful imprisonment. Its origins are traceable to the Magna Carta, signed in 1215. The issuance of the writ has no bearing on the guilt or innocence of the person whose release is sought. The object of a *habeas corpus* proceeding is merely to determine whether the person being held has been unlawfully deprived of his or her liberty without due process of law.

Article I, section 9 of the U.S. Constitution prohibits the suspension of *habeas corpus* "unless when in Cases of Rebellion or Invasion the public Safety may require it." The Judiciary Act of 1789 empowered all federal courts "to grant writs of *habeas corpus* for the purpose of an inquiry into the cause of commitment."

In 1867, Congress extended *habeas corpus* to any person claiming to be held in custody by a state in violation of the Constitution or laws or treaties of the United States.[50] According to Brennan, Congress was at that time "anticipating resistance to its Reconstruction measures and planning the implementation of the post-war constitutional Amendments"[51] designed to guarantee the rights of the freed slaves. In Brennan's view, "a remedy almost in the nature of *removal* from the state to the federal courts of state prisoners' constitutional contentions seems to have been envisaged."[52]

In other words, *habeas corpus* was to be used to prevent the unlawful jailing of African Americans and their sympathizers on trumped-up charges by the southern states in the aftermath of the Civil War. Suddenly, this purpose was again relevant and crucial in view of southern hostility to the growing civil rights movement and protesters.

By way of background Brennan explained, "Although the Act of 1867, like its English and American predecessors, nowhere defines *habeas corpus*, its expansive language and imperative tone, viewed against the background of post-Civil War efforts in Congress to deal severely with the States of the former Confederacy, would seem to make inescapable the conclusion that Congress was enlarging the *habeas* remedy as previously understood, not only in extending its coverage to state prisoners, but also in making its procedures more efficacious."[53]

To invoke *habeas corpus*, an individual "simply petitions a federal court to hear his claim that his detention by a state is a violation of federal guarantees. It avails the state nothing that the detention does no violence to state law or the state constitution. The guarantees of the federal Constitution are the higher law."[54]

The expansion of the federal courts' *habeas corpus* jurisdiction in 1867 was troublesome in two ways. First, it placed an added burden on federal courts by increasing the number of *habeas corpus* petitions. Second, it created tension and the potential for conflict between federal and state courts. State officials did not want federal judges telling them how to dispense justice in their jurisdictions.

To ease the burden and tension, the U.S. Supreme Court restricted the federal courts' *habeas corpus* power by formulating the exhaustion of state remedies doctrine. Federal courts would not consider an application for *habeas corpus* until the applicant first pursued to conclusion all remedies that might be available from the state, "including all appellate remedies in the state courts and in this Court by appeal"[55] from state court rulings. Despite the fact that a wrongfully imprisoned person might spend years in jail before all state remedies were exhausted, the Court had reaffirmed the exhaustion of state remedies doctrine as recently as 1953 in the case of *Brown v. Allen.*[56]

During the 1957–58 term, the justices heard arguments in *Irvin v. Dowd,*[57] a case that Brennan saw as an opportunity to overturn the restrictive exhaustion of state remedies rule or at least rein-terpret it more liberally. Irvin, the defendant in the case, had been convicted and sentenced to death for six murders in the state of Indiana that had aroused great indignation and drawn extensive media coverage. His *habeas corpus* petition was based on a claim that jurors had been prejudiced by the negative publicity, making it impossible for him to receive a fair trial.

Brennan prepared a lengthy draft opinion of some thirty to forty pages in which he asserted that Congress in 1867 had meant to give the federal courts broad power to release state prisoners held in violation of their federal rights. But he could persuade only three other justices—Warren, Black, and Douglas—to vote with him. Frankfurter, Harlan, Clark, and Whittaker opposed Brennan's position. The ninth justice, Potter Stewart, appointed to the Court by Eisenhower after Justice Harold Burton retired in 1958, represented the swing vote.

Stewart was born into an old, affluent family in Cincinnati, Ohio, in 1915.[58] His father served as mayor of Cincinnati[59] and also as chief judge of the Ohio state supreme court.[60] Ohio Republican Senator Robert Taft had recommended Stewart's appointment to the U.S. Court of Appeals for the Sixth Circuit, which had jurisdiction for Ohio, despite the fact that the young private attorney, who had achieved prominence as a member of the Ohio bar, was only in his late thirties.[61]

Eisenhower obliged, naming Stewart to the appellate judgeship in 1954. Subsequently, "on the basis of his record there and his high professional standing, [Ike] elevated him to the Supreme Court."[62]

As a justice, Stewart had a record that "defies easy characterization as either liberal or conservative."[63] On *habeas corpus*, he was more inclined toward the conservatives' view. Brennan saw trouble coming and plotted a different strategy. Instead of a majority opinion that broadened the federal courts' *habeas* power, he aimed simply to head off a conservative ruling that would reaffirm and thereby strengthen the existing exhaustion of state remedies doctrine.

Brennan persuaded Stewart that a narrow ruling, limited to the specific facts of the case, was all that was called for in *Irvin*. The defendant had escaped from prison while his appeal was still pending, and the Indiana state supreme court had ruled that as an escapee, he was not entitled to relief under Indiana law. The court had also stated that it did not regard the defendant's federal constitutional claims as valid. On these bases, Brennan convinced Stewart that the defendant had exhausted his state remedies.

This exhaustion having occurred, Irvin was therefore entitled, Brennan reasoned, to have the federal courts proceed with a review of his *habeas corpus* petition. Stewart agreed to concur in the result, with Brennan writing for what now became the five-member majority of the Court. But Stewart wanted it made clear that he was not voting to overturn or reinterpret the exhaustion of state remedies doctrine.

In fact, he stated as much in his short, separate concurrence, writing, "MR. JUSTICE STEWART concurs in the judgment and the opinion of the Court, with the understanding that the Court does not here depart from the principles announced in *Brown v. Allen*, 344 U.S. 443,"[64] in other words, the exhaustion of state remedies rule.

Harlan dissented. His opinion was joined by the three other conservatives—Frankfurter, Whittaker, and Clark. Frankfurter also wrote his own separate dissent. But the upshot was that while Brennan had failed to get the expansive interpretation of federal *habeas corpus* powers that he had originally sought, the continued validity of the old exhaustion of state remedies rule had been downplayed for the time being.

During the 1960–61 term, *Irvin v. Dowd*[65] was back before the Court. The defendant, Irvin, had been recaptured, and his *habeas corpus* petition had been denied by a federal district court. This time, the Supreme Court unanimously overturned the district court's denial of Irvin's *habeas corpus* petition. The state of Indiana was ordered to grant Irvin a new trial on grounds that his first trial had not been fair and impartial as required under the due process clause of the Fourteenth Amendment because of all the adverse publicity.

Again, the decision was based narrowly on the facts of the specific case. On the one hand, the exhaustion rule was not overturned, as Brennan desired. At the same time, however, justice was done without the exhaustion doctrine's being strongly affirmed.

It was not until the Court's 1963–64 term that the justices returned to the question of exhaustion of state remedies. When they did, Brennan finally got what he wanted. The composition of the Court had by that time changed. Frankfurter was gone, replaced by a liberal, Arthur J. Goldberg. Whittaker was gone as well, replaced by Byron R. White.

Consequently, in *Fay v. Noia*,[66] decided on March 18, 1963, Brennan was able to write an opinion for a 6-to-3 majority of the Court that expanded greatly the federal courts' *habeas corpus* powers. According to a former Brennan law clerk, Brennan "dusted off his original opinion in *Irvin* and it finally became the opinion of the majority."

In *Fay v. Noia*, a New York state prisoner convicted of murder in 1942 had missed the deadline for filing an appeal to the state's highest court. The U.S. District Court for the Southern District of New York had subsequently denied Noia's *habeas corpus* petition, holding that by missing the appeals deadline, he had failed to exhaust his state remedies.

The heart of the matter was that Noia's confession had been coerced, which the state admitted. The due process clause had been interpreted by the Court to prohibit the use of coerced confessions in state trials. New York's case therefore rested exclusively on Noia's failure to make timely appeal of his original conviction—in other words, on his failure to exhaust state remedies.

With regard to *habeas corpus* generally, Brennan wrote, "Although in form the Great Writ is simply a mode of procedure, its history is inextricably intertwined with the growth of fundamental rights of personal liberty. For its function has been to provide a prompt and efficacious remedy for whatever society deems to be intolerable restraints. Its root principle is that in a civilized society, government must always be accountable to the judiciary for a man's imprisonment: if the imprisonment cannot be shown to conform with the fundamental requirements of law, the individual is entitled to his immediate release."[67]

In particular regard to the exhaustion of state remedies doctrine, Brennan declared that the rule "plainly stemmed from considerations of comity rather than power."[68] He went on to state that "conventional notions of finality in criminal litigation cannot be permitted to defeat the manifest federal policy that federal constitutional rights of personal liberty shall not be denied without the fullest opportunity for plenary federal judicial review."[69] In other words, federal courts were essentially free to exercise their *habeas corpus* power as liberally as due process required.

This time around, Stewart joined Harlan and Clark in dissent. But it was too late. Congress narrowed the federal courts' *habeas corpus* powers somewhat during the 1960s in a way that was specifically intended to limit the impact of the ruling in *Fay v. Noia*. A more conservative Court narrowed those powers further during the 1970s and 1980s until finally, in 1991, *Fay v. Noia* was overruled outright.[70] But by that time the fundamental principles embodied in Brennan's opinion had remained intact and been applied by federal judges for more than a quarter-century, until a year after Brennan's retirement.

CHAPTER 15

Empowering the Suburbs: One Person, One Vote

It is not the starving urban masses who are cheated by electoral devices in the states. By and large, the chief injustice is to suburbia.

—Karl E. Meyer, in an article
for the *New Statesman* (1962)

To BILL BRENNAN, the total incorporation decisions, the rulings that applied the Bill of Rights to the states, were the most important of the Warren era, each decision a milestone on the road to realizing the full promise of due process of law for all Americans. To Earl Warren, Brennan's single most important contribution during the historic epoch over which he presided was Brennan's opinion in *Baker v. Carr,*[1] a monumental step toward achieving truly representative democracy in this country.

As *Fay v. Noia*[2] had gone beyond total incorporation by expanding the federal courts' *habeas corpus* power, *Baker v. Carr* expanded the frontiers of judicial activism by taking on the "political question" of apportionment, meaning how representatives to state legislatures and Congress are allotted among voters in the states.

Warren called it Brennan's greatest opinion because of its widespread impact. In a November 1966 article for the *Harvard Law Review*, he wrote, "Of all of them [Brennan's opinions] and without depreciating any of them, I would say that perhaps the one which is the most fundamental and which will, in the long run, most affect the lives of all the people is his historic opinion in *Baker v. Carr*. It is the foundation upon which rest all subsequent decisions guaranteeing equal weight to the vote of every American citizen from representation in state and federal government."[3]

Baker also had the effect of rendering Felix Frankfurter's philosophy of judicial restraint, or judicial abstinence, a dead letter for the time being. In fact Frankfurter's dissent in *Baker* would be the last opinion he would write before retiring from the Court.

Prior to *Baker*, the Court shied away from apportionment cases and other issues it regarded as fundamentally "political." Instead, the Court limited itself to those matters fit for "judicial" determination because they turned more on questions of law than of policy.

There was, of course, philosophical disagreement over which matters were "justiciable," meaning appropriate for the Court to address, and which were not. As Justice Douglas recalled in his autobiography, *The Court Years*, "Perhaps the deepest division in the Court in my time...concerned the 'political' question; an issue which has always plagued American law. In the federal system, Article III of the Constitution gives federal courts jurisdiction only over cases that are questions or controversies, but not every controversy presents a justiciable question. Should this country have an ambassador at the Vatican, and if so, who should be named? Which of two competing candidates should be seated by the Senate or the House? Should a law passed by Congress be approved or vetoed? Issues of that kind often present great controversies, but they are not suited for resolution from the judicial branch since, according to the Constitution, they have been entrusted to the other two branches of government for deliberation and eventual resolution."[4]

At the end of the nineteenth century, Harvard Law School dean James Bradley Thayer was an influential advocate of the philosophy of judicial restraint. This meant that Thayer was more likely than not to dub a question "political" and hence not a proper matter for the Court to consider. Thayer's thinking had a persuasive impact on Harvard Law School graduates like Oliver Wendell Holmes, who served illustriously as an associate justice of the U.S. Supreme Court from 1902 to 1932, and Felix Frankfurter.

As a young man, Frankfurter had been introduced to Holmes in Washington, D.C., sometime around 1911. Despite their age difference of some forty years, the two had struck up a friendship that lasted until Holmes's death in 1932. According to Frankfurter biographer Melvin I. Urofsky, the younger man "adored Holmes— who stood, in Frankfurter's view, for the best of Brahmin culture— and he let Holmes know his feelings."[5] Douglas believed that Frankfurter gave "special credence" to Thayer's views because Holmes adhered to them.[6]

Thayer set forth his philosophy in an article he wrote for the *Harvard Law Review* in 1893 entitled "The Origin and Scope of the American Doctrine of Constitutional Law."[7] In it, he expressed his belief that if judges interfered too frequently with the work of legislators, the citizenry would lose confidence in the courts and act to strip the judiciary of its independence. Legislators were, after all, elected; federal judges were not. Thayer therefore urged judges to defer to legislators whenever possible and refrain from overturning legislative acts on constitutional or other grounds.[8]

Quoting a passage from an 1812 decision by a South Carolina court that voiced his thinking, Thayer wrote, "The validity of the law ought not then to be questioned unless it is so obviously repugnant to the constitution that when pointed out by the judges, all men of sense and reflection in the community may perceive the repugnancy. By such a cautious exercise of this judicial check, no jealousy of it will be excited, the public confidence in it will be promoted, and its salutary effects be justly and fully appreciated."[9]

Thayer also believed that judicial restraint was desirable because it promoted civic consciousness and political awareness and involvement. As Douglas explained it, "Thayer's theory was that if a citizen could run to a court to resolve a question, the republican form of government would suffer because most citizen's complaints were better answered by the legislative branch of government, and going to the legislature would tend to promote a more active citizenry."[10]

Thayer conceded that legislators, driven by personal ambition and political expediency, were often impervious to justice. In his *Harvard Law Review* article, he wrote, "No doubt our doctrine of constitutional law has had a tendency to drive out questions of justice and right, and to fill the mind of legislators with thoughts of mere legality, of what the constitution allows. And moreover, even in the matter of legality, they have felt little responsibility; if they are wrong, they say, the courts will correct it."[11]

Nevertheless, he went on, "Under no system can the power of courts go far to save a people from ruin; our chief protection lies elsewhere."[12]

Thayer's views were frequently cited by conservative justices who sought to maintain the status quo by increasing the number and kinds of questions that were deemed "political" and hence inappropriate for the Court to review.

For example, in 1943 the Court was asked to decide in *Board of Education v. Barnette*[13] whether the state of West Virginia could lawfully compel public-school children to pledge allegiance to the flag under threat of expulsion for refusing to do so. A man named Walter Barnette and other Jehovah's Witnesses brought suit challenging the West Virginia law as an unconstitutional violation of the First Amendment's guarantee of freedom of religion. Barnette argued that the pledge violated his faith's tenet against serving gods other than the Almighty, that saluting the flag in effect amounted to idolatry.

Only three years earlier, in *Minersville School District v. Gobitis* (1940),[14] the justices had by an 8-to-1 vote upheld a similar flag-salute requirement imposed by the Minersville, Pennsylvania, school board. A challenge to that Pennsylvania requirement had been brought on behalf of Lillian and William Gobitis, sibling Jehovah's Witnesses ages twelve and ten, respectively, who had been expelled from school for refusing to take part in the flag salute.

In *Board of Education v. Barnette*, the justices reversed their ruling in *Gobitis*, the Pennsylvania case. Writing for a 6-to-3 majority in *Barnette*, Justice Robert H. Jackson did not even reach the religion question. Instead, he relied simply on the First Amendment's guarantee of freedom of speech to hold the West Virginia flag-salute statute unconstitutional. Under the free speech clause of the First Amendment, schoolchildren could not be compelled to recite the Pledge of Allegiance if, for whatever reason, they did not want to.

Frankfurter dissented, basing his argument on Thayer's theory of judicial self-restraint. Frankfurter had written the majority opinion in *Gobitis*, upholding Pennsylvania's compulsory flag salute. In *Barnette* he sought to protect West Virginia's flag-salute requirement by asserting that the entire matter was a political question that the Court was not fit to address.

Frankfurter quoted Thayer at length in his dissent, reprinting three full pages from Thayer's biography of John Marshall.[15] Marshall was the legendary chief justice whose opinion in *Marbury v. Madison*[16] in 1803 had established judicial review, the power of the Court to declare acts of Congress unconstitutional, according the judiciary a power that was unique among the world's existing systems of government. Reiterating Thayer's words, Frankfurter wrote that "there has developed a vast and growing increase of judicial interference with legislation. This is a very different state of things from what our [Founding F]athers contemplated...in framing the new [constitutional] system. Seldom, indeed, as they imagined under our system, would this great, novel, tremendous power of the courts be exerted—would this sacred ark of the covenant be taken from within the veil."[17]

Speaking for himself, Frankfurter declared, "The uncontrollable power wielded by this Court brings it very close to the most sensitive areas of public affairs. As appeal from legislation to adjudication becomes more frequent, and its consequences more far-reaching, judicial self-restraint becomes more and not less important, lest we unwarrantably enter social and political domains wholly outside our concern."[18]

He concluded, "I think I appreciate fully the objection to the [West Virginia flag salute] law before us. But to deny that it presents a question upon which men might reasonably differ appears to me to be intolerance. And since men may so reasonably differ, I deem it beyond my constitutional power to assert my view of the wisdom of this law against the view of the State of West Virginia."[19]

The *Barnette* majority was unmoved. Speaking for the Court, Jackson stated, "The very purpose of a Bill of Rights was to withdraw certain subjects from the vicissitudes of political contro-versy, to place them beyond the reach of majorities and officials and to establish them as legal principles to be applied by the courts. One's right to life, liberty, and property, to free speech, a free press, freedom of worship and assembly, and other fundamental rights may not be submitted to vote; they depend on the outcome of no elections."[20]

With regard to the right to vote, the Court had traditionally adhered to Thayer's philosophy and exercised judicial restraint even in the face of egregious and pronounced injustice. For example, the Fifteenth Amendment, ratified after the Civil War, guaranteed African Americans the right to vote. The amendment provides, "The right of citizens of the United States to vote shall not be denied or abridged by the United States or by any State on account of race, color, or previous condition of servitude." Yet throughout the South and elsewhere, African Americans were commonly turned or coerced away from the polls.

Just after the turn of the century, the Court heard arguments in *Giles v. Harris* (1902),[21] a case involving a black Alabaman named Giles who had brought suit in federal court on his own behalf "and on behalf of more than five thousand negroes, citizens of the county of Montgomery, Alabama, similarly situated and circumstanced as himself."[22] Giles's objective was to persuade the federal courts to compel the county board of registrars to permit African Americans to register to vote.

Writing for a 6-to-3 majority, Justice Oliver Wendell Holmes rejected Giles's plea that the Court take up the matter. Instead, Holmes pronounced black disenfranchisement throughout the South a political question that the Court was unfit to address. He declared, "The traditional limits of proceedings in equity have not embraced a remedy for political wrongs."[23] The term *equity*, as Holmes used it, referred to general principles of justice and fairness traditionally applied by courts when explicit legal remedies appear to be inadequate.

Holmes, whose legacy as a justice is generally associated with liberal views, went on to emphasize that "equity cannot undertake now, any more than it has in the past, to enforce political rights"[24] such as the right to vote.

In his concluding paragraph, Holmes asserted that Giles's complaint "imports that the great mass of the white population intends
to keep the blacks from voting. To meet such an intent, something
more than ordering the plaintiff's name to be inscribed upon the
lists of 1902 will be needed. If the conspiracy and the intent exist, a
name on a piece of paper will not defeat them. Unless we are prepared to supervise the voting in that State by officers of the court, it
seems to us that all that the plaintiff could get from equity would be
an empty form. Apart from damages to the individual, relief from a
great political wrong, if done, as alleged, by the people of a State and
the State itself, must be given by them or by the legislative and
political department of the government of the United States."[25]

In other words, under the guise of exercising judicial self-
restraint, the Court refused to involve itself in the struggle for black
voting rights. Instead, according to Holmes, African Americans
should turn to Congress, to the White House, or to the very people
of Alabama who were repressing them for enforcement of their
constitutional rights.

Douglas wrote years later that Holmes did the nation "a grave
injustice" with his decision in *Giles*.[26] As Holmes saw it, the denial
of black voting rights was a political question and as such called for
a political, not a judicial, remedy. "Yet imagine!" wrote Douglas.[27]
"What 'political' remedies did black people have in Alabama at the
turn of the century? The votes were with the whites, and control
was in the hands of the anti-black political machine. The voices of
blacks were muted, for they had no audience. The whites put them
in their 'proper' place, and kept them there. They were citizens by
reason of the Fourteenth Amendment, but their citizenship was
second-class."[28]

Douglas conceded, "There are, of course, as Holmes said, many
'political' issues which are left either for the executive or the
legislative exclusively, issues in which the judiciary has no hand.
But the protection of the right to vote, expressly conferred by the
Constitution, is grist for the judicial mill, as dozens upon dozens of
cases illustrate."[29]

But the "dozens of cases" to which Douglas referred came later,
not at first. With regard to apportionment, judicial abstinence was
by and large the rule. Douglas recalled, "Some judges, notably
Frankfurter, held that apportionment of votes was not a fit business

for the federal courts. The area was dubbed a 'political thicket' which the federal courts should not enter."[30]

The result was that by the early 1960s, most of the nation's state legislatures and congressional districts were grossly malapportioned, "weighted" in favor of rural voters. Douglas explained, "State legislatures frequently allowed what is known in England as 'rotten boroughs' to be created—for example, giving a district that was sparsely populated as much representation as a heavily populated district, or giving a rural district as much voting power as an urban district with twenty times the population of the rural district."[31]

In fact, tens of millions of Americans were for all practical intents and purposes disenfranchised by malapportionment all across the land. In an article entitled "Malapportionment and Judicial Power: The Supreme Court's Decision in *Baker v. Carr,*" published in the fall of 1962, Yale law professor Thomas I. Emerson offered notable examples of what he called "extreme distortion."[32]

According to Emerson, Los Angeles County in California had one state senator for its 6,038,771 people, the same as another district with a population of only 14,294.[33] Meanwhile in Connecticut, the city of Hartford's 162,178 residents elected two state representatives.[34] So did the town of Colebrook, Connecticut, with a population of only 791.[35]

Emerson pointed out that the way California was malapportioned, a majority of the state senate was elected by only 10.7 percent of the voting population.[36] In Connecticut, 12 percent of the voters elected a majority of state representatives.[37] Overall, there were thirteen states in which a majority of the state legislature was elected by a third or less of the voting populace, and only six states in which the majority of the legislature was elected by 40 percent or more of the electorate.[38]

Emerson also found that the population of congressional districts varied widely. In Michigan, for example, one congressional district encompassed 802,994 people, another only 177,431.[39] Overall, the largest congressional district was twice as large as the smallest in more than half the states.[40]

Another publication, the *Virginia Law Weekly,* reported similar findings in its April 12, 1962, edition. For example, Schuyler and Suffolk counties in New York, with populations of 15,044 and 268,530, respectively, were each represented by one member in the state assembly. More astounding was that Vermont had not reapportioned since joining the Union in 1793. As a result, the city of Burlington's 135,531 residents had no more representation in the state legislature than did the 36 people who lived in the tiny hamlet of Victory.

The *Virginia Law Weekly* also reported that control of the state senate could be won by 8 percent of the voters in Nevada, 16 percent of Montana's electorate, 18 percent of those voting in Rhode Island, and 19 percent of New Jersey voters. A mere 25 percent of Alabama voters could elect a majority in both state houses, 12 percent a majority of the legislature in California, and between 12 and 15 percent of the voters could determine control of the legislature of Florida.

The *Virginia Law Weekly* concluded that in recent years "inequality" between rural and urban voters had increased as more people moved to the cities and suburbs. As one commentator observed, "In state after state, the problem is essentially the same. The country cousins have become a minority, but refuse to yield a fair share of legislative power to the big metropolitan areas."[41]

Emerson asserted that the inequality came at the expense of urban and suburban interests, and that because of the overrepresentation of rural voters, government had become "less responsive to the progressive forces in the nation."[42] He wrote, "Housing, welfare and allocation of tax funds are examples of the kind of issues involved. The impact spreads to other problems. Thus policies in the field of race relations, minority groups being best organized and strongest in urban areas, are affected by the distortion of representation."[43]

In addition, malapportionment at the state level shaped national policy and debate. Emerson estimated that rural areas had twenty-five to thirty more seats in the U.S. Congress than they were entitled to by population.[44] Under the congressional seniority system, this overrepresentation guaranteed rural constituencies key committee chairmanships.[45] The overrepresentation also assured rural interests more influence within state party organizations that helped set the national political parties' agendas and priorities.[46]

Douglas also tended to view malapportionment as primarily a race problem. Black political power was concentrated in the cities, especially in the North. The underrepresentation of urban areas therefore minimized black political influence. To Douglas, malapportionment was just a device used to make African American votes count for less.

Nevertheless, the Court had once again persisted in being part of the problem, rather than part of the solution. In *Colgrove v. Green*,[47] decided in 1946, Illinois voters had challenged the way congressional districts were drawn under a state law. They argued that numerical inequalities among the districts violated various provisions of the U.S. Constitution.

By a 4-to-3 vote, the Court dismissed the complaint. Frankfurter, in an opinion joined by Justices Stanley Reed and Harold Burton, concluded that the Illinois apportionment was not a justiciable issue, being "of a peculiarly political nature and therefore not meet for judicial determination."[48] Justice Wiley Rutledge concurred in the result, creating a majority.

Black, Douglas, and Murphy dissented, contending that the Illinois apportionment violated the equal protection clause of the Fourteenth Amendment. Justice Jackson, who was in Europe serving as chief prosecutor at the Nuremberg tribunal, did not participate in the case. There was no ninth vote because Chief Justice Harlan Stone, recently deceased, had not yet been replaced.

After *Colgrove*, it was common for the Court to decline to hear suits challenging apportionments. Yet Douglas insisted that a true majority of the Court had "never endorsed" the views expressed by Frankfurter in *Colgrove*;[49] only two other justices had actually joined Frankfurter's opinion in that case.

By the 1960–61 term, the justices were ready to confront the apportionment question squarely. They voted 5 to 4 in conference to hear oral arguments in *Baker v. Carr*,[50] a case "which challenged the failure of Tennessee to reapportion state legislators among the counties despite substantial population changes."[51] The justices heard oral arguments in the matter during the 1960–61 term but reserved judgment, holding the case over for reargument during the 1961–62 term.

The facts of the case presented a situation that was typical of what could be found elsewhere across the country. Under Tennessee's constitution, the state was to have been reapportioned after each decennial census, with voting districts redrawn to reflect population changes. But Tennessee officials had not reapportioned the state since 1901.

Meanwhile, Tennessee's population had increased from 2,020,616 to 3,567,089 between 1901 and 1960, and the number of voters had gone from 487,380 to 2,092,891.[52] Consequently, the voting populations of the various state legislative districts varied widely. For example, six rural counties with voting populations of fewer than 7,000 people elected one representative each.[53] By contrast, Shelby County, where the city of Memphis was located, had just eight representatives for its 312,345 voters, an average of 39,345 voters per state representative.[54] Similarly, Hamilton County, which contained Chattanooga, had just three representatives for its 131,971 voters, a ratio of one representative per 43,990 voters.[55]

Wide population discrepancies were reflected in the Tennessee state senate as well. The smallest senate district comprised 25,190 voters; the largest, which included Chattanooga, had 131,971.[56]

Overall, 40 percent of Tennessee's voters elected two-thirds of the state house of representatives, whereas 37 percent of the voters elected almost two-thirds of the state senate.[57]

In 1959, a Tennessee voter named Baker, along with a number of other residents of five counties that were allegedly underrepresented in the state legislature, sued Joseph Cordell Carr, Tennessee's secretary of state, and other state officials in federal court in Nashville. Baker's suit was joined by the mayor of Nashville and by the cities of Chattanooga and Knoxville, on behalf of those cities' residents.

The plaintiffs claimed that as a result of Tennessee's failure or refusal to reapportion, sparsely populated rural voting districts were able to elect as many as or more state representatives than their more populous urban counterparts. This, the plaintiffs alleged, debased or devalued their votes in violation of the Fourteenth Amendment's equal protection clause and other constitutional provisions.

It takes four votes in conference to commit the full Court to hearing oral arguments in a particular case. Stewart, who had firmly established himself as the Court's "swing vote" on many significant issues by the time *Baker* reached the Court, had voted with the liberals—Warren, Black, Douglas, and Brennan—in favor of hearing the case. But it was not at all clear whether he was actually prepared to overturn Tennessee's apportionment. His vote was "tentative, dependent on whether thorough research and close analysis of the cases would disclose that the question was not foreclosed by prior decisions."[58]

According to Douglas, Stewart wanted to know whether past decisions had established firmly that apportionment was a political question and hence not justiciable. If they had, then Stewart was inclined to follow those precedents and leave the status quo intact, especially during such "turbulent times" and with regard to such a "controversial" issue.[59]

Warren decided initially that the best way to hold Stewart's vote and thus carry the day for the liberals was to assign Stewart to write the majority opinion. The chief justice reasoned that Stewart might be more comfortable with involving the Court in apportion-ment if he could himself set the parameters of that involvement. The result might be half a loaf, a majority opinion drawn more narrowly than the liberals would have liked. But the liberals might have to settle for that result for the time being because without Stewart's fifth vote, any movement forward was impossible.

According to Douglas, Warren ultimately changed his mind and assigned the opinion to Brennan "on the theory that if anyone could convince Stewart, Brennan was the one."[60] In fact, however, it was Douglas who persuaded Warren to assign the opinion to Brennan, something Douglas had evidently forgotten by the time he wrote his memoirs.

Brennan's case files in the Library of Congress include an undated, handwritten exchange between him and Douglas on a 3″ by 4″ piece of paper typical of those passed between justices on the bench during oral arguments. Brennan wrote, "Bill, The Chief told me this morning he's giving me #6, Baker v. Carr & that your view expressed to him yesterday had decided him. Thanks so much."[61]

Douglas replied on the same piece of paper, "He was going to give it to Potter. But I urged him to talk first with you."[62]

The opinion Brennan eventually produced, after numerous drafts incorporating suggestions and modifications offered by various Brethren, was most aptly described by Douglas as "long, scholarly but tedious."[63] In final form, it ran fifty-five pages, including an appendix. However, it accomplished the liberals' primary mission, which was to roll away the stone of the political question doctrine that had been inhibiting the Court's considera-tion of apportionment and other voting rights matters. In a memo-randum to Warren, Black, and Douglas dated January 27, 1962, Brennan proclaimed proudly that he had managed "finally to dispel the fog of another day produced by Felix's opinion in *Colgrove v. Green*."[64]

The district court judge in *Baker* had relied on the Court's holding in *Colgrove* to dismiss the plaintiffs' case. Without overrul-ing it explicitly, Brennan worked around *Colgrove* in his opinion in *Baker* by saying simply that *Colgrove* had been "misinterpreted" by the district court.[65]

He wrote, "We understand the District Court to have read the cited cases as compelling the conclusion that since the appellants sought to have a legislative apportionment held unconstitutional, their suit presented a 'political question' and was therefore nonjusti-ciable. We hold that this challenge to an apportionment presents no nonjusticiable 'political question.' The cited cases do not hold the contrary."[66]

He went on, citing precedent, "Appellants' claim that they are being denied equal protection is justiciable, and if 'discrimination is sufficiently shown, the right to relief under the equal protection clause is not diminished by the fact that the discrimination relates to political rights.'"[67]

Brennan then proceeded to redefine what he referred to as the "contours" of the political question doctrine.[68] In effect, he rewrote the doctrine more to his liking, reducing the number of subjects that should be considered beyond the purview of the Court because they are political.

In Brennan's view, the only political questions that the Court need shy away from were those involving the constitutional separa-tion of powers among the three branches of the federal government. In other words, the Court should not address matters specifically assigned either to the Congress or to the president by the Constitu-tion. But he reserved to the Court the power to determine whether a particular subject had been assigned by the Constitution to another branch.

For example, foreign relations are generally considered to be primarily within the domain of the president. Similarly, relations

with the Native American tribes are principally ascribed to Congress. Yet in Brennan's view, the Court need not show blind
deference to the other branches even in these areas. Instead, the
Court should look at the facts of each case to determine whether
judicial intervention is appropriate.

He wrote, "The doctrine of which we treat is one of 'political
questions,' not one of 'political cases.' The courts cannot reject as
'no law suit' a bona fide controversy as to whether some action
denominated 'political' exceeds constitutional authority. The cases
we have reviewed show the necessity for discriminating inquiry
into the precise facts and posture of the particular case, and the
impossibility of resolution by any semantic cataloguing."[69]

By these standards, *Baker v. Carr* was not a hard case for
Brennan. It was clearly within the Court's prerogative to decide. He
wrote, "The question here is the consistency of state action with the
Federal Constitution. We have no question decided, or to be
decided, by a political branch of government coequal with this
Court. Nor do we risk embarrassment of our government abroad, or
grave disturbance at home if we take issue with Tennessee as to the
constitutionality of her action here challenged. Nor need the
appellants, in order to succeed in this action, ask the Court to enter
upon policy determinations for which judicially manageable standards are lacking. Judicial standards under the Equal Protection
Clause are well developed and familiar...."[70]

Brennan went on, "We conclude that the complaint's allegations
of a denial of equal protection present a justiciable constitutional
cause of action upon which appellants are entitled to a trial and a
decision. The right asserted is within the reach of judicial protection under the Fourteenth Amendment."[71]

In his January 27, 1962, memo to Warren, Black, and Douglas,
Brennan had expressed confidence in being able to hold Stewart's
vote. He had written, "Enclosed is the proposed opinion in *Baker v.
Carr*, which Potter Stewart tells me entirely satisfies him."[72]
Douglas recalled, "When he [Brennan] finished the first draft, he
showed it to Stewart, who approved; and there was a broad Irish
grin on his face when he told me the fifth vote was secure."[73]

The fact was that Brennan knew how to appeal to Stewart's
moderate Republican instincts, for Brennan understood the demo-
graphic implications of the case better than his colleagues. Douglas

was wrong. Apportionment was *not* fundamentally a race issue, despite its racial overtones. Instead, what *Baker* was really all about was empowering the white, suburban middle class.

The nineteenth-century British historian and Whig statesman Thomas Macauley was convinced that America's democratic system of government would one day lead this nation to ruin. He was contemptuous of the poor, whom he regarded as incompetent and untrustworthy. Yet he foresaw the day when America's system of majority rule would bring the poor to power, displacing the rich, whom he regarded as the only class truly capable of governing properly.

In 1857, Macauley had expressed his views in a letter to an American acquaintance. "Your Constitution is all sail and no anchor," he warned.[74] "I cannot help foreboding the worst. For with you the majority is the government, and has the rich, who are always a minority, absolutely at its mercy."[75]

He went on, "The day will come when, in the state of New York, a multitude of people, none of whom has had half a dinner, will choose a legislature. Is it possible to doubt what sort of legislature will be chosen?"[76]

In an April 6, 1962, article for the *New Statesman*, Karl E. Meyer observed that the modern era had given "a fresh twist" to the problem that Macauley had anticipated.[77] As Meyer put it, "It is not the starving urban masses who are cheated by electoral devices in the states. By and large, the chief injustice is to suburbia, where, if only half a dinner is eaten, it is for reasons of dieting."[78]

Brennan expressed similar views to Stewart. As a former South Orange, New Jersey, suburbanite, Brennan was aware that suburban affluence bred liberal social views. The modern suburbanite of the early 1960s was apt to be better educated and hence more enlightened than his working-class forebears. Yet the Republican Party, especially the moderate wing of the party that had produced Stewart, was clearly making suburban inroads. The modern suburbanite of the early 1960s was as likely to be a Republican as a Democrat. Brennan saw to it that none of this thinking was lost on his Republican colleague from Ohio. In the end, however, he could not keep Stewart from writing separately and more narrowly than did Brennan.

For Brennan, the great irony was that Stewart's vote proved

marginal anyway. At the Friday conference at which the decision in *Baker* was cleared for release the following Monday, Clark announced unexpectedly that he would go along with the majority's result.[79] Douglas recalled, "Without talking to anyone, he [Clark] had changed his mind and written a short concurrence, which, if it had happened earlier, would have made Brennan's long, scholarly but tedious opinion unnecessary,"[80] for much of Brennan's writing and research had been designed to placate Stewart.

In other words, the liberals did not need Stewart. With Clark on board, they had five votes. With both Stewart and Clark concurring, the result was a 6-to-2 victory. But only Warren, Black, and Douglas actually joined Brennan, making his a plurality rather than a majority opinion. Whittaker took no part in the consideration of the case.

Frankfurter, joined by Harlan, dissented eloquently and at length. He wrote some sixty-four pages. He labeled the majority's action a "massive repudiation of the experience of our whole past"[81] and reiterated his philosophy of judicial restraint. He also asserted that how states apportioned themselves was not properly the federal courts' business. He insisted, "Apportionment battles are overwhelmingly party or intra-party contests. It will add a virulent source of friction and tension in federal–state relations to embroil the federal judiciary in them."[82]

In addition to joining Frankfurter, Harlan issued his own strongly worded dissent. In it, he contended that Tennessee's apportionment was in fact rational. Conceding, however, that his views had failed to carry the day, he concluded with his own impassioned plea for judicial restraint. He wrote, "Those observers of the Court who see it primarily as the last refuge for the correction of all inequality or injustice, no matter what its nature or source, will no doubt applaud this decision and its break with the past. Those who consider that continuing national respect for the Court's authority depends in large measure upon its wise exercise of self-restraint and discipline in constitutional adjudication will view the decision with deep concern."[83]

Critics of Brennan's opinion complained because he ordered no specific measures taken to improve the predicament of the Tennessee voters. Instead he left it to the district court to formulate a satisfactory remedy based on evidence to be presented at a trial.

Clark in his concurrence offered at least one way in which the Court could have acted to rectify the problem. He suggested, "One plan might be to start with existing assembly districts, consolidate some of them, and award the seats thus released to those counties suffering the most egregious discrimination."[84]

In subsequent rulings, however, the Court elaborated more fully on what was required in order for an apportionment to pass constitutional muster. The six so-called "reapportionment cases" followed *Baker*, involving Alabama,[85] New York,[86] Maryland,[87] Virginia,[88] Delaware,[89] and Colorado.[90] All were argued before the Court on November 13, 1963, and decided on June 15, 1964. "These cases effectively declared the apportionment of every state legislature unconstitutional."[91]

It was Douglas who actually coined the phrase "one person, one vote." He used it in writing for the majority of the Court in *Gray v. Sanders*,[92] decided in 1963. In that case, the Court by an 8-to-1 vote, with Harlan dissenting, declared unconstitutional Georgia's apportionment system under which primary elections for statewide offices and the U.S. Congress were weighted against urban areas.

Douglas wrote, "The conception of political equality from the Declaration of Independence, to Lincoln's Gettysburg Address, to the Fifteenth, Seventeenth, and Nineteenth Amendments can mean only one thing—one person, one vote."[93] *Gray* "proved to be the jurisprudential steppingstone between *Baker v. Carr* (1962) and the 1964 reapportionment cases."[94]

Writing for the Court in the Alabama apportionment case, *Reynolds v. Sims* (1964),[95] Chief Justice Warren built upon the foundation that Brennan and Douglas had laid in *Baker* and *Gray*, respectively. In *Reynolds*, Warren established that state legislative districts should be "as nearly of equal population as is practicable,"[96] based on the most recent decennial census. Essentially this became the rule for the apportionment of congressional districts as well.

Warren went on to issue his own forceful response to the conservatives' repeated calls for judicial restraint in the apportionment area. He declared, "We are cautioned about the dangers of entering into political thickets and mathematical quagmires. Our answer is this: a denial of constitutionally protected rights demands judicial protection; our oath and our office require no less."[97]

According to Douglas, *Baker v. Carr* marked "the beginning of the end of America's 'rotten boroughs.' Thus was the bugaboo of the 'political' question put to rest."[98] By the end of the 1960s, thirty-six states had reapportioned either voluntarily or under court order, making "one person, one vote" a reality nationwide.[99]

But as momentous as his opinion in *Baker v. Carr* was, it is not the decision for which Brennan is best remembered. His most famous opinion would not come until two years later, in 1964, in the case of *New York Times v. Sullivan*.[100] With his opinion in *Sullivan*, William Brennan would affix his signature to the U.S. Constitution as indelibly as those of the Founding Fathers.

CHAPTER 16

Obscenity

Congress shall make no law respecting an establishment of religion, or prohibiting the free exercise thereof; or abridging the freedom of speech, or of the press; or the right of the people peaceably to assemble, and to petition the Government for a redress of grievances.

—the First Amendment

JUSTICE BRENNAN WAS ASKED by interviewer Donna Haupt in 1989 whether he had a "favorite" part of the Constitution. He replied, "The First Amendment I expect. Its enforcement gives us this society. The other provisions of the Constitution really only embellish it."[1]

Given these sentiments, it is entirely fitting that Brennan is best remembered for his opinions that expounded upon and expanded what he called the First Amendment's "cherished rights of mind and spirit—the freedoms of speech, press, religion, assembly, association and petition for redress of grievances."[2] Many of these rulings literally shaped modern American society. For example, his opinion in 1957 in the obscenity case *Roth v. United States*[3] launched the sexual revolution. And his most famous opinion, *New York Times v. Sullivan*,[4] decided in 1964, not only made freedom of the press a reality, it ensured the success of the civil rights movement.

Looking back on his career for an article by Nat Hentoff for the March 12, 1990, edition of *The New Yorker* magazine, Brennan recalled sardonically, "For sixteen years it fell to me to write most of

182

the obscenity opinions here. They were usually assigned to me. I won't say why but they were."[5]

Prodded by Hentoff to elaborate, Brennan speculated that the cases had been given to him because "nobody else wanted to have anything to do with them."[6]

Hugo Black and William O. Douglas certainly did not. They wanted no part of the Court's acting as censor of books and movies. Black's view as to the absolute nature of the First Amendment was clear. His belief, shared by Douglas, was that the amendment barred *any* governmental interference with free expression. Both he and Douglas were adamant that the First Amendment's protections applied not only to political ideas but also to anything which might be considered obscene by the government.

Brennan was never an absolutist. Instead he developed his own pragmatic approach to applying the First Amendment. Initially his goal was to restrict the proliferation of sexually explicit material. He believed that certain kinds of speech simply did not merit the Constitution's protection and that obscenity was one of them.

The other justices' views varied. What they shared was a common conviction that it was somehow within the government's power to regulate the *obscene* or *pornographic*. But they were unable to formulate precise definitions of what terms like "obscenity" or "pornography" encompassed or, for that matter, the degree to which a publication or movie had to be obscene before the government could act.

They were also undecided about how far the government should go when it did act. Clearly the First Amendment did not protect *all* speech. No one had the right to scream "Fire!" in a crowded theater when in fact there was no fire, inciting a false panic. Nor was there a right to inform the enemy of the date the next troop ship sailed, or to commit libel or perjury. Some sorts of speech were punishable by the government in spite of the First Amendment.

And yet freedom of expression was embedded deeply in the American revolutionary consciousness. The concept was "rooted in classical writings of Western civilization, such as John Milton's *Aeropagitica* and John Stuart Mill's *On Liberty*,"[7] and freedom of expression had already been provided for in the constitutions of ten of the fourteen states that had ratified the U.S. Constitution in 1792.[8]

But cherished and deep-rooted though they were, little more than lip service was paid to First Amendment freedoms during America's first century and a half under the Constitution. As early as 1798, less than a decade after the Constitution was ratified, Congress, fearing a possible invasion by Napoleon, passed the Alien and Sedition acts aimed at stifling domestic dissent, which President John Adams believed was being instigated mostly by Irish, French, and English immigrants.[9] Among other things, the Sedition Act made it a crime to criticize government officials "in a manner intending to hold them up to public ridicule and erode their authority."[10]

The Sedition Act expired by its own terms two years after it was enacted, and when Thomas Jefferson came to power in 1801 he pardoned those still in prison for violating the law, and Congress repaid the fines levied against the offenders. But no act of Congress was struck down by the Supreme Court on First Amendment grounds until the 1960s.[11]

Meanwhile, it was not until 1925 that the Court decided that the First Amendment's free speech clause was even enforceable against the states.[12] The other First Amendment freedoms—of press, religion, assembly, and association—were not thoroughly incorporated, meaning applied in their entirety to the states, until the Warren Court era.[13]

No justice prior to Hugo Black had ever suggested that the First Amendment should be taken literally. Individual justices on occasion wrote expansively and with stirring eloquence about the sanctity of the freedoms that the First Amendment enshrined. But in reality the amendment rarely shielded from persecution or suppression those who expressed unpopular or controversial ideas. During the latter half of the twentieth century, the McCarthy era was a prime and blatant example of this sad fact.

But what was obscene? Were all portrayals or discussions of sex obscene? Was there a difference between sex and obscenity? Between obscenity and pornography? Suppose only part of a book or movie was obscene. Should the entire text or film be banned?

Furthermore, assuming obscenity could be defined, could it be restricted in such a way as to ban obscenity only, without also restricting access to socially valuable ideas? Could obscenity guidelines be formulated in such a way as to keep censors from banning unorthodox or politically unpopular works under the guise of regulating obscenity?

These were the kinds of questions the Court faced in the late 1950s. By that time, it had become abundantly clear that the lower courts needed some sort of guidance as to the relationship between obscenity and First Amendment freedom, for entirely too many criminal convictions for possessing or distributing obscene materials were based on works of obvious literary value—were, in fact, based on some of the world's great books.[14]

Titles that had been banned as obscene in various parts of the United States included *An American Tragedy* by Theodore Dreiser, *Antic Hay* by Aldous Huxley, *Ulysses* by James Joyce, *Elmer Gantry* by Sinclair Lewis, *All Quiet on the Western Front* by Erich Maria Remarque, *Casanova's Homecoming* by Arthur Schnitzler, *Strange Fruit* by Lillian Smith, and *Memoirs of Hecate County* by Edmund Wilson.[15] Something had to be done, but what?

Warren biographer Bernard Schwartz has asserted that much of the "confusion," the divergence of opinion among the justices in the field of obscenity, resulted from the fact that Earl Warren "did not play his usual leadership role."[16] According to Schwartz, "Warren was ambivalent in obscenity cases. He recognized the relationship of even the least deserving forms of expression to the First Amendment. At the same time, he could not overcome his personal abhorrence of pornography and what he called smut-peddlers."[17]

When pressed once by his law clerks to explain how he could be so liberal on race and other controversial issues but so puritanical in regard to sex, the devoutly Baptist chief justice replied, "You boys don't have any daughters yet."[18] He was subsequently quoted by *Newsweek* as telling a colleague who showed him a pornographic work, "If anyone showed that book to my daughters, I'd have strangled him with my own hands."[19]

As he had done with so many of the other complex and divisive issues confronting the Court, Warren assigned Brennan the job of writing most of the obscenity decisions. He knew that obscenity offended Brennan's Catholic sensibilities. He was confident that if anyone could figure out how to strike the proper balance between First Amendment freedoms and society's need to protect itself from the "smut-peddlers," it was Brennan. And he knew that whatever Brennan wrote would stand up intellectually.

Roth v. United States[20] was Brennan's first major obscenity opinion. Hentoff wrote in 1990 that Brennan's opinion in *Roth* "established him as the Court's spokesman on a complex, emotional issue [obscenity] that was then—as it is now—intently followed by religious groups, civil libertarians, politicians, complaining constituents, book publishers, writers, and movie producers."[21] The justices considered *Roth* during the Court's 1956–1957 term together with a companion case, *Alberts v. California*. Brennan's opinion covered both cases and was delivered on June 24, 1957.

Samuel Roth was "an old-time New York pornographer,"[22] the personification of what Warren called a "smut-peddler." He had been convicted of mailing obscene advertisements and an obscene book. Article I, section 8 of the Constitution gave Congress the power to "establish Post Offices and Post Roads"—the U.S. Post Office—and the Supreme Court had in 1877 decided that this included the power to regulate what was sent through the mail.[23] Under the federal obscenity law, nothing could be mailed that was "obscene, lewd, lascivious, or filthy."[24]

Over the years, postmasters general had at one time or another prohibited the mailing of everything from D. H. Lawrence's *Lady Chatterley's Lover* to *Esquire* magazine.[25] Appealing his conviction, Roth argued that the federal obscenity statute violated the part of the First Amendment which provides that "Congress shall make no law...abridging the freedom of speech, or of the press."[26]

In *Alberts*, the companion case, the Court considered David Alberts's appeal of his conviction under California law for possessing and advertising for sale material that was "obscene or indecent."[27] Alberts's argument was essentially the same as Roth's—namely, that the California obscenity law violated the First Amendment, which had been incorporated and applied to the states under the Fourteenth Amendment's due process clause.

Historically, the individual states had since the early nineteenth century routinely barred obscene exhibitions or prohibited the possession, sale, or distribution of obscene materials.[28] In fact, as a New Jersey state supreme court justice, Brennan had in 1953 acknowledged in the case of *Adams Theatre Co. v. Keenan*[29] that the First Amendment to the U.S. Constitution did not protect obscenity.

The *Adams Theatre Co.* case was an appeal by a Newark man who had been denied a license to open a burlesque house. Brennan overturned the denial of the license, reasoning that burlesque as a form of theatrical entertainment need not necessarily be obscene, and there was no evidence that the performances to be offered would in fact be objectionable on those grounds. He nonetheless stated clearly that First Amendment protections did not extend to "speech which is outrightly lewd and indecent."[30]

Warren was right: Brennan was disdainful of sexually explicit material, an attitude attributable in part to his fastidious father, who had been a prude. As public-safety director of Newark, New Jersey, Bill Sr. had gone so far as to try to block the showing of a film distributed by the U.S. Public Health Service to educate the public about sexual hygiene.[31] More significant than his father's influence, however, was, as Warren suspected, that of the Catholic Church.

On the one hand, Brennan believed strongly in the separation of church and state, as he had stated during his Senate confirmation hearing. In fact, his mammoth, seventy-four-page concurring opinion in *Abington School District v. Schempp*,[32] decided in 1963, still stands as one of the most powerful articulations of the idea that a wall separating church and state should be not only maintained but also kept high.

At the same time, however, his "separationist" views did not keep him from using religious tenets and canon law doctrine to inform, to supplement, his understanding of the Constitution. Nowhere was this more evident than in his decisions in the field of obscenity.

The religion, or establishment, clause of the First Amendment consists of the first ten words of the Bill of Rights. They read, "Congress shall make no law respecting an establishment of religion." Using the establishment clause as the basis for its ruling, the Court had outlawed school prayer in *Engel v. Vitale*,[33] decided on June 25, 1962. A year later the Court in effect used *Abington School District v. Schempp*, decided on June 17, 1963, to reiterate what it had already said in *Engel*—namely, that public-school prayer was not allowed under the First Amendment.

The justices felt the need to issue *Schempp* for emphasis in light of the hostile reaction to *Engel*. A Gallup poll taken during the summer of 1962 after the *Engel* decision showed that more than three-quarters of all Americans favored some sort of constitutional amendment that would permit school prayer.[34] One hundred eleven members of Congress had responded by introducing some 150 proposed constitutional amendments aimed at overturning the *Engel* decision.[35]

Nevertheless, the Court in *Schempp* by an 8-to-1 vote struck down a Pennsylvania law that required a Bible reading at the opening of school each day. *Schempp* was in fact a combination of two cases. The first involved the Schempps, "a non-Jewish family sought out by the ACLU [American Civil Liberties Union], which argued the case."[36] The other case, *Murray v. Curlett*, was brought by Madalyn Murray and her son William, professed atheists. They attacked a Baltimore city ordinance that called for Bible reading or the recitation of the Lord's Prayer each morning in the city's public schools.[37]

Brennan's concurrence in *Schempp* provided an in-depth analysis of the religion clause and its history. Quoting Jeremiah S. Black, a nineteenth-century chief justice of the Pennsylvania supreme court, Brennan wrote, "The manifest object of the men who framed the institutions of this country was to have a *State without religion*, and a *Church without politics*—that is to say, they meant that one should never be used as an engine for any purpose of the other, and that no man's rights in one should be tested by his opinions about the other. As the Church takes no note of men's political differences, so the State looks with equal eye on all the modes of religious faith.... Our [Founding F]athers seem to have been perfectly sincere in their belief that the members of the Church would be more patriotic, and the citizens of the State more religious, by keeping their respective functions entirely separate."[38]

As a Catholic, Brennan naturally feared that school prayer, Bible readings, and other religious exercises would be used to promote Protestantism, Protestants constituting this country's dominant religious group. Nevertheless, in later years he characterized his opinion in the *Schempp* case as one of the most difficult of his career, explaining, "In the face of my whole lifelong experience as a Roman Catholic, to say that prayer was not an appropriate thing in public schools...that gave me quite a hard time. I struggled."[39] Yet he insisted steadfastly until his retirement that "government has to stay away from regulating religion, and religion has to stay away from butting into any matters of government."[40]

With regard to obscenity, the canon of the Catholic Church was that obscenity was wrong, the "certain effect of obscene literature" being "the incitement to illicit sexual thought, or activity."[41] William Brennan held this view. He did not share what Justices Black and Douglas would later express, a view of obscenity as more or less benign or perhaps even beneficial. Brennan believed that obscenity was an abomination and that it incited disrespect for, and violence against, women.

In *Roth*, Brennan attacked Black and Douglas for their absolutism. He agreed that it was important to protect speech designed to bring about "political and social changes desired by the people."[42] Therefore, he conceded, "All ideas having even the slightest redeeming social importance—unorthodox ideas, controversial ideas, even ideas hateful to the prevailing climate of opinion—have the full protection of the [First Amendment] guaranties."[43]

But he asserted that there had always been certain kinds of speech that were not protected by the First Amendment, certain "limited areas" of expression that were excludable because they encroached upon "more important interests."[44] He considered obscenity to be one of these limited, unprotected areas. Insisting that "implicit in the history of the First Amendment is the rejection of obscenity as utterly without redeeming social importance,"[45] he declared on behalf of the Court, "We hold that obscenity is not within the area of constitutionally protected speech or press."[46]

Anticipating criticism from those who questioned whether reading dirty books or viewing dirty movies in fact led to criminal behavior, he acknowledged, "It is insisted that the constitutional guaranties are violated because convictions may be had without proof either that obscene material will perceptibly create a clear and present danger of antisocial conduct, or will probably induce its recipients to such conduct."[47] But he refused even to respond to those arguments. Instead, he declared that since obscenity enjoyed no First Amendment protection, it could be banned regardless of its effects, benign or otherwise.[48]

He also anticipated concern about whether his ruling would be used to ban not just obscene works but also any work that discussed or involved sex, no matter how tastefully or tangentially. He was careful, therefore, to distinguish between sex on the one hand and obscenity on the other, writing that "sex and obscenity are not synonymous."[49]

He explained, "Obscene material is material which deals with sex in a manner appealing to the prurient interest. The portrayal of sex, e.g., in art, literature and scientific works, is not itself sufficient reason to deny material the constitutional protection of freedom of speech and press. Sex, a great and mysterious motive force in human life, has indisputably been a subject of absorbing interest to mankind through the ages; it is one of the vital problems of human interest and public concern."[50]

To keep overzealous censors from going too far, Brennan established that works alleged to be obscene should be judged *as a whole* and not on the basis of isolated passages. He wrote that "judging obscenity by the effect of isolated passages...must be rejected as unconstitutionally restrictive of the freedoms of speech and press."[51]

What emerged then from *Roth* was a set of guiding principles, a framework for lower court judges to apply in obscenity cases. First, *Roth* defined obscenity as that which dealt with sex in a prurient manner, inciting lustful thoughts. Second, it made clear that obscenity was beyond the protection of the First Amendment. Third, *Roth* established that the standard for judging whether material was obscene was "whether to the average person, applying contemporary community standards, the dominant theme of the material *taken as a whole* appeals to prurient interests."[52]

Applying these standards, the Court upheld the convictions of Roth and Alberts by a 6-to-3 vote. Warren wrote a separate opinion, concurring in the result. Harlan also wrote separately, concurring in part and dissenting in part. The absolutists, Black and Douglas, filed dissents.

Shortly after *Roth* was handed down, the chief justice told his son, Earl Jr., that although he was not completely satisfied with Brennan's opinion, "It's the best we could do with what we had."[53] Liberal commentators and free speech advocates, for their part, praised the *Roth* decision. *Roth*, they believed, opened the door to freer expression because it reined in the censors, despite the facts that the decision upheld Sam Roth's conviction and declared obscenity beyond the scope of First Amendment protection. The liberals' optimism was confirmed by the rulings that followed *Roth*.

By June 1963 Anthony Lewis was prepared to exclaim in an article for *Esquire* magazine, "Applying steady pressure, nine calm men are dragging the censor, kicking and screaming, into the twentieth century."[54]

For example, during the 1956–57 term in which *Roth* was decided, the Court issued four *per curiam* orders that relied simply on *Roth* as their bases. These orders lifted the federal and state bans on a number of different kinds of material that had been treated as obscene prior to *Roth*, including nudist club newsletters and publications;[55] a gay-oriented periodical, *One—The Homosexual Magazine*;[56] and a movie that dealt with the seduction of a sixteen-year-old boy by an older woman and other "illicit sexual intimacies and acts."[57]

In 1959, in the case of *Kingsley Pictures Corp. v. Regents*,[58] the Court rejected New York State's contention that a film version of *Lady Chatterley's Lover*, adapted from the novel by D. H. Lawrence, should be banned as immoral. Writing for the Court, which was in unanimous agreement as to the result, Justice Stewart declared that motion pictures are, like newspapers, books, and speech, "within the First and Fourteenth Amendments' basic protection."[59]

Under New York law, moviemakers were required to get from the state a license to distribute their motion pictures. If a license application was denied, the film producer could appeal the ruling to the Board of Regents of the University of the State of New York. Kingsley's initial request for a license for *Lady Chatterley's Lover* had been rejected because the Education Department found that three isolated scenes in the film were "immoral" under the New York statute. Kingsley appealed, but the Regents upheld the license denial on the grounds that "the whole theme of this motion picture is immoral under said law, for that theme is the presentation of adultery as a desirable, acceptable and proper pattern of behavior."[60]

Justice Stewart explained on behalf of the Court, "It is contended that the State's action was justified because the motion picture attractively portrays a relationship which is contrary to the moral standards, the religious precepts, and the legal code of its citizenry. This argument misconceives what the Constitution protects. Its guarantee is not confined to the expression of ideas that are conventional or shared by a majority. It protects advocacy of the opinion that adultery may sometimes be proper, no less than advocacy of socialism or the single tax. And in the realm of ideas it protects expression which is eloquent no less than that which is unconvincing."[61]

Justice Black concurred in the *Kingsley* result but in a separate opinion protested the idea of the justices' even considering the relative morality of the movie's subject matter. In fact, Black objected to the justices' even viewing the film. He wrote, "If, despite the Constitution…this Nation is to embark on the dangerous road of censorship, my belief is that this Court is about the most inappropriate Supreme Board of Censors that could be found."[62]

He went on to assert that "the only way we can decide whether a State or municipality can constitutionally bar movies is for this Court to view and appraise each movie on a case-by-case basis. Under these circumstances, every member of the Court must exercise his own judgment as to how bad a picture is, a judgment which is ultimately based at least in large part on his own standard of what is immoral."[63] For example, in his separate concurrence in the *Kingsley* case, Justice Frankfurter had, citing D. H. Lawrence's *Pornography and Obscenity*, implied that the government should censor only works that make sex look ugly or less alluring than it really is.[64]

Black insisted, "The end result of such decisions seems to me to be a purely personal determination by individual Justices as to whether a particular picture viewed is too bad to allow it to be seen by the public. Such an individual determination cannot be guided by reasonably fixed and certain standards. Accordingly, neither States nor moving picture makers can possibly know in advance, with any fair degree of certainty, what can or cannot be done in the field of movie making and exhibiting. This uncertainty cannot easily be reconciled with the rule of law which our Constitution envisages."[65]

As a proponent of total incorporation, Black had argued that applying the Bill of Rights in its entirety to the states was better than leaving it to judges to decide which rights were "in" and which were "out," which rights the states were bound to respect, and which they were not. In this same way, he contended that interpreting the First Amendment literally removed or at least minimized subjectivity or unpredictability in the obscenity area.

Even before *Roth* was decided, American culture had, like American law, politics, and race relations, been undergoing profound and irresistible changes during the 1950s and early 1960s. For example, after 1959, four-letter words began to appear commonly in the works of writers like Norman Mailer, who reached wide audiences.[66] Meanwhile Beat generation writers and poets like Jack Kerouac, Allen Ginsberg, and William S. Burroughs were trampling roughshod over old taboos. During the 1950s, Kerouac wrote openly of interracial sex and romance in novels like *The Subterraneans* and of his irreverence for authority, his "calculated rejection of the social norm,"[67] in *On the Road*.

Burroughs's book *The Naked Lunch*, published in 1959 by Grove Press, reached what Anthony Lewis called "the point of no return"[68] in recounting a drug addict's cannibalistic hallucinations. Too squeamish to frame his own description of the passage, Lewis in his *Esquire* article quoted critic Stanley Edgar Hyman's account of one *Naked Lunch* episode, describing how, "after Mary has had her will of Johnny's body with finger, tongue, mouth and a rubber penis named Steeley Dan III, she kills him by hanging, 'sucks out his eyes with a pop' and 'lunches' on his genitals."[69]

The Beats drew much of their inspiration from the writings of Henry Miller, whose books, especially *Tropic of Cancer*, were renowned for their sexual explicitness. Federal customs officials battled to keep *Tropic* out of the United States from the time it was first published in France by the Obelisk Press in 1934. But thousands of bootlegged copies managed to find their way into the hands of American readers. Three million others bought the book after Grove Press, emboldened by *Roth* and its progeny, published *Tropic* in the United States in 1961. Suddenly it seemed that instead of limiting "obscene" material, *Roth* was having the unintended effect of increasing its proliferation exponentially.

For example, the high court of Massachusetts in 1962 lifted the state ban on the distribution of *Tropic* that had been in effect since Grove Press announced the book's American publication in 1961. Using *Roth* as the basis for its ruling, the Supreme Judicial Court of Massachusetts concluded in *Attorney General v. The Book Named Tropic of Cancer*[70] that "the First Amendment protects material which has value because of ideas, news, or artistic, literary, or scientific attributes. If the appeal of material (taken as a whole) to adults is not predominantly prurient, adults cannot be denied the material."[71]

Tropic of Cancer was Miller's graphic account of his experiences in Paris during the 1930s, where he lived, as he put it, without money, resources, and hope yet was the happiest man alive because he rejected all social convention. To Miller, the ideal universe would have been one in which there was "no money, no property, no executioners, no prisons, no schools," just "perfect freedom."[72]

In prewar Paris he found that freedom, his liberation, among petty thugs, prostitutes, and sexual adventurers who were part of an often decadent, alternative society. For a time, he made his living writing erotica for a dollar a page with other avant-garde writers like Anaïs Nin, Alfred Perles, and Michael Fraenkel, who made up the so-called Villa Seurat group.

Tropic was a self-described affront to contemporary values. "This is not a book, in the ordinary sense of the word," Miller explained.[73] "No, this is a prolonged insult, a gob of spit in the face of Art, a kick in the pants to God, Man, Destiny, Time, Love, Beauty...what you will."[74]

Ezra Pound said of *Tropic of Cancer*, "At last an unprintable book that is fit to read."[75] T. S. Eliot said it was "a very remarkable book, with passages of writing in it as good as any I have seen for a long time."[76] George Orwell praised Miller for his "intellectual courage," while Aldous Huxley and critic Edmund Wilson were "appreciative" of Miller's talents, and their endorsement of Miller "helped to give him his special cachet."[77]

Evidence submitted at trial had established that 85 of *Tropic's* 318 pages contained descriptions of sexual episodes.[78] All were described in "precise physical detail and four-letter words."[79] Conceding Miller's obvious talents, the trial judge was compelled to observe, "The author's descriptive powers are truly impressive and he rises to great literary heights when he describes Paris. And suddenly he descends into the filthy gutter."[80]

And yet literary experts testified that the book was the opposite of prurient, that it portrayed sex in such a graphic, undesirable, and denigrating way as to make it actually unappealing. According to Professor Harry Levin of Harvard, for example, Miller's attitude toward sex was one of "disgust," his sexual mood one of "revulsion."[81] Levin testified, "Although a lot of sex is being presented, the author, as it were, is backing away from it and even admonishing against it. It doesn't seem…[that] it would be a book to incite lustful thoughts."[82]

In one episode, the narrator describes watching his acquaintance Joe Van Norden trying to have sex with an exhausted, half-starved prostitute. She has been offered 15 francs to have sex with both men. Though her body refuses to yield to him, Van Norden is determined to consummate the arrangement.

Miller writes, "I get down on my knees behind Van Norden and I examine [them] more attentively. The girl throws her head on one side and gives me a despairing look. 'It's no use,' she says. 'It's impossible.' Upon which Van Norden sets to work with renewed energy, just like an old billy goat. He's such an obstinate cuss that he'll break his horns rather than give up. And he's getting sore now because I'm tickling him in the rump.

"'For God's sake, Joe, give it up! You'll kill the poor girl.'

"'Leave me alone,' he grunts. 'I almost got it in that time.'"[83]

Miller maintained that "Obscenity, like sex, has its rightful place in literature."[84] But he insisted he was not a pornographer and that he objected to pornography, which he defined as sex presented for purely prurient purposes. He told a *New York Times* interviewer in 1970, "The majority of readers of *Tropic of Cancer* have never read another book of mine, and they only looked for those pages where there was the sex they wanted. That disgusts me!"[85]

Feminists, for their part, have always found Miller objectionable. Kate Millet wrote in *Sexual Politics* that Miller portrays the sexes as "two warring camps between whom understanding is impossible since one (the male) is human and animal (according to Miller's perception, intellectual and sexual)—the other simply animal."[86]

Others like author Susan Griffin have complained that in some of Miller's books, as in "pornography" generally, the sexual act itself "seems to exist less for pleasure than to overpower and silence women."[87] In her book *Pornography and Silence: Culture's Revenge Against Nature*, she quotes a passage from *Sexus*, one of Miller's other novels:

"'Shut up, you bitch,' I said. 'It hurts, doesn't it? You wanted it, didn't you?' I held her tightly, raised myself a little higher to get it in to the hilt, and pushed myself until I thought her womb would give way. Then I came—right into that snail-like mouth which was wide open."[88]

But Anaïs Nin wrote the preface to *Tropic of Cancer*, welcoming it into the world as "a book which, if such a thing were possible, might restore our appetite for the fundamental realities."[89] She went on, "In a world grown paralyzed with introspection and constipated by delicate mental meals this brutal exposure of the substantial body comes as a vitalizing current of blood."[90]

Nin was Miller's friend and benefactor in Paris during the 1930s. She wrote erotica with him and, when he was utterly destitute, kept him supplied with paper by bringing him discarded sheets of New York Stock Exchange quotations from her husband's bank.[91] Parts of *Tropic* were written on the backs of these pages. To Anaïs Nin, the great significance of Miller's writing was that it revealed to her what she saw as the need for women to write more about sex and express female sensuality from their own perspective.

In her *Diaries* and in her own posthumously published erotic works such as *Delta of Venus* and *Little Birds*, Nin did exactly that. Her 1976 postscript to the preface of *Delta of Venus* acknowledged Miller's influence. She wrote, "At the time we were all writing erotica at a dollar a page, I realized that for centuries we had only one model for this literary genre—the writing of men. I was already conscious of a difference between the masculine and feminine treatment of sexual experience. I knew that there was a great disparity between Henry Miller's explicitness and my ambiguities—between his humorous, Rabelaisian view of sex and my poetic descriptions of sexual relationships in the unpublished portions of the diary. As I wrote in Volume Three of the Diary, I had a feeling that Pandora's box contained the mysteries of woman's sensuality, so different from man's and for which man's language was inadequate."[92]

In 1962, the Massachusetts high court judges were forced to conclude, "Competent critics assert...that *Tropic* has serious purpose, even if many will find that purpose obscure. There can be no doubt that a significant segment of the literary world has long regarded the book of literary importance. A majority of the court are of the opinion that the predominant effect and purpose of the book as a whole is not prurient."[93]

The court went on, "We think that the book [*Tropic*] must be accepted as a conscious effort to create a work of literary art and as having significance, which prevents treating it as hard core pornography."[94]

Times were changing. This was, after all, the same Massachusetts high court that had in May 1930 upheld the state's ban on Theodore Dreiser's *An American Tragedy*, even though that book's publication in 1925 had made Dreiser "one of America's foremost writers."[95] Dreiser has been compared to Balzac, Dickens, and Victor Hugo and is credited with making "romantic realism...possible to later American writers."[96] He was also one of the first American writers to "visualize the nature of modern business."[97]

H. L. Mencken championed Dreiser's works, as did Robert Benchley.[98] Irving Howe called *An American Tragedy* "a masterpiece, nothing less" and even went so far as to rank Dreiser "among the American giants, the very few American giants we have had."[99]

But in *Commonwealth v. Friede*,[100] decided on May 27, 1930, the Supreme Judicial Court of Massachusetts concluded that distribution of *An American Tragedy* could be barred because the book contained several isolated passages that "had a manifest tendency to incite impure thoughts, excite the sexual passions, and corrupt the morals of youths into whose hands the book might come."[101]

The real problem for the censors was, of course, the controversial nature of Dreiser's vision, including his "bold disregard of the romantic traditions of the time and his faithful descriptions of the amours of commonplace people in Chicago and New York City."[102] Moreover, Dreiser had come of age during the era of the great robber barons. He portrayed unregulated capitalism's unfettered greed as a threat to the nation's moral fabric and quality of life.

An American Tragedy was a two-volume tale of crime and punishment, based loosely on a murder that had been committed near the small town of Big Moose Lake in upstate New York during the summer of 1903.[103] A young man named Chester Gillette was found guilty and electrocuted in 1908 for the drowning death of his girlfriend, Grace ("Billy") Brown.[104] Evidently Billy, who had worked in the collar factory that Chester's uncle owned in Cortland, New York, had threatened that unless Chester married her, she would reveal to Chester's "fine friends" their illicit love affair and that she was pregnant by him.[105] Dreiser also drew elements of the plot from a number of other murders that he had covered as a newspaperman during the 1890s and early 1900s.[106]

In Dreiser's fictionalized account, the protagonist is Clyde Griffiths, the son of Christian fundamentalist parents. Fleeing to avoid responsibility for an automobile accident in his hometown, Clyde moves to another city where he works in his uncle's factory. He becomes romantically involved with two women: one a factory girl, the other a socialite. When he learns that the factory girl is pregnant, he entices her to a lake, lets her drown, and is subsequently found guilty of and executed for murder.

Dreiser's observations as a journalist had led him to the conclusion that in the United States, a certain type of crime "seemed to spring from the fact that almost every young person was possessed of an ingrowing ambition to be somebody financially and socially."[107] As one critic put it, Dreiser came to believe that "The ideals of life, liberty, and the pursuit of happiness had become no more than clichés; the ambitious American (to paraphrase [black militant] H. Rap Brown) had made murder as American as apple pie."[108]

Bill Brennan's ideal library would have had more shelf space for the works of Theodore Dreiser under the First Amendment and less, if any, for those of Henry Miller. Whatever their relative social value, Dreiser's books were less obscene than Miller's, to the extent that Dreiser's were obscene at all, and hence were less objectionable. But there seemed no way to provide the censor with a rationale for barring the works of Miller that could not also be somehow used to ban Dreiser.

Brennan forged ahead. But by the mid-1960s, the fundamental problems still were not resolved. Black and Douglas remained absolutists, and the other justices still could not agree on definitions of obscenity or pornography.

For example, on June 22, 1964, the Court decided *Jacobellis v. Ohio*[109] by a 6-to-3 vote. That decision overturned the conviction of Nico Jacobellis, manager of a movie house in Cleveland Heights, Ohio. Jacobellis had been convicted under an Ohio obscenity law for exhibiting the soft-core French film *Les Amants ("The Lovers")*. Brennan wrote the opinion for the Court, but the case is best remembered for Justice Stewart's concurrence, for in it Stewart made an extraordinarily candid admission—namely, that he could not define obscenity or pornography, other than to assert, "I know it when I see it."

He wrote, "I have reached the conclusion, which I think is confirmed at least by negative implication in the Court's [obscenity] decisions...that under the First and Fourteenth Amendments criminal laws in this area are constitutionally limited to hard-core pornography. I shall not today attempt further to define the kinds of material I understand to be embraced within that shorthand description; and perhaps I could never succeed in intelligibly doing so. But I know it when I see it, and the motion picture involved in this case is not that."[110]

Warren dissented in *Jacobellis*. The case was one of the few on which he and Brennan disagreed. But the chief justice reiterated his support for *Roth*, insisting that "For all the sound and fury that the *Roth* test has generated, it has not been proved unsound, and I believe that we should try to live with it—at least until a more satisfactory definition is evolved."[111]

By then, however, even Brennan had doubts. He had begun to wonder whether his effort to arrive at a workable formula for regulating obscenity without violating protected speech would ever bear fruit.

On November 15, 1964, he traveled to New York City to address the Jewish Theological Seminary of America on the occasion of the seminary's annual Louis Marshall Award Dinner. In his speech, he expressed concern about whether a "religiously held sexual ethic"[112] could be made to comport with the First Amendment.

He stated his view that "there is no question that society may enact laws to protect itself in the matter of sexual morality."[113] But, he pointed out, "If the complaint is made by theologians that the social norm provided by the Law is too imprecise to constitute any effective check on the publication of obscene materials, it must in turn be admitted that theologians themselves have not provided a precise definition of obscenity even for their own purposes."[114]

Referring specifically to the canon of the Catholic Church, he complained that Catholic theologians had failed to provide a definition of obscenity precise enough to serve as an acceptable basis for constitutional decision making.

"To the theologian," he asserted, quoting from an article by M. C. Slough, former dean of the University of Kansas Law School, and Father P. D. McAnany, that had recently appeared in the *St. Louis University Law Journal*,[115] "there exists no compelling reason to search for a precise definition of the term [*obscenity*], for he [the theologian] is primarily concerned with pointing out the dangers inherent in exposing one's self to the type of material one finds particularly stimulating to the sexual appetite."[116]

The inadequacy of that approach, said Brennan, was that "not all matter depicting or portraying sex is deprived of constitutional protection; therefore the judge cannot rely, as these theologians may, on the mere presence of sex, in formulating a standard."[117]

He concluded, "Judges have struggled for many decades to frame an adequate standard.... The line between protected and un-protected portrayal is dim and uncertain, and judges do experience great difficulty in making it."[118]

Meanwhile, the absolutists hardened their positions. In *Ginzburg v. United States*,[119] decided in 1966, Brennan wrote for a 5-to-4 majority, upholding the conviction of publisher Ralph Ginzburg. Ginzburg had been sentenced by a federal district court in Pennsylvania to five years in prison for sending obscene materials through the U.S. mail. The publications in question were *Eros*, a hardcover magazine; *Liaison*, a biweekly newsletter; and *The House-wife's Handbook on Selective Promiscuity*, a short book.[120] Black and Douglas took the occasion to launch some of their most eloquent and cynical attacks on government censorship.

Black wrote in his *Ginzburg* dissent that "as I have said many times, I believe the Federal government is without any power whatever under the Constitution to put any type of burden on speech and expression of ideas of any kind."[121]

In addition, Black put forth his feeling that sex was a subject about which people were not sufficiently forthcoming or informed, and that it was healthier to be candid about sex than to suppress or repress the discussion of it.

He wrote, "Sex is a fact of life. Its pervasive influence is felt throughout the world and it cannot be ignored. Like all other facts of life it can lead to difficulty and trouble and sorrow and pain. But while it may lead to abuses, and has in many instances, no words need be spoken in order for people to know that the subject is one pleasantly interwoven in all human activities and involves the very substance of the creation of life itself."[122]

He continued, "It [sex] is a subject which people are bound to consider and discuss whatever laws are passed by any government to try to suppress it. Though I do not suggest any way to solve the problems that may arise from sex or discussions about sex, of one thing I am confident, and that is that federal censorship is not the answer to these problems. I find it difficult to see how talk about sex can be placed under the kind of censorship the Court here approves without subjecting our society to more dangers than we can anticipate at the moment. It was to avoid exactly such dangers that the First Amendment was written and adopted. For myself I would follow the course which I believe is required by the First Amendment, that is, recognize that sex at least as much as any other aspect of life is so much a part of our society that its discussion should not be made a crime."[123]

Douglas was in complete agreement with Black. He expressed in his *Ginzburg* dissent his view that "the First Amendment allows all ideas to be expressed—whether orthodox, popular, offbeat, or repulsive."[124]

Pointing out that many of the tracts published by Ginzburg involved acts that were masochistic and homosexual, as well as "deviant in other respects,"[125] Douglas asked why it should be unlawful to "cater to the needs"[126] of such a readership. He wrote, "They are, to be sure, somewhat offbeat, nonconformist, and odd. But we are not in the realm of criminal conduct, only ideas and tastes. Some like Chopin, others like 'rock and roll.'"[127]

The sixty-seven-year-old justice continued, "Man was not made in a fixed mould. If a publication caters to the idiosyncrasies of a minority, why does it not have some 'social importance'? Each of us is a very temporary transient with likes and dislikes that cover the spectrum. However plebeian my tastes may be, who am I to say that others' tastes must be so limited and that other tastes have no 'social importance'? How can we know enough to probe the mysteries of the subconscious of our people and say that this is good for them and that is not?"[128]

He asserted, "I do not think it permissible to draw lines between the 'good' and the 'bad' and be true to the constitutional mandate to let all ideas alone. If our Constitution permitted 'reasonable' regulation of freedom of expression, as do the constitutions of some nations, we would be in a field where the legislative and the judiciary would have much leeway. But under our charter all regulation or control of expression is barred. Government does not sit to reveal where the 'truth' is. People are left to pick and choose between competing offerings."[129]

He concluded, "We have no business acting as censors or endowing any group with censorship powers."[130]

Douglas even went so far as to imply that "obscene" publications might have the socially beneficial effect of providing a release for those who might otherwise engage in antisocial behavior. He reiterated in his *Ginzburg* dissent a view he had expressed in the *Fanny Hill* case, *Memoirs v. Massachusetts*,[131] decided the same day.

In *Memoirs*, he wrote, "Perhaps the most frequently assigned justification for censorship is the belief that erotica produce antisocial sexual conduct. But that relationship has yet to be proven. Indeed, if one were to make judgments on the basis of speculation, one might guess that literature of the most pornographic sort would, in many cases, provide a substitute—not a stimulus—for antisocial sexual conduct."[132]

Meanwhile, the Court inevitably found itself becoming what Hugo Black had warned against, a Supreme Board of Censors. By the mid-1960s, the justices were inundated with dirty books and movies, were in effect knee-deep in smut.

Yale law professor Owen Fiss, who clerked for Brennan during the 1965–66 term, recalled a Friday night when his wife, then seven months' pregnant, came to pick him up from the office. Fiss was upstairs in the Supreme Court library, and so a guard provided her entry into Justice Brennan's chambers. The guard's eyes nearly popped out of his head when he saw the piles of sexually explicit books, magazines, and pictures strewn around the law clerks' office. The guard commented that the Supreme Court justice's chambers were no fit place for a respectable lady in a family way.

By 1968, Justice Harlan, referring to what he called the "intractable obscenity problem,"[133] pointed out that the thirteen obscenity cases decided by the Court during the eleven years since the *Roth* decision had produced a total of fifty-five separate opinions by the justices, an extraordinary divergence of viewpoints.[134] There was clearly no consensus.

Meanwhile the environment in which the obscenity debate

took place bordered on the farcical. Once a week the justices and their law clerks trooped down into the basement of the Supreme Court building for what came to be known as "dirty movie day." There they sat, in straight-backed, wooden chairs in a sterile, rectangular room with a high ceiling, bare walls, and spotless tile floor, watching movies to decide whether they were obscene. In the late 1960s and early 1970s, most of those films, such as *Vixen* or *I Am Curious (Yellow)* would be considered "soft porn" or perhaps even R-rated by comparison with the "XXX" material that would later become available.

Black and Douglas refused to attend the viewings because they believed that the Court had no business acting as censor. Privately, Black wondered aloud what men the Brethren's age could presume to know about sex anyway. He was fond of saying that if his colleagues wanted to watch dirty movies they should go to the theater and pay the cost of admission just like everybody else.[135]

Douglas, for his part, endeavored to interest his colleagues in what he regarded as more socially relevant and informative fare. He tried to organize the screening of a documentary about the environment, but no one was interested in showing up.

Warren also refused to attend "dirty movie days," but for a different reason. He skipped the viewings because he said he already knew what the objectionable material was all about. "It's all garbage," he declared.[136] "I *know* what that stuff is!"[137]

After Thurgood Marshall joined the Court in 1967, he too claimed to know what the movies were all about because, he said, he had already seen them in the theater. A raucous bear of a man at 6'4", 250 lbs., with a ribald wit, Marshall had, as lawyer for the NAACP Legal Defense and Educational Fund, traveled extensively throughout the segregated and often hostile South, arguing and winning the string of cases that laid the groundwork for his ultimate victory on *Brown*. He had seen America at its worst, had witnessed unimaginable poverty, cruelty, prejudice, and suffering and had risked his life to advance civil rights on countless occasions. Little shocked him. By time he reached the Court, his piercing cynicism was reflected in his devil-may-care attitude and humor.

Marshall never missed "dirty movie days." He looked forward to them and often primed himself for the screenings with a few martinis at lunch. Sometimes he yelled things at the screen like "Aaaah, baby!" or "I gotta get a copy of this to give to my sons when they go away to college."

Harlan commented as well. By the 1960s, his eyesight had deteriorated to the point where he was nearly blind. So he had his law clerks sit next to him and describe to him what was transpiring on screen. Every now and then he could be heard to utter a thoroughly patrician "Extraordinary!"

Even the law clerks chimed in. Usually Stewart or his clerks were given a razzing. Alluding to Stewart's claim in *Jacobellis* that although he could not define pornography, he knew it when he saw it, other justices' clerks might exclaim "That's it, I see it!" when the action on screen got especially hot and heavy.

Nevertheless, *Roth* survived until the more conservative Burger Court modified it radically to give censors a freer hand. In *Miller v. California*,[138] decided on June 21, 1973, almost sixteen years to the day that *Roth* was handed down, the Court ruled that anything which, taken as a whole, "lacks serious literary, artistic, political, or scientific value" could be banned.[139] Under *Roth* as it had evolved through interpretation, only that which was "*utterly* without redeeming social value"[140] (emphasis added) could be censored. The idea behind *Miller* was that more things could be banned as "seriously lacking" than as "utterly without." Brennan, Douglas, Stewart, and Marshall dissented from the *Miller* ruling.

Brennan used his dissent in a companion case, *Paris Adult Theatre I v. Slaton*,[141] handed down the same day as *Miller*, to break with his past and take a stand against almost all government censorship. In *Paris*, the justices by a 5-to-4 vote upheld the convictions of two Georgia movie-house operators for showing the kind of "hard core pornography" that left "little to the imagination."[142]

Brennan declared in his dissent, "I am convinced that the approach initiated 16 years ago in *Roth v. United States* ... cannot bring stability to this area of the law without jeopardizing fundamental First Amendment values."[143]

He went on to state that "after 16 years of experimentation and debate I am reluctantly forced to the conclusion that none of the available formulas, including the one announced today, can reduce the vagueness to a tolerable level while at the same time striking an acceptable balance between the protections of the First and Fourteenth Amendments, on the one hand, and on the asserted state interest in regulating the dissemination of certain sexually oriented materials."[144]

He explained, "Any effort to draw a constitutionally acceptable boundary on state power must resort to such indefinite concepts as 'prurient interest,' 'patent offensiveness,' 'serious literary value,' and the like. The meaning of these concepts necessarily varies with the experience, outlook, and even idiosyncrasies of the person defining them. Although we have assumed that obscenity does exist and that we 'know it when [we] see it'...we are manifestly unable to describe it in advance except by reference to concepts so elusive that they fail to distinguish clearly between protected and unprotected speech."[145]

He concluded, "I would hold, therefore, that at least in the absence of distribution to juveniles or obtrusive exposure to unconsenting adults, the First and Fourteenth Amendments prohibit the State and Federal Governments from attempting wholly to suppress sexually oriented materials on the basis of their allegedly 'obscene' contents."[146]

Brennan told Nat Hentoff in 1990, "I put sixteen years into that damn obscenity thing. I tried and I tried, and I waffled back and forth, and I finally gave up. If you can't define it, you can't prosecute people for it. And that's why, in the *Paris Adult Theatre* decision, I finally abandoned the whole effort."[147]

Since then, Brennan's conservative critics have blamed him for everything from the erosion of family values to the illicit sexual activity that has plagued inner-city areas. For example, in their May 18, 1984, article "The Mind of Justice Brennan" for the *National Review*, Stephen J. Markman and Alfred S. Regnery asserted, "Although ostensibly designed by Brennan as a balance between the interests of the pornographer and of the public, the [*Roth*] test has proven to be so vague and difficult to enforce as to make it, in essence, no test at all. The result is phenomena such as New York's Times Square and Washington [D.C.]'s 14th Street."[148]

Yet nothing the Court has done since 1973 has undone the sexual revolution. Four-letter words in books, magazines, movies, and even prime-time television programs are prevalent. So are erotic publications that run the complete gamut of male and female heterosexuality and homosexuality. Justice Harlan may have been right when he observed in a letter to a friend a few months before his death in December 1971 that the "ultimate solution [of the obscenity problem] must be found in a renaissance of societal values."[149]

CHAPTER 17

New York Times
v. Sullivan

Thus we consider this case against the background of a profound
national commitment to the principle that debate on public issues
should be uninhibited, robust, and wide-open, and that it may
well include vehement, caustic, and sometimes unpleasantly sharp
attacks on government and public officials.

—Justice William J. Brennan Jr.,
New York Times v. Sullivan (1964)

EW ALABAMANS READ the *New York Times* in 1960. The
newspaper, which enjoyed a total daily circulation of roughly
650,000, each day distributed only 394 copies to newsstands and
subscribers in the southern state.[1] Although it professed proudly to
carry *all* the news that was fit to print, ordinary Alabamans
regarded the *Times's* coverage as having little pertinence to their
lives. To the extent that it did report matters of interest to them, the
Times did so from the perspective of a northeastern, liberal newspaper that white Alabamans found hostile to their point of view.

For example, in the newspaper's Saturday, March 19, 1960,
edition, the *Times's* editors called upon Congress to pass civil rights
legislation that would guarantee African Americans' voting rights
at the state and local as well as federal level. This kind of legislation

would obviously have had a tremendous impact in the South, where African Americans were routinely denied the right to vote despite the fact that in many southern electoral districts they constituted sizable minorities if not majorities.

The *Times*'s editorial complained that civil rights bills pending in Congress had already been "watered down in both houses to the point where they threaten to dissolve in a muddy puddle of obfuscation."[2] The *Times* called for resistance to any further weakening of the bills and for the inclusion of strong voting-rights provisions. The editors declared, "This is the heart of the civil rights bill: the guarantee that all citizens shall have the franchise irrespective of race or color. There are other valuable provisions in the measures pending in both House and Senate; but unless the 1960 law includes a statutory method of materially advancing the Negro's right to vote in all elections, the cause of constitutionalism in this country will have again suffered a disgraceful blow."[3]

The editors warned, "The growing movement of peaceful mass demonstrations by Negroes is something new in the South, something understandable and also something ominous. Let Congress heed their rising voices, for they will be heard."[4]

Thus the *Times* had aligned itself with the civil rights movement led by Dr. Martin Luther King Jr., which was anathema to southern segregationists. Moreover, the *Times* had struck an unnerving chord with its reference to there being "something ominous" as well as understandable about the peaceful mass-protest movement. The *Times*'s clear implication was that if peaceful means failed, African Americans in the South could be expected to turn to violence in order to win respect for their long-denied constitutional rights.

As the *Times*'s editorial had asserted, King's message and methods were something new to the South—indeed, to the nation at large. The young Baptist minister, who had celebrated his thirty-first birthday just two months before the *Times* editorial appeared, was frustrated by the slow pace of progress toward racial equality. Since the mid-1950s, he had been engaged in a grassroots campaign aimed at winning passage of national civil rights legislation that would outlaw racial discrimination, common everywhere but especially virulent in the South.

In that region, second-class citizenship for African Americans was rigorously maintained by state authorities literally from cradle to grave. Hospitals and cemeteries were racially segregated. So were public accommodations, parks and recreational facilities, movie theaters and restaurants, even bathrooms and buses. The Supreme Court had in 1954 ordered the nation's public schools desegregated. But in the southern and border states (including the District of Columbia), where the public school population accounted for roughly 40 percent of the nation's total public-school enrollment, African Americans were still forced to attend racially separate and inferior schools in direct defiance of the Court's order.

Throughout the Old Confederacy, King applied the doctrine of civil disobedience used so effectively by Indian nationalist leader Mohandas K. Gandhi to gain his country's independence from Great Britain. In state after state, King engineered economic boycotts against white businesses that engaged in discriminatory practices and led nonviolent mass marches and demonstrations to protest unequal treatment.

Many of these protests had put innocent demonstrators, including children, in harm's way. In fact, King sometimes put children in the front lines of his marches. Often the demonstrators were beaten, jailed, or martyred by brutal southern police who set upon them with clubs, fire hoses, and attack dogs. Time and again the protesters offered no resistance, only songs—old Negro spirituals or "We Shall Overcome," which became the anthem of the movement. The behavior of the white police and mob violence, filmed and documented by the national news media, shocked the consciences of millions of Americans and dramatized both the desperate plight of African Americans in the South and the shameless cruelty of the white opposition.

At first, King's tactics came under attack from African Americans as well as whites. The "Old Guard," the established leaders of the civil rights movement who had masterminded victories like *Brown v. Board of Education* in the courts, regarded him as an upstart. Theirs was the logic of Aesop's tortoise; King, to them, personified the proverbial hare. *Brown* had taken at least two generations of work. The litigation strategy that won the case had been initiated by Thurgood Marshall's mentor Charles Hamilton Houston. Houston had, in turn, inherited the strategy from Nathan Margold, his predecessor as lawyer for the NAACP.

Marshall, who was generally regarded as the preeminent black leader at the time of King's emergence, saw King as a threat to this hard-won progress. Marshall wanted change to come faster, but he feared that King's arousal of the black masses would in reaction arouse the masses of whites and that African Americans, relatively weak and in the minority, would lose the ensuing power struggle. If this happened, the advances so painstakingly achieved would be lost and the cause of racial equality retarded for generations. Therefore, Marshall favored the steady, incremental approach to change advocated by the NAACP. During the late 1950s, he characterized King as "a boy on a man's errand." Privately, he criticized him for using "the bodies of children" to do the "men's work" of ending segregation.[5]

As Georgia Congressman John L. Lewis, a pioneer civil rights activist, explained, "I think it was difficult for some of the old guard leaders to understand the nature of a mass movement. They didn't understand the power, the philosophy of nonviolence. They had reservations about...the leadership of Dr. King, but even there I think they tried to be supportive. I think some of them felt threatened on the local level as well as on the national level. This was something new, this was something different, they didn't know how to deal with it. White southerners didn't know how to deal with it and the black leadership, the old guard, didn't know how to deal with it because we had been programmed or taught that we should use the courts to seek redress for our concerns, our grievances."[6]

According to Lewis, Marshall's attacks on King could also be attributed to Marshall's concern for the safety of the protesters, his fear that King's tactics "invited violence" against them. He went on, "I think Thurgood was concerned more than anything else about the young people's well-being. He didn't want to see us get hurt, he didn't want to see us get killed, and he knew that jail was not a pleasant place. He didn't want to see young people, young college students and these pretty young women from Fisk University and Spelman College [in Atlanta, Georgia], stay in jail. Thurgood was a very warm, humane, and humorous person."[7]

Lewis concluded, "He [Marshall] thought the South was so crazy, so backward, that something could happen to a group of young people in the jails of Mississippi, Alabama, and Georgia. And he was right. People did get shot. People did get killed."[8]

Eventually Marshall and the NAACP backed King's efforts and those of the organization he founded, the Southern Christian Leadership Conference (SCLC). Marshall and the NAACP provided King and the SCLC with financial support and legal assistance. Lewis recalled, "The NAACP was not there in the beginning, but later, when we needed help, needed someone to go into federal court, we had the NAACP Legal Defense Fund. So on many occasions when we got arrested, when we went to jail, the NAACP responded with lawyers like Donald Hollowell, A. T. Walden, and James Nabritt. The NAACP had lawyers all across the South, so when we would go to jail, even though Thurgood Marshall disagreed with our techniques, he would make available the legal expertise and the legal resources of the [NAACP Legal Defense and Educational] Fund, Jim Nabritt, Constance Baker Motley, Robert Carter, and a battery of just very bright and very smart people."[9]

Nevertheless, Marshall remained critical of King, who was awarded the Nobel Peace Prize in 1964, long after King was slain by a sniper in Memphis, Tennessee, in 1968. During the 1970s, Marshall told Columbia University interviewers for the university's oral history project that while King was a "great" leader, he (King) "wasn't worth diddly squat as an organizer." Marshall complained, "All he did was to dump all his legal work on us, including the bills. And that was all right with him. So long as he didn't have to pay the bills."[10]

Meanwhile, the white segregationists were by 1960 still pursu- ing their avowed campaign of massive resistance to *Brown* and subsequent desegregation rulings. Many of them decided that the key to stopping King and his movement was to intimidate his followers, kill King, or silence him in some other way.

Intimidating civil rights supporters first required "exposing" them. After they were identified, the so-called White Citizens Councils formed by southern business leaders in response to *Brown* could then carry out their stated objectives of making it "difficult, if not impossible, for any Negro who advocates desegregation to find a job, get credit, or renew a mortgage."[11]

Alabama officials decided that one way of exposing King's
supporters would be to require civil rights organizations to disclose
the names of their members and contributors or else lose their status
as nonprofit corporations licensed to do business in the state. In
1956, Alabama Attorney General John Patterson won a state court
order requiring the NAACP's Alabama chapter to surrender to
state officials all membership lists and contribution records. When
the NAACP'S Alabama branch refused to comply, the organization
was held in contempt of court and fined $100,000. The branch
subsequently disbanded, though its members carried on clan-
destinely as best they could under a different name, the Alabama
Christian Movement for Human Rights.[12]

The civil rights movement as a whole grew more militant as
efforts to silence Dr. King intensified. On February 1, 1960, four
African American students from North Carolina Agricultural and
Technical College in Greensboro, North Carolina, took seats and
demanded service at a whites-only lunch counter in a Woolworth's
store in Greensboro.[13] When asked to leave, they refused to do so,
thereby launching the "sit-in" movement that quickly spread across
the South.[14]

King immediately endorsed the North Carolina students' action. But two weeks later, he faced the prospect of imprisonment
after an Alabama grand jury indicted him for perjury in connection
with his 1956 and 1958 state tax returns.[15] Thus did Martin Luther
King Jr. become the first person in Alabama history to be charged
with felony tax evasion.[16]

Prominent supporters of King and the movement he had by now
come to personify rallied on his behalf. The Committee to Defend
Martin Luther King and the Struggle for Freedom in the South was
formed in New York City by well-known entertainers, labor leaders,
and clergymen. Among them were Harry Belafonte, Sidney Poitier,
Nat King Cole, A. Philip Randolph, Bayard Rustin, Gardner C.
Taylor, Morris Iushewitz, Father George B. Ford, Rabbi Edward E.
Klein, and Reverends Harry Emerson Fosdick and Thomas Kilgore.
The Committee's purposes were to raise money for the legal defense
of Dr. King and others and to call the nation's attention to what was
happening in the South.

On March 23, 1960, an aspiring young playwright named John
Murray began a legal controversy that would not end until four

years later. On that day, Murray placed with the *New York Times* a $4,800 full-page editorial advertisement he had helped write for the Committee.

It was not uncommon for the *Times* to run so-called editorial advertisements like the one Murray had submitted. In fact, the *Times* had published many others that were much more controversial and farfetched. For example, every couple of years since the end of the Korean War, North Korea's ruler Kim Il Sung had placed a two-page ad extolling the virtues of his communist revolution.[17] Therefore Gershon Aronson, a veteran salesperson who had worked for the *Times* for a quarter-century, made arrangements for Murray's ad to run the following week without really giving the matter so much as a second thought.[18]

The advertisement appeared on page 25 of the *Times*'s Tuesday, March 29, 1960, edition. (See Appendix for the full text of the ad.) It carried a banner headline borrowed from the *Times*'s March 19 editorial, which read "Heed Their Rising Voices." A part of the sentence from which the headline was taken appeared in italics at the top of the page: "The growing movement of peaceful demonstrations by Negroes is something new in the South, something understandable....Let Congress heed their rising voices, for they will be heard." The more disconcerting phrase "and something ominous" was dropped in order to project a more moderate tone.

The eleven-paragraph advertisement went on to relate the efforts of the students involved in the sit-in movement and to recount acts of terrorism and intimidation perpetrated against Dr. King, his family, and his followers in the South. The third and sixth paragraphs referred directly to events in Alabama. The fifth paragraph's reference to "Southern violators of the Constitution" arguably included Alabama officials. These paragraphs would serve as the bases for libel suits brought by Alabama officials against the *Times*. The paragraphs read:

In Montgomery, Alabama, after students sang "My Country, 'Tis of Thee" on the State Capitol steps, their leaders were expelled from school, and truckloads of police armed with shotguns and tear-gas ringed the Alabama State College Campus. When the entire student body protested to state

authorities by refusing to re-register, their dining hall was pad-
locked in an attempt to starve them into submission.

Small wonder that the Southern violators of the Constitution fear this new, non-violent brand of freedom fighter...even
as they fear the upswelling right-to-vote movement. Small
wonder that they are determined to destroy the one man who,
more than any other, symbolizes the new spirit now sweeping
the South—the Rev. Dr. Martin Luther King, Jr., world-
famous leader of the Montgomery Bus Protest. For it is his
doctrine of non-violence which has inspired and guided the
students in their widening wave of sit-ins; and it is this same
Dr. King who founded and is president of the Southern
Christian Leadership Conference—the organization which is
spearheading the surging right-to-vote movement. Under Dr.
King's direction the Leadership Conference conducts Student
Workshops and Seminars in the philosophy and technique of
non-violent resistance.

Again and again the Southern violators have answered Dr.
King's peaceful protests with intimidation and violence. They
have bombed his home almost killing his wife and child. They
have assaulted his person. They have arrested him seven
times—for "speeding," "loitering" and similar offenses. And
now they have charged him with "perjury"—a *felony* under
which they could imprison him for *ten years*. Obviously, their
real purpose is to remove him physically as the leader to whom
the students and millions of others—look for guidance and
support, and thereby to intimidate *all* leaders who may rise in
the South. Their strategy is to behead this affirmative movement, and thus to demoralize Negro Americans and weaken
their will to struggle. The defense of Martin Luther King,
spiritual leader of the sit-in movement, clearly, therefore, is an
integral part of the total struggle for freedom in the South.

The lower right-hand corner of the page offered a coupon with
the Committee's address, 312 West 125th Street, New York, New
York, that could be clipped out and mailed with a contribution. The
coupon requested the contributor's name and address and asked
whether the contributor sought further information or would care

to volunteer services on the Committee's behalf. Checks were to be made payable to the Committee to Defend Martin Luther King.

An impressive list of signatories appeared at the bottom of the page, among them Marlon Brando, Diahann Carroll, Dr. Alan Knight Chalmers, Richard Coe, Ossie F. Davis, Sammy Davis Jr., Ruby Dee, Anthony Franciosa, Lorraine Hansberry, Van Heflin, Nat Hentoff, Langston Hughes, Mordecai Johnson, Eartha Kitt, Hope Lange, John Raitt, Jackie Robinson, Mrs. Eleanor Roosevelt, Robert Ryan, Maureen Stapleton, and Shelley Winters.

Clergy listed as endorsing the appeal included four black Alabama ministers: Ralph D. Abernathy of Montgomery, S. S. Seay Sr. of Montgomery, Fred L. Shuttlesworth of Birmingham, and Joseph E. Lowery of Mobile.

Alabama officials were outraged by the advertisement. After all, racial discrimination existed in the North as well as in the South. To them, the *Times* ad was just another example of the northern press pillorying the South to divert attention from the North's own racial tensions. Besides, the ad contained a number of factual inaccuracies that made the situation in Alabama appear worse than it really was.

Beyond their anger, however, Alabama politicians and their clever segregationist lawyers saw an opportunity dropped in their laps. They formulated a legal strategy designed to use the advertisement to silence King, his movement, and the northern media once and for all, and to get rich in the process.

On April 8, 1960, L. B. Sullivan, a Montgomery, Alabama, city commissioner who was in charge of the police, wrote a letter to the *Times*, misdated March 8, 1960. In his correspondence, Sullivan charged that the third and sixth paragraphs of the March 29 advertisement had accused him wrongly of "grave misconduct" and "improper actions as an official of the City of Montgomery."[19]

The advertisement had not mentioned Sullivan or any Alabama official by name. Sullivan contended, however, that the police behavior complained of in the ad and presented as fact could not have occurred if he had been performing his responsibilities properly. In other words, the ad implied improper conduct by Sullivan as head of the police. Sullivan demanded "a full and fair retraction of the entire false and defamatory matter."[20]

Attorneys for the New York firm of Lord, Day & Lord replied

on the *Times*'s behalf. By letter dated April 15, 1960, the *Times*'s attorneys professed ignorance as to what in the advertisement could be taken to reflect negatively on Sullivan personally and pledged to review the matter to determine whether the ad contained any factual errors.

Meanwhile Sullivan proceeded with a planned lawsuit. On April 19, 1960, he sued the *New York Times* for libel in a state court in Montgomery. The four black Alabama ministers—Abernathy, Seay, Shuttlesworth, and Lowery—were also named as defendants. Sullivan asked for half a million dollars in compensatory damages for alleged harm to his reputation.

A short time later, Alabama Governor John Patterson followed Sullivan's lead. As state attorney general, Patterson had won the 1956 state court judgment ordering the NAACP's local chapter to surrender its membership and contributors files. On May 9, 1960, Patterson wrote to the *Times* demanding a retraction of the same two paragraphs complained of by Sullivan, and, on May 16, 1960, the *Times* did in fact publish an apology. Under a headline that read, "*Times* Retracts Statement in Ad," the newspaper reprinted Patterson's objections to the March 29 advertisement and explained, "The publication of an advertisement does not constitute a factual news report by *The Times* nor does it reflect the judgment or the opinion of the editors of *The Times*."[21]

The retraction went on to state, "Since publication of the advertisement, *The Times* made an investigation and consistent with its policy of retracting and correcting any errors or misstatements which may appear in its columns, hereby retracts the two paragraphs complained of by the Governor. *The New York Times* never intended to suggest by publication of the advertisement that the Honorable John Patterson, either in his capacity as Governor or as ex-officio chairman of the Board of Education of the State of Alabama, or otherwise, was guilty of 'grave misconduct or improper actions or omission.' To the extent that anyone can fairly conclude from the statements in the advertisement that any such charge was made, *The New York Times* hereby apologizes to the Honorable John Patterson therefor."[22]

That same day, Orvil Dryfoos, president of the New York Times Company, sent the page on which the retraction appeared to Patterson with a letter that reiterated, "to the extent that anyone can fairly conclude from the statements in the advertisement that any such charge [of misconduct or impropriety] was made, *The New York Times* hereby apologizes to the Honorable John Patterson therefor."[23]

But Patterson did not relent. His demand for a retraction had been merely a legal ploy designed to win punitive damages in addition to compensatory relief. Under Alabama law, a public official could recover punitive damages for libel only if the official had made a request for a retraction that was denied by the offending publication. In June 1960 Patterson filed his own libel action against the *Times* based on the kinds of assertions made by Sullivan— namely, that the advertisement had implied that he, as governor, had acted improperly. Like Sullivan, Patterson demanded half a million dollars in compensatory damages. He named Martin Luther King Jr. as a codefendant, along with the *Times* and the four Alabama ministers.

The parade to the courthouse was not yet over. The lawsuits were also filed by other Alabama officials, including Earl James, the mayor of Montgomery; Frank Parks, another Montgomery city commissioner; and Clyde Sellers, a former Montgomery commissioner. Each sought half a million dollars from the newspaper and the black ministers.

Lawsuits against other news organizations followed. Suddenly the "liberal" northern media was under heavy attack in the Alabama courts. For example, the Columbia Broadcasting System (CBS) became the target of $1.5 million in libel claims arising from its coverage of the civil rights movement.[24]

Meanwhile, libel claims against the *Times* soon totaled some $5 million.[25] Not all of them were related to the March 29 ad. The sum represented a tremendous amount of money in the early 1960s, even for a profitable and well-established publication of the *Times*'s stature. In fact, the newspaper's continued existence was in jeopardy.

Dr. King and the four ministers were, for their part, by no means wealthy men. Their personal residences were their only real assets. Forcing them and their families out of their homes would have in part satisfied the Alabama officials' desire for revenge. It would have taught the ministers a good lesson about "uppity" behavior. But even selling their houses would not have enabled the ministers to satisfy their share of any libel judgment. Sullivan and Patterson knew this all along; they never expected to recover significant amounts of money from the ministers. Instead, the ministers had been named as codefendants as part of another clever legal ploy aimed at keeping the libel suits in the Alabama courts.

Under federal law, a case based on a claim arising under state law—in this instance, civil libel—could be removed to a federal court only when complete diversity of citizenship existed between the plaintiffs and the defendants. To the extent that plaintiffs Sullivan and Patterson were citizens of Alabama, and the defendant *Times* was a New York corporation, that diversity was present. But the diversity was not *complete* because the defendant ministers were, like Sullivan and Patterson, Alabamans. By naming the Alabama ministers as codefendants, Sullivan and Patterson had precluded the *Times* from getting the cases removed to an impartial federal court. Thus the issues would be decided by Alabama judges and juries hostile to the northern press.

NAACP lawyers charged that southern officials' systematic efforts to suppress the civil rights movement violated the First Amendment. At first, the U.S. Supreme Court was responsive to their arguments. For example, on June 30, 1958, the Court in *NAACP v. Alabama*[26] struck down the requirement that the Alabama chapter of the NAACP reveal its membership and contributors. The disclosure requirement was held to be a violation of the freedom of assembly clause of the First Amendment, applicable to the states through the Fourteenth Amendment's due process clause.

The First Amendment guarantees "the right of the people peaceably to assemble." Writing for a unanimous Court, Justice Harlan declared that requiring the NAACP to disclose its membership would effectively preclude the members from assembling, or associating, freely. He wrote, "This Court has recognized the vital relationship between freedom to associate and privacy in one's associations."[27]

He concluded, "Inviolability of privacy in group association may in many circumstances be indispensable to preservation of freedom of association, particularly where a group espouses dissident beliefs."[28]

In another case, *NAACP v. Button*,[29] decided on January 14, 1963, the Court struck down Virginia's statute prohibiting barratry, the practice of provoking lawsuits or quarrels. The NAACP had been charged under the Virginia law with criminal solicitation for encouraging civil rights litigation. Writing for a five-man majority, Justice Brennan declared that the NAACP had a right under the First Amendment to provide legal assistance in race discrimination suits.

The ruling in *Button* gave a tremendous boost to NAACP efforts in the South. But the opinion Brennan delivered was also significant on a much broader level, for he used it to expand First Amendment freedoms generally. For example, he established that First Amendment protections extend not just to ideas and words but also to "vigorous advocacy" and "political expression" that goes beyond mere ideas or words.

He wrote, "[A]bstract discussion is not the only species of communication which the Constitution protects; the First Amendment also protects vigorous advocacy, certainly of lawful ends, against government intrusion."[30]

He continued, "In the context of NAACP objectives, litigation is not a technique of resolving private differences; it is a means for achieving the lawful objectives of equality of treatment by all government, federal, state and local, for the members of the Negro community in this country. It is thus a form of political expression."[31]

Brennan went on to state that the right to associate freely embraced not only private association but also "political association," including group litigation. He explained, "The NAACP is not a conventional political party; but the litigation it assists, while serving to vindicate the legal rights of members of the American Negro community, at the same time and perhaps more importantly, makes possible the distinctive contribution of a minority group to ideas and beliefs of our society."[32]

He concluded, "For such a group, association for litigation may be the most effective form of political association."[33]

Over the years, these words would keep the door to the courthouse open not only for the NAACP but also for advocates across a wide social and political spectrum, from lawyers on behalf of consumer and environmental protection groups to those representing prisoners, gays, women, and the underprivileged.

Yet Brennan was not saying that the First Amendment freedoms were absolute. He continued to believe that certain kinds of speech were not protected and that the government could impose reasonable regulations even on the kinds of speech that the amendment did cover. For example, the government could require political protesters to obtain a permit before parading down Main Street or prohibit a speaker from blasting his message through a bullhorn at night when people were trying to sleep.

Instead, the approach Brennan took was more subtle. The First Amendment freedoms, he went on to declare in *Button*, "are delicate and vulnerable, as well as supremely precious in our society."[34] He acknowledged that the "threat of sanctions may deter their exercise almost as potently as the actual application of sanctions."[35] Therefore, he wrote, "Because First Amendment freedoms need breathing space to survive, government may regulate in the area only with narrow specificity."[36]

By this narrow specificity standard, the Virginia barratry law was "overbroad" and "vague," for it proscribed "any arrangement by which prospective litigants are advised to seek the assistance of particular attorneys."[37] Brennan emphasized that even a "simple referral to or recommendation of a lawyer may be [unlawful] solicitation" within the meaning of the Virginia law.[38] This proscription went entirely too far since it left no room for the kind of association for group litigation that the Court determined was permitted under the First Amendment. At the very least, the Virginia law tended to frighten people away from gathering to discuss the possibility of associating for the purpose of initiating lawsuits.

Brennan at least technically left open the possibility that a barratry law could be written narrowly enough to accord First Amendment freedoms the breathing space they needed, that did not "chill" the exercise of the First Amendment rights. He sensed correctly, however, that rather than go back time and again to the drawing board, southern officials were more likely simply to plot some other course or abandon altogether their attempt to hamstring the NAACP.

Brennan's opinion in *Button* was joined by the liberals—Warren, Black, Douglas, and Goldberg. White concurred in part and dissented in part. Clark and Stewart joined Harlan in dissent.

The Court's liberals divided bitterly, however, over the question of whether sit-in demonstrations enjoyed First Amendment protection. Between 1961 and 1965, more than thirty sit-in cases came to the Court as the sit-in movement grew in size and intensity.[39] Usually the demonstrators who "sat in" at lunch counters or demanded service in retail stores where African Americans were not allowed to shop were arrested and convicted of criminal trespass, disturbing the peace, entering and remaining, vagrancy, or similar misdemeanors. Typically, lawyers for the demonstrators claimed on appeal that the state officers who made the arrests were "suppressing free speech and enforcing racial discrimination in violation of the First and Fourteenth Amendments."[40]

Matters came to a head during the Court's 1962–63 and 1963–64 terms. By that time, the southern black students who spearheaded the sit-in movement had been joined by a sympathetic generation of younger whites, many from the North. In all, some 70,000 demonstrators, black and white, were actively engaged in sit-in demonstrations throughout the South.[41]

Justice Black objected to the sit-in—or "sit-down," protests as he called them. He took the First Amendment literally, and the amendment referred explicitly to speech; it made no mention of "conduct," such as sit-ins. In addition, Black was concerned, much as Thurgood Marshall had been during the 1950s, that the civil rights mass movement would provoke the masses of whites to react negatively with protests of their own. Whites outnumbered African Americans. Therefore African Americans could not win any such mass confrontations.

Moreover, Black believed in the sanctity of private property. The Fourteenth Amendment's guarantee of equal protection of the laws had been held by the Court to apply only to state action, prohibiting racial discrimination by a state or its officers. In Black's view, the Fourteenth Amendment did not apply to private individuals, who remained free to associate, or not to associate, with whomever they chose.

Even Thurgood Marshall shared this view. Shortly after his victory in *Brown* in 1954, Marshall told an interviewer from the *Pittsburgh Courier* that it was not the NAACP's goal to force unwanted integration on private clubs or associations. Solving the race problem, Marshall insisted, "doesn't mean a man is not to determine who comes into his home, or his country club. There are lots of people I don't want around my house."[42]

As Black saw it, privately owned businesses such as restaurants, theaters, and retail stores were, like homes or country clubs, beyond the Fourteenth Amendment's reach and hence free to discriminate. He once told his colleagues in conference, "We have a system of private ownership of property and...I see nothing in the Constitution which says [that an] owner can't tell people he doesn't want to get out. Therefore, he can call the police to help protect that right. If that right is in the owner, the law must enforce that right."[43]

Douglas disagreed. He believed that private businesses that served the public should be treated as public accommodations or public utilities and that discrimination by them should be banned. Justice Brennan's papers in the Library of Congress include an impassioned memorandum from Douglas to the other justices dated October 21, 1963. In it, Douglas wrote, "Suppose a Negro enters a drug store to buy penicillin for his sick child and is arrested and convicted for 'entering' or for 'remaining.'

"Suppose a Negro is denied admission to a private hospital and is arrested and convicted for 'entering' and 'remaining.'

"Assume there is a State that has no statute requiring a common carrier to carry on-comers and a Negro is arrested and convicted for riding on one." By "common carrier" Douglas meant a form of public transportation, such as a bus.

He went on, "The question in the sit-in cases is, in other words, not whether there is state action but whether States, acting through their courts, can constitutionally put a racial cordon around businesses serving the public. If they can do it in the restaurant cases they can do it in drug stores, private hospitals and common carriers, interstate carriers apart. Property is in one case as sacrosanct as in the other. But the businesses involved in these cases are in this day and age as much affected with the public interest as were the inn-keepers and common carriers of old."

He concluded, "An affirmance [of the convictions] in these [sit-in] cases fastens apartheid tightly onto our society—a result that is incomprehensible in light of the purposes of our Fourteenth Amendment and the realities of our modern society."

Brennan, for his part, feared that if the Court's divisions over the sit-in cases were revealed, the civil rights movement would be undermined. He believed that it was still crucial for the Court to present a united front on race. Therefore he urged his colleagues not to address directly the constitutional questions posed by the sit-in cases that came to the Court during the 1963–64 term. By that time, Congress was already considering the major civil rights bill that would ultimately become the Civil Rights Act of 1964. Brennan knew that the legislation, if enacted, would prohibit the kinds of discrimination complained of by the sit-in demonstrators and hence solve the problem. In the meantime, he insisted, the justices should tread lightly.

Ultimately, Brennan's view prevailed. When the Court ruled in sit-in cases, the justices tended to side with the demonstrators. But they did so on narrow bases, dismissing the protesters' convictions on legal technicalities or declaring the vagrancy and trespassing laws under which they had been arrested "vague," "overbroad," or otherwise lacking in the requisite "narrow specificity." The Court avoided a major decision on broader constitutional grounds.

For example, in *Peterson v. Greenville*,[44] decided on May 20, 1963, the Court unanimously overturned the convictions of ten African Americans convicted of trespass for a sit-in at a lunch counter in an S. H. Kress store in Greenville, South Carolina. The store manager had refused to serve the protesters, insisting that to do so would have been "contrary to local customs"[45] and in violation of a city ordinance that required separation of the races in Greenville restaurants.

Writing for a unanimous Court, Chief Justice Warren struck down the convictions as a violation of the Fourteenth Amendment's equal protection clause. Warren held that the discriminatory city ordinance constituted state action.

In a companion case, *Lombard v. Louisiana*,[46] decided the same day, the Court threw out the criminal mischief convictions of two African American students and their white companion in connection with a sit-in at the lunch counter of the McCrory Five and Ten Cent Store in New Orleans, Louisiana. Unlike Greenville, New Orleans had no ordinance mandating racial segregation in the city's restaurants. But writing for a unanimous Court, Chief Justice Warren found state action based on comments made by city officials to the effect that the city would not permit sit-in demonstrations to succeed in securing desegregated restaurant service.

In another case, *Bell v. Maryland*,[47] Justice Brennan overturned the trespass convictions of twelve African American students for a sit-in at Hooper's Restaurant in Baltimore. Brennan based his ruling on the fact that since the convictions, Maryland had passed public-accommodations legislation outlawing discrimination in restaurants based on race. In other words, the discriminatory conduct that the students had been convicted for protesting was no longer legal in the state.

Nevertheless, the Court in *Bell* split badly. Harlan and White joined Black in a strong dissent which insisted that the Court should have addressed directly the question of whether the Fourteenth Amendment's equal protection clause required public accommodations to operate on a desegregated basis. Black expressed his previously stated view that privately owned restaurants were beyond the Fourteenth Amendment's reach.

As Brennan had hoped, however, it was not long before Congress passed and President Lyndon B. Johnson signed the Civil Rights Act of 1964. That law brought an end to discrimination in public accommodations, though it did so based on Congress's power under the Constitution's commerce clause rather than under the Fourteenth Amendment.

The commerce clause, Article I, section 8, clause 3 of the Constitution provides, "The Congress shall have the Power...To regulate Commerce with foreign Nations, and among the several States, and with the Indian Tribes." In *Atlanta Motel v. United States*,[48] decided on December 14, 1964, the Court ruled unanimously that Congress's mandate over commerce included the power to outlaw race discrimination by local, privately owned businesses that serve the general public.

The act not only made discrimination in public accommodations illegal, it also outlawed state prosecutions of people who attempted to exercise their rights under the act. Consequently the Court by an 8-to-1 vote in *Hamm v. City of Rock Hill*,[49] decided the same day as *Atlanta Motel*, overturned the convictions of demonstrators in connection with lunch counter sit-ins in South Carolina and Arkansas. In his lone dissent, Black complained that the sit-ins in question had occurred before the Civil Rights Act became law and that the act's protections should not be applied retroactively.

Meanwhile, L. B. Sullivan's libel suit against the *New York Times* had worked its way up to the U.S. Supreme Court through the Alabama state courts. At the trial-court level, a Montgomery jury had awarded Sullivan the full half million dollars in damages he had sought. The *Times* had appealed the verdict to the Alabama state supreme court but lost there on its claim that the libel judgment against the newspaper violated the First Amendment. Subsequently, the *Times* had asked the U.S. Supreme Court to review the Alabama high court's ruling. The justices agreed to do so and heard oral arguments in the case, *New York Times v. Sullivan*,[50] on January 6, 1964.

The case was considered against the backdrop of a nation in shock and mourning over the assassination of President John F. Kennedy in Dallas, Texas, on November 22, 1963. As fate would have it, the fallen president became a martyr in the struggle for racial equality. Guilt, remorse, moral uncertainty, and worry about the future propelled the nation toward passage of the sweeping Civil Rights Act of 1964, which Kennedy had proposed but that until his death had languished unfinished in the Congress.

Standing beside the slain president's flag-draped coffin as it lay in state in the Capitol rotunda, Chief Justice Warren had spoken for millions of Americans when he said, "What moved some misguided wretch to do this horrible deed may never be known to us, but we do know that such acts are commonly stimulated by forces of hatred and malevolence such as today are eating their way into the blood stream of American life. What a price we pay for this fanaticism!"[51] After November 22, 1963, the country needed a respite from hatred and intolerance.

Kennedy's death had a special impact within the Court. Warren had been appointed by President Johnson to chair the independent Commission on the Assassination of President Kennedy, known popularly as the Warren Commission. The chief justice thus was forced to divide his time between investigating and reporting on President Kennedy's death and his responsibilities at the Court.

One Warren Commission staff member recalled, "I don't know where he [Warren] got the energy. We'd start a hearing at nine in the morning. He'd preside until a few minutes before ten, then leave for the Court. At 2:30 he'd come back and sit there well into the evening. At times he was presiding at the Commission and the Court for stretches of eight and ten hours. During those last weeks, when we were finishing the report, he'd work till one in the morning, then be the first to show up next day."[52]

Overworked and distracted, Warren assigned Brennan to write the *Sullivan* opinion, which would become one of the most significant First Amendment rulings by the Court in the history of the republic. Given the monumental importance of the case and its potential consequences for freedom of speech and press and the civil rights movement, Warren might under normal circumstances have chosen to write the decision himself, lending the imprimatur of the chief justice's office to the result. In hindsight, however, it is unlikely that Warren could have done a better job than his friend and chief lieutenant.

As Brennan saw the facts of the case, Alabama's libel law was not anomalous; it was based on the customary "fair comment rule" that was on the books in most states. Under the Alabama law as applied by the state supreme court, a publication was libelous if the words it used tended "to injure a person...in his reputation" or to "bring [the person] into public contempt."[53]

But the origins of the fair comment rule were nefarious. The rule dated back to the English doctrine of seditious libel during the centuries when the Star Chamber punished almost any criticism of the government as a crime. The First Amendment had been adopted in large part as a reaction against the seditious libel doctrine. The Founding Fathers had learned through bitter experience with tyranny that "political freedom ends when government can use its powers to silence its critics."[54] As University of Chicago Law School professor Harry Kalven Jr. observed, "the presence or absence in the law of the concept of seditious libel defines the society. A society may or may not treat obscenity or contempt by publication as legal offenses without altering its basic nature. If, however, it makes seditious libel an offense, it is not a free society, no matter what its other characteristics."[55]

Yet libel, like obscenity, had always been considered beyond the scope of First Amendment protection. For example, in *Beauharnais v. Illinois*,[56] decided in 1952, the Court had upheld the conviction of a white man under an Illinois group libel statute. The Illinois law made it a crime to publish or distribute material that portrayed "depravity, criminality, unchastity, or lack of virtue of a class of citizens, of any race, color, creed or religion" and that exposed "the citizens of any race, color, creed or religion to contempt, derision, or obloquy."[57]

The group libel law had been passed in 1917 at a time when Illinois "was struggling to assimilate vast numbers of new inhabitants, as yet concentrated in discrete racial or national or religious groups—foreign-born brought to it by the crest of the great wave of immigration, and Negroes attracted by jobs in war plants and the allurements of northern claims."[58]

Joseph Beauharnais, a Chicagoan, had been fined $200 in January 1950 by a state court for distributing to his followers leaflets that said offensive things about African Americans. The flyers called upon Chicago's mayor and city council "to halt the further encroachment, harassment and invasion of white people, their property, neighborhoods and persons, by the Negro"[59] and asked "One million self respecting white people in Chicago to unite."[60] The leaflets warned, "If persuasion and the need to prevent the white race from becoming mongrelized by the negro will not unite us, then the aggressions...rapes, robberies, knives, guns and marijuana of the negro surely will."[61]

The lower right-hand corner of each leaflet offered an application in the form of a coupon for membership in the White Circle League of America, Inc., of which Beauharnais was the president. The coupon could be clipped out and mailed to the White Circle League's address, 82 West Washington Street, Chicago 2, Illinois. The coupon requested the sender's name and address and asked for a membership fee of $1.00, $3.00 for a subscription to a monthly magazine called *White News*, an unspecified contribution, or whether the sender wished to volunteer services on the League's behalf.[62]

In his opinion for the Court, Justice Frankfurter, citing precedent, declared, "There are certain well-defined and narrowly limited classes of speech, the prevention and punishment of which have never been thought to raise any Constitutional problem. These include the lewd and obscene, the profane, the libelous, and the insulting or 'fighting words'—those which by their very utterance inflict injury or tend to incite an immediate breach of the peace. It has been well observed that such utterances are no essential part of any exposition of ideas, and are of such slight social value as a step to truth that any benefit that may be derived from them is clearly outweighed by the social interest in order and morality."[63]

Frankfurter concluded, "We find no warrant in the Constitution for denying to Illinois the power to pass the law here under attack."[64]

Black and Douglas dissented from the *Beauharnais* ruling, as did Justices Robert Jackson and Stanley Reed. Black's dissent was eloquent and powerful. He wrote, "Today Beauharnais is punished for publicly expressing strong views in favor of segregation. Iron-ically enough, Beauharnais, convicted of a crime in Chicago, would probably be given a hero's reception in many other localities, if not in some parts of Chicago itself. Moreover, the same kind of state law that makes Beauharnais a criminal for advocating segregation in Illinois can be utilized to send people to jail in other states for advocating equality and nonsegregation. What Beauharnais said in his leaflet is mild compared with usual arguments on both sides of racial controversies."[65]

Douglas's dissent was prophetic. He wrote, "Today a white man stands convicted for protesting in unseemly language against our decisions invalidating [racially] restrictive [housing] covenants. Tomorrow a Negro will be haled before a court for denouncing lynch law in heated terms. Farm laborers in the West who compete with field hands drifting up from Mexico; whites who feel the pressure of orientals; a minority which finds employment going to members of the dominant religious group—all of these are caught in the mesh of today's decision."[66]

He went on, "Debate and argument even in the courtroom are not always calm and dispassionate. Emotions sway speakers and audiences alike. Intemperate speech is a distinctive characteristic of man. Hotheads blow off and release destructive energy in the process. They shout and rave, exaggerating weaknesses, magnifying error, viewing with alarm. So it has been from the beginning; and so it will be throughout time. The Framers of the Constitution knew human nature as well as we do. They too had lived in dangerous days; they too knew the suffocating influence of orthodoxy and standardized thought. They weighed the compulsions for restrained speech and thought against the abuses of liberty. They chose liberty. That should be our choice today no matter how distasteful to us the pamphlet of Beauharnais may be."[67]

He reiterated his absolutist view: "The First Amendment says that freedom of speech, freedom of press, and the free exercise of religion shall not be abridged. That is a negation of power on the part of each and every department of government. Free speech, free press, free exercise of religion are placed separate and apart; they are above and beyond the police power; they are not subject to regulation in the manner of factories, slums, apartment houses, production of oil, and the like."[68]

The *New York Times* had not been able to plead truth as a defense to Sullivan's libel action because the March 29 advertisement had indeed contained factual inaccuracies. The African American students who had staged a demonstration at the Alabama state capitol had sung the National Anthem, not "My Country 'Tis of Thee."[69] Also, the dining hall on the Alabama State College campus had never been padlocked, nor did state police at any time "ring" the campus, although they had been deployed nearby in large numbers.[70]

Furthermore, Dr. King had not been arrested seven times, but only four.[71] And some of the attempts to kill or intimidate him had occurred prior to Sullivan's tenure as commissioner, including the two bombings of King's home and three of his four arrests.[72] Nor had Sullivan had anything to do with procuring Dr. King's indictment for perjury in connection with his state income taxes as the ad could be interpreted to imply.[73] Finally, the four black Montgomery ministers had never really signed or endorsed the ad. In fact they knew nothing of it until after its publication.

The *Times* was therefore forced to base its defense on other grounds and did so, boldly taking the high road. Lawyers for the newspaper, among them former Attorney General Herbert Brownell and Herbert Wechsler, who argued the case to the justices, asserted that the First Amendment barred all libel actions for comments about government officials' conduct.

Black, Douglas, and Goldberg shared this view. They favored giving the *Times* absolute immunity from suit. But Brennan was not prepared to go that far. In 1963, he had read an article written by Yale law professor Thomas I. Emerson for the *Yale Law Journal* entitled "Toward a General Theory of the First Amendment."[74] Brennan had been persuaded by Emerson's argument that in deciding First Amendment cases, judges should apply a "balancing test." Under the test, according to Emerson, "The formula is that the court must in each case balance the individual and social interest in freedom of expression against the social interest sought by the regulation which restricts expression."[75]

Up to that time, the "articulate spokesman" on the Court for the balancing test had been Harlan.[76] Harlan saw *Sullivan* as "a classic illustration of a First Amendment problem where the public interest in discussion [had] to be accommodated with the private right not to be defamed."[77] Applying the balancing test to the circumstances of the case, Harlan was prepared to rule in the *Times*'s favor and impose "a significant restriction on the power of government to penalize libelous comments about government officials."[78] So was Brennan, who knew, as usual, that he could also count on Warren's vote.

But to arrive at unanimity or at least consensus in this crucial First Amendment case posed a challenge. Brennan knew he would have to formulate a restriction on government power stringent enough to satisfy the absolutists without alienating justices who might oppose giving the press what they regarded as a blank check to defame.

He succeeded. On March 9, 1964, Brennan announced the Court's ruling from the bench, a unanimous decision in favor of the *Times* based on a new doctrine he had formulated, the "actual malice" test. Under the novel rule, a comment about a government official could be penalized under state libel laws only if the complaining official could prove with "convincing clarity"[79] that the comment was made with actual malice, meaning "with knowledge that it [the comment] was false or with reckless disregard of whether it was false or not."[80]

The factual inaccuracies contained in the *Times*'s March 29 advertisement did not constitute actual malice, Brennan declared, because "erroneous statement is inevitable in free debate."[81] And free debate, he explained, "must be protected if the freedoms of expression are to have the 'breathing space' that they 'need...to survive.'"[82]

He insisted that anything less stringent than the actual malice standard "dampens the vigor and limits the variety of public debate," a result "inconsistent with the First and Fourteenth Amendments."[83] In what would become the passage most frequently quoted from his voluminous writings, he went on to state, "Thus we consider this case against the background of a profound national commitment to the principle that debate on public issues should be uninhibited, robust, and wide-open, and that it may well include vehement, caustic, and sometimes unpleasantly sharp attacks on government and public officials."[84]

But despite their agreement as to the result, and the unprecedented extent to which Brennan's opinion gave teeth to the guarantees of free speech and free press, the ruling did not go as far as Black, Douglas, and Goldberg would have liked. Black wrote a separate concurrence in which Douglas joined. Goldberg also concurred separately. All three expressed the steadfast belief that, as Goldberg put it, "the First and Fourteenth Amendments to the Constitution afford to the citizen and to the press an absolute, unconditional privilege to criticize official conduct despite the harm which may flow from excesses and abuses."[85]

Black complained, "'Malice,' even as defined by the Court, is an elusive, abstract concept, hard to prove and hard to disprove. The requirement that malice be proved provides at best an evanescent protection for the right critically to discuss public affairs and certainly does not measure up to the sturdy safeguard embodied in the First Amendment."[86]

Yet Black praised Brennan's work, for he was certain the result would alter the future course of American history for the better. Brennan's case files in the Library of Congress include an undated note that Black passed to him on the bench during an oral argument. Written in the Alabaman's bold scrawl, it read, "Bill, You know of course that despite my position & what I wrote I think you are doing a wonderful job in the Times case and however it finally comes out it is bound to be a very long step towards preserving the right to communicate ideas."[87]

Brennan's files also contain a note from Goldberg that was passed to him on the bench just minutes before he announced the *Sullivan* decision. In it, Goldberg explained, "The view I express that the Constitution affords an absolute immunity to press and citizen for criticism of official conduct is in the minority. The rule fashioned by the Court [in *Sullivan*] grants only a conditional privilege which does not provide the degree of safeguard to 1st and 14th Amendment rights which the Constitution I believe commands. What the Court does today however provides a far greater degree of safeguard to press and citizen in their right of free speech than the Alabama rule of libel liability which I agree is patently unconstitutional."[88]

A few hours after the Court's ruling, Arthur Ochs Sulzberger, president and publisher of the *New York Times*, issued a statement: "We are, of course, delighted with the decision of the Supreme Court. It clearly illuminates several basic issues regarding freedom of the press and therefore is of fundamental importance not only for newspapers, but other news media as well."[89]

Sulzberger concluded, "The opinion of the Court makes free-dom of the press more secure than ever before."[90]

As one legal scholar has described it, the "actual malice" test enunciated in *Sullivan* "makes no pretense of distinguishing consti-tutionally valuable from constitutionally valueless speech [such as libel]. It is instead designed solely as an instrument of policy, to attain the specific end of minimizing the chill on legitimate speech. As such, the standard epitomizes the pragmatic conception of constitutional law, a conception whose articulation and develop-ment can authoritatively be traced to Brennan."[91]

Because of Brennan's ruling in *Sullivan*, the national media were able to inform the American public about Martin Luther King Jr., the struggle for civil rights, and the often violent and abusive nature of the southern white resistance. Perhaps more than anything else, access to this information ensured King's success. Within four months of the Court's ruling in *Sullivan*, on July 2, 1964, the Civil Rights Act of 1964 was signed into law. Subsequently, President Johnson was able to push through Congress the landmark Voting Rights Act of 1965, which finally made good the promise held out by the Fifteenth Amendment to the Constitution, ratified after the Civil War to guarantee former slaves and their descendants the right to vote.

A quarter-century later, however, Brennan was forced to con-cede that the fight for racial equality still had not been won. In 1989 he told an interviewer, "Anybody who thinks that our problems of racial injustice are behind us is fooling himself. But the struggle must go on and will go on."[92] During the course of that struggle, William Brennan would find himself increasingly on the defensive as the pace of social progress began to slow just a few short years after *Sullivan*.

CHAPTER 18

The Conservative Backlash

> I think some of our judges have gone too far in assuming unto themselves a mandate...to put their social and economic ideas into their decisions.
>
> —Richard M. Nixon (1968)

THE 1960S WERE A TURBULENT TIME of protest and reaction. African Americans grew restive as changes and opportunities promised on paper failed to materialize in practice. Black militant leaders like Stokely Carmichael, H. Rap Brown, and Malcolm X labeled Martin Luther King an "Uncle Tom" for his continued commitment to nonviolence and urged instead armed resistance to racism. Between 1964 and 1967, large-scale race riots occurred in the Harlem section of New York City; the Watts area in Los Angeles, California; Detroit, Michigan; and Brennan's hometown of Newark, New Jersey. They left scores of people dead, hundreds injured, and thousands of others without homes or jobs as buildings and businesses were burned and looted.

Nearing the end of his presidency, Lyndon Johnson, the man Thurgood Marshall credited with doing more for African Americans than any other president, conceded to his biographer, Doris Kearns Goodwin, in 1967, "I moved the Negro from D$^+$ to C$^-$. He's still nowhere. He knows it. And that's why he's out there in the streets. Hell, I'd be there too."[1]

That same year, Johnson's department of labor reported to the president that the situation in America's urban ghettos was so desperate that "No conceivable increase in the gross national product would stir these backwaters. Unemployment in these areas is primarily a story of inferior education, no skills, police and garnishment records, discrimination, fatherless children, dope addiction, hopelessness."[2]

Whites were rebellious as well. As U.S. military involvement in Vietnam deepened, so did youthful opposition to the war and resistance to the draft. But dissent was not limited to the war. The youth movement represented a broad-based rejection of modern American values and the premium placed on conformity, materialism, and homogeneity.

The sense of disillusionment and disaffection manifested itself in almost every aspect of American life, from sexual permissiveness—free love—to drug use, flag burning, and the radicalization of political discussion. The powers that be were the "Establishment." The Establishment was "imperialistic." Corporate America was "plastic." Police were "pigs." American soldiers were "baby killers." The body politic was divided into "hawks" and "doves," "freaks" and "straights," people who smoked pot and those who did not. Yippie (Youth International Party) leaders like Jerry Rubin urged young people not to trust anybody over thirty.

Women burned their bras. Men grew their hair long. African Americans demanded to be called "black" instead of "Negro" and were "black and proud," donning dashikis and sporting Afro hairstyles that symbolized pride in their African heritage. The mood, even the music, of an entire generation was rebellious, countercultural, incendiary.

Nancy Brennan described the effect of the era's political and social turmoil on her father. She told interviewer Donna Haupt in 1989, "I know he would tell you today that many of the excesses in those years worried him. But I also remember him defending a good bit of what was going on at the college campuses, as long as they were nonviolent and had as their purpose more than just getting on television."[3]

But while he may have supported protests by others, Bill

Brennan wanted the members of his own family to conform to the status quo. "Acting in defiance of rules and regulations worried him," Nancy explained. "I got involved in the anti-Vietnam movement and some other less-than-commendable stuff on campus at the University of Pennsylvania. And I think dad lit four votive candles every night and hoped for the best."[4]

Yet his emphasis on conformity at home belied his liberal inclinations both as a justice and as a boss. Jeffrey T. Leeds, who clerked for Brennan during the Court's 1985–86 term, arrived for his first day of work nattily attired in conservative suit and tie, as he presumed would be expected. Little did he know that Brennan had not enforced a dress code since the 1960s. In fact, Brennan's attitude was quite the contrary.

Leeds recalled, "I walked into his chambers for the first time, and Justice Brennan said he was pleased to meet me. Then he did this thing he does every year. He kind of grabs your necktie and says, 'Do you like wearing these things?' You say no. 'Then take it off,' he says. 'You'll spend plenty of time working hard in this building. You might as well be comfortable.'"[5]

During the 1960s, Brennan's clerks shed more than just their ties. They cast off their pressed trousers, starched collars, and dress shoes in favor of blue jeans, loafers, and casual shirts that they often did not bother to keep tucked into their pants. Typically, they had long hair. And they decorated the walls of their office in a way that took full advantage of their boss's expansive view of free speech under the First Amendment, with colorful posters calling for an end to the Vietnam War or emblazoned with clenched, black fists and "black power" slogans.

None of Brennan's clerks were African American; all were white males. And women were not hired as law clerks with any regularity by any of the justices until the 1970s, so if Brennan did employ a female law clerk before that time, she was rare. But the absence of minorities and the paucity of women had more to do with scant minority and female law-school enrollment than with the attitudes of the justice. Minorities and women had long been underrepresented in the nation's law schools and in the legal profession at large, and doors long barred against them were in the 1960s only starting to open.

Brennan had never consciously tried to achieve diversity—

racial, sexual, economic, or for that matter political—among his law clerks anyway. In fact, during his first dozen years on the Court, he did not even pick them himself and often did not meet them until their first day of work. Instead, his clerks were selected for him by the late Harvard law professor Paul A. Freund, one of the century's most respected legal scholars. By the end of the 1960s, however, Brennan had decided to make the selection process more inclusive. He told Nat Hentoff in 1990, "Paul [Freund] came to me and said, 'Look, every law school in the country is madder than hell at you for taking law clerks only from Harvard. You ought to branch out.' So now I take them from everywhere. Hell, I've had them from night schools."[6]

Despite their casual appearance, long hair, and purely academic fascination with the likes of Eldridge Cleaver and Huey P. Newton, few if any of Brennan's clerks turned out to be fire-breathing, bomb-throwing radicals. Far from it. After a year or two with the justice, most went on to law professorships at places like Harvard, Yale, Columbia, New York University, and Boalt Hall, the University of California at Berkeley's law school. One former clerk, Daniel O'Hern, became a New Jersey state supreme court justice. Others became partners in top-tier law firms or did well in other businesses. Leeds, for example, became a successful investment banker.

Nevertheless, Brennan's conservative critics have always maintained that his opinions reflected his "leftist" law clerks' radical views. Federal appeals court judge Richard S. Arnold, who clerked for Brennan in 1960 and has been mentioned several times as a potential U.S. Supreme Court nominee in his own right, has acknowledged, "In the '50s and '60s, people said liberal law clerks were exercising undue influence. I think that's silly."[7]

In fact, Brennan's clerks did play a major, albeit typical, role in the writing of his opinions. Chief Justice William Rehnquist, himself a former clerk for Justice Robert H. Jackson during the 1950s, conceded in 1994 that his law clerks "do the first draft of almost all cases" and that those drafts sometimes remain "relatively unchanged."[8] The same was true with Brennan. Leeds recalled the thrill of this experience. "You go back to your office, you take a deep breath, you stare at your computer screen, and you go, 'Holy shit, I'm going to write the law of the land.'"[9] But Brennan always did the final draft himself, frequently engaging in what one former clerk called "dramatic rewriting."[10]

Brennan's law clerks' most valuable function may have been serving as their boss's eyes and ears on the rest of the Court. Thurgood Marshall said that no one on the Court "can persuade the way Brennan can persuade."[11] Marshall described Brennan as someone who "will sit down with you and talk to you and show you where you're wrong."[12] But Brennan always rejected the characterization of himself as the great conciliator who maneuvered cleverly behind the scenes to arrive at consensus. "I am not a playmaker," he often said.[13] "I don't go around cajoling and importuning my colleagues to go along with my point of view."[14]

He explained, "Rather than try to talk something out with another Justice, I sit down and write concrete suggestions as to what I don't like about what he has done or what I do like about it. I suggest changes in their drafts, and other Justices will suggest changes in what I've written. Every Justice of this Court admits that holding on to a majority can be a very difficult thing, and what we all do is try to persuade each other. From time-to-time, when I think I'm going to have a five-person majority, one of the four will write to me and say, 'I'll be happy to join with you if you delete this and this.' If you can, you do it. But there are times when I have to write back and say, 'I don't think I should, because then it wouldn't be what I wanted to say.' It's quite important to get these differences out by written exchanges."[15]

Leeds confirmed Brennan's version of his *modus operandi*, but with a key addendum. "It's true that Justice Brennan doesn't go around buttonholing other Justices, trying to persuade them to join one of his opinions. He doesn't have to do that. He gets *us* [the law clerks] to do it; that is, he gets his clerks to talk to the other clerks and find out what their Justices are thinking."[16]

By the mid-1960s, however, there was little need for buttonholing, cajoling, importuning, or play making in order to win a majority among the other justices, for Brennan was ideologically in tune with what was evolving into the most liberal Court in the nation's history. Together with Earl Warren, Hugo Black, William O. Douglas, and Abe Fortas, who replaced another liberal, Arthur Goldberg, in 1965, Brennan and the liberals usually accounted for at least five votes. And those five were committed to using the Court's power to bring about social change. Brennan's point of view was clear. As he stated in a September 29, 1964, address at the University of Pennsylvania,

"Law and social justice are inseparable. Least of all should a judge forget that law *is* an instrument of social justice."[17]

Increasingly, his opinions took on the tone and tenor of a man engaged in a desperate struggle to make American society more tolerant, less racist, less sexist, more just and compassionate, less socially and economically stratified. He promoted human dignity and championed the poor and the disadvantaged.

Between 1964 and 1965, he wrote several majority opinions designed to protect those threatened by state courts traditionally hostile to the claims of African Americans and social activists. For example, in *Dombrowski v. Pfister*,[18] decided on April 26, 1965, the Court by a 5-to-2 vote gave the federal courts broad power to halt state criminal prosecutions. Traditionally, the federal courts had adhered to the "abstention doctrine" and refused to interfere in state proceedings except in extreme circumstances.

For years leading up to *Dombrowski*, rights activists had complained about state officials' using unlawful raids and record seizures as well as criminal prosecution or the threat of it to harass or intimidate them. The plaintiffs in *Dombrowski* were all engaged in civil rights activity in Louisiana during the early 1960s and had been prosecuted under two state laws that were constitutionally suspect. One was the Subversive Activities and Communist Control Law; the other was the Communist Propaganda Control Law.

James A. Dombrowski, an officer of the Southern Conference Educational Fund, had gone into federal court seeking an injunction against Louisiana's governor, law-enforcement officers, and the chairman of the state Legislative Joint Committee on Un-American Activities to block the prosecutions.

Writing for the majority, Brennan declared that the Louisiana laws violated the First Amendment by chilling free speech. The federal courts, he ruled, were justified in intervening to stop state criminal prosecutions where First Amendment freedoms were threatened. Justice Harlan, joined by Clark, dissented, calling the ruling a threat to federal–state relations. Black and Stewart took no part in the consideration of the case.

The *Dombrowski* decision was effectively overturned by a more conservative Court in 1971.[19] In the meantime, however, Brennan's *Dombrowski* ruling unleashed "a torrent of lawsuits seeking federal court protection against state prosecutions"[20] and, like the decision in *Sullivan*, gave a tremendous boost to the civil rights movement.

Brennan also pressed forward with the expansion of First Amendment freedoms. For example, in *Keyishian v. Board of Regents*,[21] decided on January 23, 1967, he struck down as unconstitutional a New York law designed to keep "subversive" teachers out of the state university system. Harry Keyishian, who taught English at the State University of New York at Buffalo, had lost his job after he refused to sign a certificate stating that he was not a communist. Three of Keyishian's colleagues had also been dismissed or threatened with dismissal on similar grounds.

Writing for a 5-to-4 majority, Brennan held that the New York loyalty law under which the New York State Board of Regents had acted against Keyishian was unconstitutionally vague. For example, one section of the law required firing teachers for "treasonable or seditious" utterances or acts.[22] Those terms were not, however, defined with any degree of specificity. Therefore, according to Brennan, "no teacher [could] know just where the line is drawn between 'seditious' and nonseditious utterances and acts."[23]

Building on his *New York Times v. Sullivan* theme that the First Amendment requires "uninhibited, robust, and wide-open" debate, he set forth in *Keyishian* an impassioned defense of academic freedom. He declared, "Our Nation is deeply committed to safeguarding academic freedom, which is of transcendent value to all of us and not merely to the teachers concerned. That freedom is therefore a special concern of the First Amendment, which does not tolerate laws that cast a pall of orthodoxy over the classroom."[24]

Citing precedent, he concluded, "The Nation's future depends upon leaders trained through wide exposure to that robust exchange of ideas which discovers truth 'out of a multitude of tongues, [rather] than through any kind of authoritative selection.'"[25]

The importance of the Court's ruling in *Keyishian* "lay in its rejection of a state's power to make public employment conditional on surrendering constitutional rights that could not otherwise be abridged by direct state action as well as in its emphasis on academic freedom."[26] But because the vote was so close, with Clark, Harlan, Stewart, and Byron White dissenting, Harry Keyishian worried that Brennan's ruling might not stand the test of time, that it would be overturned as the composition of the Court grew increasingly conservative.

By 1990, however, the decision remained the law of the land, and Keyishian told an interviewer that Brennan's opinions "have apparently been so well drawn and so well crafted that they've held up in very hostile environments in that Court, and I hope they'll continue to do so."[27]

Brennan, for his part, felt especially gratified after he saw Keyishian interviewed by Bill Moyers on television. He told Hentoff in 1990, "It was fascinating. It was the first time I had seen him [Keyishian]. Of course, it's rare I ever see the people in the cases we deal with. The things he said on the program, the fight he and the teachers put up—I had no idea how much they had to lose personally if the case had gone the other way. They would have lost everything they had ever done as teachers."[28]

Even when he found himself in the minority, Brennan managed to make powerful and articulate statements on behalf of the civil libertarian ideals and attitudes he advocated. For example, in *Walker v. City of Birmingham*,[29] decided on June 12, 1967, the Court by a 5-to-4 vote upheld the convictions of Martin Luther King and others for conducting a protest march in Birmingham, Alabama, without a permit and in defiance of a state court order. Writing for the majority, Justice Stewart all but mentioned King by name when he declared that "in the fair administration of justice no man can be judge in his own case, however exalted his station, however righteous his motives, and irrespective of his race, color, politics, or religion."[30]

King had in fact four years earlier proclaimed the right not to be bound by "unjust" laws. In his famous "Letter from Birmingham City Jail," written in April 1963 and subsequently published to the nation by *Life* magazine, he had cited St. Augustine for the proposition that "An unjust law is no law at all."[31]

Distinguishing between just and unjust laws, King had explained, "A just law is a code that squares with the moral law or the law of God. An unjust law is a code that is out of harmony with the moral law. To put it in the terms of St. Thomas Aquinas, an unjust law is a human law that is not rooted in eternal and natural law. Any law that uplifts human personality is just. Any law that degrades human personality is unjust."[32]

He continued, "All segregation statutes are unjust because segregation distorts the soul and damages the personality. It gives the segregator a false sense of superiority, and the segregated a false sense of inferiority. To use the words of Martin Buber, the great Jewish philosopher, segregation substitutes an 'I–it' relationship for the 'I–thou' relationship, and ends up relegating persons to the status of things. So segregation is not only politically, economically and sociologically unsound, but it is morally wrong and sinful. Paul Tillich has said that sin is separation. Isn't segregation an existential expression of man's tragic separation, an expression of his awful estrangement, his terrible sinfulness? So I can urge men to disobey segregation ordinances because they are morally wrong."[33]

Obviously King did not feel bound by any court's order prohibiting him from protesting the unjust laws of segregation.

Stewart's ruling meant that King would have to pay a $50 fine and spend five days in the same Birmingham City Jail from which he had written his famous letter.[34] The decision's broader importance, however, was that it sent the wrong message to the moderate adherents to nonviolence whose leadership within the African American community was being challenged by militants who felt that the pace of racial progress was too slow, and that the nation's legal institutions were unreliable allies.

Brennan was sensitive to the politics of the situation. He regarded the Court's ruling as something of a retrenchment born of an uneasy fear that the struggle for racial equality had somehow gone too far or gotten out of hand. His dissent was joined by Warren, Douglas, and Fortas. In it he warned, "We cannot permit fears of 'riots' and 'civil disobedience' generated by slogans like 'Black Power' to divert our attention from what is here at stake— not violence or the right of the State to control its streets and sidewalks, but...patently impermissible prior restraints on the exercise of First Amendment rights, thus arming the state courts with the power to punish as a 'contempt' what they otherwise could not punish at all."[35]

The liberals were reinforced by Thurgood Marshall's arrival on the Court in 1967, providing them with a reliable sixth vote. Marshall became the first African American justice, replacing conservative Tom C. Clark. Because Marshall was committed to nonviolent, incremental change, President Johnson hoped his appointment would bolster the African American leadership's moderate elements.

Johnson told biographer Doris Kearns Goodwin that "when I

appointed Thurgood Marshall to the Supreme Court, I figured he'd be a great example for younger kids. There was probably not a Negro in America who didn't know about Thurgood's appointment. All over America that day Negro parents looked at their children a little differently, thousands of mothers looked across the breakfast table and said: 'Now maybe this will happen to my child someday.' I bet from one coast to the other there was a rash of new mothers naming their newborn sons Thurgood."[36]

But according to Goodwin, the symbolic impact of Marshall's appointment was in reality far less profound. In her biography *Lyndon Johnson and the American Dream*, she wrote, "While Johnson expected thousands of mothers to name their children after his new Supreme Court Justice, birth certificates on file in Boston and New York City revealed seven Martins, ten Luthers, eleven George Washingtons, and fifteen Franklin Delanos, but not a single Thurgood. To say this is not to take away from Johnson's action in appointing the first Negro to the Court; it was a measure of the times that achievements which would have seemed monumental in 1960 were taken as tokenism rather than progress. Militant leaders argued that whites had traditionally exercised the prerogative of choosing their own Negro leaders and choosing them on the basis of which ones were the most accommodating."[37]

By contrast, William O. Douglas regarded Marshall's appointment as tremendously symbolic. Indeed, he saw much more symbolism than substance in it. As director and general counsel of the NAACP Legal Defense and Educational Fund, Marshall had won twenty-nine of the thirty-two cases he had argued before the U.S. Supreme Court. His record, both at the NAACP and later as U.S. solicitor general, had clearly established him as the most effective lawyer of the twentieth century.

Nevertheless Douglas, who would feud with Marshall throughout his tenure over Marshall's support for the U.S. military effort in Vietnam, insisted in his autobiography that "Marshall was named [to the Court] simply because he was black," although "in the 1960s that was reason enough."[38] Douglas explained, "At that time, few black people studied law, and those who did seldom reached the top. Marshall attained the pinnacle for conspicuous service in civil rights—not civil rights generally, but civil rights in the field of race."[39]

According to Douglas, "The public needed a competent black on the Court for symbolic reasons; none was needed to put the Court right on racial problems."[40]

Douglas was correct to the extent that any sort of division between the Court's "liberals" and "conservatives" did not as yet extend to fundamental questions involving race discrimination. On school desegregation, for example, the justices continued to speak with one voice, as they had since 1954 in *Brown*, and that voice was usually Brennan's. In *Green v. County School Board of New Kent County*,[41] decided on May 27, 1968, the Court went further than it had ever gone in reaffirming its unanimous commitment to integrated schooling.

Writing for the Court, Brennan struck down as unconstitutional a "freedom of choice" plan adopted by the New Kent County, Virginia, school board. Under the plan, New Kent County schoolchildren and their parents were free to decide which of two schools the children would attend—Watkins School, which had been African American during segregation, or New Kent School, which historically had been white. There was no residential segregation in the county; persons of both races resided throughout.[42]

The problem was that the freedom-of-choice plan had failed to bring about any meaningful desegregation. But the school board argued that it had satisfied its obligation under the *Brown* ruling because the plan had "opened the doors of the former 'white' school to Negro children and of the 'Negro' school to white children"[43] whether the children and their parents in fact chose to integrate or not.

Brennan rejected this contention. Instead, he declared that *Brown* required that dual school systems be effectively abolished and that the school board's plan could not be upheld unless it effectuated a "transition to a racially nondiscriminatory school,"[44] which the New Kent freedom-of-choice plan had failed to do.

In a footnote, he quoted the findings of the United States Commission on Civil Rights. The commission had concluded, "During the past school year [1966–67], as in the previous year, in some areas of the South, Negro families with children attending previously all-white schools under free choice plans were targets of violence, threats of violence and economic reprisal by white persons and Negro children were subjected to harassment by white classmates notwithstanding conscientious efforts by many teachers and principals to prevent such misconduct."[45]

The commission's report went on to charge that southern officials had improperly dissuaded African American parents from sending their children to formerly all-white schools, and that poverty had also served as a deterrent.[46] Many poorer African American families could not afford suitable clothing for their children and were embarrassed to send them to school with better-heeled whites.[47]

Annoyed by the recalcitrance of southern officials, Brennan declared, "The burden on a school board today is to come forward with a plan that promises realistically to work, and promises realistically to work *now*."[48] He went on, "It is incumbent upon the school board to establish that its proposed plan promises meaningful and immediate progress toward disestablishing state-imposed segregation."[49]

The federal courts, he concluded, should retain jurisdiction over school desegregation cases "until it is clear that state-imposed segregation has been completely removed."[50]

But as the Court grew more liberal, American voters became more conservative. Popular support for President Johnson and the progressive Great Society he envisioned began to erode.

According to Goodwin, "The strategy he [Johnson] developed...required a relatively swift and convincing demonstration that his objectives in Vietnam were close to fulfillment, as well as the sustenance of the economic conditions that supported the Great Society. When he was unable to achieve the success his strategy demanded—when the war continued with no sign that the Communist forces were being compelled to abandon their objectives and when deteriorating [domestic] economic realities could no longer be dissolved by exhortation—his consensus began to dissolve."[51] In no time at all, "The nation was in turmoil, and the disruption worked against the President."[52]

The man who benefited most from the popular disaffection was Republican Richard M. Nixon. Eisenhower's former vice president rode to power on the crest of a conservative backlash in 1968, narrowly defeating Vice President Hubert H. Humphrey in one of the nation's closest presidential elections.

During the campaign, it often seemed that Nixon was running

President Eisenhower and administration officials with the Supreme Court justices on the White House steps in October 1956. *Front row, left to right:* William O. Douglas, Felix Frankfurter, Hugo Black, Eisenhower, Earl Warren, and Stanley Reed. Standing directly above the president is Justice John Marshall Harlan II. The man with eyes closed is Attorney General Herbert Brownell, who suggested Brennan's nomination. *(Dwight D. Eisenhower Library)*

Felix Frankfurter *(left)* and Hugo Black at a bar association luncheon in 1943. For over twenty years, the two battled over the Court's philosophical direction. Ultimately, Brennan settled into neither camp, instead cultivating a results-oriented approach based on consensus. *(Washington Post; SCUS)*

A self-described "backward country fellow," Justice Hugo Lafayette Black was in fact the intellectual leader of the Court's liberals when Brennan joined the Court in 1956. Black advocated an absolutist, or literalist, view of the First Amendment, holding that government had no power whatsoever to restrict free speech. (*Photo by Harris & Ewing; SCUS*)

Photographs from the Collection of the Supreme Court of the United States are credited SCUS.

Felix Frankfurter had been Brennan's professor at Harvard Law School. Although he had devoted much of his early life to zealous advocacy for the powerless and persecuted, he later became the principal proponent of judicial restraint, urging the Court to stay out of "political questions." Brennan complained, "After I came on the court, I was treated as one of Felix's students—and not a favorite one either." (*Photo by Ferdward Vogel; SCUS*)

The October 8, 1956, edition of *Time* magazine introduced Brennan to the public as an "affable, storytelling Irishman" and a "much-sought after-dinner speaker." Here Brennan is pictured at the podium at a Seton Hall, New Jersey, forum later that month. (*Photo by George Van; SCUS*)

"The growing movement of peaceful mass demonstrations by Negroes is something new in the South, something understandable....

Let Congress heed their rising voices,

for they will be heard."

—*New York Times* editorial
Saturday, March 19, 1960

Heed Their Rising Voices

As the whole world knows by now, thousands of Southern Negro students are engaged in widespread non-violent demonstrations in positive affirmation of the right to live in human dignity as guaranteed by the U. S. Constitution and the Bill of Rights. In their efforts to uphold these guarantees, they are being met by an unprecedented wave of terror by those who would deny and negate that document which the whole world looks upon as setting the pattern for modern freedom....

In Orangeburg, South Carolina, when 400 students peacefully sought to buy doughnuts and coffee at lunch counters in the business district, they were forcibly ejected, tear-gassed, soaked to the skin in freezing weather with fire hoses, arrested en masse and herded into an open barbed-wire stockade to stand for hours in the bitter cold.

In Montgomery, Alabama, after students sang "My Country, 'Tis of Thee" on the State Capitol steps, their leaders were expelled from school, and truckloads of police armed with shotguns and tear-gas ringed the Alabama State College Campus. When the entire student body protested to state authorities by refusing to re-register, their dining hall was padlocked in an attempt to starve them into submission.

In Tallahassee, Atlanta, Nashville, Savannah, Greensboro, Memphis, Richmond, Charlotte, and a host of other cities in the South, young American teenagers, in face of the entire weight of official state apparatus and police power, have boldly stepped forth as protagonists of democracy. Their courage and amazing restraint have inspired millions and given a new dignity to the cause of freedom.

Small wonder that the Southern violators of the Constitution fear this new, non-violent brand of freedom fighter . . . even as they fear the upwelling right-to-vote movement. Small wonder that they are determined to destroy the one man who, more than any other, symbolizes the new spirit now sweeping the South—the Rev. Dr. Martin Luther King, Jr., world-famous leader of the Montgomery Bus Protest. For it is his doctrine of non-violence which has inspired and guided the students in their widening wave of sit-ins; and it this same Dr. King who founded and is president of the Southern Christian Leadership Conference—the organization which is spearheading the surging right-to-vote movement. Under Dr. King's direction the Leadership Conference conducts Student Workshops and Seminars in the philosophy and technique of non-violent resistance.

Again and again the Southern violators have answered Dr. King's peaceful protests with intimidation and violence. They have bombed his home almost killing his wife and child. They have assaulted his person. They have arrested him seven times—for "speeding," "loitering" and similar "offenses." And now they have charged him with "perjury"—a *felony* under which they could imprison him for *ten years.* Obviously, their real purpose is to remove him physically as the leader to whom the students and millions of others—look for guidance and support, and thereby to intimidate *all* leaders who may rise in the South. Their strategy is to behead this affirmative movement, and thus to demoralize Negro Americans and weaken their will to struggle. The defense of Martin Luther King, spiritual leader of the student sit-in movement, clearly, therefore, is an integral part of the total struggle for freedom in the South.

Decent-minded Americans cannot help but applaud the creative daring of the students and the quiet heroism of Dr. King. But this is one of those moments in the stormy history of Freedom when men and women of good will must do more than applaud the rising-to-glory of others. The America whose good name hangs in the balance before a watchful world, the America whose heritage of Liberty these Southern Upholders of the Constitution are defending, is *our* America as well as theirs . . .

We must heed their rising voices—yes—but we must add our own.

We must extend ourselves above and beyond moral support and render the material help so urgently needed by those who are taking the risks, facing jail, and even death in a glorious re-affirmation of our Constitution and its Bill of Rights.

We urge you to join hands with our fellow Americans in the South by supporting, with your dollars, this Combined Appe.l for all three needs—the defense of Martin Luther King—the support of the embattled students—and the struggle for the right-to-vote.

"Heed Their Rising Voices" was the title of an editorial advertisement that ran on page 25 of the *New York Times* on March 29, 1960. The ad, which protested the treatment of Martin Luther King Jr. and his followers throughout the South, precipitated libel suits by Alabama officials. Justice Brennan's unanimous opinion for the Court in *New York Times v. Sullivan* in 1964 upheld the freedom of the press and helped ensure the success of the civil rights movement.

A liberals' power lunch at Milton Kronheim's tavern in Washington, D.C., during the late 1960s. *Seated from left:* William O. Douglas; appellate judge Woos; Milton Kronheim; Earl Warren; and Thurgood Marshall. *Standing from left:* Milton King; appellate judge David Bazelon; a former governor of Maryland; Stan Rosenweig; district court judge J. Skelly Wright; and Bill Brennan. (*SCUS*)

The Rehnquist Court from which Brennan retired in 1990. *Seated from left:* Thurgood Marshall, Brennan, Chief Justice William H. Rehnquist, Byron R. White, Harry A. Blackmun. *Standing:* Antonin Scalia, John Paul Stevens, Sandra Day O'Connor, and Anthony M. Kennedy. (*National Geographic Society*)

(At left) Justice Brennan at the peak of his power in the 1960s. Earl Warren called Brennan's "one person, one vote" ruling in *Baker v. Carr* (1962) the most significant decision of the Warren Court era. *(Photo by Bob Higbee; SCUS)*
(At right) Justice David Hackett Souter, Brennan's successor. When Thurgood Marshall learned of Souter's appointment, he flew into a rage. Marshall said his liberal ally Brennan "cannot be replaced." *(Photo by Joseph Bailey; SCUS)*

Brennan and successor Justice David Hackett Souter at a Harvard Club reception in Brennan's honor at the National Press Club in Washington, D.C., on September 30, 1992. The liberal stalwart Brennan chose conservative Souter to serve as toastmaster for the evening. *(Photo by Vincent J. Ricardel)*

Souter toasting Brennan at the Harvard Club reception. The members of the audience rose to their feet, as Souter urged, "I pray you, whether you are liberal or conservative...old or young, *drink with me now* to our great contemporary Justice Brennan!" *(Photo by Vincent J. Ricardel)*

Brennan with his second wife, Mary, alongside his official portrait in the Great Hall of the Supreme Court building. Mary was Brennan's secretary for twenty-six years before they were married. *(Photo by Franz Jantzen; SCUS)*

against the Warren Court as much as against his Democratic opponent. He made "law and order" his campaign theme and accused the Court of being soft on crime, of "seriously weakening the peace forces and strengthening the criminal forces in our society."[53] He promised to appoint to the federal bench judicial conservatives who would "interpret the Constitution strictly and fairly and objectively."[54] He said, "I think some of our judges have gone too far in assuming unto themselves a mandate...to put their social and economic ideas into their decisions."[55]

Nixon exploited the issue of forced busing, which he condemned for "forcibly mixing the races in the schools."[56] Busing was the practice of transporting students to different schools within a school district in order to achieve a racial balance in each school that reflected the racial composition of the community at large. A growing number of school districts had implemented busing plans either voluntarily or under federal court order.

Nixon explained in his memoirs, "I wanted to eliminate the last vestiges of segregation by law, and I wanted to do it in a way that treated all parts of the nation equally. I was determined that the South would not continue to be a scapegoat for Northern liberals. I was not willing, however, to impose wholesale busing, because I believe strongly in the neighborhood school. Even more important, I do not believe that schoolchildren should be torn from their home environments and, solely because of their race, be forced to go to distant schools where they might not be welcome or even safe. Compulsory segregation was wrong; but compulsory racial balancing was also wrong."[57]

By clever and timely manipulation of these emotional issues, Nixon managed to forge a coalition of white southerners and northern blue-collar suburbanites—so-called "suburban ethnics"—who did not want their children bused back into the urban communities that they had only recently managed to flee for the safety and homogeneity of the suburbs. They felt threatened by rising crime, the youth movement, the decline of patriotism, and the apparent breakdown of traditional social values. Nixon referred to these constituencies collectively as the "Silent Majority," long-suffering and forgotten.

Warren was indignant over Nixon's demagoguery. After the election, he wrote, "During the campaign, the principal issue was 'law and order.' It merely was an exercise in the rhetoric of accusation and recrimination which just increased divisiveness throughout the nation.''[58]

Brennan, for his part, rejected the underlying premises of Nixon's arguments. For example, he simply did not believe that there was any correlation between U.S. Supreme Court decisions and rising crime.

When he addressed the annual meeting of the National Council on Crime and Delinquency on May 8, 1969, in Washington, D.C., he explained, "Some of the decisions [criticized by Nixon] have set aside convictions obtained on evidence compelled from the accused or taken in an illegal search and seizure. Others have set aside convictions obtained in a criminal prosecution in which the accused was denied a speedy and public trial, or trial by jury, or information of the nature and cause of the accusation against him, or confronta-tion with the witnesses against him, or compulsory process for obtaining witnesses in his favor, or the assistance of counsel in his defense."[59]

He continued, "I have distinct reservations that any criminal is emboldened to commit his crime by decisions that require his state to honor constitutional safeguards in his prosecution. Doubtless, safeguards require judges and prosecutors to work harder in crimi-nal trials, as the police also work harder. But the convenience of prosecutors, police officers, and judges can never be the basis for the slightest diminution of rights secured by the Constitution."[60]

Brennan went on to state his belief that crime was for the most part a sociological phenomenon rooted in social and economic inequalities. He declared, "More fundamentally, there is growing recognition that the explanation of increasing crime rates may be found in long-neglected social conditions which breed crime. It is dawning on all of us that respect for law and our legal system is a direct function of society's concern with providing freedom and equality of rights and opportunities, in a realistic and not merely formal sense, to all the people of this nation: justice, equal and practical, to the poor, to the members of minority groups, to the criminally accused, to the displaced persons of the technological revolution, to alienated youth, to the urban masses, to the unrepre-sented consumers—to all, in short, who do not partake of the abundance of American life."[61]

To those who complained that the Court's insistence on strict adherence to rights guarantees often resulted in criminals' eluding punishment—that the Court had become "soft on crime"—Brennan responded that freedom for a few guilty people was a price worth paying to keep the Bill of Rights intact. In 1987, correspondent Nina Totenberg asked him during an interview for National Public Radio, "Why do you [the Court] let some of these creeps [criminals] go? They do such bad things, and on some technicality you let them go."[62]

Brennan was infuriated. He answered with his voice rising, "Honestly, you in the media ought to be ashamed of yourselves to call the provisions of the Bill of Rights 'technicalities.' They're not. They're very basic to our very existence as the kind of society we are. We are what we are because we have those guarantees, and this Court exists to see that those guarantees are faithfully enforced. They are not technicalities! And no matter how awful may be the one who is the beneficiary time and time again, guarantees have to be sustained, even though the immediate result is to help out some very unpleasant person. They're there to protect all of us."[63]

Nixon was provided with ample opportunity to appoint the kind of people he wanted to the Court. In fact, when he resigned the presidency on August 9, 1974, in the wake of the Watergate scandal, he left behind four appointees, including one present and one future chief justice.

Warren Earl Burger succeeded Earl Warren as chief justice on June 23, 1969, barely six months after Nixon took office. A native Minnesotan who was an outspoken proponent of judicial restraint, Burger had been serving on the U.S. Court of Appeals for the District of Columbia, to which he had been appointed by President Eisenhower in 1956. He had known Nixon since the two had met at the Republican National Convention in 1948.

Warren, for his part, had offered his resignation to Lyndon Johnson in June 1968, effective upon the qualification of a successor. Warren's hope was that the outgoing president would be able to appoint a liberal to replace him, but Johnson's efforts to make Abe Fortas chief justice failed. His Senate opponents accused Fortas of ethical improprieties that called his fitness into question, and the doomed nomination was withdrawn on October 4, 1968, a month before Nixon's election.

Warren, seventy-eight years old and in declining health, obliged Nixon by staying on through the end of the Court's 1968–69 term in June. By that time, the Senate had confirmed Burger by a vote of 74 to 3.

Meanwhile, Fortas's problems multiplied. Evidence of his ethical and financial misconduct proved incontrovertible, and in May 1969, Nixon's attorney general, John N. Mitchell, confronted him with a choice: resign or face impeachment and possible criminal prosecution. Fortas chose to resign. Nixon replaced him with another Minnesotan, Harry A. Blackmun, a boyhood friend of Burger's who was approved by a 94-to-0 vote of the Senate on May 12, 1970.

The liberals' ranks were further depleted when Hugo Black retired from the Court on September 17, 1971, at the age of eighty-five. Eight days later, he died. He was succeeded by conservative Lewis F. Powell Jr. of Virginia.

Harlan's departure followed on the heels of Black's. He resigned just six days after Black, on September 23, 1971, and died three months later at the age of seventy-two. He was replaced by William H. Rehnquist, the future chief justice who at the time of his appointment to the Court was serving as an assistant attorney general in Nixon's Justice Department.

Meanwhile, Douglas had been threatened, and it was not clear whether he would survive. Early in Nixon's presidency he was made the target of a Justice Department probe that called into question his relationship with Albert Parvin, a Las Vegas casino owner. Since its founding in 1967, Douglas had received remuneration for serving as president of an entity called the Albert Parvin Foundation. He managed to silence most of the criticism by severing all financial ties to Parvin.

Nevertheless Douglas, who was seventy years old when Nixon won the presidency for the first time in 1968, remained highly controversial, a lightning rod for conservative discontentment with the Court. His fourth wife, Cathy, a law student at American University in Washington, D.C., was almost a half-century his junior. And a number of his extrajudicial writings—he was the author of over 30 books, from political tracts to travel journals, memoirs, and even dime-store cowboy novels written under an assumed name—were radical.

For example, his ninety-seven-page essay *Points of Rebellion*, published in 1970, was an impassioned defense of the youth and anti–Vietnam War movements. He wrote, "We must realize that today's Establishment is the new George III. Whether it will continue to adhere to his tactics, we do not know. If it does, the redress, honored in tradition, is also revolution."[64]

He reprinted in *Points of Rebellion* a letter he had received in 1969 from a young American GI in Vietnam expressing sentiments that Douglas called "the bald truth."[65] The letter read, "Somewhere in our history—though not intentionally—we slowly moved from a government of the people to a government of the chosen few...who, either by birth, family tradition or social standing—a minority possessing all the wealth and power—now...control the destiny of mankind."[66]

The soldier continued, "You see, Mr. Douglas, the greatest cause of alienation is that my generation has no one to turn to."[67] He added, "With all the hatred and violence that exist throughout the world it is time someone, regardless of personal risk, must stand up and represent the feelings, the hopes, the dreams, the visions and desires of the hundreds of thousands of Americans who died, are dying, and will die in the search of truth."[68]

With regard to the hatred and violence here at home, Douglas blamed racist whites, not "uppity" African Americans, for the race riots that had erupted throughout the decade of the 1960s. He declared:

"Police practices are anti-Negro.

"Employment practices are anti-Negro.

"Housing allocation is anti-Negro.

"Education is anti-Negro."[69]

By mid-1970, he was the object of an impeachment effort led by then–House of Representatives minority leader (and future President) Gerald R. Ford of Michigan. Article II, section 4 of the U.S. Constitution provides that the president, vice president, and "all civil Officers of the United States," including Supreme Court justices, "shall be removed from Office on Impeachment for, and Conviction of, Treason, Bribery, or other high Crimes and Misdemeanors." Douglas's allies managed, however, to quash Ford's effort at the subcommittee level of the House Judiciary Committee.

Brennan also came under attack. Conservative members of

Congress and the press who criticized him for hiring "radical" law clerks brought matters to a head in 1966. Brennan had hired a brilliant, young Boalt Hall graduate named Michael Tigar to serve as one of his clerks during the Court's 1966–67 term. But when it came to light that Tigar had been "a leading radical activist"[70] and had, among other things, attended a youth festival in Helsinki, Finland, that had included participants from the former Soviet Union, a campaign was launched to sabotage his appointment.

Brennan recalled, "What actually happened was a deluge. The right wing deliberately set up a program—a system of pressure—that involved Abe Fortas, who was on the Court then; J. Edgar Hoover; and, more particularly, Hoover's right-hand man, Clyde Tolson. They bombarded me with all kind of letters—all having to do with Mike's participation in the Helsinki youth meeting."[71]

He went on, "Probably if I had just continued to face it down, the investigation would never have happened. But they had twenty-eight or more Congressmen protesting Mike's appointment. Clyde Tolson came over to see Fortas, and Fortas came in to see me to tell me that if I went through with this there might be an inquiry, which would be most embarrassing to Tigar and to me—and to the Court."[72]

With regard to the role played by Fortas, who was generally regarded as a liberal justice, Brennan explained, "He [Fortas] was very supportive of the First Amendment, but he was also very close to Lyndon Johnson, and also to J. Edgar Hoover. They used Fortas for a lot of things."[73]

Brennan gave in to the pressure and fired Tigar when he showed up for his first day of work. He conceded later, "I must say I've had a number of second thoughts. I suppose I should have treated it as something that would go away, but I didn't. I was very much concerned that—in the atmosphere of those days—if we got into this kind of thing it certainly would not have done the Court any good. That's what I said in the discussion I had with Mike at the time. A clerkship simply could not have that much significance—if it was going to hurt the institution."[74]

According to Brennan, "Mike understood it [Brennan's position] perfectly"[75] and harbored no resentment. Tigar joined Edward Bennett Williams's prestigious Washington, D.C., law firm and later went on to teach law at the University of Texas. In 1990, he told an interviewer, "I have enormous respect for Justice Brennan."[76]

Bill Douglas, for his part, was sorely disappointed by Brennan's handling of the matter. Brennan recalled, "Oh, he was absolutely furious at me for capitulating. He said, 'You've got to stand up to those people.'"[77]

Brennan's troubles did not end with Tigar. After Nixon was elected, federal investigators scrutinized a $10,000 real estate investment in a limited partnership that Brennan had entered into with Fortas and several liberal, lower court judges, including David L. Bazelon of the U.S. Court of Appeals for the District of Columbia Circuit and J. Skelly Wright, a U.S. district court judge for D.C.

Bazelon, Wright, and Brennan were friends. Occasionally, they "power" lunched at liquor wholesaler Milton Kronheim's warehouse in suburban Washington, D.C. Sometimes they were joined by Earl Warren, Bill Douglas, or Thurgood Marshall. According to a former Brennan law clerk who was once extended the honor of an invitation, the fare was miserable—cold-cut sandwiches wrapped in cellophane—and no alcohol was served. But the conversation was jovial, free-flowing, and *liberal*.

Brennan's detractors claimed that holding investments with lower court judges would prejudice him in favor of those judges' rulings when they came up to the Supreme Court for review. One basis for rating the quality of lower court judges was whether or not their rulings were reversed on appeal: the fewer reversals, the better the judge. Brennan cut the controversy short by divesting himself immediately. In fact, he sold off all his investments, everything from stocks and bonds to mutual funds, and determined to live on nothing but his salary.

Like Douglas, he survived. But by the time Richard Nixon resigned the presidency in August 1974, the Court's liberal heyday was clearly over, and Brennan's individual power and influence were in decline. In 1967, he had been the intellectual leader of the Court's six-member liberal majority. By August 1974 only three members of that majority remained—he, Douglas, and Marshall.

CHAPTER 19

Fighting a Rear-Guard Action

This [the Supreme Court] is an institution that has had its ups and downs for over two hundred years. By and large, it has done well, I think. There have been downturns from time to time....But we survived all that. So I don't see anything that serious, by way of changing jurisprudence, in contrast with what has happened in the past.

—William J. Brennan Jr. (1990)

WILLIAM BRENNAN VISITED EARL WARREN in his Georgetown University Hospital room at around 5:30 P.M. on Tuesday, July 9, 1974. The eighty-three-year-old former chief justice, whom Brennan referred to fondly as the "Super Chief," had been hospitalized the week before after suffering his third heart attack. Brennan found him alert and in good spirits. He was inquisitive about *Nixon v. United States*,[1] which was then before the Court. U.S. District Court Judge John J. Sirica had issued the president a subpoena to produce the Watergate tapes, clandestine recordings of Oval Office conversations that ultimately implicated Nixon in the Watergate coverup. Claiming presidential immunity, Nixon had refused to comply with the order, and the case had been taken up by the justices on appeal.

Warren knew that the Court's ruling would either seal Nixon's downfall or save him from disgrace. He suspected that the former would be the case. He had hated and distrusted Nixon for years, since the 1952 presidential campaign in which then–California Senator Nixon had pledged to support Warren's bid for the Republican nomination but switched to Eisenhower. According to his son, Earl Jr., Warren "just detested Richard Nixon with an abiding passion."[2] To Warren, Nixon was "Tricky Dick," "an evil man," "a crook and a thief."[3]

Brennan told Warren that in conference earlier that day the justices had decided the case unanimously against Nixon. The president would be ordered to hand over the tapes. Warren was ecstatic. As he had guessed, the tapes would prove to be the "smoking gun," the incontrovertible proof that Nixon had conspired with his aides to obstruct justice. According to Brennan, Warren exclaimed, "Thank God! Thank God! Thank God! If you don't do it this way, Bill, it's the end of the country as we have known it."[4]

On that note, Brennan bid a cheerful farewell. He did not know it was the last time he would see his dear friend alive. Two hours later, Earl Warren died of cardiac arrest with his wife and daughter at his bedside.

Within a year and a half of Warren's death and Nixon's departure, Douglas, too, was gone, forced by ill health to resign on November 12, 1975, after thirty-six years of service on the Court. He died on January 19, 1980. His nemesis Gerald Ford chose his successor: John Paul Stevens, a centrist midwesterner who had served since 1970 on the U.S. Court of Appeals for the Seventh Circuit. Stevens was confirmed by the Senate on December 17, 1975, by a vote of 98 to 0.

Warren Burger served as chief justice for seventeen years, from June 23, 1969, until September 26, 1986. During his tenure, the Court attained what one legal scholar has called "a general reputation for being at least moderately conservative in its use of power."[5] But for many conservatives, the Burger Court did not go far enough in reversing the judicial activist trends that characterized the Warren Court era.

For example, University of Colorado law professor Robert F. Nagel complained in 1981 that, given the Burger Court's more conservative composition, "It is perplexing...that heavy reliance on the judiciary for social and political decision-making has not moderated in the post–Warren Court years. Indeed, dependence on judicial power has become more pervasive and more routine in recent years."[6]

Nagel observed, "Judges are widely engaged in reforming schools, mental hospitals, prisons, adoption laws, and...even the census. They decide that homosexual partners must be permitted to attend high school dances, the kind of treatment that is appropriate for mental patients, where students should attend school even when the effect is to increase racial segregation, that every fifteen prisoners must have one foot of urinal trough, and so on. Like sleepwalkers following some internal vision, lower federal judges and litigants continue to use judicial power expansively."[7]

He concluded, "One possible explanation for the growth and consolidation of judicial power is that the changes in the membership of the Court simply did not achieve the announced purpose, that the Supreme Court remains committed to judicial activism."[8]

The statistics support Nagel's argument in at least one regard: The Burger Court was activist in exercising its power of judicial review and in overruling established precedent. In fact, between 1969 and 1984, the Burger Court "overturned more prior decisions, acts of Congress, and state laws than the Warren Court in its 16-year tenure."[9]

Moreover, the Burger Court's judicial restraint in some areas may have slowed social progress as much as its activism in others. After 1969, for example, there was no further incorporation of the Bill of Rights. Rights guaranteed to citizens by the Bill of Rights that must be respected by the federal government, but not necessarily enforced by state governments, include the right to indictment by a grand jury under the Fifth Amendment; trial by jury in civil cases as provided under the Seventh Amendment; the Eighth Amendment's prohibitions on excessive fines and bails; and the right to bear arms under the Second Amendment.

Liberal scholars have been highly critical of the Burger Court era. For example, Professor Robert C. Post of the University of California at Berkeley School of Law, a former clerk for both Bazelon and later Brennan, has written, "With the advent of the Burger

Court...the Supreme Court began increasingly to step back from an aggressive role in the protection of individual rights."[10]

At least one scholar, Yale law professor Akhil Reed Amar, has gone so far as to accuse the Burger Court of condoning "government-sponsored lawlessness" by thwarting "full remedies for violations of constitutional rights."[11] According to Amar, the Burger Court "pushed back remedies for segregation in public schools, denied relief to citizens threatened with racially discriminatory police brutality, cut back federal *habeas corpus* for state prisoners convicted in tainted trials, and forced lower federal courts to dismiss a broad range of suits challenging unconstitutional state conduct."[12]

Brennan was less sanguine in his criticisms. Assessing the Burger Court's legacy, he told the *Legal Times* in 1986, "There have been some retreats, but nowhere near as some have suggested may be the case—wholesale overrulings."[13]

He conceded, however, that in at least one key area of concern to civil libertarians, the Fourth Amendment's protection against unreasonable search and seizure of evidence, long-standing gains were eroded during the Burger Court era through the narrowing of the so-called "exclusionary rule." Under the exclusionary rule, evidence that has been obtained through an unconstitutional violation of a criminal defendant's rights cannot be used against the defendant by prosecutors. As future Supreme Court Justice Benjamin Cardozo once summarized the rule in 1926, "The criminal is to go free because the constable has blundered."[14]

Brennan told the *Legal Times* in 1986, "The Court has said now—over dissents—that the exclusionary rule is to be regarded merely as something that may be appropriate in some cases in order to deter [official] misconduct, but not otherwise. I think it's a very serious blow to the Fourth Amendment."[15]

Despite his less than gloomy assessment in hindsight of the Burger Court, Brennan found himself dissenting with great frequency throughout the decades of the 1970s and 1980s. Often he was joined only by Marshall, the Warren Court's other liberal holdover. As University of Virginia law professor John C. Jeffries Jr. has observed, "In most terms they [Brennan and Marshall] voted with each other more regularly than did any other two Justices.

Sometimes, their percentage of agreement reached astonishing heights. 'Brennan and Marshall' became almost a hyphenated entity, predictably aligned in the general run of cases and almost certain to vote together on the really important ones."[16]

In time Brennan came to relish the dissenter's role. The dissent, he once explained, is "offered as a corrective—in the hope that the Court will mend the error of its ways in a later case."[17] In a November 18, 1985, speech to faculty and students at the University of California's Hastings College of Law, he stated, "The most enduring dissents are the ones in which the authors speak, as the writer Alan Barth expressed it, as 'Prophets with Honor.' These are the dissents that often reveal the perceived congruence between the Constitution and the 'evolving standards of decency that mark the progress of a maturing society,' and that seek to sow seeds for future harvest. These are the dissents that soar with passion and ring with rhetoric. These are the dissents that, at their best, straddle the worlds of literature and law."[18]

He added, "[T]he dissent…safeguards the integrity of the judicial decision-making process by keeping the majority accountable for the rationale and consequences of its decision."[19]

Brennan's favorite dissent, to which he alluded often, was Justice John Harlan's refutation of the Court's majority in *Plessy v. Ferguson* (1896), which upheld racial segregation and established the separate-but-equal doctrine. Harlan's position, which no other justice shared, was that segregation was wrong and that the Constitution prohibits discrimination based on race. More than a half-century later a unanimous Court in effect embraced Harlan's view with its ruling in *Brown v. Board of Education* (1954).

The appointment of conservative justices by Republican Presidents Nixon, Ford, and Ronald Reagan did not erode Brennan's faith in the American legal system or in the Court as an institution. Marshall grew cynical, even distrustful, and to a large extent lost hope. As Jeffries, who clerked for Hugo Black's successor, Lewis Powell, during the mid-1970s, has written, "To some of his colleagues he [Marshall]…seemed withdrawn and vaguely hostile. Within two years of Marshall's appointment to the Supreme Court, the tide of judicial activism had begun to ebb. From 1972 until his retirement in 1991, Marshall saw support for the values he

held dear steadily eroding, and he could not suppress his indignation. In race cases particularly, Marshall grew increasingly bitter.
He stopped short of calling his colleagues racist—but just barely."[20]

By contrast, Brennan was philosophical. "Look," he told Nat
Hentoff in 1990, "this is an institution that has had its ups and
downs for over two hundred years. By and large, it has done well, I
think. There have been downturns from time to time. God help us,
there was Chief Justice [Roger] Taney and the *Dred Scott* decision.
But we survived all that. So I don't see anything that serious, by
way of changing jurisprudence, in contrast with what has happened
in the past."[21]

He added, "Anyway, whatever is to be, hell, we're a democracy.
The only way the citizens can have their views felt nationally is
through the Congress and the Presidency. That's our system."[22]

Besides, Brennan continued to win significant victories even
after the conservatives gained control of the Court. For example, in
Goldberg v. Kelly,[23] decided on March 23, 1970, he struck down as
unconstitutional a New York law under which welfare payments
could be terminated without according recipients a hearing at
which they could appear in person, present evidence, and cross-
examine witnesses.

The New York law allowed people to submit written statements
to authorities *after* their benefits had been cut off. But Brennan
concluded that this did not provide enough protection to satisfy the
Constitution's due process requirement. The Fourteenth Amendment's due process clause provides that no state can "deprive any
person of life, liberty, or property, without due process of law."
Writing for a 6-to-3 majority in *Goldberg*, Brennan explained,
"Written submissions are an unrealistic option for most [welfare]
recipients, who lack the educational attainment necessary to write
effectively and who cannot obtain professional assistance."[24]

He did not go so far as to declare a "right" to welfare under the
Constitution. But he did imply that while certain privileges or
benefits are not explicitly enshrined in the Constitution, they are
nonetheless fundamental to health and well-being in modern America. Therefore, they should not be taken away by the government
without adequate procedural safeguards to protect against unwarranted human hardship.

In a 1988 law review article entitled "Reason, Passion, and 'The Progress of the Law,'"[25] Brennan offered several poignant examples of human suffering that resulted from the New York law struck down in *Goldberg*:

Angela Velez's welfare benefits had been terminated by mistake. The state's welfare agency uncovered its error and her payments were resumed, but by that time Velez and her four children had been evicted from their apartment for nonpayment of rent and had gone hungry for four months.[26]

Pearl Frye had suffered similar hardship after her benefits were terminated. She and her eight children were forced to live off peanut butter and jelly sandwiches and rice given to her by friends.[27]

Another New Yorker, Esther Lett, fainted from hunger while waiting in a welfare line for a $15 emergency food payment to feed herself and her children. She was hospitalized subsequently for malnourishment.[28]

Understood in this context of human struggle, suffering, and need, Brennan's opinion in *Goldberg* was a reminder that pain is not abstract—it is real; it has a human face. He wrote, "In the bureaucratic welfare state of the late twentieth century, it may be that what we need most acutely is the passion that understands the pulse of life beneath the official version of events."[29]

He concluded, "[T]he characteristic complaint of our time seems to be not that government provides no reasons, but that its reasons often seem remote from the human beings who must live with their consequences."[30]

He achieved other major successes, as well. In *Keyes v. School District No. 1, Denver, Colorado*,[31] the "first school desegregation case to reach [the] Court which involve[d] a major city outside the South,"[32] he made clear that school desegregation was a nationwide obligation, not confined to any particular region.

The case was brought by Wilfred Keyes, an African American resident of Denver, and his daughter Christi, a seventh-grader at Denver's Smiley School. They contended that the school board had unconstitutionally segregated the schools in the city's predominantly African American Park Hill subdivision. A federal district court judge agreed. The judge concluded that the segregation of the

Park Hill schools had been achieved by, among other things, the gerrymandering of attendance zones, the use of so-called "optional zones," and the excessive use of mobile classroom units.[33]

The U.S. Supreme Court delivered its decision on June 21, 1973. Writing for a 7-to-2 majority, Brennan declared that the existence of racial or ethnic segregation in one part of a city's school system indicated the existence of a dual school system throughout, which school officials had an affirmative duty to eradicate by crosstown busing or other means.

He also insisted that faculty and staff be integrated throughout the entire system, instead of assigned on the basis of race—minority teachers to predominantly minority schools and majority teachers and staff to majority schools.

Powell, a Nixon appointee, concurred in part and dissented in part. Rehnquist dissented.

Another major victory came in *Penn Central Transportation Co. v. New York City*,[34] decided on June 26, 1978. The case arose after New York City's Landmarks Designation Committee designated Grand Central Terminal a landmark. As a result of the designation, the site's owner, Penn Central, was denied permission to build a fifty-five-story office building atop the terminal. Upon review of the plans for the office skyscraper, the Landmarks Committee declared the proposed design "nothing more than an esthetic joke"[35] that would undermine the terminal's character and architectural integrity.

Penn Central claimed that the designation amounted to a "taking" of property without just compensation in violation of the Fourteenth Amendment's due process clause. Again, the due process clause provides that no state shall "deprive any person of life, liberty, or property, without due process of law."

Writing for a 6-to-3 majority, Brennan concluded that even though the property was not worth as much to Penn Central without the office building on top of it, the diminution of value did not amount to an improper "taking" because Penn Central could still expect a reasonable return on its investment. In effect Brennan's ruling meant that a private property owner's rights would have to be balanced against the public interest in such aesthetic values as historic preservation. The decision has in effect reshaped the American urban landscape, for it has resulted in the preservation of some of the nation's most renowned and architecturally distinct structures.

Rehnquist, joined by Powell and Stevens, dissented.

By and large, however, Bill Brennan's disappointments during the Burger Court years far outweighed his successes. For example, just thirteen months after the decision in *Keyes*, the Denver case, the justices split badly in *Milliken v. Bradley*,[36] decided on July 25, 1974. In *Swann v. Charlotte-Mecklenberg Board of Education*,[37] decided on April 20, 1971, the Court had ruled unanimously that busing could be used as "one tool of school desegregation."[38] But in *Milliken*, the Court by a 5-to-4 vote refused to allow suburban Detroit schoolchildren to be bused into the city, and their counterparts in the city to be bused out to the suburbs, in order to achieve integrated schools.

Brennan, along with Douglas and White, joined Thurgood Marshall's dissenting opinion, in which Marshall warned, "Today's holding, I fear, is more a reflection of a perceived public mood that we have gone far enough in enforcing the Constitution's guarantee of equal justice than it is the product of neutral principles of law."[39]

Marshall concluded, "In the short run, it may seem to be the easier course to allow our great metropolitan areas to be divided up each into two cities—one white, the other black—but it is a course, I predict, our people will ultimately regret. I dissent."[40]

Meanwhile, Brennan also failed in his efforts to have the Court consider and negate the disproportionately harmful impact that some governmental policies or actions have on the poor. For example, in *San Antonio Independent School District v. Rodriguez*,[41] decided on March 21, 1973, the Court was asked to consider the constitutionality of the way in which Texas financed its public schools.

Under Texas's system, public schools were financed primarily with local property taxes. As a result, per-pupil expenditures in school districts with high tax bases were greater than in those with low tax bases. For example, in San Antonio's Edgewood subdivision, which was predominantly Mexican- and African American, and where property assessments were relatively low, the annual per-pupil expenditure was $356.[42] By contrast, the per-pupil expenditure in Alamo Heights, San Antonio's most affluent neighborhood, was $594, considerably more.[43]

Brennan wanted the Court to declare that education was a

"fundamental" right under the Constitution. By *fundamental*, he meant a right that was not necessarily guaranteed explicitly by the Constitution but that was nonetheless important to the effectuation of those rights that are in fact constitutionally guaranteed. For example, the Constitution expressly guarantees the right to free speech and the right to vote. Brennan would contend that neither of these rights could be exercised effectively without an education—that the right to free speech was meaningless without the ability to express oneself articulately, and that the right to vote was empty without the capacity to make an informed decision about candidates or issues.

Ordinarily, a governmental classification of an individual or group was constitutional as long as there was a rational, or reasonable, basis for the classification. In fact, the government distinguished between or among individuals or groups all the time. For example, adults were allowed to buy liquor; minors were not.

But any governmental classification that affected a *fundamental* right triggered "strict scrutiny" by the Court. This meant that the classification had to be justified by a "compelling interest," a more exacting standard than the mere rational basis test. Strict scrutiny was reserved primarily for racial classifications, or those based on national origin, status as an alien or the like, and placed the government under a heavy burden to justify any such classification that resulted in unequal treatment.

If education was a fundamental right, and any classification affecting it triggered strict scrutiny, then the government would face an uphill task justifying a scheme whereby more money was spent to educate some public-school children than others. In other words wealth, like race, would become a suspect classification, and the Texas authorities would have to come up with a way to finance their schools that did not have a disproportionately negative impact on schoolchildren who happened to live in poor neighborhoods.

The majority rejected Brennan's arguments by a narrow 5-to-4 vote. Writing for the majority, Justice Lewis Powell conceded, "The need is apparent for reform in tax systems which may well have relied too long and too heavily on the local property tax. And certainly innovative thinking as to public education, its methods, and its funding is necessary to assure both a higher level of quality and greater uniformity of opportunity."[44]

Nevertheless, Powell concluded, "It has simply never been within the constitutional prerogative of this Court to nullify statewide measures for financing public services merely because the burdens or benefits thereof fall unevenly depending upon the relative wealth of the political subdivisions in which citizens live."[45]

Stewart concurred in the result in *San Antonio*. Brennan, Douglas, White, and Marshall dissented.

Brennan also failed in his effort to have strict scrutiny applied to government actions that resulted in unequal treatment of women. On May 14, 1973, the Court decided *Frontiero v. Richardson*,[46] a case that had been brought by Sharron Frontiero, a U.S. air force lieutenant, challenging the government's refusal to let her claim her husband as a dependent for purposes of qualifying for a housing allowance and medical and dental benefits. Male air force officers were commonly granted the benefits for their wives that Frontiero sought for her husband. At the time the suit was brought, her husband, Joseph Frontiero, was a full-time student at Huntington College in Montgomery, Alabama.

Brennan's opinion for the Court struck down the air force's "dissimilar treatment for men and women who are...similarly situated."[47] But he did not limit his opinion to the narrow facts of the case. Instead he launched a broadside assault on the unequal treatment of women throughout American history. He wrote, "There can be no doubt that our Nation has had a long and unfortunate history of sex discrimination. Traditionally, such discrimination was rationalized by an attitude of 'romantic paternalism' which, in practical effect, put women, not on a pedestal, but in a cage."[48]

He went on to point out that in the past, women had been denied the right to hold public office, to serve on juries, to bring suit in their own names, to hold or convey property, or even to serve as legal guardians of their own children.[49]

He complained, "It is true, of course, that the position of women in America has improved markedly in recent decades. Nevertheless, it can hardly be doubted that, in part because of the high visibility of the sex characteristic, women still face pervasive, although at times more subtle, discrimination in our educational institutions, in the job market and, perhaps most conspicuously, in the political arena."[50]

For these reasons, he asserted that "classifications based upon sex, like those based upon race, alienage, and national origin, are inherently suspect and must therefore be subjected to close judicial scrutiny."[51]

But Brennan's was a plurality, not a majority, opinion. Although eight justices concurred in the result, leaving Rehnquist in lone dissent, Brennan's expansive ruling was joined only by Douglas, White, and Marshall. Hence there was no majority for establishing classifications based on sex as inherently suspect and therefore subject to the tougher strict scrutiny standard.

Toward the end of his career, Brennan began interchanging male and female pronouns in his opinions to emphasize his strong commitment to gender equality. Irrespective of whether a case involved a male or female plaintiff or defendant, Brennan would sometimes refer to the principal party as "she," and at other times as "he." He told Hentoff in 1990, "I do it purposely. I've been doing it for two or three years. Why? Well, why should we males be the only illustrious participants in whatever events we've been talking about?"[52]

Asked by interviewer Donna Haupt in 1989 whether there were any parts of the Constitution that he would consider changing, he replied, "I wouldn't change the Constitution except to add the Equal Rights Amendment. Today, as firmly as any time, I still think it belongs there as much as the 19th Amendment,"[53] which gave women the right to vote.

Efforts to ratify the ERA, which would have prohibited discrimination based on sex, failed during the 1970s and 1980s.

Another of Brennan's great disappointments was his inability to convince a majority of the justices to outlaw capital punishment, which he believed was prohibited by the Constitution's Eighth Amendment. The Eighth Amendment provides, "Excessive bail shall not be required, nor excessive fines imposed, nor cruel and unusual punishments inflicted." Brennan believed that the death penalty was cruel and unusual.

The question of the death penalty's constitutionality was first raised by Justice Arthur Goldberg in 1963. Frank Lee Rudolph, an indigent convicted of rape in Alabama, had appealed his death sentence to the Court, but in conference the justices by a 6-to-3 vote refused to hear his case. Goldberg, joined by Brennan and Douglas, dissented from that ruling.

In his dissent, which was circulated to the other justices on October 19, 1963, Goldberg protested that "[t]he following three questions, *inter alia*, seem relevant and worthy of argument and consideration:

"(1) In light of the trend both in this country and throughout the world against punishing rape by death, does the imposition of the death penalty by those States which retain it for rape violate 'evolving standards of decency that mark the progress of [our] maturing society,' or 'standards of decency more or less universally accepted?'

"(2) Is the taking of human life to protect a value other than human life consistent with the constitutional proscription against 'punishments which by their excessive...severity are greatly dis-proportionate to the offenses charged?'

"(3) Can the permissible aims of punishment (*e.g.*, deterrence, isolation, rehabilitation) be achieved as effectively by punishing rape less severely than by death (*e.g.*, by life imprisonment); if so, does the imposition of the death penalty for rape constitute 'unnecessary cruelty?'"[54]

In a subsequent memorandum to the conference, Goldberg analyzed in depth the history of the death penalty and of the Eighth Amendment and set forth his view that capital punishment was no longer constitutional for any crime. He wrote, "I am convinced that whatever may be said of times past, 'the evolving standards of decency that mark the progress of [our] maturing society' now condemn as barbaric and inhuman the deliberate institutionalized taking of human life by the state."[55]

He pointed out, "Many, if not most, of the civilized nations of the western world have abolished the death penalty; and few that have abolished it have ever restored it. The worldwide trend is unmistakenly in the direction of abolition."[56]

Goldberg left the Court in 1965 to serve as U.S. ambassador to the United Nations. But Thurgood Marshall, who joined the Court in 1967, shared Goldberg's opposition to capital punishment. During his years as director and general counsel of the NAACP's Legal Defense and Educational Fund, Marshall had investigated countless lynchings in the South and in the North as well, and he knew that death was a punishment meted out with greatest frequency to minorities and the poor.

His opposition was also based on his having lost a client accused of robbery and murder to the gallows when he was a struggling young attorney in Baltimore, Maryland, fresh out of Howard Law School from which he had been graduated first in his class. He recalled, "The reason why I took the case was that it was a classmate of mine in high school. When the time of execution came up, I felt so bad about it—that maybe I was responsible—that I decided I was going to go and see the execution."[57] But warned of the grisly nature of the event by a reporter who had witnessed a number of hangings, Marshall changed his mind and stayed home.

When he was asked years later whether the execution of his classmate had precipitated his lifelong opposition to capital punishment, Marshall replied, "Well, I don't know whether that...well, it did. It did because I lost the death penalty case in private practice."[58]

On June 29, 1972, the Court delivered its decision in *Furman v. Georgia*,[59] which imposed a moratorium on executions. The case was decided by a vote of 5 to 4, with Brennan, Douglas, Stewart, White, and Marshall each concurring separately.

After *Furman*, the capital punishment debate focused on five major concerns: whether it was just to punish one heinous crime—say, the taking of a life—with a punishment equally heinous, the deliberate taking of another human life; whether capital punishment served as an effective deterrent; concern over the irreversible nature of the death penalty—the fear that people later proven to be innocent had and would be executed; whether the desire for retribution, a base motivation, could properly serve as a justification for imposing the death sentence; and concern over the obvious racial bias in death sentencing, for the death penalty was much more frequently imposed upon African Americans than upon whites who committed the same or similar crimes.

Four years after the *Furman* ruling, on July 2, 1976, the moratorium was lifted by the Court's decision in *Gregg v. Georgia*.[60] By that time, a majority of the states had revised their death penalty laws to provide procedural safeguards in sentencing that alleviated the crucial concerns felt by a majority of the *Furman* Court. Seven

justices concurred in Justice Stewart's opinion for the majority in
Gregg. Brennan and Marshall dissented. They remained until their
retirements the only justices who believed that the death penalty
was by its nature cruel and unusual.

In a 1994 article for the *Notre Dame Journal of Law, Ethics and
Public Policy*, Brennan reiterated his bitter opposition to capital
punishment. He wrote, "A punishment must not be so severe as to
be utterly and irreversibly degrading to the very essence of human
dignity....The calculated killing of a human being by the state
involves, by its very nature, an absolute denial of the executed
person's humanity. The most vile murder does not, in my view,
release the state from constitutional restraints on the destruction of
human dignity. Yet an executed person has lost the very right to
have rights, now or ever. For me, then, the fatal constitutional
infirmity of capital punishment is that it treats members of the
human race as nonhumans, as objects to be toyed with and
discarded."[61]

In a frank recognition of his own mortality, he concluded, "I
have come to realize that I shall not likely live to see that 'great day
for our country...[and] our Constitution' when a majority of the
Supreme Court finally comes to accept the fact that the death
penalty 'denies the humanity and dignity of the victim and
transgresses the prohibition against cruel and unusual punishment.'
But even if it is not for me, as it was not for Justice Marshall [who
died on Sunday, January 24, 1993], to finish the work, neither were
we free to desist. The final labor, it seems, will be left to the brave
and able hands and minds of those we leave behind."[62]

Obviously his disagreements with his colleagues over the death
penalty and other of his beliefs ran deep and were passionate. Yet he
denied harboring personal animosities on account of them. Justice
Oliver Wendell Holmes once described the justices as "nine
scorpions in a bottle."[63] According to one scholar, the justices are
like "partners in an arranged marriage with no possibility of
divorce."[64]

Brennan insisted, however, that "none of that carries over—in
the slightest—to our personal relationships."[65] He told Hentoff in
1990, "It's remarkable, it really is, but it's absolutely essential in a
small body of nine people who have to work as closely as we do, and
out of sight of the public or the press or anyone else. You simply can't

afford to let your convictions affect your personal relationships. I'm not saying it has *never* happened, but I can say this: I have sat now with about a fifth of all the Supreme Court Justices there have been, and I have never had a cross word with one of them. Not with a single one of them."[66]

These comments reflected Brennan's tact and diplomacy, his determination to work collegially with others in order to achieve his goals. But the fact of the matter was that throughout much of the late 1970s and on into the early 1980s, Bill Brennan did not really feel like getting along with anybody. He was sullen and dark. He withdrew from the world as much as possible. There were no more glittering Friday night buffets in his Georgetown home with justices and law clerks intermingling in discussions of social policy over cocktails. There were no more power lunches with the boys at Kronheim's. Somehow, through sheer determination and his abiding self-discipline he managed to keep up with his work. But irreversibly, age and circumstances were beginning to take their toll.

In 1978, at the age of seventy-two, he underwent radiation treatments for a malignant tumor in his throat that almost cost him his voice and left him drained. The following year, on September 4, 1979, he suffered a small stroke that weakened his right arm and hand. Worst of all, however, was that his beloved Marjorie was losing her long battle with the cancer that would eventually kill her. For years he watched over her and cared for her while she suffered and died.

He admitted to an interviewer in 1989, "I came close, very close to crumbling under the strain. There were a couple of times when I thought I couldn't carry on, couldn't do my job. I came quite close to thinking I ought to retire. But she [Marjorie] wouldn't have any part of that. She was a great lady."[67]

Their daughter, Nancy, recalled, "Dad really did a nosedive after Mother died. And I think he really could have given up. He's so strong-willed that had he stuck by it, it would have been another case of the widower following the deceased."[68]

Fortunately, he chose life. Not long after Marjorie's death on December 1, 1982, Nancy recalled, "he asked me what I would think if he started dating Mary Fowler and I thought 'what a great idea.'"[69] Mary had been his secretary for twenty-six years, since his arrival at the Court. It was a whirlwind romance. They were married in a private ceremony on March 8, 1983. He was seventy-six; she was sixty-eight, eight years his junior.

The next day, the new Mrs. Brennan went to work and typed out her resignation. Then she prepared a one-sentence memorandum for her husband's signature to be circulated to the other justices immediately after their departure for their honeymoon. It read simply, "Mary Fowler and I were married yesterday and we have gone to Bermuda."

He returned almost miraculously renewed. The comfort of Mary's companionship, her sympathetic understanding and quiet admiration, her affection for him, buoyed his self-esteem, lifted his flagging spirits, put a certain spryness back in his step. He became jovial again. And he found his voice. His speech, made craggy and raspy by the radiation therapy, seemed to grow more forceful and assertive. He was in love, proudly and for the rest of his life. He walked hand-in-hand with Mary around the Court. A Court employee who spotted them together just after their honeymoon ducked back into his office and told his coworkers, "The love-birds are walking the halls."[70]

Later that year, Brennan said goodbye to Georgetown and moved with his bride into a luxury, high-rise condominium across the Potomac River in Arlington, Virginia. The Brennans purchased the property from Charles E. Smith, a prominent Washington, D.C.–area real estate developer who had met Brennan some twenty years earlier at a dinner party hosted by appeals court judge Bazelon.[71]

At that point in the twilight of his career, the time seemed propitious for William Brennan to retire, to go out on top, to live out the remainder of his days at home in tranquil reminiscence and modern comfort, loved and appreciated for all that he had done. Instead, he returned to the fray for one last, great battle, this time against the proponents of the so-called "Reagan Revolution."

Ronald Reagan was elected president for the first time in November 1980. His campaign had been a crusade against liberalism, which he believed had driven the country into economic downturn and despair. Disillusioned with government spending and government programs, and convinced that the American people were overtaxed, Reagan vowed to make America great again by restoring "traditional" values that he felt had been undermined by social policies dating back to Franklin Roosevelt's New Deal of the 1930s.

Reagan and his backers opposed virtually everything Brennan stood for. They sought to overturn the Supreme Court's ruling in *Roe v. Wade*,[72] decided on January 22, 1973, which had established a constitutional right to abortion. Brennan was among the Court's 7-to-2 majority in *Roe*, which had been written by Nixon appointee Harry Blackmun, and Brennan had remained an outspoken proponent of abortion rights.

The Reagan administration also opposed the Equal Rights Amendment, which failed ultimately to gain ratification, and affirmative action remedies like quotas in training, hiring, and promotions for minorities and women aimed at eradicating the persistent effects of past discrimination. Brennan was an articulate supporter of affirmative action.

Brennan had managed to maintain a low profile throughout his career, but by the mid-1980s, Reagan administration officials and conservative scholars and pundits had identified him as the nation's most powerful and effective spokesperson for liberal causes. Shortly after Reagan's landslide reelection victory in 1984, administration officials launched a vitriolic offensive against the Court in general, and Brennan in particular, which was spearheaded by Attorney General Edwin Meese III, the president's longtime adviser and confidant.

In a July 1985 address to the American Bar Association, Meese characterized several recent Court decisions as "bizarre."[73] He was especially indignant over a 1985 ruling in which the Court had struck down an Alabama law permitting moments of silence for prayer or meditation in public schools.[74]

Meese called for a return to "a jurisprudence of Original Intention," meaning that the interpretation of the Constitution should be based purely on the motives of the Framers some two centuries ago.[75] For the modern Court to interpret the Constitution otherwise, he insisted, amounted to "intellectual snobbery."[76]

In subsequent speeches, Meese criticized the Court for handing down decisions that "were, on the whole, more policy choices than articulations of constitutional principle."[77] His assistant and principal spokesperson, Terry Eastland, followed up the attorney general's remarks by characterizing Brennan as the "embodiment" of the kind of decision making that Meese had assailed.[78]

On October 12, 1985, Brennan responded to Meese's attack. He told an audience of faculty and students at Georgetown University in Washington, D.C., that professed adherence to the original intention of the Framers was "little more than arrogance cloaked as humility."[79]

He explained, "It is arrogant to pretend that from our vantage we can gauge accurately the intent of the Framers on application of principle to specific, contemporary questions. All too often, sources of potential enlightenment such as records of the ratification debates provide sparse or ambiguous evidence of the original intention. Typically, all that can be gleaned is that the Framers themselves did not agree about the application or meaning of particular constitutional provisions, and hid their differences in cloaks of generality."[80]

He concluded, "We current Justices read the Constitution in the only way we can: as Twentieth Century Americans. We look to the history of the time of the framing and to the intervening history of interpretation. But the ultimate question must be, what do the words of the text mean in our time. For the genius of the Constitution rests not in any static meaning it might have had in a world that is dead and gone, but in the adaptability of its great principles to cope with current problems and current needs."[81]

A year later, he seized the initiative and went on the offensive. In an August 8, 1986, speech to an American Bar Association panel at New York University Law School, he asserted that the Fourteenth Amendment, with its due process and equal protection clauses, was intended to serve as "the legal instrument of an egalitarian revolution" after the Civil War.[82] He contended that the intention of the Framers of the amendment had not been fulfilled. He blamed the executive branch, which had since 1969 been controlled by Republicans for all but four years, for lack of progress toward eradicating racism and other social inequalities.

He declared, "Congress and the federal judiciary have done much in recent years to close the gap between promise and fulfillment [of the Fourteenth Amendment], but who will deny that despite this great progress the goal of universal equality, freedom and prosperity is far from won and that ugly inequities continue to mar the face of our nation?"[83]

Reagan Administration officials were stung and infuriated by the rebuke. A month later, William Bradford Reynolds, the assistant attorney general for civil rights, responded on behalf of the administration in a speech delivered at the University of Missouri–Columbia School of Law on September 12, 1986. The tone of his remarks was caustic and bitter. He accused Brennan by name of harboring a "radically egalitarian jurisprudence."[84]

Reynolds went on to reiterate the administration's opposition to affirmative action as in effect reverse discrimination. And he dismissed Brennan's contributions to the field of constitutional law. Brennan's "juridical landscape," Reynolds asserted, "is, in the end, barren, featureless, and flat. There is nothing outstanding, nothing of inherent worth, nothing admirable, estimable, or truly deserving" in it.[85]

By the time he left office in January 1989, Reagan, like Nixon in the late 1960s and early 1970s, had been given ample opportunity to reshape the Court. He elevated William Rehnquist to chief justice in June 1986 upon Warren Burger's retirement. Rehnquist's appointment was confirmed by the Senate by a vote of 65 to 33 on September 17, 1986, and he was sworn in nine days later.

Reagan also appointed three associate justices. Sandra Day O'Connor, who became the first woman to serve on the Court, replaced Potter Stewart on September 25, 1981; Antonin Scalia took Rehnquist's seat and was confirmed by the Senate along with the new chief justice; and Anthony M. Kennedy succeeded Lewis F. Powell on February 18, 1988.

But Reagan's appointments failed to rejuvenate the Court's movement to the right. Instead, to the consternation of his most avid supporters, there were indications of an emerging centrist majority, averse to unsettling established precedents inherited from previous eras, including the Warren Court years.

During the late 1980s, Brennan squeezed out two last, notable victories. The first came on June 21, 1989, when the Court decided *Texas v. Johnson*,[86] the appeal of Gregory Lee Johnson, convicted under a Texas law that prohibited the desecration of venerated objects. Johnson's crime was that he had burned an American flag in front of Dallas City Hall while fellow demonstrators protesting the 1984 Republican National Convention in Dallas had looked on, chanting "America, the red, white, and blue, we spit on you."[87] The question for the Court was whether Johnson's conduct was symbolic speech protected by the First Amendment.

Writing for a 5-to-4 majority, Brennan ruled that Johnson's act of flag burning was, in fact, protected. He wrote, "If there is a bedrock principle underlying the First Amendment, it is that the Government may not prohibit the expression of an idea simply because society finds the idea itself offensive or disagreeable."[88] He went on, "We decline, therefore, to create for the flag an exception to the joust of principles protected by the First Amendment."[89]

Brennan's sympathies were not, however, with the flag burner. In fact, he asserted that by reaffirming the expansive freedom guaranteed under the First Amendment, the principles for which the flag stood would be enhanced.

He wrote, "We are tempted to say…that the flag's deservedly cherished place in our community will be strengthened, not weakened, by our holding today. Our decision is a reaffirmation of the principles of freedom and inclusiveness that the flag best reflects, and of the conviction that our toleration of criticism such as Johnson's is a sign and source of our strength."[90]

He concluded, "It is the Nation's resilience, not its rigidity, that Texas sees reflected in the flag—and it is that resilience that we reassert today."[91]

Brennan's opinion was joined by Marshall, Blackmun, Scalia, and Kennedy. His case files in the Library of Congress contain a note from Justice Blackmun, dated June 19, 1989, in which Blackmun confessed that he "struggled with this difficult and distasteful little (big?) case" but ultimately saw the issues Brennan's way.[92] More surprising, however, was Justice Scalia's support for Brennan, given Scalia's reputation for arch conservatism. Also significant was that Reagan appointee Kennedy, the Court's junior justice, seemed to belie his conservative leanings by joining Brennan's majority opinion.

Rehnquist filed a stirring dissent that extolled the virtues of the red, white, and blue and quoted at length from the national anthem, Francis Scott Key's "Star-Spangled Banner."[93] Rehnquist also reprinted in its entirety John Greenleaf Whittier's Civil War poem "Barbara Frietchie," which contains the famous lines " 'Shoot, if you must, this grey old head, / "'But spare your country's flag,' she said."[94]

The chief justice's dissent was joined by Justices White and O'Connor. Justice Stevens filed a separate dissenting opinion.

Brennan's final victory came on June 27, 1990, when the Court decided *Metro Broadcasting, Inc. v. F.C.C.*[95] In what was to be his last opinion for the Court, he wrote for a 5-to-4 majority, upholding two Federal Communications Commission affirmative action programs designed to increase African American and other minority ownership of broadcast licenses. Such minority preferences were justified, he concluded, by Congress's interest in safeguarding "the public's right to receive a diversity of views and information over the airwaves."[96]

His opinion was joined by Marshall, White, and Blackmun. Stevens filed a separate opinion concurring in the result. All four Reagan appointees—Rehnquist, O'Connor, Scalia, and Kennedy—filed dissents.

But although the Court's rightward drift may have ebbed by the close of the decade of the 1980s, there was no stemming the inexorable progression of old age. Bill Brennan was eighty-four years old at the close of the Court's 1989–90 term.

Thurgood Marshall, only two years younger than Brennan, was fond of saying, "I was appointed for a life term, and I intend to serve it."[97] In 1988, when his supporters expressed concern over the increasing number of conservative Court appointees, Marshall reassured them jauntily, "Don't worry, I am going to outlive those bastards."[98] Brennan had, on occasion, expressed similar sentiments.

By July 1990, however, it was clear to Bill Brennan that the time had come for him to leave. Both he and Thurgood had on more than one occasion dozed off during oral arguments the preceding term. By seniority they sat next to each other on the bench, and one was always there to give the other a nudge before anyone noticed, or before one or the other of them embarrassed himself by snoring. But inevitably the day came when they both fell asleep at the same time, and there was no one there to nudge either of them.

Brennan discussed his departure from the Court with Mary and his children. The difficulty would be in finding something to do, something to keep him active and interested for the remainder of his years. The sad fact was, Bill Brennan had always been a workaholic. As a justice, he had devoted the past thirty-four years of his life completely to the service of his country. He had cultivated no hobbies, no pastimes, no interests other than his family outside of his work on the Court.

Mary assured him that they would find a world of interesting things to do and share together. He had never been nice enough to himself, she said. She would see to it that he would enjoy in his retirement the comfort and leisure to which he was entitled. During his first marriage, he and Marjorie had always vacationed on Nantucket Island off the coast of Massachusetts. Mary wanted him to expand his horizons a bit, take some cruises, see the world. That boosted his confidence. He agreed to announce his retirement.

Before he did, however, he called Thurgood to inform him personally of his decision. The two men were not in reality the close friends that Court observers might have guessed. Marshall was prickly and contentious in his old age and ill health, feeling bad all the time and battling congestive heart failure. Brennan, for his part, considered Thurgood a first-rate mind but uninterested in many matters, only selectively committed to the give-and-take of viewpoints that was the essence of forging majorities on the Court.

Still the two men were ideological companions, and Brennan felt some remorse about leaving Thurgood to carry on the struggle alone.

Their chambers, like their chairs on the bench, were next to each other. But Brennan called rather than try to endure their parting in person. When Thurgood came to the phone, Brennan informed him of his decision to retire, casting it as final, irrevocable. Thurgood listened. His heart was weak; his doctors had told him not to get too upset. Then, without saying a word, Thurgood Marshall set the receiver down gently in the middle of his desk and walked away.

A few days later, Bill Brennan wrote a letter to President George Bush, dated July 20, 1990. It read, "My dear Mr. President: The strenuous demands of Court work and its related duties required or expected of a Justice appear at this time to be incompatible with my advancing age and medical condition.

"I, therefore, retire effective immediately as an Associate Justice of the Supreme Court of the United States."

CHAPTER 20

Brennan's Legacy

In the end, I hope the historical assessment of me will be that he did his best and that he did not leave anything that he needed to—or that his family would ever come to—regret.

—William J. Brennan Jr. (1989)

ON THURSDAY, JANUARY 28, 1993, William Brennan attended Thurgood Marshall's funeral at the National Cathedral in Washington, D.C. He was joined by every active or retired member of the U.S. Supreme Court, President Bill Clinton and Vice President Al Gore, most members of the U.S. Senate and House of Representatives, and several thousand mourners in tribute to the man known as "Mr. Civil Rights."

The day before the funeral, in an outpouring of gratitude and affection, some 18,000 mourners had passed by Marshall's bier as it lay in state in the Great Hall of the Supreme Court. Hour after hour from morning on into the night they had filed by to pay their respects to the man who President Clinton called "a giant in the quest for human rights and equal opportunity."[1]

It has been said that Thurgood Marshall brought the Bill of Rights to the African American people as Moses delivered the Ten Commandments to the Jews. During the august funeral services that reverberated throughout the massive Gothic cathedral, he was lionized as everything from a good-humored curmudgeon to a champion of the weak and oppressed.

275

Chief Justice William Rehnquist delivered one of the afternoon's most moving eulogies. Speaking on behalf of the Court, he proclaimed, "Inscribed above the front entrance to the Supreme Court building are the words 'Equal Justice Under Law.' Surely no one individual did more to make these words a reality than Thurgood Marshall."[2]

Brennan returned to the Supreme Court building after the funeral. Just a few months shy of his eighty-seventh birthday, he often used a wheelchair. When he did walk his gait was unsteady, and so he relied on a cane and usually had an assistant at his elbow. Justice David Souter had been kind enough to escort him up and down the aisles of the great cathedral before and after the funeral services. But now he proceeded unaccompanied through the marble corridors of the Supreme Court.

He went past his own chambers and into those Thurgood had occupied since his retirement from the Court in 1991, a year after Brennan's departure. The staff rose as he entered in deference to his status but were somewhat perplexed as to what he was doing there. He said nothing but shuffled past them into what had been Thurgood's private office. He closed and locked the door behind him. Then he moved uneasily around Thurgood's massive, mahogany desk and reclined in Thurgood's mammoth leather swivel chair, the one he had used on the bench. And there Bill Brennan sat, engrossed in thoughts of his departed friend, and his own future, until late into the evening.

The sad fact was, he and Thurgood had not ended on the best of terms. He had told Thurgood in advance of his plans to retire, and Thurgood had gone home that night and blabbed about it to his son Thurgood Jr. over dinner. Thurgood Jr. was a lawyer for the Senate Judiciary Committee. The news was somehow leaked to the press— prematurely, as far as Brennan was concerned. Once the word was out, he felt compelled to follow through with his retirement, even though at the time he was having second thoughts about it.

This was one reason why he did not go to see Thurgood before his death. Thurgood had been admitted to Bethesda Naval Hospital about a month before he died and had gone quietly downhill, in the end refusing food or nourishment, weary of his long battle with congestive heart failure. Now Brennan regretted not having visited him.

Nevertheless, he resented Thurgood's "deification." There were elementary schools, high schools, and law schools named after Marshall before he was even dead. There was the behemoth new Thurgood Marshall Federal Judiciary Building behind Union Station on Capitol Hill, where the chambers of retired Supreme Court justices would be located from then on. Thank God he had retired before they could kick him out of the Court and put him in the Thurgood Marshall Building.

He wondered who would remember him. A survey of courts and judges taken in 1989 revealed that William Brennan was virtually unknown; only about 30 of the 1,000 people interviewed could identify him. Among the justices, Sandra Day O'Connor was best known, her name recognized by almost a quarter of those surveyed. Even William Rehnquist had a higher name recognition at 90 people than did Brennan.[3] Yet it was William Brennan more than anyone else who had given the Court its foundation and direction during the latter half of the twentieth century.

At the same time, he could not begrudge Thurgood his popularity. After all, Thurgood had been quite a character, a legend and an icon, truly larger than life. Yet for all his fame, Thurgood had never taken himself too seriously, which was a rare and attractive quality in a powerful man.

As author and journalist Nicholas Lemann has written, "Marshall didn't act like a Supreme Court justice."[4] Among other things, "His un-Holmesian way of life included regular trips to the race tracks and Atlantic City casinos, copious consumption (by today's standards) of Winstons and Wild Turkey and conversation filled with profanity and a 1940s *boulevardier's* slang. (He sometimes addressed his brethren as 'baby.')"[5]

Brennan remembered with a sly smile the way Thurgood used to greet him in the morning: "You dumb bastard, don't you think you should do something to earn your pay?"[6]

As Lemann explained Marshall's behavior, "All of this was the style of a certain time and place—a time and place where no other justice or clerk had ever been—and also, perhaps, this style had some of the forced jauntiness of the combat soldier about it, having been adopted as a response to a life of unending fear and risk. But it often led those who knew Marshall only toward the end of his life to describe him patronizingly, as a colorful character, the Court's clowning token Negro."[7]

On the eve of Marshall's funeral, Brennan had told a *Washington Post* reporter, "He [Thurgood] was not valued to the extent that his learning justified because he was so funny they thought he must be stupid—my, were they wrong."[8]

He went on, "He could be irascible, but he could also be soft, sweet, and just nice. He was just a decent guy, a very good citizen."[9] Brennan concluded, "He was a stickler for the honest truth."[10]

The intercom buzzed. The phone rang. Someone was knocking and asking through the door, "Are you all right in there?" They could pound away for all Bill Brennan cared. He was not about to leave Thurgood's chair. He checked the desk drawers to see if Thurgood had a bottle hidden somewhere. One never knew with Thurgood. Or as Thurgood used to say, quoting entertainer Fats Waller, "One never knows, do one?" But he found nothing he could imbibe to toast a fond farewell.

Brennan had been more confident, more upbeat, about his legacy two and a half years earlier when he had left the Court. A statement released by his office along with a copy of his letter of retirement to the president had read, "It is my hope that the Court during my years of service has built a legacy of interpreting the Constitution and federal laws to make them responsive to the needs of the people whom they were intended to benefit and protect. *This legacy can and will withstand the test of time.*" Since then, however, his confidence had been eroded. He felt useless; he had not adjusted comfortably to retirement.

He received countless honorary degrees and awards after leaving the Court. Each was a testament to the informed public's recognition of and admiration for his work. Most notable was the Medal of Freedom, the nation's highest civilian honor, bestowed upon him by President Clinton in a White House ceremony on November 30, 1993.

Financial rewards accompanied the public recognition. For example, on February 11, 1993, he was named along with Marshall (posthumously) as a recipient of the 1993 Free Spirit Award, given by the Freedom Forum of Arlington, Virginia, for outstanding contributions to the protection of free speech. The Freedom Forum had been established by the late Frank E. Gannett, founder of the Gannett Corporation and newspapers. Along with the award came $100,000.

Several years earlier, Brennan's friend Charles E. Smith, the developer, had demonstrated his appreciation by forgiving the $120,000 balance on a loan he had extended the Brennans in connection with the purchase of their luxury condominium. When they purchased the $210,400 property in 1983, the Brennans had made a down payment of $40,000 and borrowed the remaining $170,400 from Smith under a ten-year note.

In addition, Smith had presented Bill and Mary Brennan with checks for $10,000 each, personal gifts, upon Bill's retirement from the Court. A spokesperson for Smith told the *Washington Post* in May 1991 that the gifts were "strictly friendship and the fact that Charles E. Smith respected and admired Justice Brennan so much for his contribution to the country."[11]

Smith's largesse stirred some controversy when it was revealed by Brennan in a financial disclosure statement filed before he retired. Some $60,000 of the loan for the condominium had been forgiven in 1990 while Brennan was still a sitting justice. But according to Brennan there was no violation of the American Bar Association's code of conduct, to which the justices had adhered traditionally even though the code did not apply to the Court. He emphasized, "At no time since I have lived at the condominium...did Mr. Smith or any of his companies have any matters before the court or that were affected by court decisions."[12] At the time of his retirement, Brennan's annual salary as a justice was roughly $153,600.[13]

No amount of reward or recognition seemed an adequate substitute for his work on the Court. Mary tried. She lived up to her part of their bargain by fulfilling her promise to expand his horizons by showing him the world. They traveled, and each time they were away he enjoyed it. A visit to Israel to spend Christmas in Jerusalem had been particularly memorable.

Nevertheless, when Justice Byron R. White visited Brennan's chambers in March 1993 to discuss his own retirement after thirty-one years on the Court, Brennan advised him against it, saying that his own retirement was the worst mistake he had ever made.

White replied, "I'm not like you, Bill. I like to go fishing and I'll enjoy the time with my grandchildren."

White retired at the end of the Court's 1992–93 term at the age of seventy-five and moved his chambers into the Thurgood Marshall

Building. Brennan, for his part, continued to rise early each day and make his way to his chambers in the Court where he met or corresponded with admirers and would-be biographers, worked on law review articles, and arranged for the ultimate disposition of his papers. What writer Jack Kerouac once called the "forlorn rags of growing old" left him with good days and bad days, times when he was coherent and others when he was not.

Whatever insecurities he may have harbored about his legacy were groundless. He told an interviewer in 1989, "In the end, I hope the historical assessment of me will be that he did his best and that he did not leave anything that he needed to—or his family would ever come to—regret."[14] By this modest measure, his life was unquestionably a success. But he will be remembered for much more than his personal commitment to doing his best, his impeccable work ethic, and his dedication to home and family. He will also be remembered for his monumental contributions to both his country and to humanity at large. And as he once self-confidently proclaimed, his legacy will withstand the test of time.

When William Brennan came of age in America, racism was common, virulent, and violent; inequalities between the sexes and between rich and poor were blatant and manifest; criminal justice was often arbitrary and unfair; and the First Amendment had no real teeth. After his thirty-four years of service on the Court, and in large part because of his individual contributions during that period, Americans are undeniably freer to express ideas, and less racially and gender biased, and government at both the state and federal levels is more impartial in the administration of justice and compassionate in the allocation of services and benefits, than would otherwise have been the case.

Brennan's liberal critics complain rightly that his refusal to embrace Hugo Black's absolutism left open the door for both curtailment and abuses of cherished First Amendment freedoms. Depending on who is in power, a "balancing" of the First Amendment guarantees against other governmental interests can lead to the kind of censorship of ideas that Brennan abhorred, be it under the guise of upholding community values or protecting women and minorities from the detrimental effects of "obscenity," "pornography," "hate speech," or other evils.

Moreover, the actual malice standard adopted by the Court in

New York Times v. Sullivan, although not an impregnable impedi-
ment to press censorship, has proven sturdy enough to allow for
press abuses that have often sickened and antagonized the general
public. Much of the innuendo and personal effrontery that pass
with impunity under the guise of serious journalism is deplorable.

Nevertheless, Brennan's contributions in the First Amendment
area, for which he is best remembered as a justice, gave the
guarantees of free speech and press real force and effect for the first
time in American history. Whatever abuses may have occurred as a
result have been worth the price for the fulfillment of the Founders'
promises.

In addition, Brennan's opinion for the Court in *Baker v. Carr*
put political power where it rightfully belongs in a democracy such
as ours—in the hands of the American middle class. This is not to
say, however, that Brennan was prepared to overlook or leave behind
those who, as he put it, "do not partake of the abundance of
American life." Quite the contrary, for Bill Brennan will be
remembered as a champion of the poor.

He failed in his effort to persuade the Court to regard as
inherently suspect any governmental action or classification that
has a disproportionate impact on poor people. And he could not
convince a majority of the justices that education, the ticket out of
poverty, should be regarded as a fundamental right. But with his
landmark ruling in *Goldberg v. Kelly* in 1970, in which he upheld the
right of a New York welfare recipient to a hearing before her
benefits could be terminated, he drove home at least the need for
procedural safeguards that take into account poor people's relative
powerlessness and protect them from unfair or arbitrary treatment.

Moreover, to the extent that the middle class benefited from
Brennan's jurisprudence, the changing face of that middle class may
be the greatest evidence of his influence and effectiveness on behalf
of those who were less well off to begin with.

Surveys have indicated that the growth of the suburbs that were
empowered by Brennan's decision in *Baker v. Carr* is being fed by
African Americans and other minorities who, taking full advantage
of increased educational and employment opportunities since the
demise of legal segregation, are moving up into the American
mainstream, which was one of Brennan's primary objectives.

According to University of Michigan demographer William H.

Frey, "What is going on is not so much black suburbanization as black middle-class suburbanization."[15] Between 1980 and 1990, for example, the number of African Americans living in the suburbs increased by 34.4 percent, from roughly 5.9 million to approximately 8 million.[16] Meanwhile, Hispanics and Asian-Americans experienced even higher rates of suburbanization over the same period.

Some observers regard this middle-class "flight" to the suburbs as potentially harmful to the urban populations left behind. The analogous "white flight" that began during the 1950s deprived the cities of needed tax revenue and those at the bottom of the economic ladder of needed jobs and social services.

But others view the changes as representative of an overall economic strengthening of metropolitan areas. For example, Richard P. Nathan, provost of the Nelson A. Rockefeller Institute of Government at the State University of New York at Albany, has dismissed the assertion that cities are being abandoned to the underclass. According to Nathan, only a quarter of the total number of African Americans residing in metropolitan areas in 1990 lived in poverty.[17]

As residential diversity deepens, so will equal educational opportunities, a prime focus of Brennan's work on the Court. And as minorities, suburban or otherwise, exercise their right of "one person, one vote," established by the ruling in Baker v. Carr, government at all levels will inevitably become more responsive to minority needs and aspirations. More important, the needs and aspirations of members of minority groups will coincide more routinely and inextricably with those of majority Americans.

Recognition of these and other of his contributions, monumental and far-reaching though they are, does not serve to deify William Brennan, or to enlarge him beyond the fallible justice that he was. He made mistakes, and in his haste to conciliate, forge consensus, and keep from burning bridges he may have minimized unpleasant realities.

For example, even as the Court's conservative majority solidified during the 1970s and 1980s, he was overgenerous in his assertion that he did not "see anything serious, by way of changing jurisprudence, in contrast with what has happened in the past." In reality, the Burger and Rehnquist Courts threatened to turn the clock back on civil rights and had jeopardized hard-won advances in the struggle to create a more inclusive modern society.

Fortunately, Congress intervened to undo much of the damage. For example, the Civil Rights Act of 1991, which was signed into law by President Clinton on November 21, 1991, undid the negative effects of a number of recent Supreme Court decisions that had narrowed statutory protections against employment discrimination.

But while this congressional intervention underscores the severity of the threat that had been posed to civil rights, it also lends support to Brennan's overall optimism about the American legal system, his view that while the pendulum seems to swing back and forth on fundamental questions of constitutional rights and interpretation, the system can be relied upon to right itself eventually.

After World War II, for example, the executive branch took the lead in the struggle for racial equality when President Harry Truman desegregated the armed forces early in his administration. Subsequently the Court seized the initiative with its ruling in *Brown v. Board of Education* (1954) and its unshakable commitment to racial integration throughout the next decade and a half.

Congress did not enlist in the struggle for equality until later, most notably during the 1960s, with the enactment of civil- and voting-rights legislation, fair housing laws, and other measures. But by the end of the 1980s, when the Court was engaged in a full-scale retrenchment, Congress was prepared to step in and set the Court right with the 1991 Civil Rights Act.

The extent to which the Court managed to hold the line against or at least to minimize civil rights reversals until such time as Congress was prepared to intervene is both a tribute to Brennan and unmistakable evidence of how effectively he waged his rearguard action against the Court's right wing throughout the decades of the 1970s and 1980s. For this he is owed a debt of gratitude by all Americans, not just minorities, for a threat to the rights of the few places the rights of all in jeopardy.

Since Brennan's retirement in 1990, the Court's political and social regression appears to have abated. The emergence of a centrist bloc of justices seems to have made the Court more averse to unsettling established precedents that date back to the Warren Court era. The centrists' emergence is further evidence of how effectively Brennan conducted his rear-guard maneuvers. Court

decisions delivered during the 1950s and 1960s that were assailed
originally by conservative critics as radical departures from tradition or precedent have now taken on a centrist, time-honored
character of their own.

In the future, the appointment of more and culturally diverse
women to the Court may result in the Court's reflecting more
accurately the progressive changes that have occurred in American
society at large. But this is by no means guaranteed. Women, like
men, are far from monolithic in their thinking. Nevertheless,
Brennan deserves credit for his staunch support for women's rights
as well as for minority rights, for facilitating, rather than impeding,
the inexorable progress toward gender equality.

On other issues, his views seem uncharacteristically out of
touch with modern times. For example, Brennan's emphasis on the
sociological aspects of crime, his focus on poverty, racism, and lack
of economic opportunity as factors motivating criminal behavior,
sounds antiquated. It was an attitude prevalent during the 1960s
that few people share today.

On the one hand, there is undeniably something wrong with a
society that has more people incarcerated than any other indus-
trialized nation, and in which a disproportionate number of those
incarcerated come from minority groups that have been discriminated against historically. There is, however, a growing sentiment
that in large part because of the contributions of men like William
Brennan, American society has reformed itself enough so that
everyone has an adequate chance to succeed through hard work and
diligence.

For this reason, criminal behavior is today seen less as a cry for
help or as a racist society's just deserts than as an individual
character defect, a conscious decision to behave criminally rather
than to assume individual responsibility for oneself. Consequently
there is more sympathy for the victim and less for the perpetrator,
irrespective of the perpetrator's social or economic circumstances.

All of which helps to explain the popular dissatisfaction with a
criminal justice system often regarded as "soft" on criminals, and
the contemporary appeal of capital punishment, which Brennan
opposed bitterly. In an ideal world, everyone would be as humane as
William Brennan. There is no question that it is wrong for the state,
or anyone else, to kill people.

Nevertheless, society's desire for retribution against those who commit heinous crimes may be irrepressible, at least for the time being, given current public sentiments. Brennan conceded that he would not see the day when the United States would abolish the death penalty. My suspicion is that his grandchildren and great-grandchildren will not see it, either.

William Brennan wrote 533 majority opinions, 346 concurrences, and 694 dissents during his 34 years on the U.S. Supreme Court, a prodigious legacy. As Justice David Souter pointed out at the September 30, 1992, Harvard Club of Washington, D.C., toast in Brennan's honor, one may agree or disagree with some or all of those opinions, but "their collective influence is an enormously powerful defining force in the contemporary life of this republic." It will remain so long into at least the next century.

Souter went on to rank Brennan among the greatest justices that Harvard has produced. But Harvard and the Supreme Court are inadequate scales of measurement. To the extent that William Brennan's measure can be taken, it is by comparison with the Founding Fathers, the men who wrote the Constitution. And by that measure, his rightful place is alongside James Madison, author of the Bill of Rights.

Appendix

JUSTICE BRENNAN'S UNANIMOUS OPINION in *New York Times v. Sullivan* (1964) struck a mighty blow for freedom of speech and of the press under the First Amendment and stands as his most famous decision. At issue in the case was an editorial advertisement that appeared under the headline "Heed Their Rising Voices" on page 25 of the *Times*'s Tuesday, March 29, 1960, edition. L. B. Sullivan and other Alabama officials sued the *Times* for libel, but the U.S. Supreme Court ruled in the *Times*'s favor based on the actual malice test formulated by Brennan. The advertisement in its entirety read as follows:

As the whole world knows by now, thousands of Southern Negro students are engaged in widespread non-violent demonstrations in positive affirmation of the right to live in human dignity as guaranteed by the U.S. Constitution and the Bill of Rights. In their efforts to uphold these guarantees, they are being met by an unprecedented wave of terror by those who would deny and negate that document which the whole world looks upon as setting the pattern for modern freedom....

In Orangeburg, South Carolina, when 400 students peacefully sought to buy doughnuts and coffee at lunch counters in the business district, they were forcibly ejected, tear-gassed, soaked to the skin in freezing weather with fire hoses, arrested en masse and herded into an open barbed-wire stockade to stand for hours in the bitter cold.

In Montgomery, Alabama, after students sang "My Country, 'Tis of Thee" on the State Capitol steps, their leaders were expelled from school, and truckloads of police armed with shotguns and tear-gas ringed the Alabama State College Campus. When the entire student body protested to state authorities by refusing to re-register, their dining hall was pad-locked in an attempt to starve them into submission.

In Tallahassee, Atlanta, Nashville, Savannah, Greensboro, Memphis, Richmond, Charlotte, and a host of other cities in the South, young American teenagers, in face of the entire weight of official state apparatus and police power, have boldly stepped forth as protagonists of democracy. Their courage and amazing restraint have inspired millions and given a new dignity to the cause of freedom.

Small wonder that the Southern violators of the Constitution fear this new, non-violent brand of freedom fighter...even as they fear the upswelling right-to-vote movement. Small wonder that they are determined to destroy the one man who, more than any other, symbolizes the new spirit now sweeping the South—the Rev. Dr. Martin Luther King, Jr., world-famous leader of the Montgomery Bus Protest. For it is his doctrine of non-violence which has inspired and guided the students in their widening wave of sit-ins; and it is the same Dr. King who founded and is president of the Southern Christian Leadership Conference—the organization which is spearheading the surging right-to-vote movement. Under Dr. King's direction the Leadership Conference conducts Student Workshops and Seminars in the philosophy and technique of non-violent resistance.

Again and again the Southern violators have answered Dr. King's peaceful protests with intimidation and violence. They have bombed his home almost killing his wife and child. They have assaulted his person. They have arrested him seven times—for "speeding," "loitering" and similar offenses. And now they have charged him with "perjury"—a *felony* under which they could imprison him for *ten years*. Obviously, their real purpose is to remove him physically as the leader to whom the students and millions of others—look for guidance and support, and thereby to intimidate *all* leaders who may rise in the South. Their strategy is to behead this affirmative movement, and thus to demoralize Negro Americans and weaken their will to struggle. The defense of Martin Luther King, spiritual leader of the sit-in movement, clearly, therefore, is an integral part of the total struggle for freedom in the South.

Decent-minded Americans cannot help but applaud the creative daring of the students and the quiet heroism of Dr. King. But this is one of those moments in the stormy history of Freedom when men and women of good will must do more than applaud the rising-to-glory of others. The America whose good name hangs in the balance before a watchful world, the America whose heritage of Liberty these Southern Upholders of the Constitution are defending, is *our* America as well as theirs....

We must heed their rising voices—yes—but we must add our own.

We must extend ourselves above and beyond moral support and render the material help so urgently needed by those who are taking the risks, facing jail, and even death in a glorious re-affirmation of our Constitution and its Bill of Rights.

We urge you to join hands with our fellow Americans in the South by supporting, with your dollars, this Combined Appeal for all three needs—the defense of Martin Luther King—the support of the embattled students—and the struggle for the right-to-vote.

Your Help Is Urgently Needed...NOW!!

Notes

Chapter 1: The Perfect Match of Mind and Heart

1. Michael D. Davis & Hunter R. Clark, *Thurgood Marshall: Warrior at the Bar, Rebel on the Bench* (Citadel Press, 1994), at 367–368.

2. David Souter, Remarks at the Harvard Club of Washington, D.C., Reception in Honor of Justice William J. Brennan Jr. (Sept. 30, 1992), author's files.

3. *Id.*

4. *Id.*

5. *Id.*

6. Letter from Neil L. Rudenstine, President, Harvard University, to Nicholas T. Christakos, President, Harvard Club of Washington, D.C. (Sept. 30, 1992), author's files.

7. *Id.*

8. Fax from Robert C. Clark, Dean, Harvard Law School, to Nicholas T. Christakos, President, Harvard Club of Washington, D.C. (undated), author's files.

9. *Id.*

10. Souter, *supra* note 2.

11. Stephen J. Markman & Alfred Regnery, "The Mind of Justice Brennan: A 25-Year Tribute," *National Review* (May 18, 1984), at 30.

12. *Id.* at 38.

13. Davis & Clark, *supra* note 1, at 367.

14. Souter, *supra* note 2.

15. *Id.*

16. *Id.*

17. *Id.*

18. Toni House, "Justice Brennan's Career Recalled," *The Docket Sheet* (an in-house publication of the U.S. Supreme Court) (Summer 1990), at 1, author's files.

19. *Id.*

20. Letter from Alan C. Kohn to Hunter R. Clark (July 16, 1993).

21. *See* Tim O'Brien, "William J. Brennan," in *8 Men and a Lady: Profiles of the Justices of the Supreme Court* (National Press, 1990), at 72–73.

22. *See, e.g.,* Linda Greenhouse, "Souter: Unlikely Anchor at the Court's Center," *N.Y. Times* (July 3, 1992), at A1; Linda Greenhouse, "Changed Path

for Court?: New Balance Is Held by 3 Cautious Justices," *N.Y. Times* (June 26, 1992), at A1.

23. 112 S. Ct. 2791 (1992).
24. 410 U.S. 113 (1973).
25. 112 S. Ct., at 2815.
26. 112 S. Ct., at 2815.
27. 112 S. Ct., at 2815.
28. 358 U.S. 1 (1958).
29. David J. Garrow, "Justice Souter: A Surprising Kind of Conservative," *New York Times Magazine* (Sept. 25, 1994), at 39.
30. William J. Brennan Jr., Remarks at the Meeting of the Federal Bar Association, Washington, D.C. (Nov. 29, 1956), author's files. *See also* O'Brien, *supra* note 20, at 52.
31. *See* Donna Haupt, "Justice William J. Brennan, Jr.," *Constitution* (Winter 1989), at 50.
32. William J. Brennan Jr., Remarks at the Harvard Club of Washington, D.C., Reception in His Honor (Sept. 30, 1992), author's files.
33. *Id.*

Chapter 2: "Everything I Am"

1. Marjorie R. Fallows, *Irish Americans: Identity and Assimilation* (Prentice-Hall, 1979), at 97.
2. William Shannon, "The Lasting Hurrah," *N.Y. Times Magazine* (March 14, 1976), at 75.
3. *See* Francis P. McQuade and Alexander T. Kardos, *Mr. Justice Brennan and His Legal Philosophy*, 33 NOTRE DAME LAWYER 321 (1958).
4. Sean O Murchu, "Lone Justice: An Interview With Justice William J. Brennan, Jr.," *Irish America* (June 1990), at 28.
5. *Id.*
6. *Id.*
7. *Id.*
8. Jack Alexander, "Mr. Justice From New Jersey," *The Saturday Evening Post* (Sept. 28, 1957), at 130.
9. *Id.*
10. *Id.*
11. Fallows, *supra* note 1, at 113.
12. O Murchu, *supra* note 4, at 28.
13. *Id.*
14. *See* Kim Isaac Eisler, *A Justice For All: William J. Brennan, Jr., and the Decisions That Transformed America* (Simon & Schuster, 1993), at 16.
15. *See id.*
16. *See* McQuade and Kardos, *supra* note 3, at 322.
17. *See* Eisler, *supra* note 14, at 19.
18. O Murchu, *supra* note 4, at 28.
19. *See* Eisler, *supra* note 14, at 19.
20. O Murchu, *supra* note 4, at 28.

21. *Id.*
22. *See* McQuade and Kardos, *supra* note 3, at 322; Alexander, *supra* note 8, at 130.
23. *See* Alexander, *supra* note 8, at 130.
24. O Murchu, *supra* note 4, at 28.
25. *Id.*
26. *Id.*
27. *Id.*
28. O Murchu, *supra* note 4, at 28.
29. *Id.*
30. *Id.* at 29.
31. *Id.*
32. *Id.*
33. *Id.*
34. *Id.*
35. Jeffrey T. Leeds, "A Life on the Court," *N.Y. Times Magazine* (Oct. 5, 1986), at 26.
36. *Id.*
37. *See* Eisler, *supra* note 12, at 25–26.
38. O Murchu, *supra* note 4, at 29.
39. *Id.*
40. Eisler, *supra* note 12, at 20.
41. *Newark: A Chronological and Documentary History (1666–1970)* (Arnold S. Rice ed., Oceana Publications 1977), at 21.
42. Eisler, *supra* note 12, at 25.
43. *Id.*
44. *See id.* at 24.
45. *Id.*
46. *Id.*
47. *Id.* at 21.
48. *Id.* at 24.
49. *Id.*
50. Alexander, *supra* note 8, at 132.
51. *See id.* at 21.
52. *See id.*
53. *See id.*
54. *Id.*
55. O Murchu, *supra* note 4, at 28.
56. Leeds, *supra* note 30, at 26.
57. *See* Eisler, *supra* note 12, at 23.
58. *See id.* at 22.
59. Donna Haupt, "Justice William J. Brennan, Jr.," *Constitution* (Winter 1989), at 52.
60. *Id.*
61. *Id.*
62. Eisler, *supra* note 12, at 23.

63. *Id.*

64. "An Experienced Judge for the Supreme Court," *U.S. News & World Report* (Oct. 12, 1956), at 71–72; Haupt, *supra* note 58, at 53.

65. Alexander, *supra* note 8, at 132.

66. O Murchu, *supra* note 4, at 29.

Chapter 3: Harvard Law School

1. *See* Jack Alexander, "Mr. Justice From New Jersey," *The Saturday Evening Post* (Sept. 28, 1957), at 132.

2. Kim Isaac Eisler, *A Justice For All: William J. Brennan, Jr., and the Decisions That Transformed America* (Simon & Schuster, 1993), at 28.

3. *See* Alexander, *supra* note 1, at 132.

4. *See id.*

5. *See* Francis P. McQuade and Alexander T. Kardos, *Mr. Justice Brennan and His Legal Philosophy*, 33 NOTRE DAME LAWYER 321, 322 (1958).

6. Eisler, *supra* note 2, at 27.

7. *See id. See also The Oxford Companion to the Supreme Court of the United States* (Kermit L. Hall ed., Oxford 1992), at 839.

8. *See* Eisler, *supra* note 2, at 27.

9. *See id.*

10. *See id.* at 28.

11. *See* McQuade and Kardos, *supra* note 4, at 322.

12. Eisler, *supra* note 2, at 28.

13. Frederick W. Hall, *Mr. Justice Brennan—The Early Years*, 15 HARV. C.R.-C.L. L. REV. 286, 286–287 (1980).

14. Eisler, *supra* note 2, at 30.

15. *See id.*

16. *See id.*

17. *See id.*

18. *See id.*

19. Sean O Murchu, "Lone Justice: An Interview With Justice William Brennan, Jr.," *Irish America* (June 1990), at 28.

20. Eisler, *supra* note 2, at 30.

21. *See id.*

22. *See* Alexander, *supra* note 1, at 133.

23. *See* McQuade and Kardos, *supra* note 4, at 322.

24. *See* Daniel Crystal, "Forging Judicial Greatness: Justice Brennan's New Jersey Years," *The Reporter* (publication of the Passaic County, N.J., bar association) (Spring 1984), at 22.

25. McQuade and Kardos, *supra* note 4, at 322.

Chapter 4: Counselor and Soldier

1. Kim Isaac Eisler, *A Justice for All: William J. Brennan, Jr., and the Decisions That Transformed America* (Simon & Schuster, 1993), at 41.

2. *See* Francis P. McQuade and Alexander T. Kardos, *Mr. Justice Brennan and His Legal Philosophy*, 33 NOTRE DAME LAWYER 321, 323 (1958).

3. *See* Eisler, *supra* note 1, at 34.

4. *See id.*

5. *See id.*

6. *See id.* at 33–34.

7. *See id.* at 34.

8. *See id.* at 636; *Wilson v. New,* 243 U.S. 332, 373 (1917) (Pitney, J., dissenting).

9. *See Frank v. Mangum,* 237 U.S. 309 (1915).

10. *The Oxford Companion to the Supreme Court of the United States* (Kermit L. Hall ed., Oxford 1992), at 636.

11. *Id.*

12. *Id.*

13. Daniel Crystal, "Forging Judicial Greatness: Justice Brennan's New Jersey Years," *The Reporter* (publication of the Passaic County, N.J., bar association) (Spring 1984), at 22–23.

14. *See* Eisler, *supra* note 1, at 35.

15. *See* Frederick W. Hall, *Mr. Justice Brennan—The Earlier Years,* 15 HARV. C.R.-C.L. L. REV. 286, 287 (1980).

16. *See id.*

17. *See* McQuade and Kardos, *supra* note 2, at 323.

18. *See* Eisler, *supra* note 1, at 37.

19. McQuade and Kardos, *supra* note 16, at 323.

20. Hall, *supra* note 14, at 287.

21. McQuade and Kardos, *supra* note 16, at 323.

22. *See id.*

23. McQuade and Kardos, *supra* note 16, at 323.

24. *Id.*

25. *See* Eisler, *supra* note 1, at 37.

26. *See* Jack Alexander, "Mr. Justice From New Jersey," *The Saturday Evening Post* (Sept. 28, 1957), at 132.

27. *See* McQuade and Kardos, *supra* note 16, at 323.

28. Donna Haupt, "Justice William J. Brennan, Jr.," *Constitution* (Winter 1989), at 53.

29. *See* Eisler, *supra* note 1, at 42–43.

30. *See id.* at 43.

31. *See id.*

32. *Id.*

33. *Id.*

34. *Id.*

35. *See id.*

36. *See id.* at 42.

37. *Id.* at 43.

38. McQuade and Kardos, *supra* note 16, at 323.

39. *See* Eisler, *supra* note 1, at 44.

40. *See id.*

41. *See The National Cyclopaedia of American Biography* (J. T. White, New York), vol. G, at 11.

42. *See id.*

43. *See id.*

44. *See* Eisler, *supra* note 1, at 44.

45. *Id.*

46. *See id.* at 44–45.

47. *See id.*

48. *See id.* at 45.

49. *Investigation of the National Defense Program, 1945: Hearings Before a Special Committee of the Senate Investigating the National Defense Program,* 79th Cong., 1st Sess. 14965 (1945) (statement of Sen. Mead, Chairman).

50. *Id.* (statement of Col. William J. Brennan, Chief, Labor Branch, Army Service Forces).

51. Mead, *supra* note 48, at 14966.

52. Brennan, *supra* note 49, at 14966.

53. *Id.* at 14966–67.

54. *Id.* at 14967.

55. Haupt, *supra* note 27, at 53.

56. *See* McQuade and Kardos, *supra* note 16, at 323.

Chapter 5: A Major Scandal

1. Daniel Crystal, "Forging Judicial Greatness: Justice Brennan's New Jersey Years," *The Reporter* (publication of the Passaic County, N.J., bar association) (Spring 1984), at 23.

2. Francis P. McQuade and Alexander T. Kardos, *Mr. Justice Brennan and His Legal Philosophy,* 33 NOTRE DAME LAWYER 321, 323 (1958).

3. *See* Kim Isaac Eisler, *A Justice For All: William J. Brennan, Jr., and the Decisions That Transformed America* (Simon & Schuster, 1993), at 51.

4. *See id.* at 51–52.

5. *See id.* at 52.

6. *Id.* at 54.

7. *Id.*

8. Crystal, *supra* note 1, at 23; Nat Hentoff, "Profiles: The Constitutionalist," *New Yorker* (March 12, 1990), at 48.

9. Hentoff, *supra* note 8, at 48.

10. *See Washington Post* (July 7, 1946) (op-ed page).

11. *See id.*

12. *See id.*

13. *See id.*

14. *See id.*

15. *Id.*

16. *Id.*

17. *Id.*

18. *See Investigation of the National Defense Program, 1946: Hearings Before a Special Committee of the Senate Investigating the National Defense Program,* 79th Cong., 2nd Sess. 17850 (1946) (Reading Exhibit No. 1785).

19. *See id.*

20. *See* Eisler, *supra* note 3, at 47–48.

21. *See Hearings, supra* note 16 (Reading Exhibit No. 1785).

22. *Id.* (statement of Sen. Meader).

23. *Id.* (statement of Mr. Brennan).

24. *The National Cyclopaedia of American Biography* (J. T. White, New York), vol. G (1946), at 12.

25. *Id.* at 11.

26. *Hearings, supra* note 16, at 17928 (statement of Mr. Slezak).

27. *Id.*

28. *Id.* at 17853–54; 17928 (statements of Mr. Brennan).

29. *Id.*

30. *Id.*

31. *Id.* at 17854.

32. *Id.*

33. *Id.* at 17933.

34. *Id.*

35. *Id.*

36. *Id.*

37. *Id.*

38. *Id.* at 17919–20.

39. *Id.* at 17920.

40. *Id.*

41. *Id.*

42. *Id.*

43. *Id.*

44. Eisler, *supra* note 3, at 50 (citing *The Washington Post*).

Chapter 6: Reforming the Courts

1. William J. Brennan Jr., "After Eight Years: New Jersey Judicial Reform," *American Bar Association Journal* (June 1957), at 499.

2. *See id.* at 502.

3. *Id.*

4. *Id.*

5. William J. Brennan Jr., "The Judicial Administrator," *Georgetown Law Center Bulletin* (Fall 1957), at 7.

6. *Id.*

7. *See National Cyclopaedia of American Biography* (J. T. White, New York), vol. 52 (1970), at 429.

8. *See id.*

9. *See* Kim Isaac Eisler, *A Justice For All: William J. Brennan, Jr., and the Decisions That Transformed America* (Simon & Schuster, 1993), at 35.

10. *See The National Cyclopaedia of American Biography, supra* note 7, at 429.

11. *See id.*

12. *Id.*

13. *Id.*

14. William J. Brennan Jr., *Justice Nathan L. Jacobs—Tributes From His Colleagues,* 28 RUTGERS L. REV. 209 (1974).

15. William J. Brennan Jr., "A Modern Court Structure for New Jersey," *New Jersey Law Journal* (June 12, 1947), at 1.

16. Brennan, *supra* note 14, at 209.

17. Frederick W. Hall, *Mr. Justice Brennan—The Earlier Years,* 15 HARV. C.R.-C.L. L. REV. 286, 287–88 (1980).

18. *Id.* at 288.

19. Brennan, *supra* note 1, at 499.

20. *Id.*

21. Brennan, *supra* note 5, at 7.

22. *Id.*

23. *Id.*

24. *Id.*

25. Brennan, *supra* note 1, at 565.

26. Brennan, *supra* note 5, at 7.

27. Brennan, *supra* note 1, at 500.

28. *Id.* at 501.

29. *Id.*

30. *Id.*

31. *Id.* at 502.

32. *Id.*

33. *Evening Star* (Nov. 30, 1956) (quoting William J. Brennan Jr., Address to the Federal Bar Association at the National Press Club, Washington D.C. [Nov. 30, 1956]).

34. *U.S. News & World Report,* Oct. 12, 1956, at 72.

35. Brennan, *supra* note 1, at 564.

36. *Id.*

37. *Id.* at 502, 564.

38. Jack Alexander, "Mr. Justice From New Jersey," *Saturday Evening Post* (Sept. 28, 1957), at 133.

39. *Id.*

40. Brennan, *supra* note 14, at 209.

41. *Id.*

42. *Id.*

43. Daniel Crystal, "Forging Judicial Greatness: Justice Brennan's New Jersey Years," *The Reporter* (publication of the Passaic County, N.J., bar association) (Spring 1984), at 23.

44. *See* Kim Isaac Eisler, *A Justice For All: William J. Brennan, Jr., and the Decisions That Transformed America* (Simon & Schuster, 1993), at 64.

45. *Id.* at 65.

46. *See* Crystal, *supra* note 41, at 23.

47. Frederick W. Hall, *Mr. Justice Brennan—The Earlier Years,* 15 HARV. C.R.-C.L. L. REV. 286, 288 (1980).

48. *Id.*

49. "An Experienced Judge for Supreme Court: William Joseph Brennan,

Jr.," *U.S. News & World Report* (Oct. 12, 1956), at 73.

Chapter 7: The Hinge of Fate

1. Daniel Crystal, "Forging Judicial Greatness: Justice Brennan's New Jersey Years," *The Reporter* (publication of the Passaic County, N.J., bar association) (Spring 1984), at 24.

2. William J. Brennan Jr., *Justice Nathan L. Jacobs—Tributes From His Colleagues*, 28 RUTGERS L. REV. 209, 210 (1974).

3. *Id.*

4. *Id.*

5. 65 A.2d 657 (1949).

5. 65 A.2d, at 659.

7. *See* Crystal, *supra* note 1, at 24.

8. Frederick W. Hall, *Mr. Justice Brennan—The Earlier Years*, 15 HARV. C.R.-C.L. L. REV. 286, 289 (1980).

9. *Id.*

10. 77 A.2d 183 (1950).

11. 77 A.2d, at 185.

12. 80 A.2d 641 (1951).

13. 80 A.2d, at 641.

14. 80 A.2d, at 643.

15. 80 A.2d, at 643.

16. 76 A.2d 717 (1950).

17. 76 A.2d, at 721.

18. 93 A.2d 176 (1952).

19. 93 A.2d, at 181.

20. 93 A.2d, at 181.

21. Brennan, *supra* note 2, at 209.

22. Hall, *supra* note 5, at 289.

23. *See* Jack Alexander, "Mr. Justice From New Jersey," *Saturday Evening Post* (Sept. 28, 1957), at 133.

24. *See* Kim Isaac Eisler, *A Justice For All: William J. Brennan, Jr., and the Decisions That Transformed America* (Simon & Schuster, 1993), at 77.

25. *See id.*

26. *Id.*

27. *See id.*

28. 96 A.2d 519 (1953).

29. 96 A.2d, at 521.

30. 96 A.2d, at 521.

31. *See* 96 A.2d, at 522–23.

32. 96 A.2d, at 522.

33. 98 A.2d 881 (1953).

34. 98 A.2d, at 896.

35. 98 A.2d, at 897.

36. 117 A.2d 499 (1955).

37. 117 A.2d, at 501.

38. 117 A.2d, at 501.

Chapter 8: The Shamrock and the Robe

1. Patrician scholar D. A. Binchy, *quoted in The New Encyclopaedia Britannica* (1979), vol. 13, at 1077. For a discussion of St. Patrick's life and works, *see The Oxford Illustrated History of Ireland* (R. F. Foster ed., Oxford 1991), at 8–10.

2. Sean O Murchu, "Lone Justice: An Interview with Justice William Brennan, Jr.," *Irish America* (June 1990), at 29.

3. George Reedy, *From the Ward to the White House: The Irish in American Politics* (Scribner's, 1990), at 12.

4. *Id.*

5. *See* Jack Beatty, *The Rascal King: The Life and Times of James Michael Curley (1874–1958)* (Addison-Wesley, 1992), at 392.

6. Nina Totenberg, *A Tribute to Justice William J. Brennan, Jr.*, 104 HARV. L. REV. 33, 35 (1990).

7. Nat Hentoff, "Profiles: The Constitutionalist," *New Yorker* (March 12, 1990), at 46.

8. Owen Fiss, *A Life Lived Twice*, 100 YALE L. J. 1117, 1118 (1991).

9. Michael F. Tigar, *The McCarthy Era: History as Snapshot*, 15 HARV. C.R.-C.L. L. REV. 507, 511–12 (1980) (book review).

10. 339 U.S. 382 (1950).

11. 341 U.S. 494 (1951).

12. Tigar, *supra* note 9, at 513.

13. Daniel Crystal, "Forging Judicial Greatness: Justice Brennan's New Jersey Years," *The Reporter* (publication of the Passaic County, N.J., bar association) (Spring 1984), at 20.

14. *Id.*

15. William V. Shannon, *The American Irish* (Macmillan, 1964), at 380–81.

16. *See id.* at 381.

17. *Id.*

18. *Id.*

19. *Id.*

20. *Id.*

21. Catherine B. Shannon, "Profiling Irish America," *Irish Literary Supplement* (Fall 1993), at 38 (reviewing Lawrence J. McCaffrey, *Textures of Irish America* [1992]).

22. *Id.*

23. W. Shannon, *supra* note 15, at 382.

24. C. Shannon, *supra* note 21.

25. C. Shannon, *supra* note 21.

26. W. Shannon, *supra* note 15, at 383.

27. *Id.*

28. *Id.*

29. William J. Brennan Jr., Address Before the Charitable Irish Society,

Boston, Massachusetts (Mar. 17, 1954), author's files.

30. *Id.*

31. *Id.*

32. *Id.*

33. *Id.*

34. *Id.*

35. *Id.*

36. *Id.*

37. *Id.*

38. William J. Brennan Jr., Address Before the Monmouth Rotary Club, Monmouth, New Jersey (Feb. 23, 1955), author's files.

39. *Id.*

40. *Id.*

41. *Id.*

Chapter 9: Ike's Second-Biggest Mistake

1. J. L. Bernstein, "The Philosophy of Mr. Justice Brennan," *The Reporter* (publication of the Passaic County, N.J., bar association) (Nov. 1956), (quoting Fred Rodell), *reprinted in* "Mr. Justice Brennan: Freedom's Advocate," *The Reporter* (May 1972), at 10.

2. *See The Oxford Companion to the Supreme Court of the United States* (Kermit T. Hall ed., Oxford 1992), at 552.

3. *Id.*

4. 342 U.S. 485 (1952).

5. 342 U.S. 524 (1952).

6. *See N.Y. Times,* Sept. 8, 1956, at 1, col. 1.

7. *N.Y. Times,* Sept. 8, 1956, at 8, col. 6.

8. *See id.*

9. *N.Y. Times,* Sept. 8, 1956, at 8, col. 6.

10. *N.Y. Times,* Sept. 8, 1956, at 1, col. 1.

11. *N.Y. Times,* Sept. 8, 1956, at 8, col. 4.

12. *N.Y. Times,* Sept. 8, 1956, at 1, col. 1.

13. Herbert Brownell with John P. Burke, *Advising Ike: The Memoirs of Attorney General Herbert Brownell* (University Press of Kansas, 1993), at 176.

14. *See id.* at 176–77.

15. *See id.* at 177.

16. *See id.* at 167.

17. *See id.* at 166–67.

18. *See id.*

19. *See id.* at 164.

20. Brownell, *supra* note 13, at 167.

21. *Id.*

22. *See* Bernard Schwartz, *Super Chief: Earl Warren and His Supreme Court—A Judicial Biography* (New York University, 1983), at 14–15. *See also* Michael D. Davis *&* Hunter R. Clark, *Thurgood Marshall: Warrior at the Bar, Rebel on the Bench* (Citadel Press, 1994), at 170–71.

23. Schwartz, *supra* note 22, at 15.

24. Davis & Clark, *supra* note 22, at 170–71.

25. *Id.* at 171.

26. *See id.*

27. *Id.*

28. Brownell, *supra* note 13, at 165.

29. *Id.*

30. *See id.* at 166.

31. *See id.*

32. Jack Alexander, "Mr. Justice From New Jersey," *Saturday Evening Post* (Sept. 28, 1957), at 130.

33. 163 U.S. 537 (1896).

34. 163 U.S., at 559.

35. 163 U.S., at 559.

36. *Oxford Companion, supra* note 2, at 364.

37. *Id.*

38. *Id.* at 365.

39. Brownell, *supra* note 13, at 13.

40. *See Oxford Companion, supra* note 2, at 365.

41. *See id.* at 365; Tinsley E. Yarbrough, *John Marshall Harlan: Great Dissenter of the Warren Court* (Oxford, 1992), at 86.

42. 216 F.2d 354 (2d Cir. 1954).

43. Eugene Gressman, "The New Justice Harlan," *New Republic* (April 4, 1955), at 9. *See also* Yarbrough, *supra* note 32, at 86.

44. *Id.*

45. *See* Yarbrough, *supra* note 32, at 91–92.

46. *Id.* at 91.

47. *See Oxford Companion, supra* note 2, at 365.

48. *See* Brownell, *supra* note 13, at 179.

49. *Id.*

50. 347 U.S. 483 (1954).

51. Brownell, *supra* note 13, at 179.

52. *See Oxford Companion, supra* note 2, at 365.

53. *See, e.g., N.Y. Times*, Sept. 9, 1956, at 56, col. 6.

54. Brownell, *supra* note 13, at 181.

55. *See N.Y. Times,* Sept. 12, 1956, at 33, col. 6.

56. *See id.*

57. Brownell, *supra* note 13, at 180.

58. *See id.*

59. Dwight D. Eisenhower, *The White House Years: Mandate for Change,* 1953–1956, at 226–27.

60. Brownell, *supra* note 13, 179–80.

61. *Id.* at 180.

62. *See id.*

63. *Id.* at 168.

64. *See id.* at 180.

65. *Id.*

66. *Id.*

67. Tim O'Brien, "William J. Brennan, Jr.," in 8 *Men and a Lady: Profiles of the Justices of the Supreme Court* (National Press, 1990), at 54.

68. *Id. See also* Brownell, *supra* note 13, at 180.

69. Nat Hentoff, "Profiles: The Constitutionalist," *New Yorker* (March 12, 1990), at 48.

70. Donna Haupt, "Justice William J. Brennan, Jr.," *Constitution* (Winter 1989), at 53.

71. *Id.*

72. *Time,* Oct. 8, 1956, at 25.

73. Haupt, *supra* note 70, at 53.

74. *Id.*

75. *Id.*

76. *Id.* at 53–54.

77. *Id.* at 54.

78. *Life,* Oct. 29, 1956, at 115.

79. Frederick W. Hall, *Mr. Justice Brennan—The Earlier Years,* 15 HARV. C.R.-C.L. L. REV. 286, 290 (1980).

80. O'Brien, *supra* note 67, at 54.

81. *Legal Times,* Sept. 10, 1990, at 11.

82. *Id. See also* Nat Hentoff, "Profiles: The Constitutionalist," *New Yorker* (March 12, 1990), at 45.

83. *Legal Times,* Sept. 10, 1990, at 11.

84. *Id.*

85. *See id.*

86. Brownell, *supra* note 13, at 173.

87. *Legal Times,* Sept. 10, 1990, at 11.

88. Sean O Murchu, "Lone Justice: An Interview With Justice William Brennan, Jr.," *Irish America* (June 1990), at 29.

89. *Id.*

90. Brownell, *supra* note 13, at 180.

91. Haupt, *supra* note 70, at 54.

92. *Id.*

93. *Id.*

94. *Time,* Oct. 8, 1956, at 25.

95. Haupt, *supra* note 70, at 54.

96. *Id.*

97. *Evening Star,* Oct. 16, 1956, at 1, col. 2.

98. *See id.*

99. *Id.*

100. *See id.*

101. *See id.*

102. *U.S. News & World Report,* Oct. 12, 1956, at 70.

103. *Time,* Oct. 8, 1956, at 25.

104. *Id.*

105. *Life,* Oct. 29, 1956, at 116.

106. *N.Y. Times,* Oct. 1, 1956, at 26, col. 1.

107. *N.Y. Times,* Oct. 2, 1956, at 34, col. 5.

108. *N.Y. Times,* Oct. 7, 1956, sec. 4, at 8, col. 5.

109. *N.Y. Times,* Oct. 2, 1956, at 34, col. 5.

110. *Id.*

111. Jack Alexander, *supra* note 32, at 128.

112. *Id.*

113. *Time,* Oct. 8, 1956, at 25.

114. *Id.*

115. *Life,* Oct. 29, 1956, at 115–16.

116. *Sunday Star,* Sept. 30, 1956, at A-10, col. 1.

117. *N.Y. Times,* Oct. 2, 1956, at 34, col. 5.

118. *Id.*

119. *N.Y. Times,* Oct. 2, 1956, at 34, col. 5.

120. *See Sunday Star,* September 30, 1956, at A-10, col. 2.

121. *See* Daniel Berman, "Mr. Justice Brennan," *The Nation* (Oct. 13, 1956), at 300.

122. *U.S. News & World Report,* Oct. 12, 1956, at 73.

123. Kim Isaac Eisler, *A Justice For All: William J. Brennan, Jr., and the Decisions That Transformed America* (Simon & Schuster, 1993), at 99.

124. *U.S. News & World Report,* Oct. 12, 1956, at 70.

125. *Id.*

126. *Id.*

127. *Life,* Oct. 29, 1956, at 116.

128. *Time,* Oct. 8, 1956, at 25.

129. *Sunday Star,* Sept. 30, 1956, at A-10, col. 1.

130. *Id.* at cols. 1–2.

131. *N.Y. Times,* Oct. 2, 1956, at 34, col. 5.

132. *See Oxford Companion, supra* note 2, at 970.

133. Nat Hentoff, *supra* note 82, at 50 (quoting 1987 National Public Radio interview with Brennan).

134. *Id.*

135. For descriptions of Brennan's first meeting with the other justices, *see* Eisler, *supra* note 122, at 103; Haupt, *supra* note 70, at 54; David G. Savage, "After 33 Years, Brennan Is Still for Underdogs," *L.A. Times* (Oct. 1, 1989), at 16, cols. 5–6; Schwartz, *supra* note 22, at 205.

Chapter 10: Life in Georgetown

1. *Sunday Star,* Sept. 30, 1956, at A-10, col. 1.

2. Constance McLaughlin Green, *Washington: A History of the Capital, 1800–1950* (Princeton, 1962) (vol. 2), at 398.

3. *See id.* at 14.

4. *Sunday Star,* Sept. 30, 1956, at A-10, col. 1.

5. *Sunday Star,* Sept. 30, 1956, at A-10, col. 1.

6. *Sunday Star,* Sept. 30, 1956, at A-10, col. 1.

7. Green, *supra* note 2, at 399–400.

8. *Id.*

9. *Id.* at 400.

10. *Id.*

11. *See* Tinsley E. Yarbrough, *John Marshall Harlan: Great Dissenter of the Warren Court* (Oxford, 1992), at 115.

12. *See id.*

13. *Id.*

14. *Id.*

15. *Evening Star,* Oct. 16, 1956, at A1, col. 3.

16. *See Life,* Oct. 29, 1956, at 117.

17. *Id.*

18. *Id.*

19. *See Evening Star,* Oct. 16, 1956, at A1, col. 2.

20. *See id.* at cols. 2–3.

21. *Id.* at col. 1.

22. Southern Manifesto, reprinted in Herbert Brownell with John P. Burke, *Advising Ike: The Memoirs of Attorney General Herbert Brownell* (University Press of Kansas, 1993), Appendix C, at 359–63.

23. Brownell, *supra* note 22, at 203.

24. William J. Brennan Jr., *State Constitutions and the Protection of Individual Rights,* 90 HARV. L. REV. 489, 493 (1977).

25. *Id.*

26. *See The Oxford Companion to the Supreme Court of the United States* (Kermit L. Hall ed., Oxford 1992), at 72.

27. *See id.* at 314.

28. James F. Simon, *The Antagonists: Hugo Black, Felix Frankfurter, and Civil Liberties in Modern America* (Simon & Schuster, 1989), at 69.

29. *Oxford Companion, supra* note 26, at 73.

30. *See id.* at 72.

31. *See id.*

32. Simon, *supra* note 28, at 90.

33. *Oxford Companion, supra* note 26, at 72.

34. Simon, *supra* note 28, at 90.

35. Fred Rodell, *Nine Men: A Political History of the Supreme Court from 1790 to 1955* (Random House, 1955), at 245.

36. *See Oxford Companion, supra* note 26, at 477–78.

37. *See id.* at 478.

38. *See id.*

39. *See id.*

40. *See id.*

41. *See generally id.* at 477–78.

42. *See id.* at 478.

43. *Id.* at 478.

44. *See id.*

45. Simon, *supra* note 28, at 245.

46. *Id.* at 97.

47. *Id.*

48. *Id.*

49. Rodell, *supra* note 35, at 245–46.

50. Simon, *supra* note 28, at 95.

51. *See Oxford Companion, supra* note 26, at 72.

52. *See id.*

53. Simon, *supra* note 28, at 68.

54. *Id.*

55. *See id.* at 86.

56. *Id.*

57. *Id.*

58. *Id.* at 86–87.

59. *Id.* at 83. *See also Oxford Companion, supra* note 26, at 72.

60. 332 U.S. 46, 68 (1947) (Black, J., dissenting).

61. Simon, *supra* note 28, at 176.

62. *See id.*

63. *See id.*

64. *See id.*

65. *See id.*

66. *See id.* at 176–77.

67. *Id.* at 177.

68. *Id.*

69. *Id.*

70. 211 U.S. 78 (1908).

71. 211 U.S., at 99.

72. 93 A.2d 176 (1952).

73. 302 U.S. 319 (1937).

74. 302 U.S. 328.

75. 332 U.S. 46, 65 (Frankfurter, J., concurring).

76. 332 U.S., at 65.

77. 332 U.S., at 89.

78. 332 U.S., at 89.

79. *Oxford Companion, supra* note 26, at 73.

80. Hugo L. Black, *The Bill of Rights,* 35 N.Y.U. L. REV. 865, 874 (1960).

81. *Id.* at 874–75.

82. *Oxford Companion, supra* note 26, at 314.

83. *See id.* at 315.

84. *See id.*

85. *Id.*

86. *See id.*

87. Simon, *supra* note 28, at 15.

88. *See* Howard Ball and Phillip J. Cooper, *Of Power and Right: Hugo Black, William O. Douglas, and America's Constitutional Revolution* (Oxford, 1992), at 161.

89. Simon, *supra* note 28, at 55.

90. Hunter R. Clark, "Powerbrokers," *Time* (March 8, 1982), at 26 (book review).

91. *Id.*

92. Simon, *supra* note 28, at 14.

93. *Oxford Companion, supra* note 26, at 314.

94. Simon, *supra* note 28, at 131.

95. *Id.* at 128.

96. *Oxford Companion, supra* note 26, at 316.

97. Clark, *supra* note 90, at 25. *See also* Simon, *supra* note 28, at 130 (quoting Frankfurter in conversation with Justice Frank Murphy).

98. Simon, *supra* note 28, at 128.

99. *See Oxford Companion, supra* note 26, at 394.

100. Donna Haupt, "Justice William J. Brennan, Jr.," *Constitution* (Winter 1989), at 54.

101. *Id.* at 54–55.

102. *Life,* Oct. 29, 1956, at 116.

103. Haupt, *supra* note 100, at 55.

104. *Id.*

105. Jack Alexander, "Mr. Justice From Jersey," *Saturday Evening Post* (Sept. 28, 1957), at 133.

106. *Id.*

107. *Id.*

108. James F. Simon, *Independent Journey: The Life of William O Douglas* (Harper & Row, 1980), at 328.

109. Bernard Schwartz, *Super Chief: Earl Warren and His Supreme Court—A Judicial Biography* (New York University, 1983), at 205.

110. Simon, *supra* note 28, at 235.

111. *Id.*

112. *See id.* at 236.

113. *Id.*

114. *Id.*

115. *Id.* at 238.

116. Schwartz, *supra* note 109, at 205.

117. *Id.*

118. *Id.*

Chapter 11: Justice Brennan Versus Senator McCarthy

1. *N.Y. Times,* Nov. 20, 1956, at 74, col. 2.

2. Nat Hentoff, "Profiles: The Constitutionalist," *New Yorker* (March 12, 1990), at 49.

3. *Id.*

4. *Id.*

5. *Id.*

6. *Id.*

7. *Id.*

8. *Id.*

9. *Id.* at 50.

10. *Nomination of Justice William Joseph Brennan, Jr., 1957: Hearings Before the Committee on the Judiciary of the Senate,* 85th Cong., 1st Sess., 17 (1957).

11. *Id.*

12. *Id.* at 26.

13. *Id.*

14. *Id.*

15. *Id.*

16. *Id.*

17. William J. Brennan Jr., Address Before the Monmouth Rotary Club, Monmouth, New Jersey (Feb. 23, 1955), author's files.

18. *Nomination Hearings, supra* note 10, at 27.

19. *Id.*

20. *Id.*

21. *Id.*

22. *Id.*

23. *Id.*

24. *Id.*

25. *Id.*

26. *Id.*

27. *Id.*

28. *Id.*

29. *Id.*

30. *Id.* at 28.

31. *Id.*

32. *Id.*

33. *See id.*

34. *Id.* at 34.

35. *Id.* at 32.

36. *Id.* at 33.

37. *Id.*

38. *Id.* at 34.

39. Sean O Murchu, "Lone Justice: An Interview With Justice William J. Brennan, Jr.," *Irish America* (June 1990), at 30.

40. Daniel M. Berman, *Mr. Justice Brennan: A Preliminary Appraisal,* 8 CATH. U. L. REV. 1, 7 (1958).

41. *Id.* at 7, n.26.

42. Kim Isaac Eisler, *A Justice For All: William J., Brennan, Jr., and the Decisions That Transformed America* (Simon & Schuster, 1993), at 117.

43. J. L. Bernstein, "Ordeal in Washington," reprinted in *The Reporter* (publication of the Passaic County, N.J., bar association) (Spring 1984), at 27.

44. *Id.*

45. *Id.*

46. Herbert Brownell with John P. Burke, *Advising Ike: The Memoirs of Attorney General Herbert Brownell* (University Press of Kansas, 1994), at 180.

Chapter 12: "An Incredibly Buoyant Person"

1. André Malraux, *Man's Fate (La Condition Humaine)* (Modern Library, 1934), at 359–60.

2. Jack Alexander, "Mr. Justice From Jersey," *The Saturday Evening Post* (Sept. 28, 1957), at 133.

3. Owen Fiss, *A Life Lived Twice,* 100 YALE L. J. 1117, 1119 (1991).

4. *Id.*

5. *Id.*

6. *Id.*

7. *Id.*

8. Donna Haupt, "Justice William J. Brennan, Jr.," *Constitution* (Winter 1989), at 54.

9. *Id.*

10. Bernard Schwartz, *Super Chief: Earl Warren and His Supreme Court—A Judicial Biography* (New York University, 1983), at 205–06.

11. *Id.* at 206.

12. Fiss, *supra* note 3, at 1119.

13. *Id. See also* Schwartz, *supra* note 10, at 206 ("It was Brennan to whom the Chief was to assign the opinions of some of the most important cases decided by the Warren Court."); Haupt, *supra* note 8 (quoting Sofaer).

14. Fiss, *supra* note 3, at 1120.

15. *Id.*

16. Earl Warren, *Mr. Justice Brennan,* 80 HARV. L. REV. 1, 2 (1966).

17. Schwartz, *supra* note 10, at 204.

18. *Id.*

19. *Id.*

20. *Id.*

21. *Id.* at 206.

22. *Id.*

23. *Id.*

24. *Id.*

25. Fiss, *supra* note 3, at 1120.

26. 353 U.S. 586 (1957).

27. Francis P. McQuade and Alexander T. Kardos, *Mr. Justice Brennan and His Legal Philosophy,* 33 NOTRE DAME L. REV. 321, 340 (1958).

28. *Id.*

29. *Id.*

30. 353 U.S., at 605.

31. Tinsley E. Yarbrough, *John Marshall Harlan: Great Dissenter of the Warren Court* (Oxford, 1992), at 135.

32. *Fortune,* July 1957, at 91–92.

33. *Id.* at 92.

34. 353 U.S. 657 (1957).

35. 353 U.S. 657, 670.

36. Daniel M. Berman, *Mr. Justice Brennan: A Preliminary Appraisal,* 7 CATH. U. L. REV. 1, 2 (1958).

37. 353 U.S., at 668.

38. 353 U.S., at 669.

39. 353 U.S., at 669.

40. 353 U.S., at 671.

41. *The Oxford Companion to the Supreme Court of the United States* (Kermit L. Hall ed., Oxford 1992), at 155.

42. 353 U.S., at 681–82 (Clark, J., dissenting)

43. 353 U.S., at 682 (Clark, J., dissenting).

44. *N.Y. Times,* June 5, 1957 (quoted in Berman, *supra* note 33, at 3).

45. *Id.*

46. *See* Berman, *supra* note 36, at 3, n.11.

47. *See id.*

48. Kim Isaac Eisler, *A Justice For All: William J. Brennan, Jr., and the Decisions That Transformed America* (Simon & Schuster, 1993), at 135.

49. *Id.*

50. *Id.*

51. *Id.* at 138.

52. *Id.*

53. Interview with Daniel O'Hern, associate justice of the New Jersey state supreme court (Winter 1993) (author's files).

54. *Id.*

55. *Id.*

56. Berman, *supra* note 36, at 3–4.

57. 98 A.2d 881 (1953).

58. 98 A.2d, at 896.

59. 353 U.S. 391 (1957).

60. 353 U.S., at 425 (Black, J., concurring).

61. 353 U.S., at 425 (Black, J., concurring).

62. 117 A.2d 499 (1955).

63. 117 A.2d, at 501.

64. 354 U.S. 298 (1957).

65. 354 U.S. 178 (1957).

66. 354 U.S. 234 (1957).

67. Michael F. Tigar, *The McCarthy Era: History as Snapshot,* 15 HARV. C.R.-C.L. L. REV. 507, 517 (1980) (book review).

68. *See* 354 U.S. 298, 312–27.

69. 341 U.S. 494, 579, 581.

70. 339 U.S. 382, 445.

71. 354 U.S. 298, 339 (Black, J., dissenting).

72. 354 U.S., at 339.

73. *U.S. News & World Report,* Oct. 12, 1956, at 72.

74. 354 U.S., at 187.

75. 354 U.S., at 187.

76. 354 U.S., at 195.

77. 354 U.S., at 197.

78. 354 U.S., at 197.

79. 354 U.S., at 197-198.

80. 354 U.S., at 200.

81. Tigar, *supra* note 67, at 518.

82. 354 U.S., at 202.

83. Tigar, *supra* note 67, at 518.

84. 354 U.S., at 236.

85. 354 U.S., at 237.

86. *See* 354 U.S., at 245–46.

87. 354 U.S., at 238.

88. 354 U.S., at 239–40.

89. Tigar, *supra* note 67, at 518.

Chapter 13: Faubus, Little Rock, and Justice Brennan

1. The Federalist No. 78 (Alexander Hamilton).

2. *Id.*

3. *Id.*

4. *Id.*

5. Fred Rodell, *Nine Men: A Political History of the Supreme Court From 1790 to 1955* (Rothman, 1988), at 30.

6. William J. Brennan Jr., Law and Social Sciences, The Gaston Lecture at Georgetown University, Washington, D.C. (Nov. 25, 1957) (author's files).

7. *Id.*

8. *Id.*

9. Harold D. Lasswell and Myres S. McDougal, *Legal Education and Public Policy: Professional Training in the Public Interest,* 52 YALE L. J. 203 (1943).

10. Brennan, *supra* note 6.

11. *Id.*

12. *Id.*

13. *Id.*

14. *Id.*

15. *Id.*

16. *See* Francis P. McQuade & Alexander T. Kardos, Mr. *Justice Brennan and His Legal Philosophy,* 33 NOTRE DAME LAWYER 321 (1958).

17. *Id.* at 348.

18. *Id.*

19. *Id.*

20. *Id.*

21. *Id.*

22. *Id.*

23. 347 U.S. 483 (1954).

24. Albert P. Blaustein & Clarence Clyde Ferguson, *Desegregation and the Law: The Meaning and Effect of the School Desegregation Cases* (Rutgers, 1957), at 268.

25. Brennan, *supra* note 6.

26. *Id.*

27. 208 U.S. 412 (1908).
28. 163 U.S. 537 (1896).
29. Clarence Thomas, *Toward a "Plain Reading" of the Constitution—The Declaration of Independence in Constitutional Interpretation*, 30 HOW. L.J. 983, 990 (1987).
30. *Id.*
31. *Id.*
32. *Id.* at 991.
33. *Id.*
34. *Id.*
35. Blaustein & Ferguson, *supra* note 24, at 268.
36. *Brown v. Board of Education of Topeka et al.*, 349 U.S. 294 (1955).
37. 349 U.S., at 301 (emphasis added).
38. William O. Douglas, *The Court Years (1939–1975): The Autobiography of William O. Douglas* (Random House, 1980), at 115.
39. *Id.*
40. Carl Rowan, *Dream Makers, Dream Breakers: The World of Justice Thurgood Marshall* (Little, Brown, 1993), at 233.
41. Nicholas Lemann, "The Lawyer as Hero," *New Republic,* Sept. 13, 1993, at 35 (book review).
42. Laura Kalman, "Mr. Civil Rights," *N.Y. Times Book Review,* Feb. 7, 1993, at 14 (book review).
43. Lemann, *supra* note 41, at 35.
44. *Id.*
45. Douglas, *supra* note 38, at 120.
46. 358 U.S. 1 (1958).
47. *Cooper v. Aaron*, 358 U.S. 1, 8 (1958).
48. Michael D. Davis & Hunter R. Clark, *Thurgood Marshall: Warrior at the Bar, Rebel on the Bench* (Citadel Press, 1994), at 188.
49. *See id.*
50. 358 U.S., at 8–9.
51. *See* 358 U.S., at 9.
52. 358 U.S., at 9.
53. Davis & Clark, *supra* note 48, at 189–90.
54. For a description of the violence and related events in and around Central High, *see* Davis & Clark, *supra* note 48, at 189–90.
55. Davis & Clark, *supra* note 48, at 190.
56. *Id.* at 190.
57. *See id.*
58. *See id.*
59. *Id.*
60. *Id.*
61. *See id.*
62. For a discussion of Eisenhower's handling of the crisis and Faubus's "betrayal" of the president, *see* Davis & Clark, *supra* note 48, at 190–93.
63. Interview with Ernest G. Green, managing director, Shearson Leh-

man Brothers, Inc., Washington, D.C. (March 31, 1993).

64. *Id.*

65. *Id.*

66. 358 U.S., at 12–13.

67. 358 U.S., at 13.

68. 358 U.S., at 5, note.

69. 349 U.S., at 300.

70. 349 U.S., at 300.

71. 349 U.S., at 300.

72. Davis & Clark, *supra* note 48, at 180.

73. 349 U.S., at 301.

74. Douglas, *supra* note 38, at 120 (quoting Arthur Larsen, *Eisenhower: The President Nobody Knew,* Scribner, 1968).

75. *Id.*

76. *Id.*

77. 358 U.S., at 4.

78. 358 U.S., at 4.

79. 358 U.S., at 16.

80. 358 U.S., at 16.

81. 358 U.S., at 16–17.

82. 358 U.S., at 17.

83. 358 U.S., at 18.

84. 358 U.S., at 19.

85. 358 U.S., at 19–20.

Chapter 14: Outwitting the Conservatives

1. Bernard Schwartz, *Super Chief: Earl Warren and His Supreme Court—A Judicial Biography* (New York University, 1983), at 302.

2. *Id.*

3. *Id.* at 303.

4. WJB papers, LOC, Box 14.

5. Schwartz, *supra* note 1, at 303.

6. *See id.*

7. *See id.*

8. WJB Papers, LOC, Box 14.

9. Schwartz, *supra* note 1, at 305.

10. *Id.*

11. Herbert Brownell with John P. Burke, *Advising Ike: The Memoirs of Attorney General Herbert Brownell* (Kansas, 1993), at 205.

12. *Cooper v. Aaron,* 358 U.S. 1, 25 (Frankfurter, J., concurring).

13. Letter from Carleton Putnam to Justice William J. Brennan Jr., (Oct. 13, 1958) (on file with WJB Papers, LOC, Box 14).

14. *Id.*

15. *Id.*

16. *Id.*

17. Interview with Peter Fishbein, Partner, Kaye, Scholer, Fierman, Hays

& Handler, in Washington, D.C. (April 2, 1993).

18. *Id.*

19. Donna Haupt, "Justice William J. Brennan, Jr.," *Constitution* (Winter 1989), at 55.

20. William J. Brennan Jr., *State Constitutions and the Protection of Individual Rights,* 90 HARV. L. REV. 489, 493 (1977).

21. *See* Hugo L. Black, *The Bill of Rights,* 35 N.Y.U. L. REV. 865 (1960).

22. 332 U.S. 46, 68 (Black, J., dissenting).

23. William J. Brennan Jr., *The Bill of Rights and the States,* 36 N.Y.U. L. REV. 761 (1961).

24. *Id.* at 769.

25. 332 U.S., at 124 (Murphy, J., dissenting).

26. Brennan, *supra* note 23, at 777.

27. *Id.* at 777–78.

28. *Id.* at 778.

29. Brennan, *supra* note 20, at 493.

30. *Id.* at 495.

31. William J. Brennan Jr., *The Bill of Rights and the States: The Revival of State Constitutions as Guardians of Individual Rights,* 61 N.Y.U. L. REV. 535 (1986).

32. 367 U.S. 643 (1961).

33. 370 U.S. 660 (1962).

34. 372 U.S. 335 (1963).

35. 378 U.S. 1 (1964).

36. 380 U.S. 400 (1965).

37. 386 U.S. 213 (1967).

38. 391 U.S. 145 (1968).

39. 395 U.S. 704 (1969).

40. 378 U.S. 1 (1964).

41. 211 U.S. 78 (1908).

42. Brennan, *supra* note 33, at 543–44.

43. *Id.* at 544.

44. *Id.* at 543.

45. *Id.* at 544.

46. *Id.* at 544.

47. *Id.*

48. 384 U.S. 436 (1966).

49. Brennan, *supra* note 35, at 544.

50. *See* William J. Brennan Jr., "Landmarks of Legal Liberty," in *The Fourteenth Amendment (Centennial Volume)* (Bernard Schwartz ed., New York University, 1970), at 4.

51. 372 U.S., at 415.

52. 372 U.S., at 416.

53. 372 U.S., at 415.

54. Brennan, *supra* note 51, at 4.

55. *Irvin v. Dowd,* 359 U.S. 394, 405.

56. 344 U.S. 443 (1953).
57. 359 U.S. 394 (1958).
58. *See The Oxford Companion to the Supreme Court of the United States* (Kermit Hall ed., Oxford 1992), at 837.
59. *See id.*
60. *See* Herbert Brownell with John P. Burke, *Advising Ike: The Memoirs of Attorney General Herbert Brownell* (University Press of Kansas, 1993), at 177.
61. *See* Brownell, *supra* note 58, at 177.
62. *Id.*
63. *Oxford Companion, supra* note 58, at 837.
64. 359 U.S. 394, 407 (Stewart, J., concurring).
65. 366 U.S. 717 (1961).
66. 372 U.S. 391 (1963).
67. 372 U.S., at 401–02.
68. 372 U.S., at 418.
69. 372 U.S., at 424.
70. *See Coleman v. Thompson,* 111 S. Ct. 2546 (1991).

Chapter 15: Empowering the Suburbs: One Person, One Vote

1. 369 U.S. 186 (1962).
2. 372 U.S. 391 (1963).
3. Earl Warren, *Mr. Justice Brennan,* 80 HARV. L. REV. 1, 2 (1966).
4. William O. Douglas, *The Court Years, 1939–1975: The Autobiography of William O. Douglas* (Random House, 1980), at 133.
5. Melvin I. Urofsky, *Felix Frankfurter: Judicial Restraint and Individual Liberties* (Twayne, 1991), at 5.
6. Douglas, *supra* note 4, at 134.
7. James B. Thayer, *The Origin and Scope of the American Doctrine of Constitutional Law,* 7 HARV. L. REV. 17 (1893).
8. *See id.* at 141–42.
9. *Id.* at 142 (quoting from *Administrators of Byrne v. Administrators of Stewart,* 3 Des. 466 [1812]).
10. Douglas, *supra* note 4, at 134.
11. Thayer, *supra* note 6, at 156.
12. *Id.*
13. 319 U.S. 624 (1943).
14. 310 U.S. 586 (1940).
15. James B. Thayer, *John Marshall* (Houghton Mifflin, 1901).
16. 1 Cranch (5 U.S.) 137 (1803).
17. 319 U.S., at 667–68.
18. 319 U.S., at 666.
19. 319 U.S., at 666–67.
20. 319 U.S., at 638.
21. 189 U.S. 475 (1902).
22. 189 U.S., at 482.

23. 189 U.S., at 486.

24. 189 U.S., at 487.

25. 189 U.S., at 488.

26. Douglas, *supra* note 4, at 134.

27. *Id.*

28. *Id.*

29. *Id.*

30. *Id.* at 135.

31. *Id.* at 135.

32. Thomas I. Emerson, "Malapportionment and Judicial Power: The Supreme Court's Decision in *Baker v. Carr,*" in *Law in Transition* (a publication of the National Lawyer's Guild) (Fall 1962), at 127.

33. *See id.* at 125.

34. *See id.*

35. *See id.* at 125–26.

36. *See id.* at 126.

37. *See id.*

38. *See id.*

39. *See id.*

40. *See id.*

41. Karl E. Meyer, "Shame of the States," *New Statesman* (April 16, 1962), at 478.

42. *Id.* at 127.

43. *Id.*

44. *See id.*

45. *See id.*

46. *See id.*

47. 328 U.S. 549 (1946).

48. 328 U.S., at 552.

49. Douglas, *supra* note 4, at 135.

50. 369 U.S. 186 (1962).

51. Douglas, *supra* note 4, at 135.

52. *See* 369 U.S., at 192; Emerson, *supra* note 30, at 129.

53. *See* Emerson, *supra* note 30, at 129.

54. *See id.* at 129–30.

55. *See id.* at 130.

56. *See id.*

57. *See id.*

58. Douglas, *supra* note 4, at 135.

59. *Id.*

60. *Id.* at 136.

61. WJB files, LOC, Box 70, folder 4.

62. *Id.*

63. Douglas, *supra* note 4, at 136.

64. WJB files, LOC, Box 70.

65. 369 U.S., at 209.

66. 369 U.S., at 209.
67. 369 U.S., at 209–10.
68. 369 U.S., at 210.
69. 369 U.S., at 217.
70. 369 U.S., at 226.
71. 369 U.S., at 237.
72. WJB files, LOC, Box 70.
73. Douglas, *supra* note 4, at 136.
74. Meyer, *supra* note 41 (quoting Macauley).
75. *Id.*
76. *Id.*
77. *Id.*
78. *Id.*
79. Douglas, *supra* note 4, at 136.
80. *Id.*
81. 369 U.S., at 267.
82. 369 U.S., at 324.
83. 369 U.S., at 339–40.
84. 369 U.S., at 260.
85. *See Reynolds v. Sims,* 377 U.S. 533 (1964).
86. *See WMCA v. Lomenzo,* 377 U.S. 633 (1964).
87. *See Maryland Committee for Fair Representation v. Taws,* 377 U.S. 656 (1964).
88. *See Davis v. Mann,* 377 U.S. 656 (1964).
89. *See Roman v. Sincock,* 377 U.S. 695 (1964).
90. *See Lucas v. Forty-Fourth General Assembly of Colorado,* 377 U.S. 713 (1964).
91. *The Oxford Companion to the Supreme Court of the United States* (Kermit Hall ed., Oxford 1992), at 710.
92. 372 U.S. 368 (1963).
93. 372 U.S., at 381.
94 *Oxford Companion, supra* note 91, at 346.
95. 377 U.S. 533 (1964).
96. 377 U.S., at 577.
97. 377 U.S., at 566.
98. Douglas, *supra* note 4, at 136.
99. *See id.*
100. 376 U.S. 254 (1964).

Chapter 16: Obscenity

1. Donna Haupt, "Justice William J. Brennan, Jr.," *Constitution* (Winter 1989), at 52.
2. William J. Brennan Jr., "The Meiklejohn Interpretation of the First Amendment and the Supreme Court," The Alexander Meiklejohn Lecture (April 14, 1965), Brown University, Providence, Rhode Island (author's files), at 3.

3. 354 U.S. 476 (1957).

4. 376 U.S. 254 (1964).

5. Nat Hentoff, "The Constitutionalist," *New Yorker* (March 12, 1990), at 50.

6. *Id.*

7. *The Oxford Companion to the Supreme Court of the United States* (Kermit L. Hall ed., Oxford 1992), at 298.

8. *See Roth v. United States,* 354 U.S. 476, 482 (1957).

9. *See Oxford Companion, supra* note 7, at 764.

10. *Id.*

11. *See* Michael F. Tigar, *The McCarthy Era: History as Snapshot,* 15 HARV. C.R.-C.L. L. REV. 507, 520 (1980) (book review).

12. *See Gitlow v. New York,* 268 U.S. 652 (1925).

13. *See* Brennan, *supra* note 2, at 3.

14. *See Oxford Companion, supra* note 7, at 745–46.

15. *See generally id.* at 746; Anthony Lewis, "Sex and the Supreme Court," *Esquire* (June 1963), at 82.

16. Bernard Schwartz, *Super Chief: Earl Warren and His Supreme Court—A Judicial Biography* (New York University, 1983), at 221.

17. *Id.*

18. *Id.*

19. *Id.*

20. 354 U.S. 476 (1957).

21. Hentoff, *supra* note 5, at 50.

22. Lewis, *supra* note 15, at 83.

23. *See Ex Parte Jackson,* 96 U.S. 727 (1877).

24. 354 U.S., at 480.

25. *See* Lewis, *supra* note 15, at 82–84.

26. *See* 354 U.S., at 479.

27. 354 U.S., at 481.

28. *See Oxford Companion, supra* note 7, at 745.

29. 96 A.2d 519 (N.J. 1953).

30. 96 A.2d, at 521.

31. *See* Kim Isaac Eisler, *A Justice For All: William J. Brennan, Jr., and the Decisions That Transformed America* (Simon & Schuster, 1993), at 26.

32. 374 U.S. 203, 230 (1963) (Brennan, J., concurring).

33. 370 U.S. 421 (1962).

34. *See Oxford Companion, supra* 7, at 1.

35. *See id.*

36. *Oxford Companion, supra* note 55, at 1.

37. *See id.*

38. 374 U.S., at 304 (quoting Jeremiah S. Black, "Essay on Religious Liberty," in *Essays and Speeches of Jeremiah S. Black* [Jeremiah S. Black ed., 1886]), at 53.

39. Tim O'Brien, "William J. Brennan, Jr.," in *8 Men and a Lady: Profiles of the Justices of the Supreme Court* (National Press Books, 1990), at 57;

Hentoff, *supra* note 2, at 62.

40. O'Brien, *supra* note 39, at 58 (quoting Brennan from a 1987 interview with National Public Radio).

41. Maurice Amen, C.S.C., *The Church Versus Obscene Literature,* 11 CATH. LAW 21 (1965).

42. 354 U.S., at 484.

43. 354 U.S., at 484.

44. 354 U.S., at 484.

45. 354 U.S., at 484.

46. 354 U.S., at 485.

47. 354 U.S., at 486.

48. *See* 354 U.S., at 486–87.

49. 354 U.S., at 487.

50. 354 U.S., at 487.

51. 354 U.S., at 489.

52. 354 U.S., at 489.

53. Schwartz, *supra* note 16, at 220.

54. Lewis, *supra* note 15, at 83.

55. *See Mounce v. United States,* 355 U.S. 35 (1957); *Sunshine Book Company v. Summerfield,* 355 U.S. 372 (1957).

56. *See One, Inc. v. Olesen,* 355 U.S. 372 (1957).

57. *See Times Film Corp. v. Chicago,* 355 U.S. 35 (1957).

58. 360 U.S. 684 (1959).

59. 360 U.S., at 690.

60. 360 U.S., at 685.

61. 360 U.S., at 688–89.

62. 360 U.S., at 690.

63. 360 U.S., at 690–91.

64. *See* 360 U.S., at 691–97 (Frankfurter, J., concurring). *See also* 360 U.S., at 691 (Black, J., concurring).

65. 360 U.S., at 691.

66. Lewis, *supra* note 15, at 83, 141.

67. *Id.* at 82.

68. *Id.* at 82.

69. *Id.*

70. 184 N.E.2d 328 (Mass. 1962).

71. 184 N.E.2d, at 333.

72. *N.Y. Times,* June 9, 1980, at A1. col. 1.

73. *N.Y. Times,* June 9, 1980, at A1, col. 1.

74. *N.Y. Times,* June 9, 1980, at A1, col. 1.

75. *N.Y. Times,* June 9, 1980, at A1, col. 1.

76. *N.Y. Times,* June 9, 1980, at A1, col. 1.

77. *N.Y. Times,* June 9, 1980, at A1, col. 1.

78. *See* 184 N.E.2d, at 329, n.2.

79. 184 N.E.2d, at 329, n.2.

80. 184 N.E.2d, at 329, n.2.

81. 184 N.E.2d, at 334, n.10.

82. 184 N.E.2d, at 334, n.10.

83. Henry Miller, *Tropic of Cancer* (Grove Press, 1961), at 144–45.

84. *N.Y. Times,* June 9, 1980, at A1, col. 1.

85. *N.Y. Times,* June 9, 1980, at A1, col. 1.

86. Kate Millet, *Sexual Politics* (Doubleday, 1970), at 312.

87. Susan Griffin, *Pornography and Silence: Culture's Revenge Against Nature* (Harper & Row, 1981), at 90.

88. *Id.*

89. Miller, *supra* note 83, at xxxi.

90. *Id.*

91. *See* Kathryn Winslow, *Henry Miller: Full of Life* (St. Martin's, 1986), at 23.

92. Anaïs Nin, *Delta of Venus: Erotica by Anaïs Nin* (Harcourt Brace Jovanovich, 1977), at xv–xvi.

93. 184 N.E.2d, at 334.

94. 184 N.E.2d, at 334.

95. *See Studies in An American Tragedy* (Jack Saltzman ed., Merrill Studies 1971), at ix.

96. *See The National Cyclopaedia of American Biography* (James T. White & Co., 1948), vol. 34, at 58.

97. *Id.*

98. *See Studies, supra* note 95, at x.

99. *Id.*

100. 171 N.E. 472 (Mass. 1930).

101. 171 N.E., at 473.

102. *National Cyclopaedia, supra* note 96, at 58.

103. *See Studies, supra* note 95, at v.

104. *See id.*

105. *See id.*

106. *See id.* at v–vi.

107. *See id.* at vi (quoting Theodore Dreiser, "I Find the Real American Tragedy," *The Mystery Magazine* (Feb. 1935), at 10–11).

108. *Studies, supra* note 95, at vi.

109. 378 U.S. 184 (1964).

110. 378 U.S., at 197.

111. 378 U.S., at 200.

112. Justice William J. Brennan, Address at the Louis Marshall Award Dinner of the Jewish Theological Seminary of America, in New York, New York (Nov. 15, 1964), at 11 (author's files).

113. *Id.*

114. *Id.* at 11–12.

115. M. C. Slough and P. D. McAnany, S.J., *Obscenity and Constitutional Freedom,* 8 ST. LOUIS U. L.J. 449 (1964).

116. Brennan, *supra* note 112, at 12 (quoting Slough & McAnany, *supra* note 115, at 455, n.320).

117. *Id.* at 12.

118. *Id.*

119. 383 U.S. 463 (1966).

120. *See* 383 U.S., at 466.

121. 383 U.S., at 476.

122. 383 U.S., at 481.

123. 383 U.S., at 481–82.

124. 383 U.S., at 491.

125. 383 U.S., at 489.

126. 383 U.S., at 489.

127. 383 U.S., at 489.

128. 383 U.S., at 491.

129. 383 U.S., at 491–92.

130. 383 U.S., at 492.

131. *Memoirs v. Massachusetts,* 383 U.S. 413 (1966).

132. 383 U.S., at 431–32.

133. *Interstate Circuit v. Dallas,* 390 U.S. 676, 704 (Harlan, J., concurring in part and dissenting in part).

134. *See* 390 U.S., at 705 (n.1).

135. *See* Michael D. Davis & Hunter R. Clark, *Thurgood Marshall: Warrior at the Bar, Rebel on the Bench* (Citadel Press, 1994), at 281.

136. Schwartz, *supra* note 16, at 222.

137. *Id.*

138. 413 U.S. 15 (1973).

139. 413 U.S., at 24.

140. *Memoirs v. Massachusetts,* 383 U.S. 413, 419 (1966); *Miller v. California,* 413 U.S. 15, 24–25.

141. 413 U.S. 49 (1973).

142. 413 U.S., at 52.

143. 413 U.S., at 74–75.

144. 413 U.S., at 84.

145. 413 U.S., at 84.

146. 413 U.S., at 113.

147. Hentoff, *supra* note 5, at 51.

148. Stephen J. Markman and Alfred S. Regnery, "The Mind of Justice Brennan: A 25-Year Tribute," *National Review* (May 18, 1984), at 33.

149. Tinsley E. Yarbrough, *John Marshall Harlan: Great Dissenter of the Warren Court* (Oxford, 1992), at 220.

Chapter 17: *New York Times v. Sullivan*

1. *See* Anthony Lewis, *Make No Law: The Sullivan Case and the First Amendment* (Vintage, 1991), at 9.

2. *N.Y. Times,* March 19, 1960 (op ed).

3. *N.Y. Times,* March 19, 1960 (op ed).

4. *N.Y. Times,* March 19, 1960 (op ed).

5. Michael D. Davis & Hunter R. Clark, *Thurgood Marshall: Warrior at*

the Bar, Rebel on the Bench (Citadel Press, 1994), at 214.

6. *Id.* at 216–17.

7. *Id.* at 217.

8. *Id.* at 218.

9. *Id.* at 217.

10. Davis & Clark, *supra* note 5, at 389–90.

11. *Id.* at 185.

12. *See id.* at 206.

13. *See id.* at 185.

14. *See id.*

15. *See* Lewis, *supra* note 1, at 6.

16. *See id.*

17. *See* Lewis, *supra* note 1, at 5.

18. *See id.*

19. *Id.* at 11.

20. *Id.*

21. Lewis, *supra* note 1, at 13.

22. *Id.*

23. *Id.*

24. *See N.Y. Times,* March 10, 1964, at 1, col. 5.

25. *See N.Y. Times,* March 10, 1964, at 1, col. 5.

26. 357 U.S. 449 (1958).

27. 357 U.S., at 462.

28. 357 U.S., at 462.

29. 371 U.S. 415 (1963).

30. 371 U.S., at 429.

31. 371 U.S., at 429.

32. 371 U.S., at 431.

33. 371 U.S., at 431.

34. 371 U.S., at 429.

35. 371 U.S., at 429.

36. 371 U.S., at 429.

37. 371 U.S., at 433.

38. 371 U.S., at 433.

39. *See* Howard Ball & Phillip J. Cooper, *Of Power and Right, Hugo Black, William O. Douglas, and America's Constitutional Revolution* (Oxford, 1992), at 167.

40. *Id.*

41. *See The Oxford Companion to the Supreme Court of the United States* (Kermit L. Hall ed., Oxford 1992), at 785.

42. Davis & Clark, *supra* note 5, at 180.

43. Ball & Cooper, *supra* note 39, at 167.

44. 373 U.S. 244 (1963).

45. 373 U.S., at 246.

46. 373 U.S. 267 (1963).

47. 378 U.S. 226 (1964).

48. 379 U.S. 241 (1964).

49. 379 U.S. 306 (1964).

50. 376 U.S. 254 (1964).

51. Bernard Schwartz, *Super Chief: Earl Warren and His Supreme Court—A Judicial Biography* (New York University, 1983), at 495.

52. *Id.* at 496.

53. 376 U.S., at 267.

54. Harry Kalven Jr., *A Worthy Tradition: Freedom of Speech in America* (Harper & Row, 1988), at 63.

55. *Id.*

56. 343 U.S. 250 (1952).

57. 343 U.S., at 251.

58. 343 U.S., at 259–60.

59. 343 U.S., at 252.

60. 343 U.S., at 252.

61. 343 U.S., at 252.

62. *See* 343 U.S., at 276.

63. 343 U.S., at 256–57.

64. 343 U.S., at 266.

65. 343 U.S., at 274.

66. 343 U.S., at 286.

67. 343 U.S., at 286–87.

68. 343 U.S., at 286.

69. *See* 376 U.S., at 258–59.

70. *See* 376 U.S., at 259.

71. *See* 376 U.S., at 259.

72. *See* 376 U.S., at 259.

73. *See* 376 U.S., at 259.

74. Thomas I. Emerson, *Toward a General Theory of the First Amendment,* 72 YALE L.J. 877 (1963).

75. William J. Brennan Jr., "The Meiklejohn Interpretation of the First Amendment and the Supreme Court," The Alexander Meiklejohn Lecture at Brown University, Providence, Rhode Island (April 14, 1965), at 10 (author's files) (quoting Emerson, *supra* note 74, at 912).

76. Brennan, *supra* note 75, at 10.

77. Schwartz, *supra* note 51, at 532.

78. Tinsley E. Yarbrough, *John Marshall Harlan: Great Dissenter of the Warren Court* (Oxford, 1992), at 222.

79. 376 U.S., at 285–86.

80. 376 U.S., at 279–80.

81. 376 U.S., at 271.

82. 376 U.S., at 271–72.

83. 376 U.S., at 279.

84. 376 U.S., at 270.

85. 376 U.S., at 298.

86. 376 U.S., at 293.

87. WJB files, LOC, Box 107.

88. WJB files, LOC, Box 107.

89. *N.Y. Times,* March 10, 1964, at 23.

90. *N.Y. Times,* March 10, 1964, at 23.

91. Robert C. Post, *Justice William J. Brennan and the Warren Court,* 8 CONSTITUTIONAL COMMENTARY 11, 23 (1991).

92. Donna Haupt, "Justice William J. Brennan, Jr.," *Constitution* (Winter 1989), at 57.

Chapter 18: The Conservative Backlash

1. Doris Kearns Goodwin, *Lyndon Johnson and the American Dream* (St. Martin's, 1991), at 305.

2. Michael D. Davis & Hunter R. Clark, *Thurgood Marshall: Warrior at the Bar, Rebel on the Bench* (Citadel Press, 1994), at 270.

3. Donna Haupt, "Justice William J. Brennan, Jr.," *Constitution* (Winter 1989), at 55.

4. *Id.*

5. Nat Hentoff, "The Constitutionalist," *New Yorker* (March 12, 1990), at 60.

6. *Id.*

7. Joan Biskupic, "Clerks Gain Status, Clout In the 'Temple' of Justice," *Washington Post* (Jan. 2, 1994), at A23, col. 2.

8. Marvin E. Frankel, "A Matter of Opinions" (*N.Y. Times*), May 15, 1994, at 15, col. 1.

9. Hentoff, *supra* note 5, at 60.

10. *Id.*

11. Davis & Clark, *supra* note 2, at 367.

12. *Id.*

13. Hentoff, *supra* note 5, at 59.

14. *Id.*

15. *Id.*

16. *Id.*

17. William J. Brennan Jr., "Law as an Instrument of Social Justice," Address at the Conference on School Law Commemorating the Fiftieth Anniversary of the Graduate School of Education, University of Pennsylvania, in Philadelphia, Pennsylvania (Sept. 29, 1964) (author's files).

18. *Dombrowski v. Pfister,* 380 U.S. 479 (1965).

19. *See Younger v. Harris,* 401 U.S. 37 (1971).

20. *The Oxford Companion to the Supreme Court of the United States* (Kermit L. Hall ed., Oxford 1992), at 232.

21. 385 U.S. 589 (1967).

22. 385 U.S., at 597.

23. 385 U.S., at 599.

24. 385 U.S., at 603.

25. 385 U.S., at 603.

26. *Oxford Companion, supra* note 20, at 485.

27. Hentoff, *supra* note 5, at 58.

28. *Id.*

29. 388 U.S. 307 (1967).

30. 388 U.S., at 320–21.

31. Martin Luther King Jr., "Letter From Birmingham City Jail," reprinted in *A Testament of Hope: The Essential Writings of Martin Luther King, Jr.* (James Melvin Washington ed., Harper & Row 1986), at 293.

32. *Id.*

33. *Id.* at 293–94.

34. 388 U.S., at 312.

35. 388 U.S., at 349.

36. Goodwin, *supra* note 1, at 306–07.

37. *Id.* at 307–08.

38. William O. Douglas, *The Court Years (1939–1975): The Autobiography of William O. Douglas* (Random House, 1980), at 251.

39. *Id.*

40. *Id.*

41. 391 U.S. 430 (1968).

42. *See* 391 U.S., at 432.

43. 391 U.S., at 437.

44. 391 U.S., at 437.

45. 391 U.S., at 440–41, n.5.

46. *See* 391 U.S., at 441, n.5.

47. *See* 391 U.S., at 441, n.5.

48. 391 U.S., at 439.

49. 391 U.S., at 439.

50. 391 U.S., at 439.

51. Goodwin, *supra* note 1, at 309.

52. *Id.* at 310.

53. Bernard Schwartz, *Super Chief: Earl Warren and His Supreme Court—A Judicial Biography* (New York University, 1983), at 763.

54. Robert F. Nagel, *A Comment on the Burger Court and "Judicial Activism,"* 52 U. COLO. L. REV. 223, n.1 (1981).

55. *Id.*

56. Richard M. Nixon, *RN: The Memoirs of Richard M. Nixon* (Grosset & Dunlap, 1978), at 439.

57. *Id.* at 439–40.

58. Schwartz, *supra* note 53, at 763.

59. William J. Brennan Jr., "Court Decisions and Crime," Address at the Annual Meeting of the Council of Judges, National Council on Crime and Delinquency (May 8, 1969), in 15 *Crime and Delinquency* 449, 450 (Oct. 1969).

60. *Id.* at 457.

61. *Id.* at 458.

62. Hentoff, *supra* note 5, at 65.

63. *Id.*

64. William O. Douglas, *Points of Rebellion* (Random House, 1970), at 95.

65. *Id.* at 53.

66. *Id.*

67. *Id.* at 53–54.

68. *Id.*

69. *Id.* at 45.

70. Bob Woodward & Scott Armstrong, *The Brethren: Inside the Supreme Court* (Avon, 1981), at 86.

71. Hentoff, *supra* note 5, at 61.

72. *Id.*

73. *Id. at* 61–62.

74. *Id.* at 62.

75. *Id.*

76. *Id.*

77. *Id.*

Chapter 19: Fighting a Rear-Guard Action

1. 418 U.S. 683 (1974).

2. Bernard Schwartz, *Super Chief: Earl Warren and His Supreme Court—A Judicial Biography* (New York University, 1983), at 21.

3. *Id.*

4. *Id.* at 772.

5. Robert F. Nagel, *A Comment on the Burger Court and "Judicial Activism,"* 52 U. COLO. L. REV. 223, 225–26 (1981).

6. *Id.* at 223.

F7. *Id.* at 223–24.

8. *Id.* at 224.

9. *Legal Times,* June 30, 1986, at 2, col. 3.

10. Robert C. Post, *Justice Brennan and Federalism,* 7 CONST. COMMENTARY 227, 234–35 (1990).

11. Akhil Reed Amar, *Of Sovereignty and Federalism,* 96 YALE L. J. 1425 (1987).

12. *Id.* at 1425–26.

13. *Legal Times,* June 30, 1986, at 2, col. 3.

14. *People v. Defore,* 150 N.E. 585, 587 (1926).

15. *Legal Times,* June 30, 1986, at 2, col. 4.

16. John C. Jeffries Jr., *Justice Lewis F. Powell, Jr.: A Biography* (Scribner's, 1994), at 260.

17. William J. Brennan Jr., "In Defense of Dissents," Mathew O. Tobriner Memorial Lecture, Hastings College of Law, University of California (Nov. 18, 1985), in San Francisco, California, at 4 (author's files).

18. *Id.* at 5.

19. *Id.* at 4.

20. Jeffries, *supra* note 16, at 260–61.

21. Nat Hentoff, "The Constitutionalist," *New Yorker* (March 12, 1990), at 68.

22. *Id.*

23. 397 U.S. 254 (1970).

24. 397 U.S., at 269.

25. *See* William J. Brennan Jr., *Reason, Passion, and "The Progress of Law,"* 10 CARDOZO L. REV. 3 (1988).

26. *See id.* at 21.

27. *See id.*

28. *See id.*

29. *Id.* at 22.

30. *Id.*

31. 413 U.S. 189 (1973).

32. 413 U.S., at 217 (Powell, J., concurring in part and dissenting in part).

33. *See* 413 U.S., at 188.

34. 438 U.S. 104 (1978).

35. Paul Goldberger, "Preservation's Supreme Authority," *N.Y. Times* (Sept. 16, 1990), at 44, col. 1.

36. 418 U.S. 717 (1974).

37. 402 U.S. 1 (1971)

38. 402 U.S., at 30.

39. 418 U.S., at 814.

40. 418 U.S., at 814–15.

41. 411 U.S. 1 (1973).

42. *See* 411 U.S., at 12.

43. *See* 411 U.S., at 13.

44. 411 U.S., at 58.

45. 411 U.S., at 54.

46. 41 U.S. 677 (1973).

47. 411 U.S., at 683.

48. 411 U.S., at 684.

49. *See* 411 U.S., at 685.

50. 411 U.S., at 685–86.

51. 411 U.S., at 682.

52. Hentoff, *supra* note 21, at 68.

53. Donna Haupt, "Justice William J. Brennan, Jr.," *Constitution* (Winter 1989), at 52.

54. *Rudolph v. Alabama* (Goldberg, J., dissenting) (draft circulated Oct. 19, 1963), WJB files, LOC, Box 102.

55. Arthur J. Goldberg, Memorandum to the Conference (Re: Capital Punishment) (undated), WJB files, LOC, Box 102.

56. *Id.*

57. Michael D. Davis & Hunter R. Clark, *Thurgood Marshall: Warrior at the Bar, Rebel on the Bench* (Citadel Press, 1994), at 320.

58. *Id.*

59. 408 U.S. 238 (1972).

60. 428 U.S. 153 (1976).

61. William J. Brennan Jr., *Foreword* to Symposium on Capital Punishment, 8 NOTRE DAME J.L. ETHICS & PUB. POL'Y 1, 7 (1994).

62. *Id.* at 9.

63. Jeffries, *supra* note 16, at 258.

64. *Id.*

65. Hentoff, *supra* note 21, at 58.

66. *Id.*

67. Haupt, *supra* note 53, at 56.

68. *Id.*

69. *Id.*

70. *Id.*

71. *Washington Post,* May 18, 1991, at A4, col. 1.

72. 410 U.S. 113 (1973).

73. *Newsweek,* Oct. 28, 1985, at 97.

74. *See Newsweek,* Oct. 28, 1985, at 97.

75. *Newsweek,* Oct. 28, 1985, at 97.

76. Tim O'Brien, "William J. Brennan, Jr.," in *8 Men and a Lady: Profiles of the Justices of the Supreme Court* (National Press, 1990), at 68.

77. *Id.*

78. *Id.* at 67.

79. William J. Brennan Jr., "The Constitution of the United States: Contemporary Ratification," Text and Teaching Symposium, Georgetown University, Washington, D.C. (author's files), at 4.

80. *Id.*

81. *Id.* at 7.

82. William J. Brennan Jr., "The Fourteenth Amendment," Address to the Section on Individual Rights and Responsibilities, American Bar Association, University of New York Law School, New York, New York (Aug. 8, 1986), at 1 (author's files).

83. *Id.* at 17–18.

84. William Bradford Reynolds, "Securing Equal Liberty in an Egalitarian Age," The Earl F. Nelson Memorial Lecture, University of Missouri School of Law, Columbia, Missouri (Sept. 12, 1986), at 7 (author's files).

85. *Id.* at 16.

86. 109 S. Ct. 2533 (1989).

87. 109 S. Ct., at 2536.

88. 109 S. Ct., at 2544.

89. 109 S. Ct., at 2546.

90. 109 S. Ct., at 2547.

91. 109 S. Ct., at 2547.

92. WJB files, LOC, Box 478, File 5.

93. *See* 109 S. Ct., at 2549.

94. 109 S. Ct., at 2550.

95. 110 S. Ct. 2997 (1990).

96. 110 S. Ct., at 3010.

97. Davis *&* Clark, *supra* note 52, at 3.

98. *Id.* at 5.

Chapter 20: Brennan's Legacy

1. Michael D. Davis & Hunter R. Clark, *Thurgood Marshall: Warrior at the Bar, Rebel on the Bench* (Citadel Press, 1994), at 384.

2. *Id.* at 385.

3. *Los Angeles Times,* Oct. 1, 1989, at 16, col. 2.

4. Nicholas Lemann, "The Lawyer as Hero," *New Republic* (Sept. 13, 1993), at 32 (book review).

5. *Id.*

6. *Washington Post,* Jan. 28, 1993, at A2, col. 1.

7. Lemann, *supra* note 5, at 32.

8. *Washington Post,* Jan. 28, 1993, at A2, col. 1.

9. *Washington Post,* Jan. 28, 1993, at A2, col. 1.

10. *Washington Post,* Jan. 28, 1993, at A2, col. 1.

11. *Washington Post,* May 18, 1991, at A4, col. 2.

12. *Washington Post,* May 18, 1991, at A4, col. 1.

13. *Washington Post,* May 18, 1991, at A4, col. 2.

14. Donna Haupt, "Justice William J. Brennan, Jr.," *Constitution* (Winter 1989), at 57.

15. *See Washington Post,* Aug. 15, 1994, at A12, col. 2.

16. *See Washington Post,* Aug. 15, 1994, at A12, col. 2.

17. *See Washington Post,* Aug. 15, 1994, at A12, col. 2.

Index

ABA. *See* American Bar Association
Abington School District v. Schempp,
   187–88
Abortion, 9–10, 269
Absolutism, 96, 99, 118, 154, 183, 228,
   280
Academic freedom, 239
Actual malice test, 230, 232, 280, 287
Adams, John, 184
Adamson v. California, 94–95, 155
Adams Theatre Co. v. Keenan, 55,
   186–87
Adler v. Board of Education, 72
Affirmative action, 271, 273
African Americans, 18, 62, 74, 76,
   208–24
   Beauharnais v. Illinois, 227
   Black's support, 97
   Douglas on, 170, 249
   in Georgetown, 86–87
   in 1960s, 233–34, 238, 240–45
   Putnam on, 153–54
   sit-ins, 221–24
   in suburbs, 281–82
   voting rights, 169–70, 172–73,
      207–8
   working at Supreme Court, 150
   See also Affirmative action; *Brown v.*
      Board of Education of Topeka;
      Desegregation
Alabama, 170, 207, 212, 213–14, 215,
   217, 226
Alberts v. California, 186
Alexander, Jack, 82
Amar, Akhil Reed, 255
American Bar Association, 44, 73, 77,
   279
American Communications Association
   v. Douds, 63, 125

An American Dilemma: The Negro
   Problem in Modern Democracy
   (Myrdal), 134
American Irish, The (Shannon), 65
American Tragedy, An (Dreiser),
   197–98
Apportionment. *See* Voting,
   apportionment
Arkansas, 137–38, 141
Arnold, Benedict, 69
Arnold, Richard S., 236
Aronson, Gershon, 213
Ashby, William, 18
Atlanta Motel v. United States, 224

Baker v. Carr, 164–65, 171, 173–81,
   281, 282
Barratry, 218–19, 220
Barth, Alan, 256
Batavia Metal Products Company,
   38–40
Bates, Daisy, 138
Bazelon, David L., 251
Beauharnais v. Illinois, 226–28
Bell v. Maryland, 223–24
Benton v. Maryland, 157
Berle, Adolf, 119
Berman, Daniel M., 111
Bernstein, J.L., 83–84, 104, 111–12
Big business, 118–20
Bill of Rights, 89, 94, 95–96, 99,
   154–56, 192, 254
Birmingham (Ala.), 240
Black, Hugo, 6, 83, 90–98, 102, 103,
   125, 154–55
   absolutism, 96, 99, 118, 154, 183,
      184, 280
   Adamson dissent, 95–96, 155
   background, 90

Black, Hugo (*cont'd.*)
  Beauharnais v. Illinois, 228
  Bell v. Maryland, 224
  on censorship, 202, 203
  Cooper v. Aaron, 144, 148, 152
  and Court-packing plan, 91, 92
  death, 248
  on Fifth Amendment, 123–24
  Ginzburg dissent, 200–201
  as liberal, 237
  as member of Ku Klux Klan, 93
  on movie censorship, 192
  New York Times v. Sullivan, 231
  on sit-ins, 221, 222
  on "Smith Act" trials, 125–26
  total incorporation theory, 94
Black, Jeremiah S., 188
Blackmun, Harry A., 248, 269, 272
Blacks. *See* African Americans
Blauvelt, Stella, 94
Blossom, Virgil T., 137
Blossom Plan, 137, 147
Board of Education v. Barnette, 167,
  168
Boston (Mass.), 59–61
Boston Daily Globe, 67
Brandeis, Louis D., 5, 22, 27, 97, 264
Brennan, Agnes McDermott, 13, 14, 81
Brennan, Charlie, 17, 29, 35
Brennan, Frank, 29
Brennan, Hugh Leonard, 22, 28, 86
Brennan, Marjorie, 21–23, 29, 55, 78,
  81, 85–86, 88, 101, 267
Brennan, Nancy, 22, 99–100, 234–35,
  267
Brennan, William Joseph, Jr.
  appointment to Supreme Court by
    Eisenhower, 76–84, 104
  attacks on, 249–51, 270
  Baker v. Carr, 164–65, 175–79, 181,
    281
  birth, 15
  and Black, 103
  on Burger Court, 255
  on capital punishment, 266, 285
  as champion of underdog, 61–62, 281
  and church-state separation, 187–89
  and civil rights movement, 222–24
  clerks, 235–37, 250

  commentary on Supreme Court,
    257, 266–67
  on Constitution, 270
  Cooper v. Aaron, 136, 144–50, 152,
    154
  on crime, 246–47, 284
  on desegregation, 243
  disappointments and failures, 260,
    262, 263, 281
  dissenting opinions, 255–56
  on due process, 155–56
  early decisions, 118–24
  family background, 12–20
  finances, 49, 55, 278–79
  First Amendment stance, 55, 99,
    182, 219–20, 272, 281
  first judgeship, 50–52
  and Frankfurter, 102–3, 153
  Garsson war profits case, 38–42
  in Georgetown, 86–87, 101
  Goldberg v. Kelly, 257–58, 281
  *Green v. County School Board of
    New Kent County,* 243
  and *habeas corpus,* 158–63
  at Harvard, 17, 22–25
  hate mail, 153, 154
  health, 114, 267
  Irish Catholic heritage, 12–13, 17,
    26, 27, 59, 67–68, 77, 109–11, 188
  *Keyes v. School District No. 1,
    Denver, Colorado,* 258–59
  Keyishian v. Board of Regents, 239
  as labor law specialist, 27, 30, 35–38
  on law, 131–32
  legacy, 277–85
  liberal views, 55, 79, 235, 237–40,
    269
  and McCarthy, 64–65, 68, 69–70,
    104–9, 111–12
  Malloy v. Hogan, 157
  marriage, 21–23
  and Marshall, 273, 274, 276–78
  Marshall on, 3, 7, 237
  NAACP v. Button, 219–20
  New York Times v. Sullivan, 181, 226,
    229–32, 239, 287
  obscenity opinions, 182–83, 185–87,
    189–90, 198–200, 204–5
  *Penn Central Transportation Co. v.
    New York City,* 259

personal life, 99–100, 101, 114
reform of New Jersey court system,
    43–49
retirement, 273–74, 279–80
second marriage, 267–68
as state appellate judge, 53–54, 77
as state supreme court judge, 54–56
Supreme Court swearing in, 88
testimonials to, 3–11, 278, 285
traffic accident, 100–101
Walker v. City of Birmingham, 241
and Warren, 101, 115–18, 144
and women's equality, 262–63, 284
after World War II, 34–35
during World War II, 29–33
Brennan, William Joseph, Sr., 13–16,
    18–20, 22, 23, 24–25
Brennan, William Joseph III, 22, 28,
    80, 86
"Brennan's law," 18
Brown, H. Rap, 233
Brownell, Herbert, 72–82 passim, 100,
    112, 229
Brown v. Allen, 159, 161
Brown v. Board of Education of Topeka,
    9, 10, 76, 88–89, 97, 133–40
    passim, 145, 148, 149, 209, 243,
    256, 283
Buber, Martin, 241
Burger, Warren Earl, 247, 253, 271
Burger Court, 253–55, 282
Burroughs, William S., 193
Burton, Harold H., 90, 119, 151, 160
Bush, George, 3, 274
Bush administration, 10
Busing, 245, 260

Campbell, Levin, 30
Capital punishment, 263–66, 285
Cardozo, Benjamin, 95, 99, 255
Carlson v. Landon, 72
Carmichael, Stokely, 233
Carr, Joseph Cordell, 174
Casey v. MacPhail, 52
Catholicism, 109–11, 187, 189, 199
    See also Irish Catholics
Censorship, 55–56, 191–92, 202, 281
    See also Obscenity and pornography
Central High School (Little Rock),
    136–50

Charitable Irish Society of Boston,
    59–60
Chesapeake and Ohio Canal, 101–2
Chevy Chase (Md.), 85–86
Christakos, Nicholas T., 5, 11
Church-state separation, 187–89
Civil rights, 74, 75, 208–15, 221–24,
    226, 232, 238, 239, 283
Civil Rights Act of 1964, 223, 224,
    225, 232
Civil Rights Act of 1991, 283
Clapp, Alfred C., 49
Clark, Kenneth B., 134
Clark, Robert C., 5–6
Clark, Tom C., 90, 121–22, 179, 180,
    241
Clinton, Bill, 275, 278, 283
Colgrove v. Green, 173, 176
Columbia University Law School, 22
Commonwealth v. Friede, 197
Communism, 63–65, 88, 106–9, 120,
    125–28, 239
Communist Control Act of 1954, 63
Community resistance, 145–47
Conference of Catholic Bishops, 77
Conference of Chief Justices of the
    State Courts, 77
Constitution (U.S.), 270
    See also Bill of Rights; *specific
    amendments*
Cooper v. Aaron, 10, 136, 144–54
Cornwallis, Lord, 69
Cortese v. Cortese, 54
Court system
    New Jersey, 43–49, 82–83
    state, 52
    U.S. reform, 44
    See also Judges
Court Years, The (Douglas), 135, 165
Crime, 245–47, 284–85
Cronkite, Walter, 79

Daily Worker, 109
Death penalty. *See* Capital punishment
Democracy, 131
Democracy in America (de
    Tocqueville), 129
Dennis v. United States, 64, 125
Desegregation, 88–89, 90, 134–50, 211,
    243, 258–59, 260, 283

de Tocqueville, Alexis, 129
Dewey, Thomas E., 73, 75, 76
Dirksen, Everett, 122
Dissent, 256
Dombrowski v. Pfister, 238
Double jeopardy, 157
Douglas, William O., 6, 90, 101–2, 125, 149, 155, 165, 166, 251
   absolutism, 118, 183, 228
   on African Americans, 170, 249
   on apportionment, 170–71, 172, 173, 175, 177–78, 180–81
   Beauharnais v. Illinois, 228
   controversy surrounding, 248–49
   death, 253
   and "dirty movie day," 203
   on Eisenhower, 140–41
   Ginzburg dissent, 201–2
   as liberal, 237
   on Marshall, 242–43
   "one person, one vote" phrase, 180
   on sit-ins, 222
   on Supreme Court justices, 130
   "with all deliberate speed" phrase, 135, 136
Dreiser, Theodore, 197–98
Driscoll, Alfred E., 49, 50, 54
Dryfoos, Orvil, 216
Due process, 95, 155–56, 164, 257, 259, 270
Dulles, John Foster, 76, 79
Duncan v. Louisiana, 157
Dunn, Tom, 36
Du Pont, 118–19

Eastland, James O., 109
Eastland, Terry, 269
Eckford, Elizabeth, 138
Education
   as fundamental right, 260–61, 281
   See also Desegregation
Effect of Prejudice and Discrimination on Personality Development (Clark), 134
Eighth Amendment, 263, 264
Eisenhower, Dwight D., 39, 61, 67, 71–84 passim, 104, 128, 136, 138, 140, 142, 160
Eisler, Kim Isaac, 111, 122
Emerson, Thomas I., 171, 172, 229

Engel v. Vitale, 187–88
Enola Gay, 33
Equal Rights Amendment (ERA), 263, 269
Equity, 169
Essex Country Trades and Labor Council, 15
Evening Star (Washington, D.C. newspaper), 82, 83
Exclusionary rule, 156, 255
Ex Parte Graham, 53

Fallows, Marjorie, 13, 14
Fanny Hill, 202
Faubus, Orval, 137, 138, 141, 149
Fay v. Noia, 161–63, 164
FBI, 73, 77, 120, 122
Federal Rules of Civil and Criminal Procedure, 47
Fifteenth Amendment, 169
Fifth Amendment, 54, 56, 63, 69, 70, 89, 94–95, 107, 123–24, 156, 157
Films, 191–92, 203–4
Fine, Benjamin, 138
First Amendment, 55, 96, 99, 155, 182–87, 189, 218, 219–21, 226, 228–29, 238, 239, 272, 280
Fishbein, Peter M., 144–47, 154
Fiss, Owen, 62, 113, 115, 116–17, 118, 202
Fitzgerald, John F., 61
Flag burning, 271–72
Flag salute, 167–68
Ford, Gerald R., 8, 249, 253, 256
Ford, J.W., 120
Fortas, Abe, 237, 247, 248, 250, 251
Fort Campbell (Ky.), 142
Fortune magazine, 119
Fourteenth Amendment, 89, 94, 95, 155, 170, 221–22, 223, 224, 257, 259, 270
Fourth Amendment, 89, 156, 255
Fowler, Mary, 267–68, 273, 274, 279
Francis, John J., 49
Frank, Leo, 27
Frankfurter, Felix, 5, 97–99, 119, 122, 161, 166
   Baker v. Carr, 179
   Beauharnais v. Illinois, 227–28
   and Brennan, 102–3, 153
   on censorship, 192

Colgrove v. Green, 173
Cooper v. Aaron, 144, 149, 151–53
  in Georgetown, 87
  judicial restraint philosophy, 90, 118,
    165, 168
  on states' rights, 95
  and Warren, 153
  "with all deliberate speed" phrase,
    135
Freedom Forum, 278
Free speech, 96, 99, 183–84, 226, 238,
  281, 287
  See also Obscenity and pornography
Freund, Paul A., 236
Frey, William H., 281–82
Friendly, Fred, 79–80
Frontiero v. Richardson, 262
Frye, Pearl, 258
Fundamental rights, 261
Furlough programs (World War II),
  31–32
Furman v. Georgia, 265

Gannett, Frank E., 278
Garrow, David J., 10
Garsson, Henry, 38, 39, 40
Garsson, Murray, 38
Garsson war profits case, 38–42
General Motors, 118–19
Georgetown (Wash., D.C.), 86–87, 101
Gideon v. Wainwright, 156
Giles v. Harris, 169–70
Ginsberg, Allen, 193
Ginzburg v. United States, 200–202
Goldberg, Arthur, 231, 237, 263–64
Goldberg v. Kelly, 257–58, 281
Goodwin, Doris Kearns, 233, 241, 242,
  244
Grand Central Terminal (N.Y.), 259
Gray v. Sanders, 180
Green, Constance McLaughlin, 85,
  86–87
Green, Ernest, 138–39, 141
Greensboro (N.C.), 212
*Green v. County School Board of New
  Kent County,* 243
Greenville (S.C.), 223
Gregg v. Georgia, 265–66
Griffin, Susan, 195
Grove Press, 193

Grunewald v. United States, 123

Habeas corpus, 158–63, 164, 255
Hague, Frank, 44, 52
Hall, Frederick W., 21, 24, 28, 50, 79
Hamilton, Alexander, 129, 130
Hamm v. City of Rock Hill, 224
Hardin, John Ralph, 35, 36
Harkness, Richard, 147
Harlan, John M. II, 72, 83, 87, 90, 101,
    102, 103, 119, 123, 125, 149
  background, 74–76
  Baker v. Carr, 179
  Brown v. Board of Education, 149
  Cooper v. Aaron, 152
  death, 248
  New York Times v. Sullivan, 230
  and obscenity cases, 202, 204, 206
  on privacy in group association, 218
Harlan, John Marshall, 74–75, 134,
    256
Harrison, Joseph, 49
Harvard Law School, 5–6, 17, 22–25
Harvard Legal Aid Society, 23–24
Hastie, William H., 76
Haupt, Donna, 78, 99, 100, 116, 182,
    234, 263
Hentoff, Nat, 78, 105, 182–83, 186,
    205, 236, 240, 257, 263, 266
Herter, Christian, 59
Historic landmarks, 259–60
Holmes, Oliver Wendell, 5, 22, 97,
    135, 166, 169–70, 266
Hoover, J. Edgar, 250
House Un-American Activities
    Committee, 63, 106
Houston, Charles Hamilton, 209
Hyman, Stanley Edgar, 193
Hynes, John B., 59

Illinois, 173, 226–28
In re Pillo, 54, 56, 95
Internal Security Act (1950), 63
Irish Catholics, 12–13, 26, 58–61,
  65–70
Irvin v. Dowd, 159, 160, 161, 162

Jackson, Robert H., 74, 167, 168, 236
Jacobellis v. Ohio, 198–99, 204
Jacobs, Nathan L., 45, 47, 49, 52, 54

Japanese-Americans, 73–74
Jefferson, Thomas, 184
Jeffries, John C., Jr., 255–56
Jencks v. United States, 120–23
Jenner, William, 65, 108
Jersey City (N.J.), 52
Johnson, Andrew, 91
Johnson, Gregory Lee, 271–72
Johnson, Henry, 8
Johnson, Jim, 141
Johnson, Lyndon, 225, 232, 233–34,
    241–42, 244, 247, 250
Johnson, Robert Wood, 26, 29–30
Johnston, Olin D., 104–5, 122
Journalism, 281
Judges
    and legislators, 166
    New Jersey, 47, 48
    state, 52
    Vanderbilt on, 45
    See also Supreme Court; *specific
        judges*
Judicial activism, 253–54, 256
Judicial restraint, 90, 99, 118, 165–69,
    254
Judicial system. *See* Court system;
    Judges
Judiciary Act of 1789, 91
Judiciary Act of 1869, 91–92
Judiciary branch, 129–30

Kalman, Laura, 136
Kalven, Harry, Jr., 226
Kardos, Alexander T., 132–33
Kefauver, Estes, 110
Kempton, Murray, 111
Kennedy, Anthony M., 271, 272
Kennedy, John F., 59, 61, 67, 225
Kerouac, Jack, 193, 280
*Keyes v. School District No. 1, Denver,
    Colorado*, 258–59
Keyishian, Harry, 239–40
Keyishian v. Board of Regents, 239
Keynes, John Maynard, 98
King, Martin Luther, Jr., 208–15, 217,
    229, 232, 233, 240–41, 288
Kingsley Pictures Corp. v. Regents,
    191–92
Kipp, Donald, 26, 50
Klopfer v. North Carolina, 157

Knudson, Bill, 30
Kohn, Alan C., 8
Krock, Arthur, 81–82
Ku Klux Klan, 93

Labor
    post–World War II upheavals, 35
    strikes, 27, 37
    unions, 15, 28, 37
    workers' benefits, 29
Lady Chatterley's Lover (film), 191
Langdell, Dean C.C., 22
Lasswell, Harold D., 131
Lawrence, D.H., 191, 192
Lee, Henry, 60
Leeds, Jeffrey T., 235, 236, 237
Legal Times, 79, 80, 255
Lemann, Nicholas, 136, 277
Leonard, Hugh, 22
"Letter from Birmingham City Jail,"
    240
Lett, Esther, 258
Levin, Harry, 194
Lewis, Anthony, 191, 193
Lewis, John L., 210–11
Libel, 217, 226–27, 229, 230, 287
Life magazine, 79, 81, 82, 83, 87–88,
    100, 240
Lincoln, Abraham, 91
Lindsey, Chester, 143
Liquor laws, 18–19
Little Rock (Ark.), 10, 136–50
Lodge, Henry Cabot, 59, 61, 67
Lombard v. Louisiana, 223
Lord, Day & Lord, 215
Louisiana, 238
Luce, Henry, 119
*Lyndon Johnson and the American
    Dream* (Goodwin), 242
Lyons, Dennis G., 144, 150

McAnany, P.D., 200
Macauley, Thomas, 178
McCarran, Patrick, 98
McCarran Act, 63
McCarter family, 15
McCarthy, Joseph R., 64–65, 66–67,
    68, 69–70, 88, 104–9, 111–12
McCormack, John, 17
McDougal, Myres S., 131

McQuade, Francis P., 132–33
Madison, James, 154, 156, 285
Malcolm X, 233
Malice, 231
  See also Actual malice test
Malloy v. Hogan, 156, 157
Malraux, André, 113
Man's Fate (Malraux), 113
Mapp v. Ohio, 156
Marbury v. Madison, 168
Margold, Nathan, 209
Markman, Stephen J., 205
Marshall, John, 168
Marshall, Thurgood, 3, 6, 7, 76,
    133–34, 135, 273
  and black civil rights, 209–11, 221,
    233, 275
  and Blossom Plan, 137
  and Brennan, 3, 7, 237, 273, 274,
    276–78
  on capital punishment, 264–65, 266
  on desegregation, 140, 260
  and "dirty movie day," 203–4
  dissenting opinions, 255–56
  funeral, 275–76
  increasing cynicism, 256–57
  legacy, 276–78
  as role model for blacks, 241–42
Martin, Joe, 42
Maryland, 224
Matusow, Harvey, 120
May, Andrew, 38, 39
Mead, James, 31–32, 41
Mead Committee, 31, 38, 39
Meese, Edwin III, 269–70
Memoirs v. Massachusetts, 202
Metro Broadcasting, Inc. v. F.C.C., 273
Meyer, Karl E., 178
Meyner, Robert, 83
Middle class, 281–82
Miller, Henry, 193–96, 198
Miller v. California, 204
Millet, Kate, 195
Milliken v. Bradley, 260
Minersville School District v. Gobitis,
    167, 168
Minorities, 17–18, 282
  See also African Americans
Minton, Sherman "Shay," 71–72, 76,
    79, 84

Miranda v. Arizona, 158
Missouri, 142
Mitchell, James, 82
Mitchell, John N., 248
Montgomery (Ala.), 169, 213, 215
More, Sir Thomas, 46
Movies. See Films
Muller v. Oregon, 133
Mundt, Karl, 65
Murphy, Frank, 99, 155
Murray, John, 212–13
Murray v. Curlett, 188
Murrow, Edward R., 79
Myrdal, Gunnar, 134

NAACP, 137, 209–12, 216, 218–19,
    221, 242
NAACP v. Alabama, 218
NAACP v. Button, 218–20
Nagel, Robert F., 253–54
Naked Lunch, The (Burroughs), 193
Nathan, Richard P., 282
National Labor Relations Board, 28
National Review, 3, 6–7
Newark (N.J.), 14–16, 18–19, 25
Newark Daily News, 18
Newark Evening News, 19
New Deal, 71, 90, 91, 98
New Jersey court system, 43–49,
    82–83
New Jersey Law Journal, 36, 45, 49
New Kent County (Va.), 243
New Orleans (La.), 223
New York Times, 72, 81, 82, 98, 122,
    207–8, 213, 215–18, 224–25
New York Times v. Sullivan, 181, 182,
    225, 226, 229–32, 239, 281,
    287–89
Nin, Anaïs, 194, 196
Nixon, Richard M., 59, 61, 233,
    244–48, 252–53, 256, 271
Nixon v. United States, 252

Obscenity and pornography, 182–87,
    189–206
O'Connor, Sandra Day, 9, 271, 277
Office of the Administrative Director
    of the Courts (N.J.), 47
O'Hern, Daniel, 102, 114–15, 122–23,
    236

O'Mahoney, Joseph C., 110
O Murchu, Sean, 13, 14, 15, 18, 80, 111
"One person, one vote," 180, 282
Oppenheim, Chesterfield, 119
O'Reilly, John Boyle, 60

Palestroni v. Jacobs, 53
Palko v. Connecticut, 95
Paris Adult Theatre I v. Slaton, 204–5
Parvin, Albert, 248
Patterson, John, 212, 216–18
Patterson, Robert P., 30, 34, 38–40
Penn Central Transportation Co. v.
    New York City, 259
Per curiam order, 139, 191
Peterson v. Greenville, 223
Pitney, John Oliver Halstead, 27
Pitney, Mahlon, 27, 99
Pitney, Shelton, 27, 28, 35, 36
Pitney, Hardin & Skinner, 27–28
Pitney, Hardin, Ward, and Brennan,
    35
Pittsburgh Courier, 74
Planned Parenthood v. Casey, 9, 10
Pledge of Allegiance, 167–68
Plessy v. Ferguson, 75, 134, 256
Pointer v. Texas, 156
Points of Rebellion (Douglas), 249
Police brutality, 18, 255
Pornography. *See* Obscenity and
    pornography
Pornography and Obscenity (Lawrence),
    192
Post, Robert C., 254
Pound, Roscoe, 22, 44, 133
Powell, Lewis F., 248, 261–62, 271
Prayer, 187–88, 269
Pretrial conference, 47–48
Pretrial discovery, 47–48, 56
Privacy, 218
Private property, 221–22
Protestantism, 188
Putnam, Carleton, 153–54

Rayburn, Sam, 42
Raymond, Thomas L., 16
Reagan, Ronald, 256, 268–69, 271
Reagan administration, 10, 271
Reed, Stanley F., 112
Regnery, Alfred S., 205

Rehnquist, William, 236, 248, 271,
    272, 276, 277
Rehnquist Court, 282
Reynolds, Thomas, 69
Reynolds, William Bradford, 271
Reynolds v. Sims, 180
Robinson v. California, 156
Rodell, Fred, 71, 91, 92, 130
Roe v. Wade, 9, 269
Roosevelt, Franklin, 71, 90, 91, 92, 98
Roscommon County (Ireland), 13–14
Roth v. United States, 182, 186, 189–91,
    193, 199, 204
Rowan, Carl, 135
Rudenstine, Neil L., 5
Rudolph, Frank Lee, 263
Rutgers Law Review, 52
Rutledge, Wiley B., 90, 155

Sacco, Nicola, 97
St. Patrick, 58
St. Patrick's Day, 59–60
Saltonstall, Leverett, 59
San Antonio Independent School
    District v. Rodgriguez, 260, 262
Santholm, Oscar, 19
Saturday Evening Post, 101, 114
Scalia, Antonin, 6, 271, 272
School prayer, 187–88, 269
Schwartz, Bernard, 116, 152, 153, 185
SCLC. *See* Southern Christian
    Leadership Conference
Scott, Austin Wakeman, 22
Screaming Eagle, (newspaper), 142–143
Search and seizure, 156, 255
Sedition Act, 184
Seditious libel, 226
Segregation, 240–41, 245, 255, 256
    See also Desegregation
Self-incrimination, 54, 56, 63, 69,
    94–95, 107, 123–24, 156, 157
Senate Judiciary Committee, 105
Sexual Politics (Millet), 195
Shanley, Bernard M., 50, 82, 83
Shannon, Catherine B., 66
Shannon, William V., 65, 66–67
Simon, James F., 94
Sirica, John J., 252
Sit-ins, 212, 213–14, 220–24
Sixth Amendment, 156–57

Slezak, John, 34, 40–41
Slough, M.C., 199
Smith, Charles (editor), 110
Smith, Charles E. (real estate developer), 268, 279
Smith Act, 64, 125
Society of United Irishmen, 68–69
Sofaer, Abraham, 115–16, 154
Souter, David Hackett, 3–10, 276, 285
Southern Christian Leadership Conference (SCLC), 211, 214, 288
Southern Manifesto, 88, 142
Speakman, G. Dixon, 49
Stare decisis, 9
States' rights, 89, 94, 95–96, 158
State v. Fary, 56, 124
State v. Time, 123
State v. Tune, 56
Stavis, Morton, 36
Stevens, John Paul, 8, 253
Stevenson, Adlai, 72, 104
Stewart, Potter, 117, 160–61, 162, 271
    Baker v. Carr, 174–75, 177, 178–79
    and obscenity cases, 191–92, 198–99, 204
    Walker v. City of Birmingham, 240, 241
Stone, Harlan Fiske, 22, 98
Strikes. *See* Labor
Sullivan, L.B., 215–18, 224–25, 287
Sulzberger, Arthur Ochs, 232
Supreme Court
    Brennan on, 257, 266–67
    on communism, 63–64
    Court-packing plan, 71, 91, 92
    on desegregation, 90
    "dirty movie day," 203–4
    Eisenhower's appointments, 71–84
    justices' appointment for life, 130
    justices' predilections, 130
    Reagan's appointments, 271
    "Red Monday" decisions, 124–28
    segregation in, 150
    See also specific cases and justices
Swann v. Charlotte-Mecklenburg Board of Education, 260
Sweezy v. New Hampshire, 125, 127–28

Taft, Robert, 160
Taft-Hartley Act, 64

Tennessee, 173–75, 177, 179
Texas, 260, 261
Texas v. Johnson, 271–72
Thayer, James Bradley, 165–69
Thomas, Clarence, 134–35
Thomas, Norman, 44
Tigar, Michael E., 63, 64, 127, 250
Tillich, Paul, 241
Time, Inc., 119
Time magazine, 81, 82, 83
Tolson, Clyde, 250
Tone, Wolfe, 69
Totenberg, Nina, 62
Traynor, Roger J., 131
Tropic of Cancer (Miller), 193–96
Truman, Harry, 34, 71, 121, 283
Twining v. New Jersey, 95, 157

Unions. *See* Labor
United States v. E.I. du Pont de Nemours & Co., 118–19
United States v. Flynn, 75, 76
University of Arkansas, 141
Urofsky, Melvin I., 166
U.S. News & World Report, 81, 83

Vanderbilt, Arthur T., 44–47, 49, 50, 52–53, 56, 74, 77, 78, 80, 87, 131, 133
Vanzetti, Bartolomeo, 97
Velez, Angela, 258
Vietnam, 249
Vinson, Fred, 73
Virginia, 218–19, 220
Virginia Law Weekly, 171–72
Voting
    of African Americans, 169–70, 172–73, 207–8
    apportionment, 89, 164–65, 170–81
    fraud, 52
Voting Rights Act of 1965, 232

Wagner Act, 28
Walker v. City of Birmingham, 240–41
War Manpower Commission, 39
Warren, Earl, 6, 72, 79, 80, 82, 84, 90, 102, 123, 164
    and Brennan, 101, 115–18, 144
    Brown v. Board of Education, 133, 134

Warren, Earl (*cont'd.*)
  on congressional investigations of
    suspected subversives, 126–27
  Cooper v. Aaron, 144, 149, 152
  death, 253
  and "dirty movie day," 203
  Eisenhower's appointment as chief
    justice, 73
  and Frankfurter, 153
  and Japanese-American internment,
    73–74
  on Kennedy assassination, 225
  as liberal, 237
  and Nixon, 245, 252–53
  and obscenity cases, 185, 187, 190,
    199
  Peterson v. Greenville, 223
  resignation, 247–48
  Reynolds v. Sims, 180
  and voting apportionment, 175
Warren Commission, 225

Warren Court, 245, 253, 254, 271, 283
Washington, George, 129, 143
Washington Post, 38, 39, 42
Watergate affair, 252–53
Watkins v. United States, 125, 126–27
Wechsler, Herbert, 229
Welfare payments, 257–58, 281
Welker, Herman, 65
West Virginia, 142
Wharton School, 20, 21, 46
White, Byron, 279
Whittaker, Charles E., 8, 112
Williston, Samuel, 22
"With all deliberate speed," 135–36
Women, 262–63, 284
Woods, Edward F., 101
Workers. *See* Labor
Workmen's compensation, 27
Wright, J. Skelly, 251

Yates v. United States, 125–26